Edito

This work investigates the role of Aristotelian concepts, p̶_____ mes in Thomas Aquinas's theology. The ten chapters are intended to provide an introduction to the significance of Aquinas's theological reception of Aristotle in certain major loci: the Trinity, the angels, soul and body, the Mosaic law, grace, charity, justice, contemplation and action, Christ, and the sacraments. Some of these chapters focus on the *Summa theologiae*, while others range more widely in Aquinas's corpus. Aristotelian concepts, of course, appear throughout Aquinas's theology. Jean-Pierre Torrell has pointed out that "the presence and influence of Aristotle in Thomas's writings no longer have to be shown.... Thomas retained so many important elements of Aristotle's thought that they cannot be numbered."[1] On the one hand, for quite some time, it has above all been the influence of Aristotle on Aquinas's *philosophy* that has been the center of attention. Thomas O'Meara states, "Often the approach to Thomas Aquinas during the neo-Thomist revival from 1850 to 1960 was to describe a philosophy. During that time far more books treated his philosophy than his theology.... A search through a library catalogue or a perusal of a bibliography of articles on Aquinas written prior to Vatican II yields more material on the metaphysics of an unmoved mover or the abstract description of philosophical virtues than on salvation by Jesus or the role of a sacrament."[2] On the other hand, perhaps in reaction to philosophical neo-Thomism, or perhaps because this Aristotelian influence appears no longer necessary to demonstrate, the role of Aristotle in Aquinas's *theology* presently receives less theological attention than does Aquinas's use of other authorities, especially in domains outside of theological ethics—so much so that in some theological circles the influence of Aristotle upon Aquinas's theology is no longer well understood.

When Aquinas describes his use of "authorities" in the *Summa theologiae*, he states that *sacra doctrina* accepts "the authority of philosophers in those questions in which they were able to know the truth by natural reason."[3] He carefully adds, however, that *sacra doctrina* "makes use of these authorities as extrinsic and probable arguments," by contrast to the proper and incontrovertible

---

[1] Jean-Pierre Torrell, OP, *Aquinas's Summa: Background, Structure, and Reception*, trans. Benedict M. Guevin (Washington, DC: The Catholic University of America Press, 2005), pp. 76–7.

[2] Thomas F. O'Meara, OP, *Thomas Aquinas Theologian* (Notre Dame, IN: University of Notre Dame Press, 1997), pp. xi–xii.

[3] *ST* I, q. 1, a. 8, ad 2. English translation from: Thomas Aquinas, *Summa Theologiae*, trans. Fathers of the English Dominican Province, vol. 1 (Westminster, MD: Christian Classics, 1981).

"authority of the canonical Scriptures" and the proper but only probable authority of the Fathers.[4] His vision and practice of theology firmly avoid rationalism. In this light, Torrell aptly presents Aquinas as a "spiritual master" and a "mystic": "The figure who at times seems to be known only for his philosophy is also first and foremost a theologian, a commentator on Sacred Scripture, an attentive student of the Fathers of the Church, and a man concerned about the spiritual and pastoral repercussions of his teaching."[5] Aquinas is indeed "first and foremost a theologian." As Robert Barron writes: "When one interprets Thomas as a rationalist philosopher or theologian, one misses the burning heart of everything he wrote. Aquinas was a saint deeply in love with Jesus Christ, and the image of Christ pervades the entire edifice that is his philosophical, theological, and scriptural work. Above all, Thomas Aquinas was a consummate spiritual master, holding up the icon of the Word made flesh and inviting others into its transformative power."[6]

Not least because of the success of Torrell's masterful work, scholars today tend to focus on the biblical, patristic, and liturgical sources of Aquinas's theology, as well as on Aquinas's debts to Platonic insights such as participation.[7] But for this very reason, Aquinas's theological use of Aristotle requires

---

[4] *ST* I, q. 1, a. 8, ad 2. See M.-D. Chenu's classic discussion of Aquinas's use of "auctoritates" in Marie-Dominique Chenu, OP, *Toward Understanding Saint Thomas*, trans. Albert M. Landry and Dominic Hughes (Chicago: Henry Regnery, 1964), ch. 4.

[5] Jean-Pierre Torrell, OP, *Saint Thomas Aquinas*, vol. 2, Spiritual Master, trans. Robert Royal (Washington, DC: The Catholic University of America Press, 2003), p. vii. See also Jean-Pierre Torrell, OP, *Christ and Spirituality in St. Thomas Aquinas*, trans. Bernhard Blankenhorn (Washington, DC: The Catholic University of America Press, 2011); Paul D. Murray, OP, *Aquinas at Prayer: The Bible, Mysticism and Poetry* (London: Bloomsbury, 2013).

[6] Robert Barron, *Thomas Aquinas: Spiritual Master* (New York: Crossroad, 1996), p. 13.

[7] Among many excellent studies, see Thomas F. Ryan, *Thomas Aquinas as Reader of the Psalms* (Notre Dame, IN: University of Notre Dame Press, 2000); Antoine Guggenheim, *Jésus Christ, grand prêtre de l'ancienne et de la nouvelle Alliance: Étude théologique et herméneutique du commentaire de saint Thomas d'Aquin sur l'Épître aux Hébreux* (Paris: Parole et Silence, 2004); Thomas G. Weinandy, O.F.M. Cap., Daniel A. Keating, and John P. Yocum, eds., *Aquinas on Scripture: An Introduction to his Biblical Commentaries* (London: T. & T. Clark, 2005); Matthew Levering and Michael Dauphinais, eds., *Reading Romans with St. Thomas Aquinas* (Washington, DC: The Catholic University of America Press, 2012); Paweł Klimczak, OP, *Christus Magister: Le Christ Maître dans les commentaires évangéliques de saint Thomas d'Aquin* (Fribourg: Academic Press, 2014); Fran O'Rourke, *Pseudo-Dionysius and the Metaphysics of Aquinas* (Leiden: Brill, 1992); Rudi A. te Velde, *Participation and Substantiality in Thomas Aquinas* (Leiden: Brill, 1995); Gregory T. Doolan, *Aquinas on the Divine Ideas as Exemplar Causes* (Washington, DC: The Catholic University of America Press, 2008); Michael Dauphinais, Barry David, and Matthew Levering, eds., *Aquinas the Augustinian* (Washington, DC: The Catholic University of America Press, 2007). Recent works in moral theology and philosophy have continued to explore Aquinas's debt to Aristotle: see for instance Mary M. Keys, *Aquinas, Aristotle, and the Promise of the Common Good* (Cambridge: Cambridge University Press, 2006); Nicholas E. Lombardo, OP, *The Logic of Desire: Aquinas on Emotion* (Washington, DC: The Catholic University of America Press, 2011); Daniel McInerny, *The Difficult Good: A Thomistic Approach to Moral Conflict and Human Happiness* (New York: Fordham University Press, 2006); Fabrizio Amerini, *Aquinas on the Beginning and End of Human Life*, trans. Mark Henninger (Cambridge, MA: Harvard University Press, 2013).

ARISTOTLE IN AQUINAS'S THEOLOGY

Aristotle in Aquinas's Theology

Edited by

GILLES EMERY, OP,

and

MATTHEW LEVERING

OXFORD
UNIVERSITY PRESS

OXFORD
UNIVERSITY PRESS

Great Clarendon Street, Oxford, OX2 6DP,
United Kingdom

Oxford University Press is a department of the University of Oxford.
It furthers the University's objective of excellence in research, scholarship,
and education by publishing worldwide. Oxford is a registered trade mark of
Oxford University Press in the UK and in certain other countries

Published in the United States of America by Oxford University Press
198 Madison Avenue, New York, NY 10016, United States of America

British Library Cataloguing in Publication Data
Data available

Library of Congress Cataloging in Publication Data
Data available

ISBN 978–0–19–874963–9 (Hbk.)
ISBN 978–0–19–880854–1 (Pbk.)

renewed attention, lest the study of Aquinas's theology become one-sided. Our work, therefore, highlights the significance of Aristotle in Aquinas's theology. Readers will encounter here the great Aristotelian themes, such as act and potency, God as pure act, substance and accidents, power and generation, change and motion, fourfold causality, form and matter, hylomorphic anthropology, the structure of intellection, the relationship between knowledge and will, happiness and friendship, habits and virtues, contemplation and action, politics and justice, the best form of government, private property, and the common good.

Some general background to our topic will be helpful, since Aquinas's use of Aristotle should not be viewed in isolation from the whole of Christian theology. This is especially so in an introductory work such as the present volume, whose theological audience can be assumed to possess widely differing degrees of familiarity with Aristotle's reception in Christian theology over the centuries. It is no secret, of course, that strong critiques of Aristotle have been commonplace in the history of theology. For example, Gregory of Nazianzus, though benefiting from Aristotle's philosophy in some ways, nonetheless condemned Aristotle's "mean conception of Providence, his artificial system, his mortal view of the soul, and the human-centered nature of his teaching."[8] Likewise, Augustine complained that his reading of Aristotle's *Categories* led him to think of God as simply another substance.[9] And in the thirteenth century alone, the Catholic Church's hierarchy warned against the theological use of Aristotle in 1215, 1228, 1231, 1245, 1263, 1270, and 1277.[10]

During the Renaissance and Reformation period, Aristotle often came under particularly strong attack. Thus, in his Letter to Martin Dorp (1514), Desiderius Erasmus criticized "modern theology" as "so contaminated with Aristotle, with trifling ideas thought up by men, even with secular laws, that I hardly see how it can preserve the true savor of Christ, who is pure and uncontaminated."[11] Erasmus went on to ask rhetorically: "What connection is there, I ask you, between Christ and Aristotle? or between sophistical quibbles and the mysteries of eternal wisdom? Where will these labyrinths of questions

---

[8] Gregory of Nazianzus, *Oration* 27, in Gregory of Nazianzus, *On God and Christ: The Five Theological Orations and Two Letters to Cledonius*, trans. Frederick Williams and Lionel Wickham (Crestwood, NY: St. Vladimir's Seminary Press, 2002), p. 33. Gregory equally criticizes Plato for his doctrine of ideas and his hypothesis that souls are cyclically reincarnated.

[9] Augustine, *Confessions* IV,XVI; trans. Henry Chadwick (Oxford: Oxford University Press, 1991), pp. 69–70.

[10] Ulrich G. Leinsle, *Introduction to Scholastic Theology*, trans. Michael J. Miller (Washington, DC: The Catholic University of America Press, 2010), pp. 138–41 and 144–7. See also Robert Pasnau, "The Latin Aristotle," in *The Oxford Handbook of Aristotle*, edited by Christopher Shields (Oxford: Oxford University Press, 2012), pp. 665–89.

[11] Desiderius Erasmus, "Erasmus' Letter to Martin Dorp (1514)," in *The Praise of Folly*, trans. Clarence H. Miller (New Haven, CT: Yale University Press, 1979), pp. 139–74, at 155.

get us?"[12] A few years later, Martin Luther rejected (as he put it) "the Thomistic—that is, the Aristotelian church."[13] In the course of arguing against transubstantiation, Luther observed that "Aristotle speaks of subject and accidents so very differently from St. Thomas that it seems to me this great man [St. Thomas] is to be pitied not only for attempting to draw his opinions in matters of faith from Aristotle, but also for attempting to base them upon a man whom he did not understand, thus building an unfortunate superstructure upon an unfortunate foundation."[14]

More recently, but along quite similar lines, Karl Barth affirmed that "the Christian Church certainly does not number Aristotle among its ancestors."[15] The Russian Orthodox theologian Sergius Bulgakov, for his part, warned that "within the limits of Aristotle's categories, there can be no man in general; human nature exists only in particular individuals (that is precisely why the heresy of tritheism grew out of the soil of Aristotelianism)."[16] And, voicing a representative postmodern viewpoint, the contemporary philosopher Gianni Vattimo has rejected "the attributes found in Aristotle's pure act or in Parmenides's Being, which stand radically opposed to the idea of Being as a creation of a free and loving God."[17]

As one would expect, however, defenders of the role of Aristotle in theology have not been lacking. Indeed, the depth and breadth of theological indebtedness to Aristotle over the centuries can easily go unappreciated today, even by scholars who recognize Aristotle's significance for Aquinas. Richard Rubenstein points out that for many centuries, Aristotle was utterly central in a wide variety of fields of study for Jewish, Christian, and Islamic scholars. During the medieval period, "one could not begin a discussion of metaphysics, natural science, logic, theology, ethics, aesthetics, or politics without referring

---

[12] Erasmus, "Erasmus' Letter to Martin Dorp," p. 155.

[13] Martin Luther, "The Babylonian Captivity of the Church," in *Martin Luther's Basic Theological Writings*, ed. Timothy F. Lull (Minneapolis, MN: Fortress Press, 1989), pp. 267–313, at 285. See Denis R. Janz, *Luther on Thomas Aquinas: The Angelic Doctor in the Thought of the Reformer* (Stuttgart: F. Steiner Verlag, 1989); Otto H. Pesch, *Martin Luther, Thomas von Aquin und die reformatorische Kritik an der Scholastik: Zur Geschichte und Wirkungsgeschichte eines Mißverständnisses mit weltgeschichtlichen Folgen* (Hamburg: Joachim Jungius-Gesellschaft der Wissenschaften, 1994).

[14] Luther, "The Babylonian Captivity," p. 285.

[15] Karl Barth, *Church Dogmatics*, vol. 1, The Doctrine of the Word of God, part 1, trans. Geoffrey W. Bromiley, 2nd ed. (Edinburgh: T. & T. Clark, 1975), p. 11. See also Thomas Joseph White, OP, "Introduction: Thomas Aquinas and Karl Barth, An Unofficial Catholic–Protestant Dialogue," in *Thomas Aquinas and Karl Barth: An Unofficial Catholic–Protestant Dialogue*, edited by Bruce L. McCormack and Thomas Joseph White (Grand Rapids, MI: Eerdmans, 2013), pp. 1–39.

[16] Sergius Bulgakov, *The Lamb of God*, trans. Boris Jakim (Grand Rapids, MI: Eerdmans, 2008), p. 67.

[17] Gianni Vattimo, *After Christianity*, trans. Luca D'Isanto (New York: Columbia University Press, 2002), p. 120.

to Aristotle's views and dealing respectfully with them."[18] Depending on the Latin translations that were gradually made available to them,[19] all high- and late-medieval Christian theologians in the West were in dialogue with Aristotle and with Muslim interpreters of Aristotle such as Ibn Sina (Avicenna) and Ibn Rushd (Averroes).[20]

In the Christian East, among the many Eastern Fathers who could be named, Basil the Great's *Against Eunomius* exhibits the fruitful influence of Aristotle's *Categories* and other works—as does John of Damascus's well-known *Philosophical Chapters*, which draws heavily upon the eclectic Aristotelianism of Nemesius of Emesa.[21] Indeed, Marcus Plested has demonstrated Aquinas's "continuity and affinity with a long tradition of Byzantine scholasticism going back to the Christological debates of the fifth century and recapitulated in John of Damascus."[22] The Byzantine scholasticism that Plested traces through the nineteenth century, a scholasticism that (at least with respect to the place given to Aristotelian philosophy) included Gregory Palamas, finds a parallel not only in the long tradition of Catholic scholasticism but also in the centuries of Lutheran and Reformed scholasticism, led by figures such as Francis Turretin.

---

[18] Richard E. Rubenstein, *Aristotle's Children: How Christians, Muslims, and Jews Rediscovered Ancient Wisdom and Illuminated the Dark Ages* (New York: Harcourt, 2003), p. 283.

[19] The series "Aristoteles Latinus" (medieval translations of the works of Aristotle), part of the "Corpus Philosophorum Medii Aevi," is of the greatest help in this regard. The project, still in progress, started in 1930, with the first volume being published in 1951. It is currently supervised and supported by the International Union of Academies. For instance, thanks to "Aristoteles Latinus," Marta Borgo was able to demonstrate that Aquinas's commentary on the first book of the *Sentences* makes use of no less than four different translations of Aristotle's *Metaphysics*: Marta Borgo, "La *Métaphysique* d'Aristote dans le *Commentaire* de Thomas d'Aquin au Ier livre des *Sentences* de Pierre Lombard: Quelques exemples significatifs," *RSPhTh* 91 (2007): pp. 651–92.

[20] See, for example, Marilyn McCord Adams, *Some Later Medieval Theories of the Eucharist: Thomas Aquinas, Giles of Rome, Duns Scotus, and William Ockham* (Oxford: Oxford University Press, 2010); Russell L. Friedman, *Medieval Trinitarian Thought from Aquinas to Ockham* (Cambridge: Cambridge University Press, 2010). While critical of Aristotle in certain respects—largely the very respects identified by Gregory of Nazianzus—the great medieval Muslim theologian and legal scholar Al-Ghazali likewise drew upon Aristotle, as did medieval Jewish theologians and legal scholars such as Maimonides, Gersonides, and Saadiah Gaon.

[21] See Andrew Radde-Gallwitz, *Basil of Caesarea, Gregory of Nyssa, and the Transformation of Divine Simplicity* (Oxford: Oxford University Press, 2009); Andrew Louth, *St John Damascene: Tradition and Originality in Byzantine Theology* (Oxford: Oxford University Press, 2002).

[22] Marcus Plested, *Orthodox Readings of Aquinas* (Oxford: Oxford University Press, 2012), p. 223. For a contrasting perspective, see David Bradshaw, *Aristotle East and West: Metaphysics and the Division of Christendom* (Cambridge: Cambridge University Press, 2004). Bradshaw holds that the bigger problem is Augustine: "Clearly the gulf separating Augustine from the eastern tradition is immense. It encompasses such basic issues as the nature of being, the simplicity of God, the intelligibility of God, and the final goal of human existence. What is perhaps most remarkable is that the Augustinian presuppositions we have sketched could come to dominate the thought of the West, while having virtually no influence in the East, and yet for almost a thousand years neither side recognized what had happened" (p. 229).

It is thus an exaggeration to say, as Fernand Van Steenberghen did, that in the thirteenth century, "For the first time Christian thinkers were to be confronted with Aristotle; his naturalistic view of the universe was to come face to face with the Christian outlook so long familiar to the minds of men."[23] Nonetheless, given the centuries-long absence of most of Aristotle's works from the Latin West, the thirteenth century marked in many respects a new beginning.[24] That this was so is demonstrated not least by the many commentaries on Aristotle's works authored by Aquinas and by his teacher Albert the Great.[25] This does not mean that Albert and Thomas were the first to integrate Aristotle in Latin scholastic theology. Their work had been prepared by many others, to the point that René-Antoine Gauthier suggested that Aquinas inherited an Aristotle "already entirely Christian" and that his effort was to give Aristotle a certain purity, in order to make him an instrument of his own theological reflection.[26] As Fergus Kerr remarked, "Thomas is palpably at home in Aristotle's world: a world that is saturated with purposefulness, a world that is meant to be understood in the sense that it is our nature as rational beings to inquire into the world's order and to come to understand it."[27]

Yet, what did it mean for Aquinas to be "at home in Aristotle's world"? In fact, in the late thirteenth century, some medieval thinkers such as Dietrich of Freiberg sharply criticized Aquinas for wrongly reading Aristotle,[28] that is, for submitting Aristotle to the requirements of Christian theology. In our day, the

---

[23] Fernand Van Steenberghen, *Aristotle in the West: The Origins of Latin Aristotelianism*, trans. Leonard Johnston (New York: Humanities Press, 1970), p. 59.

[24] See Ralph M. McInerny, *The Question of Christian Ethics* (Washington, DC: The Catholic University of America Press, 1993), pp. 4–5. See also Ralph M. McInerny, "Why I Am a Thomist," *American Catholic Philosophical Quarterly* 83 (2009): pp. 323–30; Jude P. Dougherty, "Wretched Aristotle," in *Indubitanter ad Veritatem: Studies Offered to Leo J. Elders SVD in Honor of the Golden Jubilee of his Ordination to the Priesthood*, edited by Jörgen Vijgen (Budel: Damon, 2003), pp. 126–32. For a rebuttal of theological and philosophical efforts to distance Aquinas from Aristotle, see also Ralph M. McInerny, *Praeambula Fidei: Thomism and the God of the Philosophers* (Washington, DC: The Catholic University of America Press, 2006).

[25] For the relationship between Albert's work and Aquinas's, see the introductions provided by Simon Tugwell in Simon Tugwell, OP, ed., *Albert and Thomas: Selected Writings* (Mahwah, NJ: Paulist Press, 1988).

[26] On this, see Jean-Pierre Torrell, OP, *Saint Thomas Aquinas*, vol. 1, The Person and his Work, trans. Robert Royal, rev. ed. (Washington, DC: The Catholic University of America Press, 2005), p. 238.

[27] Fergus Kerr, *Thomas Aquinas: A Very Short Introduction* (Oxford: Oxford University Press, 2009), p. 28.

[28] See Ruedi Imbach, "Pourquoi Thierry de Freiberg a-t-il critiqué Thomas d'Aquin? Remarques sur le *De accidentibus*," *Freiburger Zeitschrift für Philosophie und Theologie* 45 (1998): pp. 116–29. On this anti-Thomistic reception of Aristotle, see Catherine König-Pralong, "Dietrich de Freiberg: Métaphysicien allemand antithomiste," *RThom* 108 (2008): pp. 57–79. This issue of the French *Revue thomiste* (108/1) is entirely dedicated to anti-Thomism in medieval and modern thought.

degree of Aquinas's real indebtedness to Aristotle has been questioned by Mark Jordan in his *The Alleged Aristotelianism of Thomas Aquinas*.[29] Wayne Hankey and Fran O'Rourke have emphasized the Neoplatonic character of Aquinas's thought, often against the view that Aristotle is Aquinas's primary philosophical source.[30] Hankey remarks with regard to Aquinas's philosophy of *esse*, for example, "What served to distinguish Thomas from Aristotle in this regard . . . in fact rather serves to distinguish his position as Neoplatonic as opposed to Aristotelian. Indeed, the characteristics meant to place Thomas and Avicenna together in the tradition of Exodus rather serve to identify their common filiation from Porphyry."[31] In light of Jordan's work and that of others, Kerr observes that calling Aquinas an "Aristotelian" "requires nuancing, in the light of recent scholarship, even if it is plausible at all."[32]

In the period leading up to the Second Vatican Council, Aristotle's role in Catholic theology became a matter of intense debate. Scholars associated with what came to be called the *nouvelle théologie* found the regnant scholastic forms of theology to be dry and overly abstract. They blamed much of this on the influence of Aristotle, as well as on Aquinas's baroque commentators who seemed to them to have minimized the biblical and patristic sources of Aquinas's thought and to have maximized the Aristotelian elements. At issue, in large part, was what is required to ensure the "scientific" character of dogmatic theology.

Marie-Dominique Chenu's early contribution to this debate, *Une École de théologie: Le Saulchoir*, was placed on the Index of Forbidden Books in 1942 and led to his removal from his teaching position.[33] In later works, he

[29] See Mark D. Jordan, *The Alleged Aristotelianism of Thomas Aquinas* (Toronto: Pontifical Institute of Mediaeval Studies, 1992).

[30] See O'Rourke, *Pseudo-Dionysius*; Wayne J. Hankey, *God in Himself: Aquinas' Doctrine of God as Expounded in the* Summa Theologiae (Oxford: Oxford University Press, 1987). See also the balanced and erudite study by te Velde, *Participation and Substantiality*.

[31] Hankey, *God in Himself*, p. 6. See also the numerous more recent studies by Wayne J. Hankey, including his "Denys and Aquinas: Antimodern Cold and Postmodern Hot," in *Christian Origins: Theology, Rhetoric and Community*, edited by Lewis Ayres and Gareth Jones (London: Routledge, 1998), pp. 139–84. Simon Tugwell rightly observed that "Thomas had a much sharper awareness than Albert did of the differences between Aristotelianism and Platonism" (Simon Tugwell, OP, "Aquinas: Introduction," in *Albert and Thomas*, pp. 201–351, at 203).

[32] Fergus Kerr, *After Aquinas: Versions of Thomism* (Oxford: Wiley–Blackwell, 2002), p. 9.

[33] For discussion see Hans Boersma, *Nouvelle Théologie and Sacramental Ontology: A Return to Mystery* (Oxford: Oxford University Press, 2009), pp. 135–48; McInerny, *Praeambula Fidei*, ch. 5: "The Chenu Case"; Janette Gray, R.S.M., "Marie-Dominique Chenu and Le Saulchoir: A Stream of Catholic Renewal," in *Ressourcement: A Movement for Renewal in Twentieth-Century Catholic Theology*, edited by Gabriel Flynn and Paul D. Murray (Oxford: Oxford University Press, 2012), pp. 205–18. See also the particularly important article by Thomas Joseph White, OP, "The Precarity of Wisdom: Modern Dominican Theology, Perspectivalism, and the Tasks of Reconstruction," in *Ressourcement Thomism: Sacred Doctrine, the Sacraments, and the Moral Life: Essays in Honor of Romanus Cessario, OP*, edited by Reinhard Hütter and Matthew Levering (Washington, DC: The Catholic University of America Press, 2010), pp. 92–123.

addressed our topic directly. Thus, in *Toward Understanding Saint Thomas*, Chenu took note of "the innumerable Aristotelian threads that run through the warp and woof of the *Summa theologiae*," and he praised the ways in which Aquinas appropriated and transformed Aristotle's anthropology, "just as grace perfects nature without violence to its original structure."[34] At the same time, he cautioned that Aquinas can only rightly be called an "Aristotelian" so long as we recall that Aquinas's use of Aristotle, like Aelred of Rievaulx's use of Cicero, is "New wine in old skins!"[35] Chenu was critical of the Aristotelianism that he found in the neo-scholastic tradition, and he often complained of the confines of Aristotelian logic when taken too strictly.[36]

From the same time period, Josef Pieper's *Guide to Thomas Aquinas* devoted a good bit of attention to Aquinas's use of Aristotle. For Pieper, it was necessary to insist that Aquinas is not an "Aristotelian," lest the Platonic and Neoplatonic aspects of Aquinas's thought be overlooked.[37] Of course Pieper did not thereby mean to deny that Aquinas made extensive recourse to Aristotle. On the contrary, "We find Thomas giving us ever new shades of the fundamental Aristotelian position. Aristotle, he says, refuses to withdraw from the realities present to the senses, refuses to be distracted from those things that are evident to the eyes. And Thomas himself emphatically accepted this principle."[38] Yet Aquinas did not do so, Pieper emphasized, in the manner of some earlier medieval students of Aristotle, who embraced Aristotle's thought as an antidote to the spiritual symbolism that had previously dominated the medieval worldview. Pieper held that Aquinas instead "succeeded in uniting this hearty worldliness with the radicality of the evangelical spirit, which has always rather tended toward negation of the world, or at least toward unworldliness."[39] Entranced by the creation, Aquinas could embrace "Aristotle's fundamental attitude toward the universe, in his affirmation of the

---

[34] Chenu, *Toward Understanding Saint Thomas*, pp. 29 and 31.

[35] Chenu, *Toward Understanding Saint Thomas*, p. 29. For its force, Chenu's comparison requires that one know that one third of Aelred's *Spiritual Friendship* (along with the structure of this work) is drawn directly from Cicero's *De amicitia*.

[36] See for example Marie-Dominique Chenu, OP, *Is Theology a Science?*, trans. Adrian H. N. Green-Armytage (London: Hawthorn Books, 1959), p. 78. Nonetheless, Chenu affirmed that "the Church's preference for Thomism is based upon the coherence of a system which, through centuries of flux in philosophy and religious experience, has proved the best adapted to keep the truths of religion in their right place—truths which may easily become distorted by their very attractiveness, whether in the passionate preaching of the Gospel or in the discovery of the powers of pure reason. The maintenance of a wise balance guarantees the breadth of his thought" (p. 112). See also Pope John Paul II's reflections on Aquinas and Aristotle in his *Memory and Identity: Conversations at the Dawn of the Millennium* (New York: Rizzoli International Publications, 2005), pp. 39–41.

[37] Josef Pieper, *Guide to Thomas Aquinas*, trans. Richard and Clara Winston (San Francisco: Ignatius Press, 1991), p. 43.

[38] Pieper, *Guide to Thomas Aquinas*, p. 44.

[39] Pieper, *Guide to Thomas Aquinas*, p. 48.

concrete and sensuous reality of the world" precisely on theological grounds.[40] In Pieper's phrase, Aquinas could be both *"for* the 'Gospel' and *for* 'Aristotle.'"[41] Pieper concluded: "Thomas was neither Platonist nor Aristotelian; he was both."[42]

When Chenu and Pieper were writing, the theological interpretation of Aquinas generally emphasized his indebtedness to Aristotle. If today the theological situation is quite different, especially outside of the domain of theological ethics, it behooves us to examine why Aquinas found Aristotle's philosophy so valuable for all areas of theology. It is not possible in a short work to examine each of the *Summa*'s "innumerable Aristotelian threads." The scope of the present work is limited. But the studies contained here, written by theologians, philosophers, and medievalists, should help readers to see how and why Aquinas found Aristotle useful in Christian theology.

As a final step, let us briefly survey the ten chapters of this work. Some of them take as their main goal a faithful historical exposition of Aquinas's use of Aristotle on a particular topic. Others, while striving to describe Aquinas's use of Aristotle with historical accuracy, envision a primarily constructive and contemporary context for their work. The ordering of the chapters follows the plan of the (unfinished) *Summa theologiae*, beginning with God and ending with the sacraments. The opening chapter, by Gilles Emery, delves into Aquinas's use of Aristotle in his theology of the Trinity. As Emery shows, Aristotle is a major source for the structure, the concepts, and language that Aquinas employs in order to deepen his theological account of the revealed mystery. Serge-Thomas Bonino treats Aristotle's role in the angelology of Aquinas, both in his *Summa theologiae* and in other works such as his *De substantiis separatis*. Aquinas uses Aristotle to reflect upon the integrity of angelic nature and angelic action, the possible modes of angelic movement and knowledge, the immateriality of angels, and the fact that each angel is its own specific form. Raymond Hain treats Aristotle's influence on Aquinas's doctrine of the soul. Aquinas thinks that Aristotle considers the soul to be separable and immortal, but even so, the soul is the form of the body and thus is genuinely united to matter. On this basis, Hain addresses the issue of the resurrection of the body and the soul's existence after death. Matthew Levering takes up Aristotle's role in Aquinas's treatise on the Old Law. Aquinas uses Aristotle to help him show that the Mosaic law is a good and reasonable law, the kind of law that one would want one's community to have. Simon Francis Gaine examines Aristotle's role in Aquinas's theology of grace, and shows how Aquinas employed Aristotle to clarify important matters pertaining to our deification. Guy Mansini argues that Aquinas's understanding of charity as

---

[40] Pieper, *Guide to Thomas Aquinas*, p. 49.   [41] Pieper, *Guide to Thomas Aquinas*, p. 49.
[42] Pieper, *Guide to Thomas Aquinas*, p. 22. Pieper refers here to Louis-Bertrand Geiger, OP, *La participation dans la philosophie de S. Thomas d'Aquin* (Paris: Vrin, 1942).

friendship accords, both strictly and analogously, with Aristotle's definition of friendship. Christopher A. Franks presents Aquinas's use of Aristotle with respect to the virtue of justice. Aquinas takes his definition of justice from Aristotle, so that our rights flow from our concretely embodied relational duties rather than grounding these relational duties. Mary Catherine Sommers discusses Aquinas's theology of contemplation and action. She notes that Aristotle offers eight arguments in support of the view that the contemplative life is better than the active life, and Aquinas uses all of them in *ST* II-II, q. 182. Yet Aquinas holds that Christ, though he did not live the contemplative life, lived the most perfect life. Corey L. Barnes reflects upon Aquinas's Christology as exhibiting what it means to do theology as an Aristotelian *scientia*, with particular attention to fittingness, *actiones sunt suppositorum*, instrumentality, and Christ's resurrection. Lastly, John P. Yocum traces Aquinas's use of Aristotle in his teaching on the sacraments. Aquinas combines Augustine's theory of signs with Aristotle's views of human learning through the senses. Aquinas also employs Aristotle's doctrine of causality to express the way in which the sacraments cause grace and lead us to our supernatural fulfillment.

We wish to express our particular thanks to Émile Friche, a doctoral candidate at the University of Fribourg who currently serves as Gilles Emery's Research Assistant. Émile unified the style of references in the footnotes, he helped to draw up the final bibliography and the indices, and he also contributed in numerous other ways to the preparation of this work.

Gilles Emery, OP
Matthew Levering

Contents

Abbreviations

Ang.	*Angelicum*
De malo	Thomas Aquinas, *Quaestiones disputatae de malo*
De potentia	Thomas Aquinas, *Quaestiones disputatae de potentia*
De veritate	Thomas Aquinas, *Quaestiones disputatae de veritate*
In Physic.	Thomas Aquinas, *Expositio libri Physicorum* (or *Commentaria in octo libros Physicorum Aristotelis*)
In Sent.	Thomas Aquinas, *Scriptum super Sententiis* (I *Sent.* = commentary on Book I of the *Sentences*, and so on)
Leonine ed.	Thomas Aquinas, *Opera omnia iussu Leonis XIII P. M. edita*, Cura et studio Fratrum Praedicatorum (Rome–Paris: Commissio Leonina, 1882–)
Marietti ed.	Thomas Aquinas, *Opera* (Marietti: Turin)
PG	*Patrologia Graeca*, ed. J.-P. Migne, Paris
RSPhTh	*Revue des sciences philosophiques et théologiques*
RThom	*Revue thomiste*
SCG	Thomas Aquinas, *Summa contra Gentiles*
Sent. Ethic.	Thomas Aquinas, *Sententia libri Ethicorum*
Sent. Metaph.	Thomas Aquinas, *Sententia libri Metaphysicae* (or *In duodecim libros Metaphysicorum Aristotelis expositio*)
ST	Thomas Aquinas, *Summa theologiae* (*ST* I = *Prima Pars*; *ST* I-II = *Prima Secundae*; *ST* II-II = *Secunda Secundae*; *ST* III = *Tertia Pars*)
Thom.	*The Thomist*
TS	*Theological Studies*

References to Aquinas's and Aristotle's works follow the standard divisions of these works and in some cases also include paragraph or line numbers of the relevant editions. In the references to Aquinas's works, numbers given in parentheses (no./nos.) refer to the paragraphs of the Leonine and Marietti editions. For details about editions and English translations of these works, see the bibliography.

In addition to abbreviations for Aquinas's works, we make use of other common abbreviations:

a.	*articulus*
aa.	*articuli*
ad	reply to an argument (to an objection)
arg.	argument (= objection)
ch(s).	chapter(s)

col.	column
dist.	*distinctio(nes)*
lect.	*lectio*
q.	*quaestio*
qq.	*quaestiones*
un.	*unicus*

The names of Bible books are abbreviated according to Michael D. Coogan, ed., *The Oxford Encyclopedia of the Books of the Bible*, vol. 1, Acts–LXX (Oxford: Oxford University Press, 2011), pp. xxiii–xxx.

List of Contributors

Corey L. Barnes is Associate Professor of Religion at Oberlin College in Oberlin, Ohio.

Serge-Thomas Bonino, OP, is Dean of the Faculty of Philosophy at the Pontifical University of St. Thomas Aquinas (Rome) and is the General Secretary of the International Theological Commission.

Gilles Emery, OP, is Professor of Dogmatic Theology at the University of Fribourg, Switzerland.

Christopher A. Franks is Associate Professor of Religion at High Point University in High Point, North Carolina.

Simon Francis Gaine, OP, is the Regent of Blackfriars in Oxford.

Raymond Hain is Assistant Professor of Philosophy at Providence College in Providence, Rhode Island.

Matthew Levering is James N. and Mary D. Perry Jr Chair of Theology at Mundelein Seminary in Mundelein, Illinois.

Guy Mansini, OSB, is Professor of Systematic Theology at St. Meinrad Seminary in St. Meinrad, Indiana.

Mary Catherine Sommers is Professor of Philosophy at the Center for Thomistic Studies, University of St. Thomas, Texas.

John P. Yocum teaches theology at Sacred Heart Major Seminary in Detroit, Michigan.

1

Central Aristotelian Themes in Aquinas's Trinitarian Theology

Gilles Emery, OP

This chapter asks the following question: what are the central Aristotelian themes that Aquinas uses in his Trinitarian theology? Or, more generally: what is Aristotle's influence on Aquinas's account of the Trinity? In what follows, after some preliminary observations, I will limit myself to *explicit references* made to Aristotle in the context of Trinitarian writings by Aquinas, with no pretense of being exhaustive.

Two preliminary observations are in order. Firstly, in *ST* I, qq. 27–43, Aristotle is far from being the main source quoted or mentioned by Aquinas. That honor belongs, not surprisingly, to Holy Scripture. Aristotle is cited or mentioned explicitly twenty-four times (if we count a reference in an objection and its discussion in the reply as one single occurrence)—roughly the same as the number of references to Boethius. It is fewer than the number of citations of Hilary of Poitiers, and four times fewer than references to St. Augustine (whom Aquinas mentions a little more than one hundred times). Certainly, the mere number of explicit quotes and references is not enough in order to evaluate the importance of Aristotle (and of other authors as well), since Aristotle is present in the background of many texts that do not explicitly mention him. So, for example, there is no explicit mention of Aristotle in the first article of *ST* I, q. 27 on the processions, but the parallel article in the *De potentia* shows an explicit use of Aristotle (see section 1.3). A complete study of Aristotle's presence in Aquinas's Trinitarian theology goes beyond the scope of the present study. The metaphysics of being, act, and simplicity is omnipresent and plays a decisive role that will not be examined here.

Secondly, when St. Thomas deals with the mystery of the Trinity, his discourse proceeds on two levels. The first is that of the mystery itself, namely, the mystery of the Trinity as the "object" of faith and of theological contemplation, the mystery confessed and taught. Aristotle, not surprisingly, does not appear on this level; indeed, he is explicitly excluded from this level, since philosophers were not able to discern that God is Triune, a truth that only revelation makes known. The second level is that of the *concepts* that allow us to account for the faith, and that of the analysis of our *language*, our mode of speaking about God (*intellectus fidei*). These two levels are closely interconnected but their distinction is essential in order to avoid confusions. The use of Aristotle is of capital importance on the second level. I have distinguished three spheres of influence: firstly, structural themes that shaped Aquinas's Trinitarian theology; secondly, central concepts of Trinitarian theology that are explicitly marked by the influence of Aristotle; and thirdly, the place of Aristotle's logic of signification and of predication, and of the Aristotelian doctrine on human knowledge.[1]

1.1. STRUCTURAL THEMES OF TRINITARIAN THEOLOGY DRAWN FROM ARISTOTLE

1.1.1. Immanent Action

At the very start of the study of "what concerns the Trinity of the persons in God" (*ST* I, q. 27, a. 1), Aquinas explains that the fundamental mistake of both Arianism and Sabellianism was to understand the divine processions as directed toward something external, so that neither of them posited a procession *within* God himself. The only way to do justice to the faith is to take the divine processions not as involving an action directed toward something external, but as involving an action that remains within the agent and that gives rise to a procession *ad intra*. Here, Aquinas does not refer to Aristotle, but in the parallel article of *De potentia* (q. 10, a. 1, corpus) he gives three references to Aristotle: *Metaphysics* X, to show how words implying movement—and that primarily apply to sensible things—can be attributed to immaterial beings;[2]

---

[1] Aquinas's indebtedness to Aristotle's *doctrines*, *concepts*, and *method* (including predication in Trinitarian theology) is underlined by James Doig, "Aquinas and Aristotle," in *The Oxford Handbook of Aquinas*, edited by Brian Davies and Eleonore Stump (Oxford: Oxford University Press, 2012), pp. 33–44, at 39–41. My references to St. Thomas's works are taken from the Leonine edition; when a work has not been published in the Leonine edition, I use the Marietti edition, with two exceptions: *Summa theologiae*, ed. Institutum Studiorum Medievalium Ottaviense, 5 vols. (Ottawa: Harpell, 1941–1945); *Scriptum super libros Sententiarum*, vol. 1, ed. Pierre Mandonnet (Paris: Lethielleux, 1929). English translations of St. Thomas are taken, with some modifications, from "St. Thomas Aquinas' Works in English," Dominican House of Studies, Washington, DC, accessed February 20, 2015, <http://dhspriory.org/thomas/>. English translations of Aristotle (including the division of Aristotle's works in books and chapters) are taken from *The Works of Aristotle*, trans. William D. Ross, 2 vols. (Chicago: Encyclopædia Britannica, 1952). In the limits of this study, I do not specify (apart from a few exceptions) the Latin translations of Aristotle used by Aquinas.

[2] Aristotle, *Metaphysics* X,4 (1055a8–10); see also Aquinas, *ST* I, q. 67, a. 2, ad 3; *ST* I-II, q. 7, a. 1, corpus; *Quaestio disputata de virtutibus in communi*, a. 11, corpus.

De anima III, to show that "movement" (*motus*) can be taken in a broad sense for any kind of operation, including understanding as *actus perfecti*;[3] and *Physics* III, to distinguish such operation from movement as *actus imperfecti*.[4] It is on this basis that Aquinas develops his explanations of two kinds of operations that give rise to processions in creatures, and that are also said of God by analogy: firstly, "transitive operation" that leads to the procession of something external (creation, conservation, government); and secondly, "immanent operation" that gives rise to an immanent procession. The most illuminating reference to Aristotle is found at the beginning of the second book of the *Summa contra Gentiles*:

> There are, however, two sorts of operation, as Aristotle teaches in *Metaphysics* IX: one that remains in the agent and is a perfection of it, as the act of sensing, understanding, and willing; another that passes over into an external thing, and is a perfection of the thing made as a result of that operation, such as the acts of heating, cutting and building. Now, both kinds of operation belong to God: the former, in that he understands, wills, rejoices, and loves; that latter, in that he brings things into being, preserves them, and governs them.[5]

Although Aristotle had hardly any idea of the "immanent procession" of a term really distinct from its principle in the acts of understanding and willing,[6] he provided Aquinas with the fundamental key that allows an account of the generation of the Son and the procession of the Holy Spirit, in order to avoid the pitfalls of Arianism and Sabellianism.

1.1.2. "Ordo Disciplinae": Processions, Relations, and Persons

Aquinas inherits the tradition that the divine persons are distinguished by *relative* properties; names like "Father" and "Son" signify a relation. However, he goes further than that in affirming that the divine persons are *constituted* by a relation ("personal relation"), and that the divine persons *are* relations that

---

[3] Aristotle, *De anima* III,7 (431a6–7); see also Aquinas, *ST* I, q. 18, a. 1, corpus.

[4] Aristotle, *Physics* III,1 (201b31–32); see also (among other references) Aquinas, *De veritate*, q. 4, a. 1, ad 1.

[5] *SCG* II, ch. 1 (nos. 853–854): "Est autem duplex rei operatio, ut Philosophus tradit, in IX *Metaphysicae*: una quidem quae in ipso operante manet et est ipsius operantis perfectio, ut sentire, intelligere et velle; alia vero quae in exteriorem rem transit, quae est perfectio facti quod per ipsam constituitur, ut calefacere, secare et aedificare. Utraque autem dictarum operationum competit Deo: prima quidem in eo quod intelligit, vult, gaudet et amat; alia vero in eo quod res in esse producit, et eas conservat et regit." Aristotle, *Metaphysics* IX,8 (1050a23–b3). See also Aquinas, *Sent. Metaph.* IX, lect. 8 (nos. 1862–1865); *Sent. Ethic.* I, lect. 1, with the same reference to *Metaphysics* IX (Leonine ed., vol. 47/1, p. 6).

[6] Aristotle, *Metaphysics* IX,8 (1050a34–b1): "Of some there is no product (*ergon*) apart from the act (*energeia*); the act exists in them: so the seeing is in the one seeing, the contemplation is in the one contemplating, and life is in the soul."

subsist. In order to show this, the *Summa theologiae* unfolds in a precise order: firstly, processions (q. 27); secondly, relations (q. 28); and thirdly, persons (q. 29). This order is rooted in Aristotle's teaching on relation. Aquinas often recalls, with reference to Aristotle, that real relations can have only two foundations, that is, two causes that make a real relation exist in a subject: (1) quantity, and (2) action/passion. "According to the Philosopher in *Metaphysics* V, every relation is based (*fundatur*) either on quantity, e.g. double and half; or on action and passion, e.g. maker and made, father and son, master and servant, and the like."[7] In fact, Aristotle's text mentions three kinds of "relatives."[8] Aquinas's commentary on the *Metaphysics* specifies that quantity and action/passion are the foundations of relations according to which "things are relative" insofar as these things are referred to something else, and not because something else is referred to them.[9] Put otherwise, only quantity and action/passion can be the cause of relations that are bilaterally real. On the one hand, quantity must be excluded from God. On the other hand, there is no "passive" in God: "The only 'passive' that we posit among the divine persons is grammatical (*solum grammatice loquendo*), according to our mode of signifying; i.e. we speak of the Father *begetting* and of the Son *being begotten*."[10] Thus, only actions remain to account for real relations. In God, these are "notional acts" (to beget, to spirate) that give rise to processions (to be begotten, to proceed), namely processions that correspond to actions that remain within the agent.[11]

This Aristotelian analysis of relation explains the structure of the first three questions of the *Summa*'s Trinitarian treatise: since the divine person will be understood as a subsisting relation (q. 29), the study of the person requires a teaching on relations (q. 28), which in turn presupposes a study of the processions (q. 27). The order of teaching will therefore be: processions,

---

[7] *ST* I, q. 28, a. 4, corpus: "Respondeo dicendum quod, secundum Philosophum, in V *Metaphys.*, relatio omnis fundatur vel supra quantitatem, ut duplum et dimidium; vel supra actionem et passionem, ut faciens et factum, pater et filius, dominus et servus, et huiusmodi." *In I Sent.*, dist. 26, q. 2, a. 2, ad 4: "Ut patet ex Philosopho, V *Metaph.*, ubi dicit, quod quaedam fundantur supra quantitatem et quaedam supra actionem." *In Physic.* III, lect. 1 (no. 280): "Hanc igitur divisionem manifeste expressit Philosophus in V *Metaphys.*; sed hic breviter tangit, dicens quod *ad aliquid* aliud quidem est secundum superabundantiam et defectum; quod quidem fundatur super quantitatem, ut duplum et dimidium; aliud autem secundum activum et passivum, et motivum et mobile." Explicit references to Aristotle on the foundation of relations are found in other places, for instance in *De potentia*, q. 7, a. 9, corpus; q. 8, a. 3, arg. 7; q. 10, a. 3, arg. 2; *In I Sent.*, dist. 27, q. 1, a. 2, arg. 3.

[8] Aristotle, *Metaphysics* V,15 (1020b26–1021b11). The third kind concerns the relative "as the measurable to the measure, and the knowable to knowledge, and the perceptible to perception."

[9] Aquinas, *Sent. Metaph.* V, lect. 17 (no. 1026).

[10] *ST* I, q. 41, a. 1, ad 3. In God, "to proceed" is an *act*. See *In I Sent.*, dist. 20, q. 1, a. 1, ad 1: "It is by one and the same operation that the Father begets and the Son is begotten, but this operation is in the Father and in the Son according to two distinct relations (*sed haec operatio est in Patre et Filio secundum aliam et aliam relationem*)."

[11] *ST* I, q. 27, a. 5, corpus: "Processiones in divinis accipi non possunt nisi secundum actiones quae in agente manent."

then relations, and finally persons. This order rests largely on Aristotle's teaching on the foundation of real relations.

1.1.3. Relative Opposition

Relative opposition is central to St. Thomas's Trinitarian theology: the divine persons are distinguished by virtue of relative opposition (which also accounts for the equality and consubstantiality of the divine persons).[12] The Trinitarian theme of "opposition" comes from St. Basil of Caesarea,[13] and was then elaborated in the Latin West by St. Anselm of Canterbury: Aquinas did not invent it, but developed his teaching in the line of St. Anselm. What characterizes Aquinas's teaching on relative opposition is the systematic analysis of "opposition," which is guided by Aristotle.

Firstly, Aquinas refers to Aristotle in order to show that "every distinction or division is either by quantity or by form," so that there can be no distinction among immaterial things except by some opposition.[14] Since there is no quantity in God, the distinction of the divine persons has to do with an opposition of the formal order:

> Every formal distinction is by reason of some opposition, especially in things of the same genus: because a genus is divided by contrary differences, by which the species are distinguished, as is said in *Metaphysics* X. Accordingly, if there be a distinction between the divine processions, this must be by reason of some opposition.[15]

---

[12] *ST* I, q. 28, a. 3.

[13] Basil of Caesarea, *Against Eunomius* II,28, in Basil of Caesarea, *Contre Eunome, Suivi de Eunome, Apologie*, trans. Bernard Sesboüé (Paris: Cerf, 1983), p. 120; see also II, 26 (p. 108): "antithesis." On this, see Gilles Emery, OP, *The Trinity: An Introduction to Catholic Doctrine on the Triune God*, trans. Matthew Levering (Washington, DC: The Catholic University of America Press, 2011), pp. 87–8.

[14] *In I Sent.*, dist. 26, q. 2, a. 2, corpus: "Et ideo dicimus, quod nihil aliud est principium distinctionis in divinis, nisi relatio. Cujus ratio est, quia omnis distinctio vel divisio est vel per quantitatem vel per formam, secundum Philosophum. Secundum quantitatem vel materiam, divisio in divinis non est, cum non sit ibi quantitas et materia. Omnis autem distinctionis formalis principium est aliqua oppositio." *SCG* IV, ch. 24 (no. 3612): "In rebus enim, remota materiali distinctione . . . non inveniuntur aliqua distingui nisi per aliquam oppositionem." *In Physic.* III, lect. 12 (no. 394): "Est autem duplex divisio: una formalis, quae est per opposita; et alia secundum quantitatem." *Compendium theologiae* I, ch. 60: "Formalis distinctio non est nisi per oppositionem." See also *Sent. Metaph.* IV, lect. 3 (no. 566).

[15] *De potentia*, q. 10, a. 2, arg. 2: "Omnis autem formalis distinctio est per aliquam oppositionem, et maxime eorum quae sunt unius generis: nam genus dividitur contrariis differentiis, per quas species distinguuntur, ut dicitur in X *Metaph*. Oportet ergo, si processiones distinguantur in divinis, quod hoc sit ratione alicuius oppositionis." The argument is conceded. Aristotle, *Metaphysics* X,8 (1058a9–10): "For all things are divided by opposites (ἀντικειμένοις)." Aquinas, *Sent. Metaph.* X, lect. 10 (nos. 2120–2121): "Videmus enim quod omnia genera dividuntur per opposita. Quod quidem necesse est. Nam ea quae non sunt opposita, possunt

Secondly, Thomas receives from Aristotle's *Categories* 10 (11b15–13b35),[16] *Metaphysics* V,10 (1018a20–21), and *Metaphysics* X,4 (1055a38–b1), the four kinds of "opposites" that he discusses in the context of Trinitarian theology: contradictories, contraries, opposites according to privation and possession, and relatives. He therefore holds: (1) the opposition of affirmation and negation; (2) the opposition of contrariety (*contrarietas*, which implies a diversity of form); (3) the opposition of possession and privation; and (4) the opposition of relation. On this basis, Aquinas notes (once again with Aristotle) that the oppositions of negation, contrariety, and privation either remove the other term or include an opposition of contradiction—which is not the case with relatives.[17]

According to Aquinas's interpretation of Aristotle, the opposition of relation is the only one that *does not suppress* one of the terms, and which, in itself, *does not imply any imperfection* in one term by comparison with the correlative term.[18] This trait holds special interest for Trinitarian theology: it allows one to show that the divine persons are *distinguished* by "opposed relations of origin," while preserving the perfect *equality* and *consubstantiality* of these persons.

1.1.4. Two Immanent Actions in an Intellectual Nature: Understanding and Willing

Aquinas's account of the Trinity retains only two immanent actions in God, namely, *intelligere* and *velle*, which give rise to the processions of the Word (the Son) and of Love (the Holy Spirit).[19] The analogical foundation of this thesis can be found in the following statement: "In an intellectual nature, there are only two [operations that remain within the agent], namely, understanding and willing."[20] The analogy ("similitude") of the "diction of the word" and of

---

simul existere in eodem." In *De potentia*, q. 10, a. 5, corpus, Aquinas also refers to Aristotle's *De caelo* I,9 (278b1–8).

[16] On things "opposed as relatives," see Aristotle, *Categories* 10 (11b24–33).

[17] *De potentia*, q. 7, a. 8, ad 4: "Oppositio relationis in duobus differt ab aliis oppositionibus: quorum primum est quod in aliis oppositis unum dicitur alteri opponi, in quantum ipsum removet: negatio enim removet affirmationem, et secundum hoc ei opponitur; oppositio vero privationis et habitus et contrarietatis includit oppositionem contradictionis, ut IV *Metaph.* dicitur. Non autem est hoc in relativis." Aristotle, *Metaphysics* IV,6 (1011b15–22).

[18] *In I Sent.*, dist. 26, q. 2, a. 2, corpus; *SCG* IV, ch. 24 (no. 3612); *De potentia*, q. 7, a. 8, ad 4; *De potentia*, q. 8, a. 1, ad 13.

[19] *ST* I, q. 27, a. 5, corpus: "Processiones in divinis accipi non possunt nisi secundum actiones quae in agente manent. Huiusmodi autem actiones in natura intellectuali et divina non sunt nisi duae, scilicet intelligere et velle.... Relinquitur igitur quod nulla alia processio possit esse in Deo, nisi Verbi et Amoris."

[20] *De potentia*, q. 9, a. 9, corpus: "operationes quae non transeunt extra, sed manent in operante. Hae autem in natura intellectuali sunt solum duae, scilicet intelligere et velle."

the "spiration of love," on which the entire Trinitarian treatise of the *Summa* is built, rests precisely on this.

The absence of the theme of "memory" in *ST* I, qq. 27–43 represents a certain shift from Augustine's *De Trinitate*.[21] This shift is not completely new. Before Thomas, Albert the Great (who adopted an Arabic–Aristotelian epistemology) had proposed a reductive reading of Augustinian illumination, by replacing Augustinian memory with the agent intellect (whereas, for Augustine, memory is the site of the mind's illumination, the place where God dwells): in Albert's Dionysian commentaries, memory plays almost no role.[22] Thomas continued the trajectory that Albert started.

Aquinas's discussion of memory is extremely complex, and reveals an evolution of his own thought.[23] In the limited scope of this study, I will consider only one aspect of his teaching. For Aquinas, the "memory belonging to the mind" (by contrast with the sensitive memory) pertains to the intellect: "Memory is not a power distinct from the intellect."[24] To be more precise, memory is the place of the conservation of intelligible *species*, and it is part of the possible intellect (*intellectus possibilis*). Aquinas grounds this view in his reading of Aristotle: "From its nature, the memory is the treasury or storehouse of species. But in *De anima* III, the Philosopher attributes this to the intellect ... Therefore the memory is not another power from the intellect."[25] The tension between the Augustinian heritage and Aristotelian psychology comes to the fore in the following objection, taken from the *De veritate*: "Different acts belong to different powers. But the possible intellect and memory, as part of the mind, have the same act, namely, to preserve species (*species retinere*). Now, *Augustine assigns this function to memory and the Philosopher assigns it to the possible intellect*."[26] Consequently, since the soul's powers are distinguished from one another by their acts and by the formal nature of their objects, Aquinas assigns memory to the intellect, here again

---

[21] The triad of memory, understanding, and will or love, is discussed in the context of the image of the Trinity (*ST* I, q. 93), but not in *ST* I, qq. 27–43.

[22] See Bernhard Blankenhorn, OP, "How the Early Albertus Magnus Transformed Augustinian Interiority," *Freiburger Zeitschrift für Philosophie und Theologie* 58 (2011): pp. 351–86. For what follows, I am indebted to Bernhard Blankenhorn, OP, "Aquinas as Interpreter of Augustinian Illumination in Light of Albertus Magnus," *Nova et Vetera* 10 (2012): pp. 689–713.

[23] See Marco F. Manzanedo, *La imaginación y la memoria según Santo Tomás* (Roma: Herder, 1978).

[24] *ST* I, q. 79, a. 7, corpus: "Memoria non est alia potentia ab intellectu."

[25] *ST* I, q. 79, a. 7, sed contra; cf. a. 6, ad 1. Aristotle, *De anima* III,4 (429a27–29): "It was a good idea to call the soul 'the place of forms,' though this description holds only of the intellective soul, and even this is the forms only potentially, not actually."

[26] *De veritate*, q. 10, a. 3, arg. 1 (emphasis mine). The answer reads: "Although memory as belonging to the mind is not a power distinct from the possible intellect, there is a distinction between memory and possible intellect according to orientation to different things" (*De veritate*, q. 10, a. 3, ad 1).

drawing on his reading of Aristotle's *De anima*.[27] Aquinas thus denies that memory may be a power different from the intellect.[28]

In the treatment of the *imago Dei* in *ST* I, q. 93, although St. Thomas does value the triad "memory, understanding, and will,"[29] memory plays no essential role. In Aquinas's view, Augustine "locates the image of the divine Trinity more in *actual understanding and actual willing*, than in these as existing in the habitual retention of the memory; although even thus the image of the Trinity exists in the soul in certain way."[30] The image of the Trinity is found primarily in the *acts* of the soul—acts that have God as their object and that have a likeness with God's own acts (the diction of the Word, and the spiration of Love).[31] This modest place given to memory is due, at least in part, to the prevalence of Aristotelian psychology.

1.2. CENTRAL CONCEPTS OF TRINITARIAN THEOLOGY

A good number of concepts central for Trinitarian theology are explained in direct reference to Aristotle. With no pretense of being exhaustive, I will limit myself to a presentation of the most significant ones.

1.2.1. Substance

In his discussion of the "person," Aquinas explains the word "substance" in reference to Aristotle. A special attention is paid to the distinction between "first substance" and "second substance" according to *Metaphysics* V,8 (1017b23–26) and *Categories* 5.[32] Aquinas specifies that, although the singular as such cannot be defined, Aristotle's definition of "first substance" ("the ultimate subject, which is not predicated of something else") concerns what pertains to the "common *ratio* of singularity."[33]

---

[27] *ST* I, q. 79, a. 7, corpus; cf. q. 77, a. 3, sed contra.

[28] On the interpretation of St. Augustine by Aquinas, see *ST* I, q. 79, a. 7, ad 1: "Augustine does not take these three (memory, intelligence, and will) as three powers; but by memory he understands the soul's habit of retention; by intelligence, the act of the intellect; and by will, the act of the will." See also *ST* I, q. 93, a. 7, ad 3. We should note that, in his commentary on the *Sentences*, Aquinas accepted that every property (*proprietas*) consecutive to the essence of the soul may be called a "power of the soul" (*potentia animae*), so that "there are three powers distinct from another: memory, intelligence, and will" (*In I Sent.*, dist. 3, q. 4, a. 1, corpus).

[29] See, for instance, *ST* I, q. 93, a. 7, ad 2.   [30] *ST* I, q. 93, a. 7, ad 3 (emphasis mine).

[31] *ST* I, q. 93, a. 8.   [32] *ST* I, q. 29, a. 2, corpus; *De potentia*, q. 9, a. 1, corpus.

[33] *ST* I, q. 29, a. 1, ad 1.

When discussing whether, in Boethius's definition of the person as *rationalis naturae individualis substantia*, "substance" refers to the first substance or to the second substance ("second substance" signifies the "nature of the genus absolutely in itself," while "first substance" signifies "that nature as subsisting individually"), Aquinas insists that the division of *substantia* into "first substance" and "second substance" should not be taken as a division into genus and species, but rather as a division "according to different modes of being" (*secundum diversos modos essendi*), since this division is analogous.[34] He also specifies that, in Boethius's definition of the person, it is preferable to take the word *substantia* according to what is common to first and second substances: it belongs to the addition of *individualis* to make clear that the person is a hypostasis (first substance).[35] The claim that *substantia* applies first and principally to "particular substances" (first substances) is made with reference to Aristotle's *Categories* 5 (2a11–14).[36] Aquinas also takes up from Aristotle's *Metaphysics* VII,6 (1032a5–6) the conception that simple substances are their essence.[37]

1.2.2. Nature

In the context of the "person," the concept of *natura* and the development of its meaning (starting from generation and birth, *natura* has come to signify the intrinsic principle of movement, and then the essence) are explained with reference to Aristotle, especially *Metaphysics* V,4 (1014b16–1015a19) and *Physics* II,1 (192b8–23).[38] In Boethius's definition of the person, "nature" is not taken as the principle of movement, but as signifying the specific difference, that is, the essence.[39]

Aquinas also explains the "order of nature" in the Trinity (the order of the divine persons according to the communication of the divine nature) with the help of Aristotle's discussion of "nature" in *Metaphysics* V,4 (1014b17–18): the concept of "nature" implies the idea of "origin."[40]

---

[34] *De potentia*, q. 9, a. 2, ad 6.   [35] *De potentia*, q. 9, a. 2, ad 7.

[36] *In I Sent.*, dist. 23, q. 1, a. 1, corpus.

[37] *De potentia*, q. 9, a. 1, corpus. See also Aristotle, *Metaphysics* VIII,6 (1045a36–b7). In the same context (the person as substance), the distinction between substance and accidents clearly draws on Aristotle's *Categories* and *Metaphysics*; see, for instance, *ST* I, q. 29, a. 1; *De potentia*, q. 9, a. 2, corpus.

[38] See, for instance, *ST* I, q. 29, a. 1, arg. 4 (*Physics* II,1) and ad 4 (*Metaphysics* V,4).

[39] *ST* I, q. 29, a. 1, ad 4. See also *De potentia*, q. 9, a. 2, ad 11; *ST* III, q. 2, a. 1, corpus (and a. 2, corpus).

[40] *In I Sent.*, dist. 20, q. 1, a. 3, quaestiuncula 1, corpus: "Ordo originis signatur cum dicitur ordo naturae, secundum quod dicitur natura a Philosopho, V *Metaph.*, ex qua pullulat pullulans primo. Unde nomen naturae importat rationem originis." For this Arabic–Latin translation, see *Aristotelis opera cum Averrois commentariis*, vol. 8, *Aristotelis Metaphysicorum libri XIII cum*

1.2.3. Individual

Two aspects (among others) of the *individuum* are worth a special mention. Firstly, Aquinas uses Aristotle when he discusses the meaning of the "individual" in Boethius's definition of the person (the person is an *individual* substance of rational nature). The word "individual" (*individuum*) is a "name of intention" (second intention), that is, it does not signify the singular thing itself, but rather "the intention of singularity."[41] How are we, then, to understand the concept of individual in the definition of the person? Aquinas explains:

> Since the essential differences of things are often unknown and unnamed, we are sometimes under the necessity of employing accidental differences to designate substantial distinctions, as the Philosopher teaches in *Metaphysics* VIII. Thus it is that *individual* is included in the definition of *person*, in order to indicate an individual mode of existence (*individualem modum essendi*).[42]

On the one hand, this reference to Aristotle justifies the use of a "name of intention" in the definition of the person; on the other hand, it allows Aquinas to locate the principle of distinction of the divine persons in the relations, insofar as these relations denote a "distinct mode of existence."[43]

This teaching can be interpreted as Aquinas's appropriation of Cappadocian theology: the divine hypostases are characterized by a distinct "mode of

---

Averrois Cordubensis in eosdem commentariis et Epitome (Frankfurt am Main: Minerva, 1962), p. 107B: "Et etiam dicitur natura illud, in quo pullulat pullulans primo." See also Aquinas, *In I Sent.*, dist. 34, q. 2, a. 1, ad 3: "Natura semper habet rationem principii" (with reference to Aristotle's *Physics* II). On the use of Aristotle's *Metaphysics* in the commentary on the *Sentences*, see the enlightening study by Marta Borgo, "La *Métaphysique* d'Aristote dans le *Commentaire* de Thomas d'Aquin au Ier livre des *Sentences* de Pierre Lombard: Quelques exemples significatifs," *RSPhTh* 91 (2007): pp. 651–92.

[41] See, for instance, *In I Sent.*, dist. 23, q. 1, a. 3, corpus: "Non significat rem singularem, sed intentionem singularitatis."

[42] *De potentia*, q. 9, a. 2, ad 5, with reference to *Metaphysics* VII,12 (or to *Metaphysics* VIII,2 [?]). Aquinas makes a similar statement in his commentary on *Metaphysics* VII, lect. 12 (no. 1552). For other references to the same passage, see *In II Sent.*, dist. 3, q. 1, a. 6, corpus; *In IV Sent.*, dist. 44, q. 2, a. 1, quaestiuncula 1, ad 1; *Sententia de generatione* I, ch. 3, lect. 8 (Leonine ed., vol. 3, p. 293); *Sententia libri De anima* I, ch. 1 (Leonine ed., vol. 45/1, p. 7). For further references, see Marie-Dominique Roland-Gosselin, OP, *Le "De ente et essentia" de S. Thomas d'Aquin* (Paris: Vrin, 1948), p. 40. The same principle is invoked, in the same context (but with no explicit reference to Aristotle), in *ST* I, q. 29, a. 1, ad 3.

[43] *Individuum* designates a "mode of being" (*De potentia*, q. 9, a. 2, ad 5), and the person as substance indicates a "special mode of existing" (*De potentia*, q. 9, a. 2, ad 6; q. 9, a. 3, corpus). On this, see Lawrence Dewan, *Form and Being: Studies in Thomistic Metaphysics* (Washington, DC: The Catholic University of America Press, 2006), pp. 229–47. The role of relations is well expressed in *De potentia*, q. 2, a. 5, ad 5: "Sicut una et eadem est essentia trium personarum, non tamen sub eadem relatione, vel secundum eumdem modum existendi est in tribus personis." *De potentia*, q. 3, a. 15, ad 17: "Licet eadem natura sit Patris et Filii et Spiritus Sancti, non tamen eumdem modum existendi habet in tribus, et dico modum existendi secundum relationem."

subsisting" (*tropos tēs huparxeōs*)—an understanding that Aquinas may have known from, among other sources, St. John Damascene's *De fide orthodoxa*.[44]

Secondly, Aquinas refers to Aristotle's *Metaphysics* VII,11 (1037a5–10) to distinguish between the essence and the individual: "As body and soul belong to the nature of man, so *this* soul and *this* body belong to the understanding of *this* man, as it is said in *Metaphysics* VII: and by these is this particular man distinguished from all other men."[45] This Aristotelian teaching is applied to the understanding of the *person* with respect to *essence*: "Thus, 'hypostasis' and 'person' add the individual principles (*principia individualia*) to the *ratio* of the essence, and they are not the same as the essence in things composed of matter and form."[46] In God, the individuating principle ("quasi principle of individuation")[47] that accounts for the "individual" is the relation of origin.[48] To be more precise: the relations of origin, or relative properties, are the *principle of distinction* of the three divine persons.[49] This allows Aquinas to distinguish *materialiter* between the definition of the human person and the definition of the divine person (beyond Boethius's common definition that applies analogically to both human beings and God): the "material" signification of the human person includes individuation by matter, whereas the divine person signifies a relation or a relative.[50]

1.2.4. Principle

In the *Summa theologiae*, the meaning of the word "principle" (*principium*), a key term of Trinitarian theology, is discussed in reference to Aristotle's *Metaphysics* IV,2 (1003b24) and *Metaphysics* V,1 (1013a16–17). Aquinas begins his question on the Father by noting that Aristotle considered "principle" (*principium: archē*) and "cause" (*causa: aitia, aition*) as equivalent.[51] His commentary on the *Sentences* offers a similar reference to Aristotle.[52] According to St. Thomas, the Greeks use the words "cause" and "principle" indifferently,

---

[44] John Damascene, *De fide orthodoxa* I,8, in John Damascene, *De fide orthodoxa: Versions of Burgundio and Cerbanus*, ed. Eligius M. Buytaert (New York: Franciscan Institute St. Bonaventure, 1955), p. 35: "modum existentiae."

[45] *ST* I, q. 33, a. 2, corpus.

[46] *ST* I, q. 29, a. 2, ad 3 (without explicit reference to Aristotle).

[47] *SCG* IV, ch. 14 (no. 3503): "quasi individuationis principium."

[48] *ST* I, q. 29, a. 4, corpus (without explicit reference to Aristotle, but with the same explanation as in q. 33, a. 2, corpus).

[49] *ST* I, q. 33, a. 2, corpus.   [50] *De potentia*, q. 9, a. 4, corpus.

[51] *ST* I, q. 33, a. 1, arg. 1: "Principium enim et causa idem sunt, secundum Philosophum."

[52] *In I Sent.*, dist. 29, q. 1, a. 1, arg. 2: "Quod est principium alicujus videtur esse causa ejus: quia, sicut dicit Philosophus in V *Metaph.*, quot modis dicitur causa, tot modis dicitur principium vel initium." This clearly refers to Aristotle's statement in *Metaphysics* V,1; see also Aquinas, *Sent. Metaph.* V, lect. 1 (nos. 751–760).

when speaking of God (the Father is the Principle and Cause of the Son and of the Holy Spirit). But the Latin doctors do not use *causa*: rather, they employ the word *principium*, since the term *causa* implies diversity and dependence, whereas *principium* may signify a pure order (*ordo*), without any diversity between the principle and what issues from it.[53] The same explanation is found in Aquinas's commentary on *Metaphysics* V,1: "The term principle (*principium*) implies an order, whereas the term cause (*causa*) implies some influence on the being of the thing caused."[54]

This is especially important for Trinitarian theology: when we say that a divine person is the principle of another person, we only mean an order of origin, that is, a relation of origin. In a similar context, when explaining that the Son is both "from the Father" and "principle of the Holy Spirit" (the Son is *principium de principio*),[55] Aquinas discusses the following affirmation from Aristotle's *Physics* I,6 (189a30–31): "What is a principle (*archē*) ought not to be the predicate of any subject: if it were, there would be a principle of the principle." How, then, can the Son be the principle of the Holy Spirit? Thomas answers that, in this passage, Aristotle had in view the "first principles" (*principia prima*), so that Aristotle's statement can be applied to the Father: "The first principle, so to say, is the principle from no principle, and that is the Father."[56]

1.2.5. Relation

The doctrine of relation offers a striking example of the importance of Aristotle in Aquinas's Trinitarian theology: on this topic, the number of references to Aristotle is quite impressive. I have already discussed the theme of relative opposition (in section 1.1.3) and the foundation of real relations (in section 1.1.2). Aquinas's teaching on relations draws essentially on *Metaphysics* V,15 and *Categories* 7 (as well as on some passages of *Physics* that consider relation with respect to movement and predication). Since I have dealt with this topic at some length in a recent essay,[57] my discussion here will be limited to only six aspects.

---

[53] *ST* I, q. 33, a. 1, ad 1. Cf. *In I Sent.*, dist. 29, q. 1, a. 1, ad 2. For more on this, see Gilles Emery, OP, *The Trinitarian Theology of Saint Thomas Aquinas*, trans. Francesca A. Murphy (Oxford: Oxford University Press, 2007), pp. 156–8.

[54] *Sent. Metaph.* V, lect. 1 (no. 751).

[55] For the formula "principum de principio," see for instance *In I Sent.*, dist. 29, q. 1, a. 4, sed contra 1; *ST* I, q. 39, a. 8, corpus; *ST* I, q. 45, a. 6, ad 2.

[56] *De potentia*, q. 10, a. 4, ad 16: "Principium autem primum, ut ita dixerim, est principium non de principio, quod est Pater." Cf. arg. 16: "De ratione principii est quod non sit ab alio, secundum Philosophum in I *Physicorum*."

[57] Gilles Emery, OP, "*Ad aliquid*: la relation chez Thomas d'Aquin," in *Saint Thomas d'Aquin*, edited by Thierry-Dominique Humbrecht (Paris: Cerf, 2010), pp. 113–35; updated and expanded

[1] The major definition of the "relatives" and of "relation" that St. Thomas uses in Trinitarian theology is the second definition of the "relatives" found in Aristotle's *Categories* 7: "*Sunt 'ad aliquid' quibus hoc ipsum esse est ad aliquid quodam modo habere*" (Boethius's Latin translation).[58] Aquinas thus explains: "Relatives (*ea quae ad aliquid dicuntur*), according to their own proper *ratio*, signify only a relationship to another (*solum respectum ad aliud*)"; "The specific reason of a relative consists in being referred to another (*cum ratio specifica relativi consistat in hoc quod ad aliud se habet*)"; "The being [the essence] of a relative is to be referred to another (*relativi esse est ad aliud se habere*)"; "Relation . . . consists only in the fact of being referred to something else (*relatio . . . consistit tantum in hoc quod est ad aliud se habere*)."[59]

[2] Aquinas draws on Aristotle to show the existence of *real* relations in our world, that is to say, relations that are not only conceptual but that exist in the reality of "extramental things" (which are, for Aquinas, the object of the *Categories*).[60] This aspect is central for the analogical use of relation in Trinitarian theology, since, if there were no *real* relations in our world, the attribution of real relations to God would mean nothing to us.

[3] St. Thomas refers to Aristotle in order to distinguish between "real relations" and "relations of reason." This appears especially when Aquinas discusses the difference between the relation of knowledge to the thing known (which is a real relation), and the relation of the thing known to knowledge (which is a relation of reason). It is precisely this point (namely, that there is a difference between the formal *ratio* of the

---

version in English: "*Ad aliquid*: Relation in the Thought of St. Thomas Aquinas," in *Theology Needs Philosophy: Essays in Honor of Ralph McInerny*, edited by Matthew Lamb (Washington, DC: The Catholic University of America Press, forthcoming 2016). For sources and historical background, see Gilles Emery, OP, "La relation dans la théologie de saint Albert le Grand," in *Albertus Magnus: Zum Gedenken nach 800 Jahren: Neue Zugänge, Aspekte und Perspektiven*, edited by Walter Senner (Berlin: Akademie Verlag, 2001), pp. 455–65.

[58] Aristotle, *Categories* 7 (8a31–32). Latin translation from: Aristotle, *Categoriae vel Praedicamenta*, ed. Lorenzo Minio-Paluello, "Aristoteles Latinus I.1–5" (Bruges: Desclée de Brouwer, 1961), p. 22. See also 8a39–b1: "Relativis autem hoc est esse, ad aliquid quodammodo habere" (p. 22). The translation by William of Moerbeke (around 1266) stresses even more the formal reason of the relatives: "Sunt ipsa ad aliquid quibus esse idem est cum hoc quod est ad aliquid aliquo modo se habere" (p. 101).

[59] Respectively: *ST* I, q. 28, a. 1, corpus; q. 32, a. 2, corpus; q. 40, a. 2, ad 4; *In Physic.* III, lect. 1 (no. 280).

[60] See especially *De potentia*, q. 7, a. 9, corpus, with reference to *Metaphysics* V,7 (1017a7–30): "In nullo enim praedicamento ponitur aliquid nisi res extra animam existens. Nam ens rationis dividitur contra ens divisum per decem praedicamenta, ut patet V *Metaph*. Si autem relatio non esset in rebus extra animam non poneretur *ad aliquid* unum genus praedicamenti." Aquinas, *Sent. Metaph.* V, lect. 9 (nos. 885–892). See also Aristotle, *Metaphysics* V,15. In *De potentia*, q. 7, a. 9, corpus, Aquinas refers as well to *Metaphysics* XII,10 (1075a11–15) to show the existence of a real "order" (real relations) in the created universe.

relation on the one hand, and the relation's *existence* in a subject on the other) that accounts for the special "mode of signifying" of relations, a matter that Aquinas again explains with reference to Aristotle: although the real relation is an accident that "inheres" in a subject, "it does not signify as some *thing* of the subject in which it is found, but as *towards something exterior.*"[61] This difficulty is also linked with the discussion of the famous thesis that considered relations as "assistant" (*assistentes*) or "externally affixed" (*extrinsecus affixae*).[62]

[4] Among the properties of "relatives" (πρός τι) that Aquinas finds in Aristotle's *Categories*, two are of special importance for Trinitarian theology. First, relatives *as such* are simultaneous.[63] To be more precise: the simultaneity of nature (*simul natura*) is found in the *relativa* which have the same reason for their mutual relationship (e.g. father and son, master and servant, double and half), or which are in act *as relatives* (e.g. the known and the science). Put otherwise: the subjects, considered in themselves, are not necessarily simultaneous by nature (a father, *as a human being*, exists before his son), but the *relations* themselves are by nature simultaneous.[64] Aquinas refers to this property in order to show that there is no priority of one divine person over another. Relations allow him to show that the divine persons are *co-eternal*, in response to Arianism that could not accept the eternity of the Son's generation.[65]

[5] The second property concerns the mutual implication of relatives: according to Aristotle, the understanding of a relative includes the understanding of its correlative, and conversely. "It is plain that, if a man definitely apprehends a relative thing, he will also definitely apprehend that to which it is relative."[66] Following this view, Aquinas states: "In one relative is found the notion of the other relative."[67] By this very fact, knowing one divine person implies knowing the others: "As the Philosopher says, whoever knows a relative term also knows its

---

[61] *De potentia*, q. 8, a. 2, corpus: "*Ad aliquid* vero non significatur secundum rationem accidentis: non enim significatur ut aliquid eius in quo est, sed ut ad id quod extra est. Et proper hoc etiam dicit Philosophus, V *Metaph.*, quod scientia, inquantum est relatio, non est scientis, sed scibilis." See *Sent. Metaph.* V, lect. 17 (nos. 1028–1029). Aristotle, *Metaphysics* V,15 (1021a29–33).

[62] *ST* I, q. 28, a. 2, corpus; *De potentia*, q. 8, a. 2, corpus.

[63] *In I Sent.*, dist. 9, q. 2, a. 1, corpus: "Relativorum autem est simul esse natura, secundum Philosophum in *Praedicam.*" *ST* I, q. 42, a. 3, ad 2: "Manifestum est quod relativa sunt simul natura et intellectu." Aristotle, *Categories* 7 (7b15).

[64] *De potentia*, q. 7, a. 8, ad 1; *ST* I, q. 13, a. 7, arg. 6. These texts refer to Aristotle, *Categories* 7 (7b22–8a12).

[65] *In I Sent.*, dist. 9, q. 2, a. 1, corpus. See also *ST* I, q. 40, a. 2, ad 4.

[66] Aristotle, *Categories* 7 (8a35–37).

[67] *De potentia*, q. 7, a. 10, ad 4: "In uno enim relativo est intellectus alterius relativi." *In I Sent.*, dist. 19, q. 3, a. 2, corpus: "In uno relativorum intelligitur aliud."

correlative."[68] This property also allows St. Thomas to account for the mutual indwelling of the divine persons ("the Father is in the Son," "the Son is in the Father").[69]

[6] Finally, according to Aristotle's *Physics*, "there is no motion (*kinēsis*) in respect of the relative (πρός τι): for it may happen that when one correlative changes, the other, although this does not itself change, is no longer applicable, so that in these cases the motion is accidental."[70] When commenting on this text, Aquinas explains that there is no movement per se in the predicament *ad aliquid*, but only "per accidens."[71] This characteristic is used to show that the Trinitarian processions do not threaten God's immutability. Since "generation signifies a relation by way of operation,"[72] and because relation per se is not subject to movement, relation allows one to account for the *immutability* of the Son's generation, once again in response to Arianism.[73] Under all these aspects, Aquinas's use of Aristotle's teaching on "relatives" proves to be of the utmost importance for his account of the Trinitarian faith.

1.2.6. Generation

The analogical definition of generation in *ST* I, q. 27, a. 2 is inspired by the Aristotelian concept of generation–birth, as it is found, for instance, in *Physics* I,7–9 and II,1. From Aristotle, Aquinas takes up the double meaning of "generation" with which he begins his discussion: (1) the common process of generation, that is, the passage from nonexistence to existence; (2) the generation proper to living things, in which sense generation means "the origin of a living being from a conjoined living principle: and this is properly called birth."[74] To the latter definition, Aquinas adds the following

---

[68] *In I Sent.*, dist. 1, q. 2, a. 2, corpus: "Sicut enim dicit Philosophus, qui novit unum relativorum, cognoscit et reliquum." See also *In II Sent.*, dist. 38, q. 1, a. 4, corpus: "Qui novit unum relativorum, novit et reliquum" (with reference to Aristotle's *Categories*); *De veritate*, q. 2, a. 3, sed contra 2.

[69] *ST* I, q. 42, a. 5, corpus: "Secundum etiam relationes, manifestum est quod unum oppositorum relative est in altero secundum intellectum."

[70] Aristotle, *Physics* V,2 (225b11–13).

[71] Aquinas, *In Physic.* V, lect. 3 (no. 666): "Motus non est per se in *ad aliquid*, sed solum per accidens."

[72] *In I Sent.*, dist. 20, q. 1, a. 1, ad 1: "Generatio significat relationem per modum operationis." See also *De potentia*, q. 2, a. 5, ad 8.

[73] *In I Sent.*, dist. 9, expositio textus: "Et ita adventu relationis non potest concludi aliqua mutabilitas" (with reference to Aristotle's *Physics* V,2). See also *De potentia*, q. 7, a. 8 (with the same reference to *Physics* V,2).

[74] *ST* I, q. 27, a. 2, corpus. For this, and for what follows, see Hyacinthe-François Dondaine in: Thomas Aquinas, *Somme théologique: La Trinité*, vol. 1 (Paris: Desclée, 1950), p. 163.

specification: properly speaking, generation applies to "what proceeds by way of similitude."[75] This specification is important, since it will allow him to distinguish the Son's generation from the procession of the Holy Spirit (which does not occur "by way of similitude," but "by way of love"). References to Aristotle also appear in the context of the immutability of the generation in God. In *Physics* V,1 (225a12–17), Aristotle writes that generation (*genesis: generatio*) is a change. But this cannot apply to God.[76] Aquinas's answer draws on Aristotle himself: "Operation differs from movement (*differt operatio a motu*), according to the Philosopher, since 'operation' is the act of a perfect thing, but 'movement' is the act of an imperfect one."[77] We find, here again, the Aristotelian reference (*De anima* III,7 [431a6–7]) noted above (section 1.1.1) in the context of "immanent action."

1.2.7. Power

Aquinas grounds his discussion of "notional power" (the power to beget, the power to spirate) in Aristotle's definition of active power (*dunamis*) as "principle of acting."[78] He does not stick to only one of the definitions given by Aristotle (*Metaphysics* V,12 [1019a15–1020a6]), but he takes what is most common in them, namely, the idea that power is the principle of an act,[79] and the principle of what is produced by an action.[80] He notes, with reference to *Nicomachean Ethics* I,1 (1094a3–5)[81] and *Metaphysics* IX,8 (1050a23–b1),[82] that power does not always produce something, since many operations have no product (*non habent aliquid operatum*), so that "power is always the principle of action or operation."[83] This distinction is important for the clarification of

---

[75] *ST* I, q. 27, a. 2, corpus.   [76] *In I Sent.*, dist. 4, a. 1, arg. 1.

[77] *In I Sent.*, dist. 4, q. 1, a. 1, ad 1. Cf. *In I Sent.*, dist. 7, q. 1, a. 1, ad 3; *Sententia libri De anima* III, ch. 6 (Leonine ed., vol. 45/1, p. 230). See also *Sententia libri De anima* I, ch. 6 (Leonine ed., vol. 45/1, p. 30): "Motus autem et operatio differunt quia motus est actus imperfecti, operatio vero est actus perfecti."

[78] *ST* I, q. 41, a. 5, arg. 1: "Dicitur enim potentia activa esse principium agendi, ut patet in V *Metaphys.*"

[79] *ST* I, q. 41, a. 4, corpus: "Cum potentia nihil aliud significet quod principium alicuius actus."

[80] *De potentia*, q. 2, a. 2, corpus: "Potentia . . . sit principium . . . et eius quod est per actionem productum."

[81] See *Sent. Ethic.* I, lect. 1 (Leonine ed., vol. 47/1, p. 6): "Duplex est operatio, ut dicitur in IX Metaphysicae: una quae manet in ipso operante, sicut videre, intelligere et velle, et huiusmodi operatio proprie dicitur actio; alia autem est operatio transiens in exteriorem materiam, quae proprie dicitur factio."

[82] See *Sent. Metaph.* IX, lect. 8 (no. 1865): here Aquinas distinguishes between actions in which "nothing else is produced in addition to the action of the power" (*non est aliquod opus operatum praeter actionem potentiae*), and actions that "pass over into something external in order to perfect it" (*transit in aliquid exterius perficiendum*).

[83] *De potentia*, q. 2, a. 2, corpus: "Semper enim potentia est actionis vel operationis principium."

notional power, since "when speaking of God, words that signify a principle in respect of operation are not employed as denoting a personal property (*non dicuntur notionaliter*), but only those that signify a principle in respect of the term of an operation (*respectu eius quod est operationis terminus*)."[84] Notional power is the power *to beget the Son*, and the power *to spirate the Holy Spirit*. This leads to the conclusion that notional power "signifies the divine nature directly (*in recto*), and the relation indirectly (*in obliquo*)."[85]

In applying Aristotle's understanding of power to "notional power" in the Trinity, Aquinas underlines that "what is power is the very thing which is the principle of action,"[86] so that in God "notional power" signifies primarily the divine nature itself. Aquinas also explains the meaning of *virtus* (an attribute appropriated to the three divine persons)[87] by taking up the translation of Aristotle's *De caelo* I,11 (281a7–8 and 281a14–15) by Gerard of Cremona: *virtus* is "the utmost of power in a thing" (*ultimum quod est in re de potentia*), or "the utmost of power" (*ultimum potentiae*),[88] that is to say, the perfection of power and the ultimate influence of power.[89]

1.2.8. Equality

The concept of *aequalitas* by means of which Aquinas accounts for the divine persons' equality in nature, eternity, and power (a central theme of Trinitarian doctrine), comes principally from two passages of Aristotle's *Metaphysics*. The first is *Metaphysics* V,15 (1021a11–12),[90] where Aristotle gives the following

---

[84]   *De potentia*, q. 2, a. 2, corpus. In this context, St. Thomas is especially careful to put aside any idea of change.

[85]   *ST* I, q. 41, a. 5, corpus.

[86]   *De potentia*, q. 2, a. 2, corpus: "Nam si id quod est potentia, est ipsa res quae est principium actionis, oportet naturam divinam esse id quod est principium in divinis." *ST* I, q. 41, a. 5, ad 1: "Potentia . . . significat id quod est principium; non quidem sicut agens dicitur principium, sed sicut id quo agens agit, dicitur principium." On this, see Emmanuel Perrier, OP, *La fécondité en Dieu: La puissance notionnelle dans la Trinité selon saint Thomas d'Aquin* (Paris: Parole et Silence, 2009), pp. 106–7.

[87]   *In I Sent.*, dist. 34, q. 2, a. 1, ad 1. In *ST* I, q. 39, a. 8, corpus, Aquinas appropriates *virtus* to the Son and to the Holy Spirit, without mentioning Aristotle.

[88]   For this Latin translation, and for other occurrences of *virtus* as "ultimum potentiae," see the note by René-Antoine Gauthier, OP, on Aquinas's *Quodlibet* IV, q. 2, a. 1, arg. 1, in the Leonine edition (vol. 25/2, p. 320).

[89]   *Quaestio disputata de virtutibus in communi*, a. 1, corpus. By comparison with power (*potentia*), the notion of *virtus* emphasizes three aspects or nuances: perfection, immediacy, and the production of a maximal effect; a fourth aspect consists in the special use of *virtus* when Aquinas explains instrumental causality in relation to a principal agent. See Mireille Fornerod, "La distinction entre *virtus* et *potentia Dei* selon saint Thomas d'Aquin," *Revue théologique de Louvain* 45 (2014): pp. 502–32. Fornerod notes that, besides the influence of Neoplatonic and Dionysian thought, these aspects are "above all" part of the "Aristotelian heritage" (p. 529).

[90]   Among other passages, see also Aristotle, *Metaphysics* X,3 (1054a29–b3).

definitions: "Those things are the same whose substance is one; those are like whose quality is one; those are equal whose quantity is one."[91] The second text is *Metaphysics* X,5 (1056a22–24): "The equal is that which is neither great nor small...and it is opposed to both as a privative negation." In the *Summa theologiae*, Aquinas's treatment of divine equality begins with the latter definition,[92] which allows a clear and simple exclusion of all inequality between the divine persons (since there is neither "greater" nor "smaller" in God), and a direct identification of the persons' equality with their single essence. As for the first definition, it requires an explanation about how quantity can be said of God: not, of course, as "dimensive quantity" (*quantitas dimensiva*, which is found only in corporeal things), but as "quantity of force" (*quantitas virtutis*, *quantitas virtualis*) which is taken from the perfection of a nature or a form (we thus speak of the "greatness" of a spiritual thing), and from the effects of such a form. It is in this sense ("quantity of force") that equality applies to the divine persons.[93]

1.2.9. "Being In"

When discussing the reciprocal indwelling or mutual "being in" (*esse in*) of the divine persons (Aquinas does not call it explicitly *perichoresis*, though St. Bonaventure and other contemporaries used this word), St. Thomas refers to Aristotle's *Physics* IV,3 (210a14–24) on the modes according to which a thing may be said to "be in another." He counts eight modes, which are explicitly listed in the commentary on the *Sentences*: as the whole is in its parts; as the parts are in their whole; as the genus is in its species; as the species is in its genus; as something is in a place; as the form is in matter; as things are in what moves them; and as something is in its end.[94] The *Summa theologiae* refers to the same passage from the *Physics*, though without enumerating all these modes.[95] In both works, Aquinas denies that the Father may be in the Son—and the Son in the Father—according to any of these modes.

---

[91] For these definitions from Aristotle see, for instance, *In I Sent.*, dist. 19, q. 1, a. 1, corpus (in the context of Trinitarian equality): "Sicut dicit Philosophus, unum in substantia facit idem, unum in quantitate aequale, unum in qualitate facit simile." *In I Sent.*, dist. 8, q. 4, a. 3, arg. 2: "Philosophus dicit: unum in substantia facit idem, in quantitate aequale, in qualitate simile." *ST* I, q. 42, a. 1, arg. 1: "Aequalitas enim attenditur secundum unum in quantitate, ut patet per Philosophum, V *Metaphys.*" See also *Sent. Metaph.* V, lect. 17 (no. 1022).

[92] *ST* I, q. 42, a. 1, corpus: "Secundum Philosophum...aequale dicitur quasi per negationem minoris et maioris" (with explicit reference to Aristotle's *Metaphysics*).

[93] *ST* I, q. 42, a. 1, ad 1.

[94] *In I Sent.*, dist. 19, q. 3, a. 2, arg. 1. As in the *Summa* (*ST* I, q. 42, a. 5, arg. 1) the discussion *begins* with Aristotle.

[95] *ST* I, q. 42, a. 5, arg. 1. I thank Marta Rossignotti Jaeggi who pointed this out to me.

In the commentary on the *Sentences*, he specifies that Aristotle's modes do not cover all the ways according to which a thing may be in another, except "by some reduction of similitude" (*per quamdam similitudinis reductionem*). If, then, we apply such "reduction of similitude," the mutual indwelling of the divine persons can be linked with some of Aristotle's modes: so, the Trinitarian "co-immanence" by reason of the unity of essence can be led back to the presence of the genus in the species, in some improper fashion (since there is neither genus nor species in God); in the same way, the mutual indwelling by reason of the divine relations may be led back to the presence of a thing in what moves and causes it (although the Father is not an efficient principle with respect to the Son).[96] Aquinas gives a similar detailed answer when he examines "whether the properties (of the divine persons) are in the persons themselves, and in the essence."[97]

The *Summa theologiae* also teaches that none of the modes enumerated by Aristotle can properly account for the mutual "being in" of the divine persons. Here, Aquinas specifies that "the mode the most nearly approaching to the reality is the one according to which a thing is said to be in its originating principle (*esse in principio originante*), except that the unity of essence between the principle and what proceeds from this principle is not found among created things."[98] The presence of Aristotle in the question of the mutual "being in" of the divine persons is especially interesting for our topic, since it shows both the help offered by natural philosophy and its limits in theology: "What is found in creatures does not sufficiently represent what is in God."[99] In the commentary on the *Sentences*, as a conclusion to the discussion of *Physics* IV,3 on the modes of "being in another," Aquinas recalls the Augustinian rule taught by the Fourth Lateran Council (in a Trinitarian context as well): between God and creatures, "the dissimilarity is greater than any similarity."[100]

1.2.10. Oneness and Plurality

St. Thomas draws on Aristotle to define unity and plurality—concepts that are central to Trinitarian theology. In statements such as "God is one" or "the Father is one," the word "one" means the transcendental one, that is, the one convertible with being. Accordingly, Trinitarian plurality is explained in terms

---

[96] *In I Sent.*, dist. 19, q. 3, a. 2, ad 1.

[97] *In I Sent.*, dist. 33, q. 1, a. 3, ad 4 (see arg. 4, with explicit reference to Aristotle's *Physics* IV).

[98] *ST* I, q. 42, a. 5, ad 1.

[99] *ST* I, q. 42, a. 5, ad 1: "Ea quae in creaturis sunt, non sufficienter repraesentant ea quae Dei sunt."

[100] *In I Sent.*, dist. 33, q. 1, a. 3, ad 4: "in his omnibus major dissimilitudo quam similitudo."

of "transcendental multiplicity."[101] The idea of "transcendental multiplicity" is Aquinas's own, but he holds from *Metaphysics* V,6 (notably 1016b3–6) and *Metaphysics* X,1 (1052b15–16) the understanding of the *one* as "that which is not divided," in such a way that "one" adds nothing positive to being, but only the negation of a division.[102] In the same context, when explaining how this negation ("non-division") applies to God, Aquinas refers to Aristotle's discussion of the meanings of "privation."[103] The clarification of the distinction between the numerical one ("one" which is the principle of number, and pertains to quantity) and the one "convertible with being" also rests on Aristotle.[104] The different meanings of "multiplicity" with respect to "unity" are equally clarified with the aid of Aristotle's *Metaphysics* (X,3 and X,6).[105] In a similar context, the discussion of words that can or cannot be properly used to signify unity and plurality in God, e.g. "alone" (*solus*),[106] "diverse" (*diversum*), and "different" (*differens*), is made with reference to definitions found in Aristotle's *Metaphysics*.[107]

Aquinas refers to Aristotle in order to define several other concepts, which I will not present in the limited scope of this study. We should note, among others, the concepts of "privation" and "negation" by means of which St. Thomas explains the Father's property of "unbegottenness";[108] the attribution

---

[101] *ST* I, q. 30, a. 3, corpus; cf. ad 2: "multitudo transcendens." On this, see Emery, *The Trinitarian Theology of Saint Thomas Aquinas*, pp. 137–41.

[102] *Quodlibet* X, q. 1, a. 1, sed contra 1 and corpus: "Est enim unum *quod non diuiditur*, secundum Philosophum.... Sic ergo intelligendum est, secundum opinionem Aristotilis et Commentatoris eius, quod unum quod conuertitur cum ente non superaddit enti rem aliquam, set solum negationem diuisionis." See the texts quoted in notes by Fr. René-Antoine Gauthier, the Leonine editor (Leonine ed., vol. 25/1, pp. 123–4), especially *In I Sent.*, dist. 24, q. 1, a. 3, sed contra 2; *De potentia*, q. 9, a. 7, sed contra 10.

[103] *Quodlibet* X, q. 1, a. 1, sed contra 2, with reference to Aristotle's *Metaphysics* X,3 (1054a20–26); see also Averroes's text quoted in note by the Leonine editor (Leonine ed., vol. 25/1, p. 123). *De potentia*, q. 9, a. 7, ad 11, with reference to Aristotle's *Metaphysics* V,22.

[104] See, for instance, *In I Sent.*, dist. 24, q. 1, a. 3, corpus and ad 4. For the "one" as identical with "being," see Aristotle, *Metaphysics* X,2 (1054a13–19); Aquinas, *Sent. Metaph.* X, lect. 3 (nos. 1974–1982).

[105] See, for instance, *Quodlibet* X, q. 1, a. 1, arg. 2, with reference to Aristotle's *Metaphysics* X,3 (1054a20–26); *De potentia*, q. 9, a. 7, ad 7, with reference to Aristotle's *Metaphysics* X,6 (1056b3–1057a17). See also *Sent. Metaph.* X, lect. 8 (nos. 2075–2096, especially 2076–2077, 2081–2082, and 2090–2091).

[106] *In I Sent.*, dist. 21, q. 1, a. 1, quaestiuncula 1, corpus; *ST* I, q. 31, a. 3, arg. 1. Aristotle, *Sophistici Elenchi* 22 (178a39–b1): "not with another." See also *In I Sent.*, dist. 21, q. 2, a. 1, arg. 2 (if the Augustinian affirmation "*Trinitas est solus Deus*" is true, is the statement "*Trinitas est Deus solus*" also true?), with reference to Aristotle's *Peri hermeneias* 10 (20b1–2).

[107] Aquinas, *De potentia*, q. 7, a. 3, ad 2: "Differens et diversum differunt, ut Philosophus dicit." *De potentia*, q. 9, a. 8, arg. 2: "Secundum Philosophum in X *Metaph.*, diversum dicitur absolute, differens vero relative." Aristotle, *Metaphysics* X,3 (1054b23–31). The Latin translation "differentia vero et diversitas aliud," and then "diversum ... differens," is found, for instance, in the *Translatio Anynoma sive Media* (it is found in the translation by William of Moerbeke as well). See also Aristotle, *Metaphysics* V,9 (1018a9–15).

[108] *In I Sent.*, dist. 28, q. 1, a. 1, ad 2 and ad 3 (with explicit reference to Aristotle).

of operations to distinct individuals (*actus sunt suppositorum*, an Aristotelian principle that Aquinas will employ in his Christology but that he first uses in the context of Trinitarian theology);[109] the different meanings of "necessity," in order to explain in which sense the generation of the Son is necessary;[110] the meaning of "gift," in the discussion of the Holy Spirit as *Donum*;[111] the "causality of what comes first," by means of which Aquinas links creation to the Trinitarian processions;[112] and several aspects of the understanding of "motion" with respect to "procession."[113] The themes and concepts that have been considered with some detail are enough to realize the extraordinary importance of Aristotle in Aquinas's teaching on the Trinity.

1.3. ARISTOTELIAN LOGIC: SIGNIFICATION, ATTRIBUTION, AND ARGUMENTATION

When Aquinas takes up an Aristotelian concept, he often recalls the rules of signification and analogy, as explained in *ST* I, q. 13, with reference to *ST* I, q. 3 (on God's simplicity): "We cannot speak of simple things except by the mode of the composite things from which we take our cognition."[114] These composite things determine our mode of understanding (*modus intelligendi*) and our mode of signifying (*modus significandi*): under these aspects, our words do not properly apply to God (since they are bound to the mode according to which things exist in the created world); but the "perfections signified" (*perfectiones significatae*) are properly attributed to God, in a way that respects God's incomprehensibility.

The influence of Aristotelian epistemology and logic can be found throughout the treatise on the Trinity. St. Thomas is constantly working at the purification of our language, in order to make it appropriate for a correct understanding of the faith. The careful distinction between ontological levels

---

[109] *In I Sent.*, dist. 26, q. 2, a. 2, corpus: "omnis operatio est individuorum distinctorum, secundum Philosophum"; dist. 27, q. 1, a. 2, sed contra 1: "operatio, secundum Philosophum, est individuorum distinctorum, vel singularium." See also *ST* I, q. 39, a. 5, ad 1: "actus sunt suppositorum"; q. 40, a. 1, ad 3: "Actus autem suppositorum sunt." For the Christological use of this principle, see section 2 of Chapter 9 in this work: "*Actiones Sunt Suppositorum.*"

[110] *In I Sent.*, dist. 6, q. 1, a. 1, corpus (with explicit reference to Aristotle).

[111] *In I Sent.*, dist. 18, q. 1, a. 2, corpus; *ST* I, q. 38, a. 2, corpus (with explicit reference to Aristotle).

[112] See Gilles Emery, OP, *La Trinité créatrice: Trinité et création dans les commentaires aux Sentences de Thomas d'Aquin et de ses précurseurs Albert le Grand et Bonaventure* (Paris: Vrin, 1995), pp. 276–80 and 533.

[113] Among other texts, see Aquinas, *De potentia*, q. 10, a. 1, corpus.

[114] *ST* I, q. 3, a. 3, ad 1.

(material things, created spiritual things, God) allows an analogical use of names and concepts on the epistemological level.

A good example is found in *De potentia*, q. 10, a. 1, dealing with "procession" ("whether there is a procession in God"). Here, Aquinas begins by recalling that our intellectual knowledge starts from the senses. Referring to Aristotle, he gives the example of "distance" (*distantia*), a concept which was first applied to place (*locus*) and was afterwards used to designate any difference of forms. In this way, "procession" (*processio*) was first used to signify a local movement from one place to another; then its use was extended (*transumitur*) to signify any emanation of a thing from another, according to an "order" (*ordo*). With this background, Aquinas explains that there are two kinds of operations: transitive operations, and immanent operations (an Aristotelian theme again). At this point, Aquinas refers to Aristotle's *De anima* III (by contrast with *Physics* III) in order to show that "movement" (*motus*) can apply to any operation, including the operations of sensing and understanding as *actus perfecti*: taken in this sense, "movement" (self-motion) serves to define living things. Aquinas continues by attributing both transitive and immanent operations to God (according to the rules of analogy), in order to show that, in God, the "speaking of the Word" and the "spiration of Love" must be grasped as immanent operations. The Aristotelian frame of the discussion of "procession" is especially striking.

Aquinas's understanding of "signification" is based on his reading of Aristotle's *Peri hermeneias*: "The signification of a name does not refer to the thing immediately but through the intellect (*mediante intellectu*), since spoken words are the signs of the soul's passions, and the conceptions of the intellect are similitudes of things, according to the Philosopher at the beginning of *On Interpretation*."[115] This teaching plays a central role in the Trinitarian doctrine of the Son as *Word*. The confrontation with Aristotle inspired Aquinas to develop a new view on the Word, by integrating Aristotelian and Augustinian theories of cognition.[116] His mature exposition of the Word starts with the following affirmation: "According to the Philosopher, the vocal sound signifies what is conceived by the intellect."[117] Aquinas also draws on Aristotle's *De anima*: "And again, as [the Philosopher] puts it in *De anima*, the vocal sound proceeds from the imagination."[118] Aquinas's commentary on St. John explains

---

[115] *De potentia*, q. 7, a. 6, corpus. Aristotle, *Peri hermeneias* 1 (16a3–4).

[116] Harm Goris, "Theology and Theory of the Word in Aquinas: Understanding Augustine by Innovating Aristotle," in *Aquinas the Augustinian*, edited by Michael Dauphinais, Barry David, and Matthew Levering (Washington, DC: The Catholic University of America Press, 2007), pp. 62–78.

[117] *ST* I, q. 34, a. 1, corpus: "Vox enim significat intellectus conceptum, secundum Philosophum, in libro I *Periherm.*" Explicit references to Aristotle's *Peri hermeneias* in Aquinas's teaching on the divine Word are also found in other works, e.g. *Compendium theologiae* I, ch. 37.

[118] *ST* I, q. 34, a. 1, corpus: "Et iterum vox ex imaginatione procedit, ut in libro *De anima* dicitur." Aristotle, *De anima* II,8 (420b32).

with greater detail that the "exterior word" signifies neither the intellect itself, nor the intelligible *species*, nor the act of understanding, but what the intellect *forms* or *expresses* when it understands, that is to say, the "inner word" (*verbum interius*).[119]

Aquinas unites Augustinian theological heritage with Aristotelian philosophy. This new synthesis goes beyond Aristotle, by distinguishing clearly between abstraction and formation of the inner word. St. Thomas refers again to Aristotle's *De anima* III,6 (430a26–28) when he explains that the "inner word" is found in *the two operations of the intellect*: the "understanding of indivisibles" and the "operation by which the intellect unites and separates" (that is, the formation of a definition, and the formation of an enunciation).[120] Aristotle's *Metaphysics* IV,7 (1012a23–24) is also invoked on this point: "So the Philosopher says that the *ratio* which a name signifies is its definition."[121] Although the conclusion is derived from the Augustinian tradition, it is presented as consistent with the reading of Aristotle: "Hence, what is thus expressed, i.e. formed in the soul, is called an *interior word*."[122] Among other aspects of the same topic, we should also note the following affirmation: "The intellect, insofar as it understands in act, becomes one with the thing understood." This teaching comes from Aristotle: Aquinas uses it to show that the Word is perfectly one with the Father.[123] These Aristotelian resources are of central importance, since they allow an analogical account of the divine Word and of his essential unity with the Father.

The Aristotelian principle according to which "what is signified by a name is its definition"[124] is applied as well to Boethius's analogical definition of the

---

[119] *Lectura super Ioannem*, ch. 1, lect. 1 (no. 25). See also *SCG* IV, ch. 11 (no. 3466): here Aquinas specifies that the "inner word" is neither the substance of the intellect, nor the thing which is understood; in the same chapter, when dealing with the divine Word as *Imago*, St. Thomas makes a similar statement with reference to Aristotle (no. 3476): "Ratio enim hominis in intellectu non est homo, nam, ut Philosophus dicit, lapis non est in anima sed species lapidis." Aristotle, *De anima* III,8 (431b29–432a1).

[120] *Lectura super Ioannem*, ch. 1, lect. 1 (no. 25). An explicit reference to the *De anima* is found in the same Trinitarian context in *De potentia*, q. 9, a. 5, corpus: "Hoc ergo est primo et per se intellectum, quod intellectus in seipso concipit de re intellecta, sive illud sit definitio, sive aliqua enuntiatio, secundum quod ponuntur duae operationes intellectus in III *De anima*." For Aquinas's interpretation of this passage, see his *Sententia libri De anima* III, ch. 5.

[121] *Lectura super Ioannem*, ch. 1, lect. 1 (no. 25): "Unde dicit Philosophus quod ratio, quam significat nomen, est definitio." For this Latin translation, see the note in Aquinas's *Expositio Libri Peryermenias* I, lect. 2 (Leonine ed., vol. 1*/1, p. 13).

[122] *Lectura super Ioannem*, ch. 1, lect. 1 (no. 25): "Unde dicit Philosophus quod ratio, quam significat nomen, est definitio. Istud ergo sic expressum, scilicet formatum in anima, dicitur verbum interius."

[123] *ST* I, q. 27, a. 1, ad 2: "Intellectus secundum hoc quod actu intelligit, secundum hoc fit unum cum intellecto. Unde . . . necesse est quod Verbum divinum sit perfecte unum cum eo a quo procedit, absque omni diversitate." Aristotle, *De anima* III,4 (430a3–5); *De anima* III,5 (430a19–20); *Metaphysics* XII,9 (1075a1–5).

[124] This principle appears in various formulations. For instance, see *De potentia*, q. 7, a. 2, sed contra 3: "Nomen enim proprie significat substantiam et quidditatem, ut habetur IV *Metaph.*"

person.[125] Along with Aristotle (*Metaphysics* IV,4), St. Thomas also specifies that what a name signifies must be one: the name *persona* cannot signify equally both essence and relation (a position held by Simon of Tournai and William of Auxerre, though in different ways),[126] since what this name signifies must be one.[127] As noted above (in section 1.2.1 on "Substance"), Aquinas holds that Boethius offered a *common* (analogical) definition of the person. If we look further for a "*formal* signification," the divine person must be grasped as "a distinct subsistent in the divine nature." And, according to its "*material* signification," the divine person signifies a relation or a relative.[128] This raises a difficulty: if "what is signified by a name is its definition," and if we accept the definition of the person by Boethius, how can it be said that the "divine person" signifies a subsisting relation? Aquinas's answer reads: "In the meaning of 'individual substance'—that is to say, distinct and incommunicable [substance]—in God, we understand a relation."[129] Similarly, Aquinas explains that the Aristotelian principle according to which "spoken words are the signs of what is conceived by the intellect" (*Peri hermeneias* 1 [16a3–4]) is still true when we understand the divine person as a subsisting relation: the "substance" that is conceived by the intellect is said to be "absolute" in the sense that it exists by itself, whereas the "relative" (the divine person as a relation) only "excludes the absolute that is not referred to another."[130]

Similar principles are invoked in other contexts as well. For instance, the rules of *appellatio* and *denominatio* are applied to the understanding of names such as "Begetter" (*genitor*) and "Father" (*pater*),[131] and to the formula "*Pater et Filius diligunt se Spiritu Sancto*."[132] In sum, Aquinas takes up Aristotle's

---

[125] *In I Sent.*, dist. 25, q. 1, a. 1, ad 2; *De potentia*, q. 9, a. 4, arg. 7 and corpus; *ST* I, q. 29, a. 4, arg. 3.

[126] See Emery, *The Trinitarian Theology of Saint Thomas Aquinas*, pp. 115–16.

[127] *De potentia*, q. 9, a. 4, corpus: "Quia quod non significat unum, nihil significat. Unde omne nomen significat unum in una acceptione, ut dicit Philosophus in IV *Metaph.*" Aristotle, *Metaphysics* IV,4 (1006b7): "For not to have one meaning is to have no meaning." See also Aristotle, *Metaphysics* VII,11 (1037a17–20); *Metaphysics* VII,12 (1037b24–27). We should note as well that Aristotle's *Metaphysics* VII,4 (1030b5–6) is invoked in the discussion about the divine persons as *tres res* (a theme of the Augustinian tradition): Aquinas, *In I Sent.*, dist. 25, q. 1, a. 4, ad 2.

[128] *De potentia*, q. 9, a. 4, corpus; cf. arg. 7, with reference to Aristotle's *Metaphysics* IV,7 (1012a23–24).

[129] *ST* I, q. 29, a. 4, ad 3 (see arg. 3, with the same reference to Aristotle's *Metaphysics* IV,7: "what is signified by a name is its definition").

[130] *De potentia*, q. 9, a. 4, arg. 10: "Voces, secundum Philosophum, sunt signa intellectuum; intellectus autem qui concipitur ex hoc nomine *persona* est intellectus substantiae primae . . . qua nihil est magis absolutum, cum sit per se existens"; and ad 10: "Relativum autem excludit absolutum quod ad aliud non refertur" (provisional text of the Leonine edition).

[131] *ST* I, q. 33, a. 2, ad 2: "Secundum Philosophum in II *De anima*, denominatio rei maxime debet fieri a perfectione et fine. Generatio autem significat ut in fieri: sed paternitas significat complementum generationis." Aristotle, *De anima* II,4 (416b23–24).

[132] *ST* I, q. 37, a. 2, corpus: "Cum res communiter denominentur a suis formis . . . Contingit autem aliquid denominari per id quod ab ipso procedit." On "denomination" and its roots in

fundamental principles on naming and signification: he not only shows their validity when applied to our speech about God, but he also (and primarily) uses them in order to refine his account of Trinitarian language.

Last but not least, we can observe Aristotle's influence on Aquinas's understanding of the task and purpose of speculative Trinitarian theology. Although there is no explicit mention of Aristotle's epistemology in *ST* I, q. 32, a. 1 ("whether the Trinity of the divine persons can be known by natural reason"),[133] I will make an exception to the method of the present study, since this topic is worth a special mention. When explaining how human intelligence can manifest the Trinity, St. Thomas distinguishes between two kinds of "reasons" (*dupliciter inducitur ratio*). The first kind offers a proof sufficient to demonstrate a fundamental thesis or a "principle" (*radix*). The second kind cannot furnish a sufficient proof for such a principle; but it can show that, once this principle is posited (*radici iam positae*), the effects that follow from it are fitting or consistent (*congruere*) with this principle and with other observations.[134] "Reasons" brought forward in order to show the existence of the Trinity (God's goodness and beatitude, the analogy of the word and love, and similar arguments) belong to the second case: they do not prove the existence of three divine persons—since faith in the Trinity rests exclusively on revelation—but they "manifest" the Trinity to the mind of believers, that is to say, they make the Trinitarian mystery more luminous to the mind of believers.

On the one hand, this description of the non-demonstrability and faithful acceptance of the Trinity can be linked to Aristotelian logic, in which a proposition established by a higher science is received as a "given" (*suppositio*) by an inferior science that cannot prove it: the inferior science "assumes" this proposition as a foundation for its own explanations, as Aquinas writes in his commentary on the *Posterior Analytics*.[135] On the other hand, the nature of

---

Aristotle's *Categories* 1 (1a12–15), see Jean Jolivet, "Vues médiévales sur les paronymes," *Revue internationale de philosophie* 29 (1975): pp. 222–42.

[133] Here, Aristotle appears in objection 1 and in its reply, concerning "the number three, through which we bring ourselves to acknowledge the greatness of one God": Aristotle, *De caelo* I,1 (268a13–15). According to Aquinas, Aristotle only "wished to say that the ancients used the threefold number (*ternarius numerus*) in their sacrifices and prayers, on account of some perfection residing in the number three." But the parallel article in the *De veritate* (q. 10, a. 13, corpus) does refer to Aristotle's theory of knowledge: "Primorum autem principiorum cognitio a sensibilibus ortum sumit, ut patet per Philosophum in II Posteriorum; ex sensibilibus autem non potest perveniri ad cognoscendum propria personarum sicut ex effectibus devenitur in causas." Aristotle, *Posterior Analytics* II,19 (100a10–11).

[134] *ST* I, q. 32, a. 1, ad 2: "Ratio . . . quae radici iam positae ostendat congruere consequentes effectus . . . Secundo modo se habet ratio quae inducitur ad manifestationem Trinitatis: quia scilicet, Trinitate posita, congruunt huiusmodi rationes; non tamen ita quod per has rationes sufficienter probetur Trinitas personarum."

[135] *Expositio Libri Posteriorum* I, lect. 5 (Leonine ed., vol. 1*/2, p. 25): "Alique propositiones suppositiones dicuntur. Sunt enim quedam propositiones que non possunt probari nisi per

arguments used to "manifest" the Trinity is illustrated by the theory of
"eccentrics" and "epicycles" proposed by Ptolemaeus and Hipparchus.[136]
The commentary on Aristotle's *De caelo* shows that Aquinas knew the weakness of such astronomical theories: they are "assumptions" (*suppositiones*) by
means of which some astronomers attempted to account for the movements of
planets ("assumptions that save the appearances"); but perhaps the movements of planets can be explained in some other way that is not yet known.[137]
Put otherwise, such explanations are probable. In a similar manner, though
with significant differences (the comparison bears on the impossibility of
proving the Trinity by necessary reasons), the theologian receives from God,
by revelation, this mysterious "principle": there are three persons in God.
Once this principle is posited by faith (*Trinitate supposita*), theology develops
arguments of fittingness to "manifest" the Trinity.[138]

In the first chapters of the *Summa contra Gentiles*, St. Thomas explains the
purpose of this work by noting the twofold task of the wise man: to speak the
truth, and to refute the opposing error. As Fr. René-Antoine Gauthier pointed
out, this twofold office of the wise man comes from Aristotle's *Sophistical
Refutations*.[139] On this basis, Aquinas distinguishes between the truths that
can be known by the natural light of human reason, and those truths that are
beyond the reach of human reason. The first kind of truths (e.g. that God
exists, that he is one) can be proved by demonstrations (*demonstrative*).[140] But
in the domain of truths that belong exclusively to the faith (e.g. that God is
Trinity), the arguments advanced by the theologian do not have demonstrative force; rather, they are "likely arguments" (*rationes verisimiles*) or "probable arguments" (*rationes probabiles*).[141] Aquinas insists that the second kind

principia alterius sciencie, et ideo oportet quod in illa sciencia supponantur, licet probentur per
principia alterius sciencie."

[136] *ST* I, q. 32, a. 1, ad 2: "Sicut in astrologia ponitur ratio excentricorum et epicyclorum ex
hoc quod, hac positione facta, possunt salvari apparentia sensibilia circa motus caelestes: non
tamen ratio haec est sufficienter probans, quia etiam forte alia positione facta salvari possent."

[137] *Sententia libri De caelo* II, lect. 17, no. 2 (Leonine ed., vol. 3, pp. 186–7): "Licet enim,
talibus suppositionibus factis, apparentia salvarentur . . . forte secundum aliquem alium modum,
nondum ab hominibus comprehensum, apparentia circa stellas salvantur."

[138] See Hyacinthe-François Dondaine in: Thomas Aquinas, *Somme théologique*, vol. 1,
pp. 198–200 and 253–8. The phrase "Trinitate supposita" is taken from Aquinas, *De veritate*,
q. 10, a. 13, corpus, in the context of the knowledge of the Trinity through "appropriated"
essential attributes: "Per essentialia quae personis appropriantur, sicut potentia Patri, . . . Trinitas
perfecte cognosci non potest . . . sed Trinitate supposita huiusmodi attributa propter aliquam
similitudinem ad propria personarum appropriantur personis."

[139] *SCG* I, ch. 1 (no. 7); cf. ch. 2 (no. 9). Aristotle, *Sophistici Elenchi* 1 (165a25–27). Boethius's
translation reads: "Est autem . . . in unoquoque opus scientis non mentiri quidem eum de quibus
nouit, mentientem autem manifestare posse." René-Antoine Gauthier, OP, *Saint Thomas d'A-
quin, Somme contre les Gentils: Introduction* (Paris: Éditions Universitaires, 1993), pp. 147–56,
at 148.

[140] *SCG* I, ch. 3 (no. 14); cf. ch. 9 (no. 55): "rationes demonstrativas."

[141] *SCG* I, ch. 9 (nos. 54–55).

of truths cannot be contrary to the principles of natural human reason. Hence, arguments brought forward against the faith "do not have demonstrative force (*nec demonstrationis vim habent*), but are either probable reasons (*rationes probabiles*) or sophisms (*rationes sophisticae*)" that can be answered.[142] This tripartite classification (namely: *demonstrative, probable,* and *sophistical* arguments) is very close to the three kinds of syllogisms mentioned at the beginning of Aristotle's *Topics*.[143]

Aquinas uses Aristotelian logic in order to clarify his approach as a theologian. Admittedly, Aquinas's "probable reasons" differ from Aristotle's "dialectical syllogism" (at least in this context). "Likely reasons" or "probable reasons" are brought forward for the exercise and encouragement of the faithful (*ad fidelium quidem exercitium et solatium*), and not in order to convince opponents.[144] Such "reasons" show that "what the faith proposes is not impossible."[145] Aquinas also refers to Aristotle when he notes that an indication of the Catholic truth can be gathered from Trinitarian heresies (Arianism, Sabellianism), since errors contradict not only the truth, but also each other.[146] Aristotelian logic is put to use by Aquinas in service of the Augustinian project of "faith seeking understanding."

Despite the limited scope of this study, it clearly appears that Aristotle plays a decisive role in Aquinas's Trinitarian theology. Aristotelian resources concern all the major fields of Aquinas's account of the Trinity: method (structural themes), metaphysics, natural philosophy, anthropology, psychology, epistemology, language, and logic. Aquinas's recourse to Aristotle also supports and strengthens the unity of Trinitarian theology with the treatment of other theological domains. Obviously, on such a topic, Aquinas goes totally beyond what Aristotle could have imagined. But he never uses Aristotle as a mere expedient. Rather, he adopts Aristotelian notions because of their truth value, and he assimilates them (with some adjustments or complements) into a Christian discourse. In constant reference to the *Philosophus*, Thomas integrates Aristotle into his own theology—and this in several ways: he

---

[142] *SCG* I, ch. 7 (no. 47; cf. no. 42).

[143] Aristotle, *Topics* I,1 (100a25–101a4): "demonstration (*apodeixis*)," "dialectical reasoning (*dialektikos syllogismos*) from reasons that are generally accepted," and "contentious reasoning (*eristikos syllogismos*)." For the relationship between "dialectical syllogism" and "probable reasons," see Aquinas, *Expositio Libri Posteriorum* I, lect. 1 (Leonine ed., vol. 1*/2, p. 6): "syllogismus dyaleticus ex probabilibus est, de quo agit Aristotiles in libro Topicorum."

[144] *SCG* I, ch. 9 (no. 54). For more on this, see Gilles Emery, OP, *Trinity, Church, and the Human Person: Thomistic Essays* (Naples, FL: Sapientia Press, 2007), pp. 49–65.

[145] *ST* II-II, q. 1, a. 5, ad 2: "Rationes quae inducuntur a Sanctis ad probandum ea quae sunt fidei non sunt demonstrativae, sed persuasiones quaedam manifestantes non esse impossibile quod in fide proponitur."

[146] *SCG* IV, ch. 7 (no. 3426): "Nam vero, ut Philosophus dicit, etiam falsa attestantur: falsa vero non solum a veris, sed etiam ab invicem distant." Aristotle, *Prior Analytics* II,2 (53b4–10); *Posterior Analytics* I,32 (88a20–30).

structures his exposition of the Trinity around Aristotelian principles; he starts theological discussions with Aristotle (in the objections or in the body of articles); he elaborates central theological theses with the aid of Aristotle; he takes up Aristotelian definitions in order to clarify theological doctrines; he solves objections by referring to Aristotle; and he interprets Aristotelian themes to make them fit into his own theological discourse. As I recalled at the beginning of this chapter, Aristotle is far from being the main source quoted or mentioned by Aquinas, but the use of Aristotle really shapes Aquinas's Trinitarian theology, and contributes greatly to its originality, coherence, and strength.

2

Aristotelianism and Angelology According to Aquinas

Serge-Thomas Bonino, OP

Angelology, with its cascade of spiritual beings, intermediaries between humankind and God, seems to be an impregnable bastion (or perhaps a Trojan horse?) of Platonism in Christian theology.[1] Is it not Plato himself that St. Thomas Aquinas considers to be the "inventor" of the suprasensible world?[2] As a matter of fact, Plato is the first (apart from the incomplete attempt by Anaxagoras) to understand how to move beyond the materialism of the first philosophers. Transcending imagination by way of the intellect, he was unique in raising his intellectual gaze toward the fundamental causes of reality and in recognizing the existence of immaterial substances.[3] Do not Denys and

---

[1] This chapter has been translated from the French by Benjamin Heidgerken.

[2] Aquinas, *De substantiis separatis*, ch. 1 (Leonine ed., vol. 40, p. D 42): "Unde Plato sufficientiori via processit ad opinionem primorum Naturalium evacuandam."

[3] The "history of fundamental philosophy," in the form of broad frescos, is laid forth in several texts in St. Thomas's corpus. St. Thomas generally focuses on the progressive discovery of superior forms of causality, up to the radical ultimate causality that is the work of creation. In parallel fashion, especially in the text of *De substantiis separatis*, he also identifies how the human spirit became aware of the superior principles that are separate substances. See *SCG* II, ch. 37 (nos. 1129–1130) (around 1261–1262); *De potentia*, q. 3, a. 5 (around 1265–1266); *ST* I, q. 44, a. 2 (1266/1268); *In Physic.* VIII, lect. 2 (1268/1269); *De substantiis separatis*, ch. 9 (around 1271). These texts have been the object of numerous interpretations: Jacques Maritain, *La philosophie bergsonienne*, 2nd ed. (Paris: M. Rivière, 1930), p. 426; Étienne Gilson, "É. Gilson à J. Maritain: 15 avril 1931," in Étienne Gilson and Jacques Maritain, *Correspondance 1923–1971: Deux approches de l'être*, ed. Géry Prouvost (Paris: Vrin, 1991), pp. 46–51; Étienne Gilson, *L'esprit de la philosophie médiévale*, vol. 1 (Paris: Vrin, 1932), pp. 240–2; Joseph de Finance, *Être et agir dans la philosophie de saint Thomas* (Paris: Beauchesne, 1945), p. 126, n. 1; Anton C. Pegis, "A Note on St. Thomas, *Summa Theologica*, 1, 44, 1–2," *Mediaeval Studies* 8 (1946): pp. 159–68; André Hayen, *La communication de l'être d'après saint Thomas*, vol. 2, L'ordre philosophique de saint Thomas (Paris: Desclée de Brouwer, 1959), pp. 38–43; Étienne Gilson, *Introduction à la philosophie chrétienne* (Paris: Vrin, 1960), pp. 27–44: "La cause de l'être"; Jan A. Aertsen, *Nature and Creature: Thomas Aquinas's Way of Thought* (Leiden: Brill, 1988), pp. 196–201; Leo Elders, S.V.D., *La théologie philosophique de saint Thomas d'Aquin: De l'être à la cause première*, trans.

St. Augustine, the authoritative masters (with their different accents) of Christian angelology for the Latin theologians of the thirteenth century, both profoundly internalize just such a predominantly Platonic philosophy?[4]

Subsequently, one can ask what effect the arrival of Aristotelianism in thirteenth-century Christendom had on the theology of angels. This particular historical question raises another one, more universal and still relevant: to what degree is Christian theology affected by a change in its philosophical referent, as in the movement from Platonism to Aristotelianism? If one judges that theology is directly dependent on philosophy, then this movement in the thirteenth century would have necessarily put traditional angelology in crisis—unless the difference between Platonism and Aristotelianism was less sharp for the medieval spirit than it is for us today, who are the children of historical criticism. In this case, a certain tendency in the medieval period to harmonize Plato and Aristotle could have softened the consequences of the change in philosophical referent. If, by contrast, one thinks that theology is a completely different thing than a philosophy applied to religious questions,

Moines de l'abbaye Notre-Dame de Fontgombault (Paris: Téqui, 1995), pp. 459–64; Carlos Arthur Ribeiro do Nascimento, "Thomas d'Aquin et l'histoire de la philosophie grecque," in *Was ist Philosophie im Mittelalter?*, edited by Jan A. Aertsen and Andreas Speer (Berlin: W. de Gruyter, 1998), pp. 293–7; Rudi A. te Velde, "The Progress of Philosophical Reason towards Creation," in *Participation and Substantiality in Thomas Aquinas* (Leiden: Brill, 1995), ch. 8; Rudi A. te Velde, *Aquinas on God: The "Divine Science" of the* Summa Theologiae (Aldershot: Ashgate, 2006), pp. 132–8; Gilbert Dahan, "*Ex imperfecto ad perfectum*. Le progrès de la pensée humaine chez les théologiens du XIIIᵉ siècle," in *Progrès, réaction, décadence dans l'Occident médiéval*, edited by Emmanuèle Baumgartner and Laurence Harf-Lancner (Genève: Droz, 2003), pp. 171–84; Jan A. Aertsen, "La scoperta dell'ente in quanto ente," in *Tommaso d'Aquino e l'oggetto della metafisica*, edited by Stephen L. Brock (Roma: Armando Editore, 2004), pp. 35–48; Gregory P. Rocca, OP, *Speaking the Incomprehensible God: Thomas Aquinas on the Interplay of Positive and Negative Theology* (Washington, DC: The Catholic University of America Press, 2004), pp. 224–31. Aquinas also retraces the history of the ideas related to "separate substances," angels and demons, in *ST* I, q. 110, a. 1, ad 3; *De potentia*, q. 6, a. 6; *De malo*, q. 16, a. 1; *Quaestio disputata de spiritualibus creaturis*, a. 5.

[4] On the authority of Denys in matters concerning angelology, see Aquinas, *De substantiis separatis*, ch. 18 (p. D 71): "It remains for us to set forth what the Christian religion affirms on each of these subjects [concerning angels]. For that, we will make particular use of the texts of Denys, who exposited more excellently than any other that which concerns spiritual substances (*Restat ostendere quid de singulis habeat christianae religionis assertio. Ad quod utemur praecipue Dionysii documentis, qui super alios ea quae ad spirituales substantias pertinent excellentius tradidit*)." On the Platonic influence on Denys according to St. Thomas, see Aquinas, *Expositio super librum Dionysii De divinis nominibus*, ch. 5, lect. 1 (no. 634); *De malo*, q. 16, a. 1, ad 3. On St. Augustine's Platonism according to St. Thomas, see *De veritate*, q. 21, a. 4, ad 3: "Augustine follows the opinion of Plato in a good number of cases, when it can be made to conform to the truth of the Christian faith (*Augustinus in multis opinionem Platonis sequitur, quantum fieri potest secundum fidei veritatem*)"; *Quaestio disputata de spiritualibus creaturis*, a. 10, ad 8 (Leonine ed., vol. 24/2, p. 113); *ST* I, q. 84, a. 5, corpus: "Whenever Augustine, who was imbued with the doctrines of the Platonists, found in their teaching anything consistent with faith, he adopted it: and those things which he found contrary to faith he amended." English translation from: Thomas Aquinas, *Summa Theologiae*, trans. Fathers of the English Dominican Province, 5 vols. (Westminster, MD: Christian Classics, 1981). *ST* I, q. 77, a. 5, ad 3.

and that it enjoys a real epistemological transcendence in relation to the philosophies that it uses, must one conclude that the arrival of Aristotelianism did not profoundly modify the corpus of the traditional angelological doctrine?

To begin to respond to these questions, which concern more than the history of doctrine, I propose in this chapter to evaluate the influence of Aristotelian philosophy[5] on the angelology of St. Thomas, especially in the two sections of the *Prima Pars* of the *Summa theologiae* that are dedicated to the subject—the one concerning angelic creatures as such (qq. 50–64) and the other concerning their participation in the divine rule (qq. 106–114)—while also referring to other texts by St. Thomas.[6]

In a first section, I will try to clarify the epistemological status that St. Thomas attributes to his consideration of angels. The goal is to evaluate the degree to which theological angelology is theoretically susceptible, according to St. Thomas, to be modified by a "new" philosophy. I will then examine St. Thomas's reception of Aristotle's explicit teachings concerning "separate substances" (that is, separate from matter), which Aquinas identifies roughly with the angels of the Christian tradition. Finally, in a third section I will concern myself with the way in which some Aristotelian ideas, while lacking a direct connection to the question of separate substances, influenced St. Thomas's reflections on angels.

2.1. ANGELOLOGY: FAITH AND/OR REASON?

Without ever having treated the subject systematically, St. Thomas has a very clear idea of the epistemological status of angelological doctrines. It corresponds to his understanding of the relationships between faith and reason, such as it is presented, for example, at the beginning of Book I of the *Summa contra Gentiles*. There, St. Thomas explains that there are three kinds of truths: purely natural truths (accessible to human reason and not having been the object of any revelation); revealed natural truths—that is,

---

[5] By "Aristotelian philosophy," I mean here the philosophical positions that St. Thomas Aquinas and his contemporaries attributed to Aristotle and not those that historical criticism today considers to have their origin in him.

[6] Concerning St. Thomas's angelology in general, see James D. Collins, *The Thomistic Philosophy of the Angels* (Washington, DC: The Catholic University of America Press, 1947); Jean-Marie Vernier, *Les anges chez saint Thomas d'Aquin: Fondements historiques et principes philosophiques* (Paris: Nouvelles Éditions Latines, 1986); Tiziana Suarez-Nani, *Les anges et la philosophie: Subjectivité et fonction cosmologique des substances séparées à la fin du XIIIe siècle* (Paris: Vrin, 2002); Tiziana Suarez-Nani, *Connaissance et langage des anges selon Thomas d'Aquin et Gilles de Rome* (Paris: Vrin, 2002); Serge-Thomas Bonino, OP, *Les anges et les démons: Quatorze leçons de théologie catholique* (Paris: Parole et Silence, 2007).

truths that are contained in revelation but that can be correctly grasped and affirmed by reason and especially by philosophical reflection;[7] and finally strictly supernatural truths.

Revelation contains teachings concerning angels. These teachings thus pertain to Christian doctrine, contained in the canonical Scriptures and proposed by the Church to be adhered to in faith by Christians.[8] For example, the Christian faith teaches "very firmly" that angels are creatures[9] and that they were created in time.[10] On the basis of revelation, the Fathers and doctors of the Church developed angelological (hypo)theses, sometimes mutually contradictory, which remain in the realm of theological opinion and which do not belong to the faith as such. St. Thomas mentions, for example, the divergences between the *sancti doctores* on the question of the chronological relationship between the creation of the invisible universe and that of the visible universe,[11] or again on the determination of the angelic orders from which the demons came.[12] He also identifies any reflection about the "place" of the creation of angels as pertaining solely to theological opinion.[13]

But human reason as such, apart from the light of faith, can also attain some knowledge of the world of spiritual creatures. This "natural knowledge" found rational expression in the work of the great philosophers of antiquity, especially Aristotle.[14] It is true that philosophers spoke of "separate substances" or of "Intelligences" rather than of "angels" and that, among those philosophers who acknowledged the existence of demons, their rather "ontological" definition of demons does not fully correspond to theologians' "ethical" definition. But St. Thomas, following Maimonides,[15] does not hesitate to identify the

---

[7] See Paul Synave, OP, "La révélation des vérités divines naturelles d'après saint Thomas d'Aquin," in *Mélanges Mandonnet: Études d'histoire littéraire et doctrinale du moyen âge*, vol. 1 (Paris: Vrin, 1930), pp. 327–70.

[8] In *De substantiis separatis*, St. Thomas uses the following expressions to designate the content of revelation: *doctrina catholica* (Prologue, p. D 41); *sententia catholicae fidei* (ch. 9, p. D 58); *christianae religionis assertio* (ch. 18, p. D 71); *christiana traditio* (ch. 18, p. D 71); *christiana doctrina* (ch. 18, p. D 72, two times); *assertio catholicae fidei* (ch. 18, p. D 72); *catholicae doctrinae sententia* (ch. 19, p. D 74).

[9] *De substantiis separatis*, ch. 18 (p. D 71). Cf. *ST* I, q. 61.

[10] *De substantiis separatis*, ch. 18 (p. D 72).   [11] *ST* I, q. 61, a. 3.

[12] *De substantiis separatis*, ch. 20 (p. D 79); *ST* I, q. 63, a. 7.   [13] *ST* I, q. 61, a. 3.

[14] St. Thomas generally knows how to distinguish what pertains *in principle* to rational knowledge from what the philosophers *in fact* discovered. He knows that the two domains do not necessarily coincide and that one cannot identify natural reason with the thought of Aristotle. In any case, he does not often use this distinction in matters of angelological doctrine.

[15] Moses Maimonides, *The Guide for the Perplexed* II, ch. 6; trans. Michael Friedländer, 2nd ed. (New York: Dover, 1904), p. 160: "Angels are incorporeal. This agrees with the opinion of Aristotle: there is only this difference in the names employed—he uses the term 'Intelligences,' and we say instead 'angels.' His theory is that the Intelligences are intermediate beings between the Prime Cause and existing things, and that they effect the motion of the spheres, on which motion the existence of all things depends. This is also the view we meet with in all parts of Scripture; every act of God is described as being performed by angels."

separate substances of philosophy with the angels of the Bible—a position that was not self-evident in his time.[16] Under different names, and to a greater or lesser degree, philosophers and theologians in fact speak of the same thing. Between true philosophy and the Christian faith, St. Thomas argues that there is not only noncontradiction and compatibility, but also a certain continuity, with philosophy in some way preparing the ground for faith. There is thus a continuity between the discourse of philosophers about separate substances and the angelology of Christian theologians. The Prologue of St. Thomas's *De substantiis separatis* presumes this continuity:

> Our intention being to express the perfection of the holy angels, it is necessary to begin with what human conjecture in antiquity deduced about angels. If we find something there that is in harmony with the faith, we will take it, but anything that contradicts Catholic doctrine we will refute.[17]

The interest of the theologian, in this encounter with the philosophers, is centered on the revealed natural truths attained by the philosophers. Thus, in chapter 3 of *De substantiis separatis*, St. Thomas identifies three aspects of angelology on which Plato and Aristotle converge (which itself is already a sign of truth!) and which correspond to the teaching of the Christian faith. The first concerns the mode of existence (*modus existendi*) of immaterial substances. According to the interpretation proposed by St. Thomas, Plato and Aristotle both recognized that immaterial substances are dependent on God for their existence and that they are caused by God.[18] The second concerns a remarkable property of angelic nature: angels are incorporeal and immaterial (which does not exclude, for them, a certain potentiality).[19] And the third concerns the participation of angels in the divine governance.[20] This is a point to which St. Thomas often returns in order to emphasize the fundamental agreement between philosophers and Christian faith. He writes, for example,

---

[16] In his *In II Sent.*, dist. 3, a. 3, Albert the Great poses the question: "Do we call 'angels' these separate substances that the philosophers call 'intelligences,' as some dare to defend with polemics? (*Utrum nos vocemus angelos substantias illas separatas quas philosophi intelligentias vocant, ut quidam contentiose defendere praesumunt*)"; Albert the Great, *Opera omnia*, vol. 27, *Commentarii in II Sententiarum*, ed. Auguste Borgnet (Paris: Louis Vivès, 1894), pp. 64–6. In favor of this identity between the angels of religion and the Intelligences of philosophy, Albert cites Avicenna ("This is what Avicenna affirms: the intelligences are what the people and the interpreters of the law call angels [*Ita dicit Avicenna, quod intelligentiae sunt quas populus et loquentes in lege angelos vocant*]"), Al-Ghazali, and Maimonides. But Albert's own response is in the negative: the properties that the philosophers attributed to Intelligences are incompatible with Christian dogma.

[17] Aquinas, *De substantiis separatis*, Prologue (p. D 41). The reasoning of *De substantiis separatis* evokes in many ways that of the *SCG*.

[18] *De substantiis separatis*, ch. 3 (p. D 46). Cf. ch. 17. One will note the similarity of these texts to the argumentation of *ST* I, q. 44, a. 1. In the latter text, St. Thomas makes reference to the same arguments in favor of creation, attributed there as well to Plato and to Aristotle.

[19] *De substantiis separatis*, ch. 3 (p. D 46); cf. ch. 18.

[20] *De substantiis separatis*, ch. 3 (pp. D 46–D 47).

that "all corporeal things are ruled by the angels. This is not only laid down by the holy doctors, but also by all philosophers who admit the existence of incorporeal substances."[21] St. Thomas emphasizes elsewhere in his work other points of convergence between philosophy and theology, at times boldly, as when he brings together the theological distinction, dear to St. Gregory the Great, between angels that serve (*administrantes*) and those that remain always before God (*assistentes*), with the philosophical distinction between the souls of the heavenly spheres and the separate Intelligences;[22] or when he relates the demonology of John of Damascus to Platonic demonology.[23] He is always concerned to show the eminent philosophical fittingness of Christian angelology.

If philosophy effectively speaks of the same reality as theology, though under another light, and if by means of "separate substances" philosophy is able to advance truths that anticipate or confirm in their own way the Christian doctrine of angels, still St. Thomas does not delude himself as to the real significance of this philosophical knowledge of angels. He knows that human reason, left to itself, is extremely fragile, so much so that he develops this very point each time that he wants to ground rationally the moral necessity of a revelation of some essentially natural truths:[24]

> Human reason is insufficient for a full knowledge of separate substances, though nature still knows them quite well. Looking toward them, our intellect is like the eye of an owl looking toward the sun, as it is said in Book II of the *Metaphysics*. This is why it is said in Book II of *On Animals* that we can only know very little about that subject by reason, even though what one *can* know is dear and well-loved. And this is why the philosophers said nothing in a definitive manner (*demonstrative*)[25] about them and quite little about them even in an argumentative manner (*probabiliter*), which explains their divergence concerning the number of angels.[26]

---

[21] *ST* I, q. 110, a. 1, corpus. See *De veritate*, q. 5, a. 8; *SCG* II, ch. 99 (no. 1849); *ST* I, q. 110, a. 3; *Responsio ad lectorem Venetum de 36 articulis*, a. 1; *Responsio ad magistrum Ioannem de Vercellis de 43 articulis*, a. 3. On the cosmological function given to angels by St. Thomas and on its significance, see Suarez-Nani, *Les anges et la philosophie*, pp. 91–171. The comparison that Suarez-Nani makes between the responses that Albert the Great, Robert Kilwardby, and Thomas Aquinas made to an inquiry of John of Vercelli on the movement of the heavenly bodies confirms that "the position of Thomas Aquinas is the only one that attributes to angels a cosmological function and the only one that thereby confers to spiritual creatures a philosophical legitimacy" (p. 133).

[22] See Aquinas, *In II Sent.*, dist. 10, q. 1, a. 2. Cf. *In II Sent.*, dist. 3, q. 3, a. 2; *De veritate*, q. 16, a. 1.

[23] In *ST* I, q. 63, a. 7, St. Thomas underlines a convergence between the thesis of John of Damascus according to which the fallen angels belonged to the lowest rung of the angelic hierarchy, and the Platonic doctrine of demons.

[24] See *SCG* I, ch. 4 (nos. 22–25).

[25] St. Thomas relativizes, for example, the properly demonstrative value of philosophical arguments in favor of the cosmic action of separate substances by grouping those arguments among the arguments from supreme fittingness. See his *Responsio ad lectorem Venetum de 36 articulis*, a. 2.

[26] *In II Sent.*, dist. 3, q. 1, a. 3, corpus.

As the Prologue of *De substantiis separatis* states, philosophical doctrine concerning separate substances rests on "human conjecture (*humana coniectura*)," a notion that St. Thomas elsewhere opposes to the certainty of faith.[27] It is not surprising, then, that even the best philosophers contradicted themselves, failed ever to attain true certitude, and, finally, became entangled in grave error concerning angels. They maintained, for example, that angels had been created from eternity[28] and again, succumbing to the charm of Neoplatonic ideas about mediation, that angels exercised a properly creative action vis-à-vis bodily creatures.[29]

Let us specify one last aspect of St. Thomas's conception of the relationship between natural knowledge and the knowledge of faith about angels. If it is true that the philosophy of separate substances can confirm some aspects of Christian doctrine concerning angels, it also develops purely philosophical theses that have no direct connection to Christian faith. In this case, St. Thomas encourages us not only to respect the freedom of philosophical research (which is not his main concern) but also to avoid causing scandal before nonbelievers (*irrisio infidelium*) by incorrectly leading them to think that the truths of faith depend upon unconvincing philosophical arguments (this is his main preoccupation).[30] This strategy, constant in Aquinas, is particularly clear in his *Responsio de 43 articulis*, of which the first articles concern precisely some questions of cosmological angelology. From the start, St. Thomas protests:

> Many of these articles pertain not to the doctrines of faith but rather to the teachings of the philosophers. But it is harmful to affirm or to deny, as if they concerned sacred doctrine, things that do not belong to the teaching of piety.... It seems to me that the most certain course is neither to affirm these shared ideas of the philosophers, when they do not contradict our faith, as if they were dogmas

---

[27] Generally speaking, *coniectura* is the opposite of indubitable science. Specifically, *humana coniectura* is the opposite of supernatural faith and its certitude: see *ST* II-II, q. 1, a. 3, ad 3: "Sed illa determinatio temporis, in qua decipiebatur, non erat ex fide, sed ex coniectura humana. Possibile est enim hominem fidelem ex coniectura humana falsum aliquid aestimare. Sed quod ex fide falsum aestimet, hoc est impossibile."

[28] See *De substantiis separatis*, ch. 18 (p. D 72): "Est autem christianae doctrinae contrarium ut sic dicantur spirituales substantiae a summa deitate originem trahere quod fuerint ab aeterno, sicut Platonici et Peripatetici posuerunt; sed hoc habet assertio catholicae fidei quod coeperunt esse postquam prius non fuerant."

[29] See *De veritate*, q. 5, a. 8; q. 8, a. 8. In any case, the philosophers recognize that this creative action is instrumental; see *De potentia*, q. 3, a. 4, corpus: "Nec etiam ipsi Philosophi posuerunt Angelos vel intelligentias aliquid creare, nisi per virtutem divinam in ipsis existentem." Which is none the less false: see *ST* I, q. 45, a. 4 and parallels. The error that attributes to angels a creative action leads to another concerning the mode of angelic knowledge of material substances. See *De veritate*, q. 8, a. 8.

[30] See *ST* I, q. 32, a. 1, corpus: "Cum enim aliquis ad probandam fidem inducit rationes quae non sunt cogentes, cedit in irrisionem infidelium, credunt enim quod huiusmodi rationibus innitamur, et propter eas credamus"; *Quodlibet* III, q. 14, a. 2.

of faith, even if sometimes these dogmas are introduced under the name of philosophers, nor to deny them as contrary to the faith, so as not to give occasion to the wise of this world to despise the doctrine of faith.[31]

After having explored different points of view (on the animation or lack thereof of heavenly bodies, on the intervention of angels in the movement of the heavens, and so forth), at the end of the examination of the articles that were submitted to him, St. Thomas concludes: "In brief, all these articles have little or nothing to do with the doctrine of the faithful, but rather they come completely from philosophy."[32]

2.2. STRENGTHS AND WEAKNESSES OF ARISTOTELIAN ANGELOLOGY

In the sections of the *Prima Pars* of the *Summa theologiae* that constitute most particularly the material object of our study, St. Thomas twice refers to an explicit teaching of Aristotle about separate substances.[33] The first occurrence (in q. 50, a. 3) concerns the number of angels, and the second (in q. 110, a. 1) pertains to the influence of separate substances on the material world. In both cases, Aristotle's position is put in relation to that of Plato.

In order better to apprehend the way in which Aquinas conceives of the relationships, on the one hand, between Aristotle and Plato and, on the other hand, between the "philosophers" and the Christian faith, a detour through the *De substantiis separatis* is necessary. In that treatise, which was written around 1271 and which bears witness on these points to the highest maturity attained by his thought, St. Thomas proposes to assess the excellence of angels. In the Prologue, in a good Aristotelian fashion that sees in the history of ideas a privileged path toward the specification of the *veritas rerum*, St. Thomas states that he will begin his exposition with a critical examination of the "conjectural" teachings of the ancients concerning separate substances.

In this reconstruction, Plato appears as the first to have gone, in a coherent way, beyond the materialism of the "physicists." He identified the existence of

---

[31] *Responsio ad magistrum Ioannem de Vercellis de 43 articulis*, Prooemium.

[32] *Responsio ad magistrum Ioannem de Vercellis de 43 articulis*, a. 7. *De malo*, q. 16, a. 1, corpus: "Sive demones habeant corpora sibi naturaliter unita sive non habeant hoc non multum refert ad fidei christiane doctrinam."

[33] Aristotle explicitly treats the subject of separate substances in Book XII of the *Metaphysics*. St. Thomas seems to think, at least up until *De unitate intellectus* (1270), that we have lost a section of this text in which Aristotle would have developed the question of separate substances. See Aquinas, *De unitate intellectus*, ch. 1 (Leonine ed., vol. 43, p. 299); ch. 5 (p. 313). See Alain de Libera, *L'unité de l'intellect: Commentaire du* De unitate intellectus contra Averroistas *de Thomas d'Aquin* (Paris: Vrin, 2004), pp. 132–5.

a complex world of intellectual substances in which one can distinguish, situated between God and the human soul, four "classes": the Ideas or secondary gods, the separate intellects, the souls of the heavenly bodies, and the demons (both good and evil).[34] For St. Thomas, this Platonic teaching, while in need of some modification to its vocabulary, could be compatible with Christian faith, if its truth were confirmed at the philosophical level.[35] But such is not the case. Basically, the philosophical foundation of the Platonic discourse concerning separate substances is flawed. It is vitiated by Plato's fundamental error, often denounced by Aquinas in the manner of Aristotle.[36] Confusing intelligibility in itself (*in se*) with intelligibility for us (*quoad nos*), due to a deficient anthropology that underestimates the rootedness of human cognitive activity in sense perception, Plato is the victim of the illusion of an ontological–logical parallelism. He projects on the real what are in fact the elaborations of human thought (which is not a direct reflection of the ontological structures of reality). He is thus led unduly to hypostasize abstractions, attributing, for example, the status of subsistent subjects to universals.[37]

Aristotle, for his part, begins with firmer foundations since he draws on experience and borrows the "*via motus*" in order to approach separate substances.[38] Starting with the diverse movements of which we have a sensible experience, principally the movement of the heavenly bodies, he highlights their physical and metaphysical conditions of possibility. Reasoning from effects to their causes, he establishes the existence of immaterial substances that are the principles of the diverse cosmological movements.[39] These immaterial substances are of two types: the souls of the heavenly bodies, the immanent principles of their movement; and substances separated from all matter, whose perfection and goodness exert on the souls of the heavenly bodies an attracting force of the order of final causality.[40]

St. Thomas's judgment of Aristotelian "angelology" is mixed. On the one hand, he recognizes that it offers a more solid foundation than the Platonic doctrine of Ideas, and he does not hesitate to defend Aristotle's model by

---

[34] *De substantiis separatis*, ch. 1 (p. D 43): "Sic igitur patet quod inter nos et summum Deum quatuor ordines ponebant, scilicet deorum secundorum, intellectuum separatorum, animarum caelestium, et daemonum bonorum seu malorum."

[35] *De substantiis separatis*, ch. 1 (pp. D 42–D 43).   [36] *ST* I, q. 88, a. 1.

[37] *De substantiis separatis*, ch. 2 (pp. D 43–D 44).

[38] *De substantiis separatis*, ch. 2 (p. D 44): "Thus, see why Aristotle, in his investigation of the substances separated from matter, proceeds according to a more obvious and more dependable way, to whit, the way of movement (*Et ideo Aristoteles manifestiori et certiori via processit ad investigandum substantias a materia separatas, scilicet per viam motus*)." The two adjectives *manifestior* and *certior* are also applied to the *prima via* toward the existence of God in *ST* I, q. 2, a. 3, corpus: "Prima autem et *manifestior* via est, quae sumitur ex parte motus. *Certum* est enim, et sensu constat, aliqua moveri in hoc mundo."

[39] *Super Boetium De Trinitate*, q. 5, a. 4, ad 3.

[40] *De substantiis separatis*, ch. 2 (pp. D 44–D 45).

showing that its validity is not intrinsically linked to the affirmation, effectively heretical, of the eternality of the world and its movement.[41] But, on the other hand, he is critical of two particular conclusions of Aristotle's angelology. This twofold critique, while finding clearest expression in the *De substantiis separatis*, is constant in Aquinas's work. It is therefore already found in the angelological questions of the *Prima Pars*.

The first criticism concerns Aristotelian "naturalism." Aristotle acknowledges the influence of separate substances on our world, but he considers their action—universal though it may be—always to be mediated by the heavenly bodies. The separate substances thus never interfere directly in this lower world but only by means of the natural course of cosmic motion: "Aristotle held that immaterial substances are not the species of sensible bodies, but something higher and more universal; and so he did not attribute to them any immediate presiding over single bodies, but only over the universal agents, the heavenly bodies."[42]

Not only is such mediation heretical[43] but, according to St. Thomas, it contradicts the realist intention of Aristotelian thought, an intention that is precisely to give an adequate explanation for the diverse movements that we observe. Aristotle's explicit conclusions are opposed to Aristotle's principles! Certain sensible phenomena cannot be explained by the mere *mediated* action of separate substances through the natural and regular movement of the heavenly bodies: these phenomena rather suppose a direct act by these personal substances.[44] St. Thomas is thinking here about the diverse phenomena produced by magic or which accompany the different forms of demonic "possession." Aristotle's disciples tried to attribute such phenomena to astrological influences, but in St. Thomas's estimation they did so without success.[45] For him, these extraordinary phenomena are not miracles, properly speaking, since they do not exceed the capabilities of creatures as such,[46] but

---

[41] *De substantiis separatis*, ch. 2 (p. D 46): "Potest etiam alicui videri praedictum Aristotilis processum ad substantias immateriales ponendas inconvenientem esse, eo quod procedit ex sempiternitate motus, quae fidei veritati repugnat. Sed si quis diligenter attendat rationem eius processus, non tollitur etiam aeternitate motus sublata; nam sicut ex aeternitate motus concluditur motoris infinita potentia, ita etiam hoc idem concludi potest ex motus uniformitate."

[42] *ST* I, q. 110, a. 1, ad 3.

[43] *In I Sent.*, dist. 37, q. 3, a. 1, corpus: "Circa hoc [= the angel's localization] triplex est opinio. Una opinio est philosophorum, quod intelligentiae vel angeli nullo modo sunt in loco; ponunt enim quod intelligentia est quaedam essentia denudata a materia et ab omnibus conditionibus materialibus, et quod intelligentia movet orbem per animam ejus conjunctam ipsi orbi, sicut desideratum ab ipsa; et ideo nullam applicationem ad corpus vel ad locum habet, quia non immediate operatur circa aliquod corpus. Haec autem opinio haeretica est; quia secundum fidem nostram, ponimus angelos immediate circa nos operari." See also *De potentia*, q. 6, a. 3.

[44] See *De substantiis separatis*, ch. 2 (p. D 45).

[45] See *De substantiis separatis*, ch. 2 (p. D 45).

[46] See *ST* I, q. 114, a. 4; *In II Sent.*, dist. 7, q. 3, a. 1; *Lectura super Ioannem*, ch. 10, lect. 5 (no. 1431); *ST* I, q. 110, a. 4, ad 2. The question of demonic "miracles"—the wonders produced by

they do attest that separate substances exercise a free and direct action on the physical world:

> But [Aristotle] did not say that there were any spiritual substances with immediate rule over the inferior bodies, except perhaps human souls; and this was because he did not consider that any operations were exercised in the inferior bodies except the natural ones for which the movement of the heavenly bodies sufficed. But because we assert that many things are done in the inferior bodies besides the natural corporeal actions, for which the movements of the heavenly bodies are not sufficient; therefore in our opinion we must assert that the angels possess an immediate presidency not only over the heavenly bodies, but also over the inferior bodies.[47]

From this point of view, the Platonists, despite their errors concerning the bodily nature of demons (good or evil),[48] were perhaps closer to the truth than the Aristotelians since they recognized that demons have the ability to act directly here below. Be that as it may, St. Thomas clearly refuses to reduce angels to a simple cog in the cosmic machine. Separate substances in Christianity are not bound to heavenly bodies as asses yoked to the mills they turn.[49] They are personal subjects who enjoy an authentic freedom of initiative. It is this fact that places them, in the hierarchy of beings, well above the heavenly bodies and forbids subordinating them to these bodies.[50]

The second criticism that Aquinas voices concerning Aristotelian angelology flows from this refusal to subordinate angels to the heavenly bodies. It concerns the number of separate substances. Because of his (correct) starting point for his reflection on separate substances, namely cosmic movement, Aristotle is unfortunately led to fix their number as a function of the number of heavenly movements.

> There have been various opinions with regard to the number of the separate substances. Plato contended that the separate substances are the species of sensible things; as if we were to maintain that human nature is a separate substance of itself: and according to this view it would have to be maintained

---

Pharaoh's magicians (cf. Exod 7–9) or those expected of the Antichrist (2 Thess 2:9–10)—is treated at length by St. Augustine: *City of God* XX,xix,4; XXI,vi,1.

[47] *ST* I, q. 110, a. 1, ad 2.

[48] In *ST* I, q. 115, a. 5, Aquinas distinguishes three positions concerning demons: that of the Aristotelians, that of the Platonists, and the Catholic position. The Peripatetics denied the existence of demons and attributed to the heavenly bodies actions that are claimed to be performed by demons; the Platonists attributed to demons a body and consequently subsumed them to the universal action of the heavenly bodies over nature.

[49] The image comes from William of Auvergne (*De Universo* I-II, ch. 5) who uses it to denounce Avicenna's vision of separate substances. Cited in Étienne Gilson, "Pourquoi saint Thomas a critiqué saint Augustin," *Archives d'histoire doctrinale et littéraire du moyen âge* 1 (1926–1927): pp. 5–127, at 51, n. 1.

[50] On the heavenly bodies in the thought of St. Thomas, see Thomas Litt, *Les corps célestes dans l'univers de saint Thomas d'Aquin* (Louvain: Publications Universitaires, 1963).

that the number of the separate substances is the number of the species of sensible things. Aristotle, however, rejects this view (*Metaph.* I) because matter is of the very nature of the species of sensible things. Consequently the separate substances cannot be the exemplar species of these sensible things; but have their own fixed natures, which are higher than the natures of sensible things. Nevertheless Aristotle held (*Metaph.* XI) that those more perfect natures bear relation to these sensible things, as that of mover and end; and therefore he strove to find out the number of the separate substances according to the number of the first movements.[51]

Aristotle's fundamental error is to have thought of separate substances only as a function of heavenly bodies and to have neglected to think of them in themselves.[52] Two attenuating circumstances helped, in St. Thomas's eyes, to excuse him for this error. On the one hand, Aristotle had the wisdom to propose his calculation of the number of separate substances only under the form of a probable solution. As he often does when Aristotle seems to be in opposition to Christian faith, for example concerning the eternity of the world,[53] St. Thomas insists: Aristotle affirms nothing as if it were strictly proven.[54] On the other hand, Aristotle was the victim of a method which, in itself, was wholly appropriate: "He was forced to make use of this argument, since only through sensible things can we come to know intelligible ones."[55] His weakness was his inability to separate himself sufficiently from his starting point. In any event, Aristotle was clearly wrong to invert the order of finalities, that is, to confuse end and means. Spiritual substances, far from being subordinate to material substances and, as it were, in their service, subordinate the material substances to themselves.[56] The bodily movements that they cause are the habitual means through which they diffuse in the material world the forms that exist spiritually in them as ideas, thus manifesting the

---

[51] *ST* I, q. 50, a. 3, corpus; cf. *SCG* II, ch. 92 (no. 1783).

[52] St. Thomas considers (1) the identification of angels with the forms of the heavenly bodies and (2) the determination of their number as a function of the number of heavenly bodies as one and the same "error of the philosophers." Christian angelology avoids these errors by affirming the transcendence of angels with regard to any given physical body. See *In II Sent.*, dist. 8, q. 1, a. 1. The same refusal to identify angels with their cosmic function is found, for example, in Albert the Great: see Albert the Great, *In II Sent.*, dist. 2, a. 1 (p. 45) and dist. 3, a. 2 (p. 61).

[53] See *ST* I, q. 46, a. 1.

[54] Aquinas often falls back in this context to the reservation demonstrated by Aristotle in *Metaphysics* XII,8 (1074a16). See *Sent. Metaph.* XII, lect. 10 (no. 2586); *SCG* II, ch. 92 (no. 1785); *ST* I, q. 50, a. 3, ad 3; *De substantiis separatis*, ch. 2 (p. D 46); *De unitate intellectus*, ch. 5 (p. 313). See Libera, *L'unité de l'intellect*, pp. 462–70. The merely "probable" character of Aristotle's teaching on the subject is already underlined by Maimonides, *The Guide for the Perplexed* II, ch. 3 (p. 51): "The opinions that Aristotle puts forward on the causes of the movements of the spheres, and from which he concludes the existence of *separate Intelligences*, [are] in any case hypotheses incapable of demonstration."

[55] *ST* I, q. 50, a. 3, ad 3.

[56] See *In II Sent.*, dist. 3, q. 1, a. 3, ad 4; *ST* I, q. 50, a. 3, ad 3; *De unitate intellectus*, ch. 5 (p. 313).

generous goodness that motivates their providential action on the cosmos. Angels are therefore not in any way unemployed (*otiosi*) if they do not work directly to move the heavenly spheres! They have other, far more important tasks.

Aristotle's reductionistic thesis had already given rise to two developments among his disciples. But these did not find much favor in St. Thomas's eyes. The first is that of Avicenna, who increased the number of separate substances by raising the number of heavenly movements taken into consideration. But this purely "quantitative" correction remains a prisoner of the methodological defect that consists in subordinating separate substances to heavenly bodies.[57] The second is that proposed by Maimonides.[58] Maimonides tried to reconcile the Aristotelian thesis that ties the number of separate substances to the number of heavenly movements with the biblical texts that make reference to a profusion of innumerable angels. Maimonides interpreted these biblical texts on the basis of this Aristotelian thesis: in the Bible, the word "angel" refers to many other realities than solely the separate Intelligences, not only to human messengers but also to physical and psychic faculties written into the nature of things by God. This exegesis does not much appeal to St. Thomas, who rejects it as forcing the sense of Scripture.[59]

As for St. Thomas, each time that he wants to account for the scriptural affirmations about the great number of angels, he has recourse in a very significant way to a priori arguments that draw upon the divine intention in the creative act, which is nothing other than the manifestation of God's glory.[60] In good theological form, he avoids reducing our knowledge of the angelic world to what we can ascertain solely by the philosophical path, that is to say, by a posteriori arguments that reason from the effects to the cause. He does not call the validity of this way into question, provided that it does not set itself up as an exclusive method for speaking of the angels. He integrates it into a much wider perspective. Furthermore, in order not to destabilize the philosophical approach to angels, he tries hard to show that nothing prevents the attribution of a cosmological function to the abounding multitude of angels if one envisions them as forming an ordered series of movers, in which causality is communicated from the highest angels, who participate more in the desirability of the Good, all the way down to those that are the closest to the heavenly bodies.[61] But from a strictly philosophical point of view, one can only deduce from the movement of a heavenly body the necessity of a proximate

---

[57] See *De substantiis separatis*, ch. 2 (p. D 44); *In II Sent.*, dist. 3, q. 1, a. 3. Cf. Avicenna (Latin), *Liber de Philosophia prima sive Divina scientia*, V–X, tract. IX, ch. 3; ed. Simone van Riet (Leuven: Peeters, 1989), pp. 464–76.

[58] See Maimonides, *The Guide for the Perplexed* II, ch. 6 (pp. 160–2).

[59] See *In II Sent.*, dist. 3, q. 1, a. 3; *SCG* II, ch. 92 (no. 1794); *ST* I, q. 50, a. 3.

[60] See, for example, *In II Sent.*, dist. 3, q. 1, a. 3; *ST* I, q. 50, a. 3.

[61] See *SCG* II, ch. 92 (no. 1785).

mover (and of a first Mover), without it being possible to determine whether or not an ordered series of subordinate second movers intervenes between the proximate mover and the first Mover. If, for example, someone falls upon a typed manuscript of which I am the author, he can deduce with certainty, first, the existence of an author endowed with reason and, second, the existence of a word processor. But he could not affirm nor deny the mediation of a secretary who could have typed the text under my dictation. Yet, if he knows by other means that I have a secretary in my service, then he could suppose with a good deal of probability that I made use of his or her services.

2.3. INDIRECT INFLUENCES FROM ARISTOTLE ON AQUINAS'S ANGELOLOGY

Aristotle's influence on Aquinas's angelology is not limited to the critical assimilation of Aristotle's (rather slender) explicit teaching on separate substances. More profoundly, Aristotle's philosophy constitutes for Aquinas and his contemporaries, in varying degrees, a sort of *koine*, a language or common referential framework. The adoption of this philosophical "vulgate" led theologians to reformulate, and to make precise, certain problems in angelology by way of Aristotelian concepts.[62] It is clear for example that the highly technical developments concerning the manner in which angels relate to place and move about borrows a great deal from the Aristotelian analysis of movement in the *Physics*, even if the problem itself is in no way truly Aristotelian.[63]

The ubiquity of this basic Aristotelianism makes it difficult to determine the real degree of influence that Aristotle as such had on St. Thomas's angelology as such. It seems to me however that over and above the utilization of new philosophical categories, Aristotelianism led St. Thomas to develop some of his own theses concerning angels, or, at least, provided him with the means to do so. By way of illustration, then, I will first examine the role of the Aristotelian notion of "nature" in St. Thomas's angelology. I will next evaluate

---

[62] Unless I am mistaken, there are seventy-six explicit references to Aristotle in qq. 50–64 of the *Prima Pars* (fifteen questions) and only fifteen in qq. 106–114 (nine questions). Even if the theology of angelic action in the cosmos refers to an Aristotelian theme (five of the fifteen explicit references are found in q. 110, which is dedicated to the governance of angels over the physical world), Aristotle offers few resources for questions relative to the internal organization of the angelic world and to the ministry of angels toward human beings. It is a different situation in qq. 50–64. The presence of Aristotle is discrete in the question concerning the "history" of angels (eight explicit references in qq. 61–64). On the contrary, the references to Aristotle are numerous in the questions concerning the structure of being and the action of angels. The strongest concentrations pertain to angelic knowledge (eleven references in q. 58; ten in q. 54) and the ontological status of angels (eight references in q. 50).

[63] See *ST* I, qq. 52–53 and parallels.

the influence of Aristotle's philosophy in the properly Thomistic analysis of the metaphysical structure of angels. Finally, I will briefly examine the paradoxical use to which St. Thomas puts the epistemology of *De anima* in his angelology.

Aristotle's fundamental contribution consists of the notion of *physis*. Thanks to Aristotle, Christian thought in the thirteenth century was better able to articulate that the beings that comprise the sensible world are not simply inconsistent reflections of the real world of Ideas. In themselves, these sensible beings enjoy a real autonomy in the order of being, of intelligibility, and of action. Each being has an immanent "nature." This nature is defined by specific purposes or goals and by the whole ensemble of interconnected capabilities to act that make it possible to attain those goals. Moreover, because they exercise on each other a real action through causality, the beings of this world form an order, a Nature, made up of stable relationships of which the mind can grasp the intelligibility and express it under the form of laws.

How does this physical universe's autonomy harmonize with its radical dependence vis-à-vis a free and transcendent God as well as with the action in it of "supernatural" agents, such as angels or demons? This was the great question that Christian thought in Aquinas's day had to address. St. Thomas had to avoid, on the one hand, the rationalistic naturalism that subsumes God and angels under Nature, reducing them to nothing but elements of a rational Whole that contains them. On the other hand, he had to avoid the occasionalism that destroys the regularities of the natural order under the pretext of doing justice to the divine and angelic freedom to act. In this context, the position of St. Thomas concerning the action of angels in physical nature represents a remarkable equilibrium. On one side, as we have already seen in section 2.2, St. Thomas (like Avicenna) refutes the Aristotelian naturalist thesis according to which separate substances only act in this world mediately through the movement of heavenly bodies. But on the other side, in the name of Aristotelianism, he challenges the "occasionalist" and Platonizing thesis of Avicenna that reserves for the Intelligences the prerogative of directly introducing substantial forms in unformed matter, a thesis that is connected to the heretical one that attributes to angels a participation in creation:[64]

> The Platonists asserted that the forms which are in matter are caused by immaterial forms, because they said that the material forms are participations of immaterial forms. Avicenna followed them in this opinion to some extent, for he said that all forms which are in matter, proceed from the concept of the *intellect*; and that corporeal agents only dispose [matter] for the forms. They seem to have been deceived on this point, through supposing a form to be something made per se, so that it would be the effect of a formal principle. But, as the

---

[64] St. Thomas excels at making one philosopher refute another and at judging them both in light of Christian faith. See *In III Sent.*, dist. 16, q. 1, a. 3, ad 3.

Philosopher proves (*Metaph.* VII [VI,8]), what is made, properly speaking, is the *composite*: for this properly speaking, is, as it were, what subsists.[65]

According to Avicenna, a form (the physical form that informs unformed matter, as much as the psychological form that forms the potential intellect) can only be made, in some sense *ex nihilo*, by a separate Intelligence that is itself a pure form. This is the famous occasionalist thesis of the "Giver of forms" that reduces physical or psychological processes to simple preparations of the matter in view of the reception of a form that comes from elsewhere. St. Thomas refutes this thesis in the name of an Aristotelian conception of nature:

> In the opinion of Aristotle, however, and of those who follow him, the above view cannot stand. Aristotle in fact advances two arguments to prove that forms are not stamped on matter by a separate substance, but are brought into act from the potentiality of matter by the action of a form existing in matter.[66]

Whatever distant and mediated influence angels have in generation through the action of heavenly bodies (*hominem generat sol et homo*),[67] it is always a subject composed of matter and form that is the immediate cause of the generation of another subject composed of matter and form, for the form of a physical being never exists in a state of ontological independence vis-à-vis the composite, except in the case of humans. The action of angels thus is never directly exercised upon prime matter (against Avicenna), but rather this action always occurs through a local movement impressed upon composite hylomorphic beings. This local movement is produced indirectly through the movement of heavenly bodies but (against Aristotle) it can also be the effect of a direct initiative of a separate substance.[68]

But the notion of nature that, in Aristotle, primarily concerned the sensible substances of this world, takes in St. Thomas a larger, transcendental significance. Aquinas transfers it analogically to the order of created spiritual substances. This application of the idea of nature to angelic creatures, far from the "naturalization" of the spiritual world that some have imagined it to be, is the source of a remarkable theological clarification. It permits St. Thomas to distinguish with precision what, in the angelic subject, arises from "nature" and what arises from its supernatural vocation to divinization. St. Thomas makes systematic use of this distinction (without separation) between the natural order and the supernatural order in the angel. He insists particularly

---

[65] *ST* I, q. 110, a. 2, corpus. See also *ST* I, q. 45, a. 8; q. 65, a. 4; q. 91, a. 2; *De potentia*, q. 3, a. 8. In *In II Sent.*, dist. 7, q. 3, a. 1, St. Thomas declares that Avicenna's thesis is combated just as well by the philosophers (in the name of Aristotelian cosmological mediation) as by the theologians.

[66] *De potentia*, q. 6, a. 3, corpus; *On the Power of God (Quæstiones disputatæ de potentia Dei)*, Book 2, trans. English Dominican Fathers (Eugene, OR: Wipf & Stock, 2004), pp. 172–3.

[67] See Aristotle, *Physics* II,2 (194b13); Aertsen, *Nature and Creature*, pp. 302–10.

[68] See *De malo*, q. 3, a. 4, corpus. On the question of the modalities of angelic action in the physical world, see Bonino, *Les anges et les démons*, pp. 77–85.

on the permanence of natural structures in the supernatural order among both the blessed angels and the fallen ones.[69] Christian theology certainly did not await the thirteenth-century Aristotelian contribution to have recourse to the idea of nature or to distinguish between the natural and supernatural orders, but this contribution did permit a more precise and systematic use of the distinction.

St. Thomas's reflection on the metaphysical nature of the angels also owes much to the indirect influence of Aristotelian philosophy. Two typically Thomistic theses are partly connected with Aristotelian physics and epistemology. The first is the affirmation of the pure immateriality of the angel, a thesis that was not self-evident up to the thirteenth century.[70] To establish it, St. Thomas relies both on a strictly Aristotelian interpretation of hylomorphism, which leads him to reject the idea of spiritual matter and the thesis of universal hylomorphism,[71] and on the Aristotelian theory of intellectual knowledge, which supposes that the intellect is "something incorporeal and immaterial, as the Philosopher proves in Book III of *On the Soul*."[72] Angels, being pure intellect, are necessarily immaterial.

The second thesis affirms that each angelic subject is a species unique to itself.[73] Highly controversial, it was condemned in March 1277, above all in the way it seemed to set a limit to the omnipotence of God.[74] In any case, this

---

[69] See, for example, *ST* I, q. 62, a. 7, sed contra: "So long as a nature endures, its operation remains. But beatitude does not destroy nature, since it is its perfection. Therefore it does not take away natural knowledge and love." Denys, concerning the fallen angels, had already emphasized that "their natural gifts remain intact (*dona naturalia in eis manent integra*)." See Pseudo-Dionysius, *The Divine Names* IV,23, in Pseudo-Dionysius, *The Complete Works*, trans. Colm Luibheid (Mahwah, NJ: Paulist Press, 1987), p. 91. See Bernard Quelquejeu, OP, "'Naturalia manent integra': Contribution à l'étude de la portée, méthodologique et doctrinale, de l'axiome théologique 'gratia praesupponit naturam,'" *RSPhTh* 49 (1965): pp. 640–55.

[70] *ST* I, q. 50, aa. 1–2. See Bonino, *Les anges et les démons*, pp. 115–25.

[71] On the Thomistic critique of universal hylomorphism and its context, see Erich Kleineidam, "Das Problem der hylomorphen Zusammensetzung der geistigen Substanzen im 13. Jahrhundert, behandelt bis Thomas von Aquin" (Diss. Breslau, 1930); Aimé Forest, *La structure métaphysique du concret selon saint Thomas d'Aquin* (Paris: Vrin, 1931), chs. 4 and 5; Odon Lottin, OSB, "La composition hylémorphique des substances spirituelles: Les débuts de la controverse," *Revue néo-scolastique de philosophie* 34 (1932): pp. 21–41; Collins, *The Thomistic Philosophy of the Angels*, pp. 42–75; Fernand Brunner, *Platonisme et aristotélisme: La critique d'Ibn Gabirol par saint Thomas d'Aquin* (Louvain: Publications Universitaires, 1965); James A. Weisheipl, OP, "Albertus Magnus and Universal Hylomorphism: Avicebron," in *Albert the Great: Commemorative Essays*, edited by Francis J. Kovach and Robert W. Shahan (Norman: University of Oklahoma Press, 1980), pp. 239–60; Pilar Ferrer Rodríguez, "La inmaterialidad de las sustancias espirituales (Santo Tomás versus Avicebrón)" (Diss. Universidad de Navarra, Pamplona, 1988).

[72] *De substantiis separatis*, ch. 19 (p. D 75).

[73] See *ST* I, q. 50, a. 4 and the numerous parallels. See Rega Wood, "Angelic Individuation according to Richard Rufus, St. Bonaventure and St. Thomas Aquinas," in *Individuum und Individualität im Mittelalter*, edited by Jan A. Aertsen and Andreas Speer (Berlin: W. de Gruyter, 1996), pp. 209–29; Suarez-Nani, *Les anges et la philosophie*, pp. 35–50.

[74] See David Piché, ed. and trans., *La condamnation parisienne de 1277* (Paris: Vrin, 1999), p. 104: "81 (43). Quod, quia intelligentie non habent materiam, deus non posset plures ejusdem

thesis, constant in St. Thomas, proceeds immediately from the application to angelology of the philosophical doctrine of individuation by quantified matter, a doctrine that is connected to the Aristotelian understanding of hylomorphism.[75] Since the multiplicity of individuals partaking of the same specific form is only explicable in light of the reception of this form in distinct portions of matter, the absence of all matter in a spiritual subject such as the angel necessarily requires the uniqueness of its species. Each angel is its own species. It is by its very form, its intelligible type, that an angel is distinct from another angel. The angel Gabriel is distinguished from the angel Raphael as horses are distinguished from lions, and not as Bucephalus distinguishes itself from Rocinante. For Aquinas, this doctrine of the uniqueness of the species of each separate substance is that of the "philosophers."[76]

Finally, with regard to angelic knowledge, St. Thomas carries out a fascinating—because paradoxical—exercise. Thanks to Aristotle's *De anima*, Thomas is in possession of a wholly coherent epistemology. But Aristotelian epistemology is distinct from Platonic epistemology precisely in the way it takes into consideration the fleshly condition of the human spirit. In this regard, the distinction between intelligibility in itself and intelligibility *quoad nos* is characteristic of Aristotelianism. The human spirit is not directly engaged with the intelligible world but only accesses it through the mediation of the sensible. St. Thomas makes this "incarnated" epistemology his own. One sees this clearly in the way he accounts for the action of angels on the human *psyche*.[77] In supranatural dreams, angelic action harmoniously inserts itself into the physical–psychical processes of dreams described by Aristotle, by reorienting these dreams processes from the inside and not by replacing them.[78] His study of angelic knowledge is thereby rendered even more paradoxical. In effect, it is on the basis of this Aristotelian epistemological model, which distinguishes so clearly the human mode of knowledge from that of separate substances, that St. Thomas proposes to think analogically about the modalities of the knowledge of pure spirits like the angels! The exercise is delicate, as attested by the numerous difficulties that are born of a too-rapid transition to

---

speciei facere"; and p. 108: "96 (42). Quod deus non potest multiplicare individua sub una specie sine materia." See John F. Wippel, "Thomas Aquinas and the Condemnation of 1277," *The Modern Schoolman* 72 (1995): pp. 233–72, at 243–8; Suarez-Nani, *Les anges et la philosophie*, pp. 75–85: "L'individualité des anges et la condamnation de 1277." On the reception of the condemnation of this thesis, see John F. Wippel, *The Metaphysical Thought of Godfrey of Fontaines: A Study in Late Thirteenth-Century Philosophy* (Washington, DC: The Catholic University of America Press, 1981), pp. 366–9.

[75] See Aristotle, *Metaphysics* VII,8 (1034a37); Marie-Dominique Roland-Gosselin, OP, *Le "De ente et essentia" de S. Thomas d'Aquin* (Paris: Vrin, 1948), pp. 49–134: "Le principe de l'individualité." Aquinas attributes to Aristotle the thesis of individuation by matter; see *Sent. Metaph.* VII, lect. 7 (no. 1435); *De veritate*, q. 10, a. 5.

[76] See *De potentia*, q. 3, a. 10, corpus.   [77] See *ST* I, q. 111.

[78] See *ST* I, q. 111, a. 3.

angelic knowledge from the epistemological model constructed by Aristotle to give an account of human thought.[79] And yet, the necessity that the theologian has of thinking simultaneously about human knowledge and angelic knowledge (to say nothing of divine knowledge), clarifying the one by means of the other, enables St. Thomas to elaborate an epistemology, at once general and particular, of rare depth.

Christian theology, such as it was understood and practiced by St. Thomas, is not philosophy applied to religious questions. It has its own object, its own light, its own method, its own end, and, if it has recourse to philosophy, it is as a "teacher" and never as a "servant."[80] It is in the light of his or her own principles and methods that the theologian assumes and integrates in a critical way certain notions and doctrines elaborated by philosophers. The history of theology, therefore, cannot be a mere reflection of the history of philosophy.

It remains true, however, that the evolution of philosophical ideas has repercussions on theology. Thus, as we have seen in this chapter, assimilation of Aristotelian philosophy incontestably left its mark on the angelology of St. Thomas. But this is a completely different thing than an "Aristotelianization" of Christian theology. St. Thomas only retains those doctrines of Aristotle that seem to him helpful for clarifying the Christian mystery because, by reason of their intrinsic truth, they provide a solid foundation for the analogical process that leads to the *intellectus fidei*.

Even more, because of the transcendence of theology over all philosophy, the theologian avoids pledging himself or herself to a particular philosophical school, and instead he or she seeks to gather together a sort of philosophical "common good." Thus, it is clear that, while conscious of the divergences between Plato and Aristotle, St. Thomas does not try to contrast Platonism and Aristotelianism systematically. Persuaded that "all truth, whoever speaks it, comes from the Holy Spirit,"[81] he takes what is good wherever he finds it. Eclecticism? Certainly not. Rather, the *doctor communis* looks in the history of philosophy for the common truths that unify before he looks for the particularities that divide. This is perhaps the way in which the theologian puts into practice the fifth beatitude: *Beati pacifici . . .*

---

[79] The references to the epistemology of Aristotle are numerous in the objections of qq. 54–58 of the *Prima Pars*. See *ST* I, q. 54, a. 4, arg. 1; *ST* I, q. 57, a. 2, arg. 1.

[80] See *ST* I, q. 1, a. 5, ad 2.

[81] See Serge-Thomas Bonino, OP, "'Toute vérité, quel que soit celui qui la dit, vient de l'Esprit-Saint': Autour d'une citation de l'*Ambrosiaster* dans le corpus thomasien," *RThom* 106 (2006): pp. 101–47.

3

Aquinas and Aristotelian Hylomorphism

Raymond Hain

Thomas Aquinas, dissatisfied with the inadequacies of the ancient materialists as well as those of the Platonic dualists, was convinced that an Aristotelian account of human nature preserved both the genuine unity of the human person and our unique status as intellectual, and so immortal, creatures. Materialists denied the immortal character of human beings, while dualists denied that the body was a genuine part of the self. Aristotle's account of form and matter provided Aquinas the solution, but Aquinas's appropriation of Aristotle nevertheless entails a set of difficulties rooted in this attempt to combine real body/soul unity with the unique status of the intellectual soul. Here I will first develop Aquinas's account of Aristotle in his *De anima* commentary and the relationship between that commentary and Aquinas's own mature account of the soul in the *Summa theologiae*, keeping in mind Aquinas's two central concerns: body/soul unity and the status of the intellectual soul. I hope then to make clear how a series of problems arises for Aquinas's position based on whether we emphasize body/soul unity or the special status of the intellectual soul, and I will take as my main example the status of the disembodied soul between death and resurrection. I will offer a somewhat radical solution to this problem, the consequences of which I am not yet clear about; but I am convinced that for those of us who find Aquinas's appropriation of Aristotle convincing (as I myself certainly do), a development of some sort, whether in the direction I will propose or some other, is necessary.

3.1. AQUINAS AND ARISTOTLE'S *DE ANIMA*

St. Thomas knew Aristotle's *De anima* through William of Moerbeke's Latin translation, and Aquinas's commentary on Aristotle's text, the first of his twelve Aristotelian commentaries (including his incomplete ones), comes towards the end of his life (1267–1268), just before his second appointment as Dominican regent master in Paris.[1] Here I am interested not in whether Aquinas correctly understood Aristotle himself, or for that matter whether he correctly interpreted the Aristotelian text produced by Moerbeke—instead, I begin with how Aquinas himself understood Aristotle's *De anima*, both because this helps us see to what extent Aquinas saw himself following in Aristotle's footsteps, and because it will clarify what mattered most to Aquinas in his own account of the soul. Aristotle opens the second book of the *De anima* with his definition of "soul": "Soul is the first actuality of a physical body potentially having life."[2] Aquinas summarizes Aristotle's argument for his definition of the soul as follows:

> When there are two things, both of which we speak of as being something or as doing something, then one of them—the one that is first—serves as the form, whereas the other serves as the matter. Soul, however, is the first thing through which we live, although we live through soul and body. Therefore soul is the form of a living body. And this is the definition of soul introduced earlier: that soul is the first actuality of a physical body potentially having life.[3]

A living thing possesses two elements: form and matter, actuality and potentiality, a "first actuality" and a "physical body potentially having life." By the soul, we mean the form of a living thing, that which makes a thing actually alive, that which is joined to those elements able in themselves to become living if once united to a soul.

There are three things to note about what Aquinas takes Aristotle to have done by defining soul as "the first actuality of a physical body potentially having life." First, the materialism of the ancients has been refuted. Aquinas begins his own account of human nature in the *Summa theologiae* by asking whether the soul is a body. He responds by defining the soul as "the first principle of life in those things which live," and then argues that only an *act* could possibly be this first principle (hence Aristotle's definition calls the soul

---

[1] Here and elsewhere I follow Torrell on the dating of Aquinas's works. See Jean-Pierre Torrell, OP, *Saint Thomas Aquinas*, vol. 1, The Person and his Work, trans. Robert Royal, rev. ed. (Washington, DC: The Catholic University of America Press, 2005).

[2] Aristotle, *De anima* II,1 (412a28), p. 117. Quotations from the *De anima* will be from the version Moerbeke prepared and so will occasionally vary from the critical Aristotelian texts available today. Page references will be to Robert Pasnau's English translation in Thomas Aquinas, *A Commentary on Aristotle's* De anima, trans. Robert Pasnau (New Haven, CT: Yale University Press, 1999).

[3] *Sententia libri De anima* II, lect. 4 (no. 271) = ch. 4, lines 163–170, p. 146. References to Aquinas's commentary will be by book and lesson (lesson number from the Marietti edition), and then chapter and line numbers from the Leonine edition (vol. 45/1). Numbers in parentheses refer to the Marietti paragraph numbers. Page references are to the English translation in *A Commentary on Aristotle's* De anima, trans. Robert Pasnau (New Haven, CT: Yale University Press, 1999); for the discrepancy between the Leonine and other editions in the numbering of chapters, see *A Commentary on Aristotle's* De anima, pp. xxiv–xxv.

the first *actuality*, and not merely the first *principle*, as Aquinas does before he has responded to the ancients). He takes this conclusion to be a refutation of "the philosophers of old, ... [who] asserted that only bodies were real things; and that what is not corporeal is nothing."[4] Aquinas's argument is brief and difficult (and it is not my purpose here to develop it),[5] but he is following the opening passages of *De anima* II,1 in which Aristotle argues that the soul must be an actuality. Aquinas's own commentary on that opening passage emphasizes that a body is alive only in virtue of something else (it cannot be that simply *being a body* makes that body alive, otherwise all bodies would be alive). Aquinas thought that the ancients only believed in the existence of material causes,[6] and he takes Aristotle here to have shown that formal causes must also exist, and that the soul is precisely the formal cause of living things.

Second, though the soul is the form of the body, the status of the intellect is still unclear (and therefore so is, for example, whether or not some part of an intellectual living being might be able to survive death). Towards the end of Aristotle's discussion of his definition, he says the following:

> As for intellect and the analytic power, nothing is yet clear. But it seems that it is a different sort of soul and that only this can be separated, in the way that what is everlasting [is separated] from what can be corrupted. It is clear from these [earlier considerations], however, that the remaining parts of the soul are not separable, as some say they are.[7]

Aquinas, commenting on this passage, repeats first that "it is not yet clear" whether the intellect has a bodily organ, and then claims that at least superficially it appears that the intellect "has a different mode of existing."[8] Though Aristotle and Aquinas both believe that the ancient materialists, by ignoring formal causes, possessed an impoverished metaphysics, this does not necessarily imply that human beings somehow survive death; for most ensouled beings, if not all of them, when their material and formal causes are separated from one another in death, each one's "first actuality" ceases to exist.

Finally, though this is not obvious, Aquinas believes that Platonic dualism has also been refuted. Because the soul must be an actuality, the ancient materialists were mistaken, but Aristotle remarks that "it is unclear whether soul is the actuality of the body, as a sailor is of his ship."[9] And Aquinas adds:

---

[4] *ST* I, q. 75, a. 1, corpus. English translations of the *ST* are from Thomas Aquinas, *Summa Theologiae*, 5 vols., trans. Fathers of the English Dominican Province (Westminster, MD: Christian Classics, 1981).

[5] For a clear and careful discussion of this argument (though one with which I am not always in agreement), see Robert Pasnau, *Thomas Aquinas on Human Nature: A Philosophical Study of* Summa theologiae Ia 75–89 (New York: Cambridge University Press, 2002), pp. 25–44.

[6] *Sent. Metaph.* VIII, lect. 4 (no. 1737).

[7] Aristotle, *De anima* II,2 (413b24–29), p. 141.

[8] *Sententia libri De anima* II, lect. 4 (no. 268) = ch. 4, lines 108 and 114, p. 145.

[9] Aristotle, *De anima* II,1 (413a9), p. 128.

Because Plato supposed that soul is the actuality of body not as a form is but as a mover is, Aristotle adds that it is not yet clear whether soul is the actuality of the body as a sailor is the actuality of his ship—that is, as a mover only.[10]

But, as Aristotle develops his demonstration of the definition of soul in *De anima* II,2 by arguing that the soul is the *first* actuality of a body potentially having life, Aquinas thinks that he thereby refutes Platonic dualism. Even though it is not obvious in the commentary that Aquinas believes this, in *ST* I, q. 76, a. 1, where Aquinas asks if the intellectual principle is united to the body as its form, Aquinas refers to Aristotle's argument in *De anima* II,2 as decisive:

> It is clear that the first thing by which the body lives is the soul. And as life appears through various operations in different degrees of living things, that whereby we primarily perform each of all these vital actions is the soul. For the soul is the first principle of our nourishment, sensation, and local movement; and likewise of our understanding. Therefore this principle by which we primarily understand, whether it be called the intellect or the intellectual soul, is the form of the body. This is the demonstration used by Aristotle.

Aquinas is referring to Aristotle's demonstration at *De anima* II,2 (414a4–14), which Aquinas carefully develops in his commentary. In this way, thinks Aquinas, Aristotle's definition of soul as the form of living things excludes both ancient materialism and Platonic dualism, but leaves open the peculiar nature of the intellect and its implications for intellectual living beings.

After discussing the nutritive and sensitive powers, Aristotle returns to the intellect in *De anima* III,4. Because the intellect is able to understand all things, it must not actually be any of them.[11] That is, the intellect as potentially all things (or, as Aquinas says, the "possible intellect") cannot be corporeal, nor can it operate through a corporeal organ (as does the power of vision, for example).[12] Aquinas comments:

> Since our intellect is naturally suited to have intellective cognition of all sensible and corporeal things, it must lack every corporeal nature . . . If intellect had any

---

[10] *Sententia libri De anima* II, lect. 2 (no. 243) = ch. 2, lines 153–157, p. 132.

[11] Aristotle, *De anima* III,4 (429a18), p. 341.

[12] Certain recent commentators have been very skeptical of this argument, but some years ago Herbert McCabe explained its force with remarkable simplicity: "Now one of the characteristic things about a picture is that it is first of all something in its own right—a piece of canvas or wood—and then it resembles something. Now it is just the things that the picture has in its own right that must be forbidden to the picture in the mind. If it were a picture on wood, it would not serve to distinguish a cow from a cow painted on wood; if it were made of cast iron it would not help to tell a cow from a cast iron lawn-cow. There is no *mental stuff* that the picture could be made of—it must have everything the cow has and nothing else. It cannot *resemble* a cow because anything except the sheer resemblance will be an alien element like wood or cast iron. It must be simply everything that a cow has and nothing else. And what is this except to be the nature of the cow?" See Herbert McCabe, OP, "The Immortality of the Soul: The Traditional Argument," in *Aquinas: A Collection of Critical Essays*, edited by Anthony Kenny (Notre Dame, IN: University of Notre Dame Press, 1976), pp. 297–306, at 304–5.

determinate nature, the nature that was natural to it would prevent it from having cognition of other natures. That is why [Aristotle] says for something appearing within it will prevent and block the cognition of what is outside it—i.e., will hamper intellect, veil it in a certain way, and close it off from contemplating other things.[13]

In the same way it is reasonable that it not be mixed with a body—i.e., that it have no corporeal organ in the way that the soul's sensory part has. For if there is any corporeal organ for intellect in the way that there is for the sensory part, then it will follow that it has a determinate nature drawn from the natures of sensible things.[14]

It is in the discussion of the intellect that Aquinas makes his most extensive and interesting arguments that go beyond a literal interpretation of the text, and they begin here with the discussion of the possible intellect. Aristotle concludes his discussion of the unmixed nature of the possible intellect with the sentence: "For it [the possible intellect] is separated, whereas what is sensory does not exist without a body."[15] Aquinas begins a lengthy comment on this sentence with this: "Some people have been so deceived by this passage, however, that they have posited a possible intellect separated in existence from the body, like one of the separated substances."[16] And after a detailed discussion of the issue and Averroes's position in particular, he concludes with the following:

It is astonishing, though, how carelessly [the proponents of this position] went wrong because of his saying that intellect is "separated," since the meaning of this word is available from his text: intellect is called separated because it does not have an organ as a sense does. And that can be true because the human soul in virtue of its superior status surpasses the capability of corporeal matter and cannot be wholly encompassed by it. That is why it is endowed with an action that corporeal matter has no share in, and because of this its power for that action has no corporeal organ. And *that* is how intellect is separated.[17]

After this discussion of the intellect as potentially all things, Aristotle argues that the intellect must also be active:

Indeed there is intellect of the sort in which all things are brought about [the possible intellect, just discussed], and, on the other hand, [there is] that by which it serves to bring about all things, as a sort of condition . . . And this latter intellect is separable, unaffectable, and unmixed, being actual in substance.[18]

---

[13] *Sententia libri De anima* III, lect. 7 (no. 680) = ch. 1, lines 139–142 and 147–154, p. 345.
[14] *Sententia libri De anima* III, lect. 7 (no. 684) = ch. 1, lines 198–204, p. 346.
[15] Aristotle, *De anima* III,4 (429b5), p. 341.
[16] *Sententia libri De anima* III, lect. 7 (no. 689) = ch. 1, lines 277–280, p. 348.
[17] *Sententia libri De anima* III, lect. 7 (no. 699) = ch. 1, lines 372–383, p. 350.
[18] Aristotle, *De anima* III,5 (430a13–16), p. 364.

Because, as Aquinas says, an agent is superior to what is affected by it, and because the intellect as active, the "agent intellect," affects the possible intellect, the agent intellect must be separated, unaffectable, and unmixed, as is the possible intellect. And "on this basis it is also clear that [the agent intellect] is in actuality as regards its substance, since the agent is superior to its patient and its matter only insofar as it is in actuality."[19] The intellectual soul is able to become all things, but since, as Aquinas said earlier,[20] the intellect knows by means of the forms in sensible things, and sensible things cannot themselves affect the possible intellect (which is superior to them), the intellect itself must abstract those forms from matter and use them as that by which it knows. This is the intellect as active, and it must be the highest part of the intellectual soul.

Again, we find Aquinas careful here to defend a particular interpretation of Aristotle and to rule out a rival, and very influential, interpretation: "On the basis of the things said in this passage some people[21] have claimed that agent intellect is a separated substance and that it differs in substance from possible intellect."[22] But, among other reasons, this claim "runs contrary to Aristotle's position. He expressly says that 'these [two] different things [agent intellect and possible intellect] are *in soul*' (430a12–14), by which he expressly lets it be understood that they are parts or powers of soul, not separated substances."[23] Instead, the proper interpretation of Aristotle's claims about the nature of the agent intellect is that the intellectual soul survives death and is of its very nature imperishable:

> [Aristotle] says, first, that only separated intellect is that which truly is. This claim, of course, must be understood, not as regards agent intellect or possible intellect alone, but as regards both; for it was in regard to each of them that he said earlier that "it is separated" [III.7.429b5; cf. 430a17]. And so it is clear that he is speaking here of the whole intellective part, which is called separated, of course, because it has its operation without a corporeal organ. Now at the beginning of this work [I.2.403a10–11] he said that if any operation of soul is special (*propria*) to it, then it can be the case that soul is separated. And thus he concludes that that part of soul alone, the intellective part, is imperishable and everlasting. This is what he presupposed earlier in Book II [4.413b25–27]: that this sort of soul is separated from the others "as the everlasting from the perishable." It is called everlasting, however, not because it always was but because it always will be. Thus the Philosopher says in *Metaphysics* XII [1070a21–26] that a form never exists before its matter, but soul remains after its matter—"not all of it, but intellect."[24]

---

[19] *Sententia libri De anima* III, lect. 10 (no. 733) = ch. 4, lines 83–86, p. 366.
[20] *Sententia libri De anima* III, lect. 10 (no. 731) = ch. 4, lines 54–63, p. 366.
[21] This includes, among others, Ibn Sina (*Liber de anima* V,5) and Ibn Rushd (*De anima* III,17).
[22] *Sententia libri De anima* III, lect. 10 (no. 734) = ch. 4, lines 89–92, p. 366.
[23] *Sententia libri De anima* III, lect. 10 (no. 736) = ch. 4, lines 123–127, p. 367.
[24] *Sententia libri De anima* III, lect. 10 (nos. 742–743) = ch. 4, lines 202–220, p. 369.

Aquinas is consistent with his earlier interpretation of the word "separated," and here claims that for Aristotle the intellectual soul is indeed immortal. But the state of such a disembodied soul is an impoverished one, for without the body and its concomitant sense powers, the agent intellect has nothing on which to work, and so, says Aquinas:

> Without this perishable part of soul... our intellect intellectively cognizes nothing, because it does not intellectively cognize anything without a phantasm (as will be said below [III.12.431a16–17]). And so when the body is destroyed, the knowledge of things does not remain in the separated soul in the same way in which it now intellectively cognizes.[25]

Notice here at the end that, while Aquinas explains that for Aristotle the intellect exists without understanding after death, Aquinas argues that the possibility that the intellect after death will have knowledge by some other means is left open. He ends here with the simple but suggestive remark that "to discuss the way [the intellect] intellectively cognizes then is no part of the present plan."[26]

Just as Aquinas is careful to exclude readings of Aristotle that place the intellectual powers of the soul outside of the actual form of the living being, so here he is careful to show that Aristotle merely proves that the intellect cannot have knowledge after death in the same way that it has knowledge during life. Aquinas's most extended remark on this comes much earlier, as he comments on the Prologue of the *De anima* in which Aristotle says: "Having intellective cognition, however, seems above all else special [to soul]. But if this too is a kind of phantasia, or does not occur without phantasia, then it will not be possible even for this to occur without body."[27] Aquinas comments on this as follows:

> It is important to know, therefore, that there is one kind of operation or state of soul that needs a body as instrument *and* as object. In this way seeing needs a body (i) as an object, since color (the object of sight) is a body, and also (ii) as an instrument, since vision, even if it is from soul, occurs only through the organ of sight (through the pupil, that is, which serves as an instrument). And in this way seeing belongs not only to soul but also to the organ. There is another kind of operation, however, that needs a body not as its instrument but only as its object. For intellective cognition does not occur through a corporeal organ but needs a corporeal organ. For as the Philosopher says in Book III [12.431a14–15], phantasms are related to intellect in the same way that colors are related to sight. But colors are related to sight as objects; therefore phantasms are related to intellect as objects. Therefore, since phantasms do not occur without a body, it follows that intellective cognition does not occur without a body—but in such a way that the body serves as the object, not as the instrument.[28]

---

[25] *Sententia libri De anima* III, lect. 10 (no. 745) = ch. 4, lines 242–248, p. 370.
[26] *Sententia libri De anima* III, lect. 10 (no. 745) = ch. 4, lines 248–249, p. 370.
[27] Aristotle, *De anima* I,1 (403a7–10), p. 12.
[28] *Sententia libri De anima* I, lect. 2 (no. 19) = ch. 2, lines 50–69, p. 15.

Because the body serves as the object, and not the instrument, it is conceptually possible for the intellect to have knowledge after death, since the object is in no way a part of the intrinsic nature of intellectual activity, though such activity depends on, for the living being, the body. This makes it possible for the separated soul to have knowledge in some other fashion, say by the special grace of God.

Aristotle concludes the *De anima* with remarks on appetite and on the order between the powers of the soul. Here I need only mention a very brief discussion of the intellectual appetite or will. Moerbeke's Latin of Aristotle's brief passage is translated as:

> Moreover, there is the appetitive part, which certainly seems to be different from all [the others] both conceptually and in potentiality. . . . In the reasoning part it becomes will, and in the irrational part concupiscence and anger. If the soul is three, however, there will be appetite in each.[29]

Aquinas takes this as a very straightforward acknowledgement of the existence of the rational appetite or will, though Aristotle does not return to this particular form of appetite again in the *De anima*, nor does Aquinas bring it up elsewhere in his commentary. In this way, therefore, all the major elements of Aquinas's own account of the soul are already present in Aristotle's *De anima*, and even those that are not (like the knowledge of the separated soul) require no fundamental changes to Aristotle's claims.

3.2. *SUMMA THEOLOGIAE* I, QQ. 75–89

Aquinas's own most extensive and mature treatment of the human soul, qq. 75–89 of the *Prima Pars* of the *Summa theologiae*, is contemporaneous with his commentary on Aristotle's *De anima*; both were written in Rome and finished towards the end of 1268, just before his journey to Paris. Aquinas accepts in these questions as his own all of Aristotle's views outlined above (in section 3.1) and regularly repeats Aristotle's arguments in his own account of human nature. Indeed, he never explicitly rejects any of Aristotle's claims in the *De anima*, though there are perhaps some minor discrepancies here and there between Aquinas's interpretation of Aristotle and Aquinas's own views.[30] In many ways he develops, and in places supplements, Aristotle's

---

[29] Aristotle, *De anima* III,9 (432b3–7), p. 393.

[30] Pasnau, requiring an example to show that we cannot assume that Aquinas simply accepts absolutely everything said in the *De anima*, chooses a difficulty about the relationship between the internal sense power of *phantasia* and the workings of the external senses. Perhaps Aquinas does disagree with Aristotle here, but the fact that Pasnau, who knows these texts extremely well,

account, but the connection between Aristotle's own arguments in the *De anima* and these fifteen questions is remarkably close.

This connection to Aristotle is evident even in the way Aquinas constructs the interplay of authorities and arguments. For instance, of the eighty-nine articles that make up these fifteen questions, Aquinas refers to Aristotle in the *sed contra* forty times (Augustine is a distant second at nineteen, with Damascene next at six). Particularly striking is the use of Aristotle in the *sed contra* of the first article of the final question of the treatise (q. 89: "whether the separated soul can understand anything?"), a question about which we might suppose Aristotle would have nothing to say, and that Aquinas fills with references to Scripture and the Fathers:

> The Philosopher says, "If the soul had no proper operation, it could not be separated from the body." But the soul is separated from the body.[31] Therefore it has a proper operation, and above all, that which consists in understanding. Therefore the soul can understand when it is apart from the body.

It is worth noting, too, that even the omission of Aristotle is suggestive. Aristotle is absent from the *sed contra* of each of the seven articles that make up the beginning of the treatise, q. 75, in which Aquinas asks what pertains to the essence of the soul. The authorities are rather Augustine and Dionysius, even in the article that asks "whether the soul is man?" (Aquinas reminds us of Augustine's approval of Varro's comment that "man is not a mere soul, nor a mere body, but both soul and body").[32] Though references to Aristotle make up the bulk of Aquinas's references in the treatise, he is careful here to begin his defense of Aristotelian theses with orthodox authorities.

The structure of these fifteen questions also mirrors that of *De anima* II–III remarkably closely (see Table 1). The most interesting discrepancy involves Aquinas's discussion of the will, which has almost no parallel in the *De anima*, and most of Aquinas's references to Aristotle here are to the *Nicomachean Ethics* rather than the *De anima*. But Aquinas himself, though he discusses the nature of the rational appetite, does not talk about the acts of the will here because "the acts of the appetitive part of the soul come under the consideration of the science of morals; wherefore we shall treat of them in the second part of this work."[33] Aristotle, we might suppose, likewise saved a fuller discussion of the will for his ethical works. Aquinas also slightly rearranges material in order to follow Dionysius: "Since Dionysius (*Ang. Hier.* xi) says that three things are to be found in spiritual substances—essence, power, and operation—we shall treat first of what belongs to the essence of the soul;

is limited to such a minor question is very telling. See his introduction to *A Commentary on Aristotle's* De anima, pp. xi–xxv, here at xx.

[31] Notice that Aquinas is again consistent in his use of the word "separated."
[32] *ST* I, q. 75, a. 4, sed contra.   [33] *ST* I, q. 84, Prologue.

Table 1. Comparative Structures of *De Anima* II–III and *ST* I, qq. 75–89

De anima	Summa theologiae I
II,1–2 (definition of "soul")	75–76 (the essence of the soul)
II,3 (the soul's powers)	77–78, a. 1 (the powers of the soul in general)
II,4 (vegetative powers)	78, a. 2 (vegetative powers)
II,5–12 (external senses)	78, a. 3 (external senses)
III,1–3 (internal senses)	78, a. 4 (internal senses)
III,4 (possible intellect)	79, aa. 1–2 (possible intellect)
III,5 (agent intellect)	79, aa. 3–5 (agent intellect)
No corollary	79, aa. 6–13 (memory, reason, synderesis, conscience, etc.)
III,9 (appetitive powers)	80 (appetitive powers in general)
III,10–11 (sense appetite)	81 (sense appetite)
No corollary	82–83 (the will and free choice)
III,6–8 (acts of the intellect)	84–88 (how the intellect knows when united to the body)
No corollary	89 (the knowledge of the separated soul)
III,12–13 (the order of the parts of the soul)	*No corollary*

secondly, of what belongs to its power; thirdly, of what belongs to its operation."[34] For this reason, discussion of the acts of the intellectual power is moved to the end, rather than grouped with discussion of the power itself as in the *De anima*. Finally, as Aquinas says,[35] Aristotle is discussing soul in general, whereas Aquinas, as a theologian, is properly concerned with the intellectual and appetitive powers only (in which the virtues reside), and so naturally we can leave behind certain things (such as *De anima* III,12–13, on the order between the different types of souls) and de-emphasize others (like the vegetative and sense powers).

I have suggested already that Aquinas, in appropriating Aristotle's *De anima* to construct an account of human nature that is philosophically convincing and nevertheless compatible with Christianity, must argue most especially for two things: first, that there is something about human beings that will of its nature exist forever; and secondly, that this immortal part of us is indeed genuinely *ours*, such that for it to last forever is for us to have the potential to last forever. This is precisely where Aquinas is most emphatic in his interpretations of Aristotle in the *De anima* commentary, and this makes up the heart of his opening discussion in the treatise on human nature.

The purpose of the first question of the treatise, q. 75 ("What pertains to the essence of the soul"), is to show that the human soul is in itself immortal. Aquinas progressively separates the human soul from that which corrupts (it is not a body, nor does it depend on a body for its subsistence, nor is it similar to the souls of animals), concluding in a. 6 that the soul is naturally incorruptible because, as we have seen already (in section 3.1), it possesses an

---

[34] *ST* I, q. 75, Prologue.   [35] *ST* I, q. 78, Prologue; q. 84, Prologue.

operation that is neither corporeal nor dependent instrumentally speaking on a body. But then he reminds us in the concluding seventh article that we are not as separate from the material world as are the angels. Q. 75, then, separates the soul as much as possible, though not completely, from the material world with an eye towards immortality. But then q. 76, "Of the union of body and soul," reverses the direction of argument and unites the soul as much as possible to the material world in order to preserve a genuine union with the body. So the soul must be the form of the body; every unique person has his or her own unique soul; the intellectual soul is the *only* form of the body; there is nothing that mediates between the union of the soul and the body (neither accidents nor other bodies); and therefore the soul is united such that it is wholly present in every part of the body.

It is no accident that Aquinas must make central his defenses of the immortal character of the intellectual soul and the genuine unity between that same soul and the material world. One can, indeed, understand the main objections this account faces as the consequences of oscillation between a more "materialistic" interpretation of Aristotle's account of human nature and a more "immaterial" account. Given Aristotle's general claim that the human being is the result of a union between form and matter, then if we emphasize the importance of our bodily nature for Aristotle, and that what genuinely exists is the whole, the substance, then we will naturally conclude that upon death the material and formal aspects of ourselves are destroyed. It is the whole that matters, and that constitutes us, and without the whole we will be no more. Death is therefore the end of us. We preserve genuine unity between body and soul only at the cost of immortality.

On the other hand, if we emphasize the unique character of the intellect, its immaterial nature and its operation independently of a corporeal organ, then it seems natural that such a thing would be immortal, for what could destroy something that neither has parts that could be separated from one another, nor could be injured by the injury of any other material thing whatsoever? The cost is that it now appears much harder to argue that this immaterial and immortal power is in any real way closely united to the material world. And we human beings must be either wholly mortal though we possess access of some sort to this immortal power, or we are ourselves immortal and no longer genuinely united to the material world.

Aquinas, in his appropriation of Aristotle, is as we have seen (in the present section 3.2) careful to argue both for immortality and for union, and so excludes these two interpretations. But Aquinas's interpretation of Aristotle is, in the history of Aristotelianism, a minority one. So, for example, Alexander of Aphrodisias argued in the third century that the human intellect, since a power of a form united to matter, must cease to exist upon the death of the human being. And Ibn Rushd argued in the twelfth century that an intellectual power that was "separate" and "unmixed" must be different from the soul that was the substantial form of the body, though it made possible that soul's knowledge.[36]

Yet even if we assume that Aquinas's appropriation of Aristotle (whether it agrees with Aristotle himself or not) is coherent and persuasive, Aquinas's account itself is open to the same struggle between a more "materialistic" or a more "immaterial" interpretation. As with the interpretation of Aristotle, what is at stake is again, on the one hand, the immortal character of the human being and, on the other, the real unity between body and soul. The motivation here, however, is often Christian. According to Aquinas's interpretation of Aristotle, the intellectual soul is incorruptible and survives death, but its separated existence is an impoverished one, for its sense powers are gone and its intellectual powers are inoperative without access to phantasms.[37] But the Christian believes that the blessed after death will not only live, but live more fully than they ever did here on earth. The solution is an obvious one: God at the resurrection will reunite the substantial form that is our soul with the matter of our body, and we will then enjoy a supernatural but embodied bliss for all eternity by means of God's grace. This solution, however, raises a number of serious difficulties.

For example, if we emphasize the bodily side of Aquinas's account, the genuine unity between form and matter and the necessity of both for the presence of the whole human being, then it will be the case that my soul must be reunited with precisely the *same* matter with which it was once united. Only material continuity, as well as formal continuity, will allow my resurrection (after all, if I am to get the same table back, it must be the same wood *and* it must be once again in the same shape it was before). And this seems to be what Aquinas says:

> None of man's essential principles yields entirely to nothingness in death, for the rational soul which is man's form remains after death . . . ; the matter, also, which was subject to such a form remains in the same dimensions which made it able to be the individual matter. Therefore, by conjunction to a soul numerically the same man will be restored to matter numerically the same.[38]

---

[36] For an excellent study of Aquinas's maneuvering between Alexander and Ibn Rushd, among others, see Anton C. Pegis, "Some Reflections on *Summa contra Gentiles II, 56*," in *An Etienne Gilson Tribute: Presented by his North American Students with a Response by Etienne Gilson*, edited by Charles J. O'Neil (Milwaukee: Marquette University Press, 1959), pp. 169–88.

[37] *Sententia libri De anima* III, lect. 10 (nos. 744–745) = ch. 4, lines 221–249, pp. 369–70.

[38] *SCG* IV, ch. 81 (no. 6 [Marietti ed.: no. 4151]), p. 303. Page references are to the English translation in *On the Truth of the Catholic Faith: Summa contra Gentiles*, vol. 4, Salvation, trans. Charles J. O'Neil (Garden City, NY: Image Books, 1957); repr. as *Summa contra Gentiles* (Notre Dame, IN: University of Notre Dame Press, 1975). See also *SCG* IV, ch. 84 (no. 7 [Marietti ed.: no. 4201]), p. 321, in which Aquinas argues that the resurrected man must have numerically the same body if he is to be identically the same individual.

For Aquinas, one does not require all the matter that was united to one's form during life, but at least a part is required, in which case God will supply the rest. This is made clear by the case of cannibalism, in which the same matter was united to more than one human soul: "If [a man] ate human flesh only, what rises in him will be that which he drew from those who generated him, and what is wanting will be supplied by the Creator's omnipotence."[39] But this emphasis on numerically the same matter, and so on the deep union between body and soul, raises a puzzle, for it is not difficult to imagine that, over the course of the human species (millions of years? billions? trillions?) two persons could conceivably have been generated from numerically the same matter, and perished before adding to that matter. Perhaps the generating matter can be shared between them, but how many could share it? And if there is a limit, is it inconceivable that over time the limit will be reached and one person will, so to speak, be left empty handed at the resurrection?

Instead, we could say that Aquinas's account requires only that the same body *qualitatively* speaking is required for resurrection, but not the same numerical body.[40] But then the body begins to look less necessary than it was at first to the human person, for it is not *this* body that is necessary for my resurrection, but instead simply *some body or other* that possesses certain qualities. It will then be the case that my body is not an essential part of me. Instead, what is essential is that *I be embodied*, but no physical part of me is itself essential to me as such. This contrasts sharply with my soul, which is indeed essential as such to me; I can "switch bodies" and still be myself, but I cannot switch souls.

Here is another difficulty that arises in a similar way. If we begin by emphasizing the immaterial and immortal part of human nature, and most especially the intellectual part of the soul, then while the body might be necessary for the resurrection, it serves little purpose beyond this in the full life that awaits the saved. And this again seems to be what Aquinas says: "Since man's perfect Happiness consists in the vision of the Divine Essence, it does not depend on the body. Consequently, the soul can be happy without the body."[41]

Yet Aquinas recognizes, as the objections make clear, that this seems to make the body superfluous, and so he allows that the body does indeed contribute to happiness:

---

[39] *SCG* IV, ch. 81 (no. 13 [Marietti ed.: no. 4158]), p. 307.

[40] This is the solution defended by, for example, Bruno Niederbacher, S.J., "The Same Body Again? Thomas Aquinas on the Numerical Identity of the Resurrected Body," in *Personal Identity and Resurrection: How Do We Survive our Death?*, edited by Georg Gasser (Burlington, VT: Ashgate, 2010), pp. 145–59, and Eleonore Stump, *Aquinas* (New York: Routledge, 2003), p. 208.

[41] *ST* I-II, q. 4, a. 5, corpus.

We must, however, notice that something may belong to a thing's perfection in two ways. First, as constituting the essence thereof; thus the soul is necessary for man's perfection. Secondly, as necessary for its well-being; thus, beauty of body and keenness of wit belong to man's perfection. Wherefore though the body does not belong in the first way to the perfection of human happiness, yet it does in the second way.[42]

It is not clear that this is a satisfying defense of the importance of the body for our eternal happiness (how does the presence of "well-being" *both* add nothing essential to my happiness *and* add to my happiness in a way that justifies the need for my body?), and for this reason some have argued that Aquinas's view cannot be strictly speaking correct if we are going to do justice to our embodied nature.[43] Even granting that my soul must be united to my body in order for the person that is myself to exist, this would provide only an instrumental role for the body when it comes to happiness; there is nothing necessarily *bodily* about my eternal happiness, though I need my body as an essential constituent of myself. Aquinas sees this and argues that, in a sense, for the sake of my well-being, my body must participate in genuine happiness, but the difficulty here is understanding well-being in a way that preserves both a genuine dependence on the body and the unique status of the intellectual soul in possession of the beatific vision.

I hope my general point is clear enough. On these questions and others, whether you will tend towards a more "material" or "immaterial" resolution of the difficulty will be determined by what you consider most important: the genuine unity of the body/soul composite, or the special status of the intellectual soul. Though Aquinas's main purpose, in his appropriation of Aristotle, is to hold these two together and to give each their proper due within Christian theology, at the very least he has left us significant puzzles that, even now, await satisfying conclusions.

3.3. THE STATUS OF THE DISEMBODIED SOUL

I turn now in the remainder of this study to one very pressing puzzle of special relevance to Christians that is again a reflection of this general tension: the

---

[42] *ST* I-II, q. 4, a. 5, corpus, and compare with *SCG* IV, ch. 79 (no. 11 [Marietti ed.: no. 4156]), p. 299.

[43] See, for example, John Morreall, "Perfect Happiness and the Resurrection of the Body," *Religious Studies* 16 (1980): pp. 29–35. Morreall is not directly discussing Aquinas and considers this problem from the general perspective of the Christian account of the beatific vision and the general resurrection, but he presses on precisely the difficulty faced by Aquinas. For an argument centered on Aquinas, see Germain Grisez, "The True Ultimate End of Human Beings: The Kingdom, Not God Alone," *TS* 69 (2008): pp. 38–61.

status for Aquinas of the disembodied soul between death and resurrection. Here again, one's interpretation of this status depends on whether one emphasizes body/soul unity or instead the special status of the intellectual soul.

If the human person is essentially a body/soul composite, then it seems natural to say that when the body and soul are separated and the composite dissolved, the person must cease to exist. And this is precisely what Aquinas says:

> The soul is a part of the human species; and so, although it may exist in a separate state, yet since it ever retains its nature of unibility, it cannot be called an individual substance, which is the hypostasis or first substance, as neither can the hand nor any other part of man; thus neither the definition nor the name of person belongs to it.[44]

And again:

> Not every particular substance is a hypostasis or a person, but that which has the complete nature of its species. Hence a hand, or a foot, is not called a hypostasis, or a person; nor, likewise, is the soul alone so called, since it is a part of the human species.[45]

We might think that the loss of personhood between death and the resurrection of the body is perhaps not that significant (that is, perhaps I myself can exist at one time as a person and at another time as a nonperson). But consider the following objection and reply:

> Objection. Further, the soul of Peter is not Peter. If therefore the souls of the saints pray for us, so long as they are separated from their bodies, we ought not to call upon Saint Peter, but on his soul, to pray for us: yet the Church does the contrary. The saints therefore do not pray for us, at least before the resurrection. Reply. It is because the saints while living merited to pray for us, that we invoke them under the names by which they were known in this life, and by which they are better known to us: and also in order to indicate our belief in the resurrection, according to the saying of Ex. 3:6, "I am the God of Abraham," etc.[46]

Aquinas seems to accept that the soul of St. Peter is not St. Peter, and here says that we call upon the soul of St. Peter by the name "St. Peter" according to synecdoche,[47] whereby a part is used to refer to the whole, rather than in the full sense in which we might use this name after the general resurrection. Here is another passage:

> Abraham's soul, properly speaking, is not Abraham himself, but a part of him (and the same as regards the others). Hence life in Abraham's soul does not suffice to make Abraham a living being, or to make the God of Abraham the God

---

[44] *ST* I, q. 29, a. 1, ad 5.   [45] *ST* I, q. 75, a. 4, ad 2.

[46] *ST* II-II, q. 83, a. 11, arg. 5 and ad 5.

[47] As Aquinas says: "Through synecdoche, sometimes only a part of man is called man, especially the soul, which is the more noble part of man" (*De veritate*, q. 13, a. 5, ad 3).

of a living man. But there needs to be life in the whole composite, i.e., the soul and body: and although this life were not actually when these words were uttered, it was in each part as ordained to the resurrection. Wherefore our Lord proves the resurrection with the greatest subtlety and efficacy.[48]

It seems therefore that the disembodied soul is neither a person nor strictly speaking the object of a proper noun. When we pray to St. Peter, we are not praying to Peter himself, but to Peter's soul, and we keep our use of his name both in honor of his life and in prospect of his resurrection. But St. Peter strictly speaking has ceased to exist, and he will return to existence only when his soul is reunited with his body at the resurrection. This is a natural conclusion if we wish to emphasize the genuine unity between the form and matter that constitute a human being. Once that union is dissolved, we have a significant (for St. Thomas, a substantial[49]) change such that the particular person ceases to exist. The soul remains, and so the possibility of personal immortality is preserved, but it should not surprise us that this position follows from what Aquinas has said about the union between body and soul.

Nevertheless, it is a deeply disturbing conclusion, and though it seems clear to me that St. Thomas accepts it,[50] many readers of Aquinas have strongly resisted it. Consider Eleonore Stump's strategy, for example. She argues against this interpretation in precisely the way we should expect if we were to react against the focus on body/soul unity and turn instead to the unique character of the intellectual soul; she emphasizes the personal characteristics of the human soul itself and, drawing on the particularly Christian focus on the special status of the human soul, the theological difficulties we face if we do not exist between the time of our death and our resurrection. First, as Aquinas argues, the separated soul has an intellect and a will, it can (among other things) know singulars and universals and can suffer the pains of hell and enjoy the bliss of heaven.[51] But are not these activities things that only *persons* do? And therefore if the separated soul of St. Peter is not Peter, it must be

---

[48] *ST, Supplementum*, q. 75, a. 1, ad 2. See also *In IV Sent.*, dist. 43, q. 1, a. 1, quaestiuncula 1, ad 2; and *In III Sent.*, dist. 22, q. 1, a. 1, arg. 6.

[49] *Quaestiones disputatae de anima*, q. 1.

[50] In addition to the passages already discussed, the best textual defense of this that I know of is Patrick Toner, "St. Thomas Aquinas on Death and the Separated Soul," *Pacific Philosophical Quarterly* 91 (2010): pp. 587–99.

[51] See *ST* I, q. 89 in regards to the knowledge of the separated soul. That the separated soul must possess rational appetite as well as intellect can be inferred from many claims about the activity of the separated soul; for instance, Aquinas argues that the desire of the separated soul in possession of the beatific vision is entirely at rest (*ST* I-II, q. 4, a. 5, ad 5). See also Stump's discussion (which omits references) in Eleonore Stump, "Resurrection, Reassembly, and Reconstitution: Aquinas on the Soul," in *Die menschliche Seele: Brauchen wir den Dualismus?*, edited by Bruno Niederbacher and Edmund Runggaldier (Frankfurt: Ontos Verlag, 2006), pp. 153–74, esp. 157–9.

someone else, and this involves insurmountable difficulties (why should someone else suffer for me, and why should my resurrection force someone else to perish and lose eternal bliss?). And secondly, for Aquinas as well as the Christian tradition more generally, things happen to separated souls that apparently must happen to the persons themselves. For example, when Christ harrowed hell after his death, Abraham was brought to heaven from limbo. But if Abraham ceased to exist upon his death and will return only at the resurrection of his body, then strictly speaking Abraham was never in limbo and has not yet entered heaven. This, suggests Stump, seems both heretical and preposterous.

Instead, Stump argues that for Aquinas the whole human being is greater than (and so also other than) the sum of its parts. I might at any one time be constituted of my soul and matter, but over time the matter will change, will increase or decrease, and yet I remain. At no time, therefore, am I identical to the various parts of which I consist (since those parts can admittedly come and go, say if my leg is amputated), and therefore, she says, my identity is not equivalent to my constitution:

> A human person is not identical to his soul; rather, a human person is identical to an individual substance in the species *rational animal*. A particular of that sort is normally, naturally, composed of form and matter configured into a human body. Because constitution is not identity for Aquinas, however, a particular can exist with less than the normal, natural complement of constituents. It can, for example, exist when it is constituted only by one of its main metaphysical parts, namely, the soul. And so although a person is not identical to his soul, the existence of the soul is sufficient for the existence of a person.[52]

Therefore Aquinas means that the soul of St. Peter is not (identical to) the person that is St. Peter, but St. Peter the person can exist, constituted by his soul alone, as a whole that is greater than its parts (or, in this case, part).

But even if it is true that the whole is greater than its parts for human beings (and so the human person, St. Peter, is not merely "matter + form"), there is a problem here. Some parts are necessary such that the whole that is greater than them can exist only if they are present. So of course the normal, natural complement of constituents for human beings includes two arms, two legs, form, and matter. But while the person can survive the removal of his or her arms and legs, it is not at all clear that the same person could survive the destruction of all matter, just as we would think the person could not survive the destruction of the soul (if the soul ceased to exist, surely the person would too). Stump avoids this distinction between essential natural parts and un-essential natural parts by using words like "naturally," "ordinarily," and "normally." It seems true, however, *both* that the whole person is greater

---

[52] Stump, "Resurrection," p. 170.

than its individual parts, *and* that some natural parts are essential to the existence of the person. But if some parts are essential, then the distinction between constitution and identity allows us to avoid the loss of personhood in the case of the disembodied soul *only* if matter itself is a natural part in the sense that arms and legs are rather than in the sense that a person's form is a natural part. But then Stump's argument is question-begging, since this is precisely the claim made from the perspective of genuine body/soul unity: the body, matter itself, is an essential constituent of human beings, and to take that away is to dissolve the greater whole of which it was a part, even if that greater whole is not identical to any part or to the sum of its parts.

And yet, even though Stump's strategy seems to me a failure, her arguments against the claim that St. Peter ceases to exist at his death and will only exist again after the resurrection are powerful ones. From a Christian perspective,[53] it seems to me an undoubtedly repugnant conclusion that St. Peter does not exist between his death and the general resurrection, for there are things that St. Peter (as well as others of the dead) is supposed to be doing between death and resurrection. The intercessions of the saints are, for example, meant to be genuine intercessions made on our behalf by the saints themselves; it seems an inadequate consolation, if those saints do not actually exist, to be reminded that at least their souls exist and can pray for us—at the very least, it radically revises the meaning of traditional pious practice, if not the doctrine of the communion of the saints. Consider again Aquinas's reply to the objection concerning prayers to St. Peter. Aquinas appears to accept that the saints themselves do not pray for us; only their souls do. And we invoke their souls by the names of the persons to whom they were attached in remembrance of their lives on earth and in anticipation of their life to come. But we will be unable to say that St. Peter himself prayed for all those for whom his disembodied soul prayed, and this seems to make a mockery of the communion of saints.

Here is another disturbing consequence that follows if we also accept the doctrine of purgatory (as Aquinas certainly did): if I die in the state of grace but needing purification, then I must suffer in purgatory before entering eternal life. This purification, though perhaps lengthy, need not last until the general resurrection (for we say that the prayers of the just can release souls from purgatory), and let us suppose that I am admitted to heaven before the resurrection of my body. But if we say that I myself cease to exist upon my death and only return to existence at the resurrection of my body, then it will

---

[53] There is of course no *one* "Christian perspective," and therefore some Christians will have no difficulty accepting that the dead do nothing of a "personal" sort between death and resurrection. This is not Aquinas's position, nor the position of the majority of the Christian tradition, nor is it my own position. But it does represent a rather different way out of these difficulties.

be true that I never suffered in purgatory, even though my soul did. How are we to understand this? That I cease to exist at death, and so lose consciousness and awake the next moment (so it seems to me) in eternal bliss? But this appears manifestly unjust, for I myself was never punished. It cannot be enough to say that a part of me was punished (my soul) and so I myself am punished. It is obvious that burning my dead body causes me no real suffering, so why should burning my disembodied soul cause me suffering? Perhaps when I come back into existence, I will possess memories of the pain experienced by my soul that went through purification. But since I am now in heaven, these memories themselves cannot constitute punishment (for to be in heaven means I need no punishment); but on the other hand merely knowing that a part of myself suffered is not in itself equivalent to *me* suffering (after all, I was not present during this suffering, and merely knowing that suffering existed does not make one suffer, since this would entail that God must suffer).

I do not see a tidy way out of this problem, a problem reflective of the tension that follows on Aquinas's appropriation of Aristotle's account of the human soul. If we emphasize genuine body/soul union, it is perfectly reasonable that the person ceases to exist at death and returns only at the resurrection. But if we emphasize the extraordinary characteristics of the intellectual soul (characteristics that are very much consonant with Christian traditions about the activities of souls between death and resurrection), it is very hard to deny that what is left over after death is the same person, however defective he or she might be.

But perhaps, for those of us who consider Aquinas's appropriation of Aristotle (and its combination with Christianity) a more fruitful way of thinking about human nature than either materialism or dualism, we should turn from our frequent preoccupation with the formal element of human nature to a re-examination of the material character of human nature. When we speak of "matter" we often imply that we mean a certain sort of "stuff," such that my arm, for example, is a bit of my matter. If I lose an arm, we might think, I lose part of my matter. This way of speaking is exemplified most of all by the phrase "body and soul," where "soul" refers to my form and "body" apparently refers to my matter. But this is an imprecise way of speaking for Aquinas. Strictly speaking, my body is itself the composite of matter and form; this is clear even in Aristotle's initial definition of "soul" in *De anima* II,1: "Soul is the first actuality of a physical body potentially having life." It is only a physical body *potentially* having life that is properly joined to the soul, and when we consider the body in this way we intend an abstraction from any particular living body. My living body, here and now, consists of both form and matter.[54] Indeed, it is impossible to "point to" a piece of my matter, for any part of me is ensouled and so no part is simply material.

---

[54] Aquinas distinguishes these senses of "body" in *De ente et essentia*, ch. 2. Also helpful is Joseph Bobik's commentary on Aquinas's discussion. See Joseph Bobik, *Aquinas on Being and*

When we speak of matter, therefore, we should not mean this or that visible part of the physical world. Instead, matter properly speaking signifies potentiality[55] (so prime matter is pure potentiality), and the composition of actuality (form) and potentiality (matter) results in the visible physical objects we see around us. If we therefore speak of matter as potentiality, in what sense are human beings material or physical creatures? We are physical in the sense that human beings possess a set of potentialities related to one another in such ways as that together they result in the experience of "materiality" that we call the physical world. Because I am material, I can sense objects in space and experience movement through time, affect other substances by means of particular causal powers, and so on. To call me material is in this way to call me changeable according to a certain set of rules that determine how substances like myself in important ways are able to interact with one another. A human being is most properly material, therefore, because he or she possesses the potency to change (both actively and passively) in ways we collectively call "physical." This means that to call St. Peter a mixture of form and matter is to say that he essentially possesses a potency to change in ways characteristic of so-called "material" things.

Given this way of expressing the material character of human beings, it is possible for us to understand death not as a substantial change such that St. Peter loses all his matter and is reduced to his soul alone (or perhaps ceases to exist), but instead as an accidental change (albeit an extraordinarily severe one) such that the matter of St. Peter is not completely separated from his form. St. Thomas expressly denies this[56] (and for this reason I am not yet clear as to whether or not this account of death will require too much deep revision of Aquinas's account of human nature such that the baby would be thrown out with the bathwater), but if we pursue this line of thinking it will allow us to escape some of the puzzles Aquinas's account raises while nevertheless maintaining all the major elements of his Aristotelian account of human nature.

What is needed to make this plausible is a way of understanding the disembodied soul as nevertheless still joined in some sense to matter. When we call human beings material, we mean that they possess the potentiality to interact in "physical" ways by means of certain causal powers. For the most part, it seems clear that death removes this potentiality, but it does not do so completely. After all, it is true of me (or my soul) after death but before the resurrection that I have the potentiality to engage with the world in the normal

---

Essence: A Translation and Interpretation (Notre Dame, IN: University of Notre Dame Press, 1965), pp. 81–8.

[55] See *De principiis naturae*, § 1, in which Aquinas develops the Aristotelian account of matter as potentiality and says: "Just as anything that is in potency can be called matter, so anything from which something has existence, whatever kind of being it is, whether substantial or accidental, can be called form."

[56] *Quaestiones disputatae de anima*, q. 1.

physical way; the fact that after the resurrection I will be able to do so means that whatever is left of me immediately after death is related to the physical world in a way utterly different from the way in which, say, angels are related to that world. An angel never has the potential to interact with the physical world in a genuinely "physical" way, simply because it is no part of angelic nature to possess the necessary causal powers to do so. If the other animals survived death in some sense, then they too would still possess the kind of materiality I mean here, but of course when they die genuine substantial change occurs and the animal in question ceases to exist. Human beings (or what is left of them), therefore, after death but before the resurrection, still possess an orientation towards fully physical existence that is properly understood as the possession of a certain set of potentialities. And as such, so I claim, they can still be understood as importantly material beings. Aquinas does recognize to a certain extent what I am emphasizing, since he says that after death, though the nutritive and sensitive powers are no longer present in the soul, it is nevertheless true that "they remain virtually in the soul, as in their principle or root."[57] This virtual presence is not possible for angels, and is possible for human beings after death only because after death they retain the potentiality to again be fully material (that is, *full of* certain potentialities).

This implies that we must think of death as an extraordinarily debilitating injury done to the very heart of our being, such that Aristotle's original claim is correct—left to ourselves, after death we would possess an impoverished (and unconscious) existence. It is only by the grace of God that the separated soul possesses knowledge, for example. This is analogous to the way we sometimes understand the genuine rationality of severely disabled (or extremely young) human beings. The manifestation of their rationality is blocked in some fashion, or the requisite parts of themselves are missing (that is, intellectual activity in human beings naturally requires concomitant sensory activity as well—so the intellect turns to phantasms in order to actively know, and the absence of phantasms implies the absence of intellectual activity). After death, I no longer have the ability to interact with the world in an immediate and physical way, and since such interaction is natural to me, I am severely wounded. But in a sense I still possess the ability, though it is "blocked" or "hindered" in a significant way, and I am not able on my own to recover the immediate fullness of this ability (it takes the special intervention of God in the resurrection).

It is clear that this response to the question of the status of the separated soul avoids the problems that arise if we deny the personhood of St. Peter after his death, and so it maintains the importance of the intellectual, personal aspect of human nature. But it also maintains genuine body/soul unity, for the

---

[57] *ST* I, q. 77, a. 8, corpus.

material part of my nature is essential, without it I would be nothing, and a full and whole human life is a fully material one in which my material capacities are fully formed and available to me. This, it seems to me, preserves the very real pain of death as well as the true joy (and miracle) of resurrection. This perhaps does not yet solve all the difficulties attached to the tension between Aquinas's two central theses; for example, it is not clear that this will resolve the problem of the role that the body should play in eternal happiness. And it is of course possible that this will require too great a change to Aquinas's understanding of human nature for this to be a helpful development. But, to my mind at least, it is a promising and potentially very fruitful beginning.

4

Aristotle and the Mosaic Law

Matthew Levering

Should a student of the Mosaic law seek the help of Aristotle? Today, it seems highly unlikely that any theological or exegetical study of the Mosaic law would employ Aristotle, and yet Thomas Aquinas, in his *Summa theologiae*, freely did so.[1] One hardly knows what to think about this element of Aquinas's approach to the Mosaic law. Did it assist him in seeing things that are present in Scripture and that today we might not easily recognize, or did it fundamentally distort his vision of the Mosaic law? Since in Aquinas's *sacra doctrina* Aristotle has much less authority than does Scripture, did Aquinas use Aristotle's ideas in ways that remained governed by the text of Scripture? Or, despite Aquinas's claims regarding Aristotle's much lesser authority, did Aquinas at times allow Aristotle to lead him away from the biblical matrix of the Mosaic law?

4.1. ARISTOTLE IN AQUINAS'S TREATISE ON THE "OLD LAW": PRELIMINARY OBSERVATIONS

In exploring these questions, I will focus on Aquinas's treatise on the "Old Law" in the *Prima Secundae* of the *Summa theologiae*.[2] My conclusion is that

---

[1] Since much of Aquinas's treatise on the Old Law consists in the presentation and interpretation of biblical texts, further research needs to be done into the relationship of Aquinas's biblical interpretation to that of his medieval contemporaries, such as the *Postillae in totam Bibliam* compiled by the Dominican Hugh of Saint Cher (and others) as a supplement to the *Glossa ordinaria*. For the use of the *Postillae* in the thirteenth century in Paris and in Dominican schools, see M. Michèle Mulchahey, *"First the Bow is Bent in Study . . . ": Dominican Education before 1350* (Toronto: Pontifical Institute of Mediaeval Studies, 1998), pp. 485–501.

[2] For the indebtedness of the *Summa theologiae*'s treatise on the Old Law to the *Tractatus de praeceptis et legibus* found in the *Summa* ascribed to Alexander of Hales, see Beryl Smalley, "William of Auvergne, John of La Rochelle and St. Thomas Aquinas on the Old Law," in *St. Thomas Aquinas 1274–1974: Commemorative Studies*, vol. 2, edited by Armand A. Maurer

Aquinas's use of Aristotle helps him to appreciate the law of Israel *as law* in a way that most modern Christian theologians are unable to do. The bulk of my study seeks to determine precisely how each citation of Aristotle in Aquinas's treatise impacts his reading of the Mosaic law. Since six of the eight questions in Aquinas's treatise contain only a total of four citations of Aristotle,[3] I focus on the two questions where Aristotelian citations abound. Those two questions are q. 100, where Aquinas cites Aristotle's *Nicomachean Ethics* sixteen times and Aristotle's *Politics* once; and q. 105, where the balance is reversed and Aquinas cites Aristotle's *Politics* fourteen times, the *Nicomachean Ethics* twice, and the *Physics* once.[4] Occasionally, I also refer to Aquinas's commentary on Aristotle's *Nicomachean Ethics* (*c*.1271–1272) and his unfinished commentary on Aristotle's *Politics* (*c*.1269–1272).[5]

(Toronto: Pontifical Institute of Mediaeval Studies, 1974), pp. 11–71, at 47–68. For this background, see also my *Christ's Fulfillment of Torah and Temple: Salvation according to Thomas Aquinas* (Notre Dame, IN: University of Notre Dame Press, 2002), pp. 6–7; Jean Tonneau, OP, "The Teaching of the Thomist Tract on Law," *Thom.* 34 (1970): pp. 13–83, at 23–4. All medieval works on the Old Law are indebted to Augustine's *Contra Faustum*, on which see Paula Fredriksen, *Augustine and the Jews: A Christian Defense of Jews and Judaism* (New York: Doubleday, 2008), pp. 213–352.

[3] In three of the eight questions of this treatise (q. 98, "On the Old Law," q. 101, "Of the ceremonial precepts in themselves," and q. 103, "Of the duration of the ceremonial precepts"), Aquinas does not cite Aristotle at all. I have also excluded three other questions in the treatise, which contain a total of four citations of Aristotle: q. 99, "Of the precepts of the Old Law," q. 102, "Of the causes of the ceremonial precepts," and q. 104, "Of the judicial precepts."

[4] For Aquinas on the *Nicomachean Ethics*, see Vernon J. Bourke, "The *Nicomachean Ethics* and Thomas Aquinas," in *St. Thomas Aquinas 1274–1974: Commemorative Studies*, vol. 1, edited by Armand A. Maurer (Toronto: Pontifical Institute of Mediaeval Studies, 1974), pp. 239–59, with a focus on Aquinas's *Sent. Ethic.*; Terence H. Irwin, "Historical Accuracy in Aquinas's Commentary on the *Ethics*," in *Aquinas and the Nicomachean Ethics*, edited by Tobias Hoffmann, Jörn Müller, and Matthias Perkams (Cambridge: Cambridge University Press, 2013), pp. 13–32. In his "Thomas Aquinas and the Politics of Moses," *Review of Politics* 52 (1990): pp. 84–104, Douglas Kries insightfully examines Aquinas's account of the judicial precepts in relation to Aristotle's *Politics*, and in this study I cover some of the same terrain. John Y. B. Hood, *Aquinas and the Jews* (Philadelphia: University of Pennsylvania Press, 1995), p. 57, observes: "In isolating the 'judicial' precepts for special analysis, Aquinas followed John of La Rochelle . . . But when John wrote, Aristotle's *Politics* had not yet been translated. Access to this work enabled Thomas to see the *iudicialia* as a polity as well as a civil and criminal code . . . This interpretation helped focus the notion that the Mosaic Law had constituted the Jews as a *populus*" (cf. pp. 41 and 59). In his "The Teaching of the Thomist Tract on Law," p. 31, Jean Tonneau provides a table that lists all the authorities cited in *ST* I-II, qq. 90–108. Aristotle, who is cited forty-eight times in qq. 90–97 and forty-eight times in qq. 98–108, is second only to Augustine. Niceto Blázquez, OP, argues that Aquinas's use of Aristotle in the treatise is analogous to his use of Maimonides in the treatise: see Niceto Blázquez, OP, "Los tratados sobre la ley antigua y nueva en la 'Summa Theologiae,'" *Scripta theologica* 15 (1983): pp. 421–67, at 442–3. Mary Keys shows how Aristotle's understanding of legal or general justice informs Aquinas's view of the Mosaic law and especially of the Decalogue: see Mary M. Keys, *Aquinas, Aristotle, and the Promise of the Common Good* (Cambridge: Cambridge University Press, 2006), pp. 185–94.

[5] See Jean-Pierre Torrell, OP, *Saint Thomas Aquinas*, vol. 1, The Person and his Work, trans. Robert Royal, rev. ed. (Washington, DC: The Catholic University of America Press, 2005), pp. 333 and 343–4.

Douglas Kries has insightfully observed that "Thomas understands the Mosaic law as belonging to that realm of truth which is supernaturally revealed by God to humanity. The precepts of the Old Law reflect the wisdom of the divine intellect and to regard them as anything less than a perfect code of righteousness would be impious."[6] Aquinas considers that, from the standpoint of human reason, Aristotle's moral and political philosophy can shed light on the wisdom of the Mosaic law, whose wisdom he affirms in faith.[7] Yet, would Aquinas have done better to read the Mosaic law without this Hellenistic instrument? My intensive survey of Aquinas's citations of Aristotle in qq. 100 and 105 aims to show that the use of Aristotle allows Aquinas to reflect upon the Mosaic law in a manner that does justice to its main preoccupations and original legal context.

4.2. THE MORAL PRECEPTS OF THE OLD LAW (*ST* I-II, Q. 100)

I begin with the second article of q. 100, where Aristotle's *Nicomachean Ethics* helps Aquinas inquire into the scope of the moral precepts. Recall that in *Nicomachean Ethics* V, Aristotle shows that justice can be understood as "complete virtue or excellence, not in an unqualified sense, but in relation to our fellow men," so that such justice "is not a part of virtue but the whole of virtue."[8] Taking up this definition of justice in the third objection, Aquinas raises a question: if "of all the virtues justice alone regards the common good, as the Philosopher says," then are the moral precepts "only about the acts of justice"?[9] In his *respondeo*, Aquinas makes clear that the answer is no, because (as Aristotle himself goes on to explain in *Nicomachean Ethics* V) all virtuous acts belong to the general virtue of justice, but there is also a special virtue of justice, namely to give what is due to another. Human law has to do with the special virtue of justice rather than with the general one. Referring to

---

[6] See Kries, "Thomas Aquinas and the Politics of Moses," p. 88. Kries adds that "Thomas insists that a rational understanding of the judicial precepts is attainable by the unaided human intellect, and he spares no effort in attempting to grasp the inherent reasonableness of the Mosaic regime (Ia-IIae, q. 104, a. 2, ad 3)" (p. 88).

[7] For Aquinas on Moses, see (in comparison with Maimonides on prophecy) Avital Wohlman, *Thomas d'Aquin et Maïmonide: Un dialogue exemplaire* (Paris: Cerf, 1988), pp. 294–304. For Aquinas's use of Maimonides in his treatise, see especially Juan Fernando Chamorro, OP, "Ley nueva y ley antigua en Santo Tomás," *Studium* 7 (1967): pp. 317–80, at 355–80.

[8] Aristotle, *Nicomachean Ethics* V,1, trans. Martin Ostwald (Englewood Cliffs, NJ: Prentice Hall, 1962), p. 114.

[9] *ST* I-II, q. 100, a. 2, arg. 3. English translation from: Thomas Aquinas, *Summa Theologiae*, trans. Fathers of the English Dominican Province, 5 vols. (Westminster, MD: Christian Classics, 1981).

Aristotle's text, Aquinas observes that "human law makes precepts only about acts of justice; and if it commands acts of other virtues, this is only in so far as they assume the nature of justice."[10] Human law is satisfied so long as we give what is due to our neighbor; it does not require that we be interiorly virtuous.

It would therefore seem that the moral precepts of the Mosaic law only have to do with the special virtue of justice. Aquinas also points out in the *respondeo* of the second article, however, that a divine law must command giving what is due to God. To give what is due to God is possible only when we have a virtuous soul. This requires all the virtues, both intellectual and moral, because "the intellectual virtues set in good order the acts of the reason in themselves: while the moral virtues set in good order the acts of the reason in reference to the interior passions and exterior actions."[11] For this reason, *divine* law, as opposed to mere human law, must include much more than precepts involving the special virtue of justice. Thus the Mosaic law proposes "precepts about the acts of all the virtues," while taking care to distinguish between obligations and counsels.[12]

In arguing in a. 2 that the people of Israel required a different set of laws from those of other human communities, Aquinas draws as well upon Book IV of Aristotle's *Politics*. In the passage that Aquinas cites in his *respondeo*, Aristotle holds that the constitution, which determines the end or goal of the community, should determine the laws.[13] A different constitution should mean different laws; a monarchy requires different laws from a democracy or an oligarchy. Applying this principle to the people of Israel, Aquinas concludes that a community ruled by God, whose end is nothing less than union with God, will need different laws from those of any merely human community. Although he does not here cite any particular precepts of the Mosaic law, he has in view such precepts as "you shall not covet your neighbor's wife" (Exod 20:17), which by commanding temperance, an interior virtue of the soul, goes farther than mere human law can go.

In *Nicomachean Ethics* X, Aristotle notes that different activities have different pleasures, and that different people take pleasure in different things. Aquinas refers to this passage in q. 100, a. 4, where, in replying to the third objection, he explains the fittingness of the Decalogue's distinction between two kinds of covetousness, namely coveting one's neighbor's wife and coveting one's neighbor's goods. The diversity of the things in which humans take pleasure requires the Decalogue to divide covetousness in this fashion.

---

[10] *ST* I-II, q. 100, a. 2, corpus. See Jeffrey Hause, "Aquinas on Aristotelian Justice: Defender, Destroyer, Subverter, or Surveyor?," in *Aquinas and the* Nicomachean Ethics, edited by Tobias Hoffmann, Jörn Müller, and Matthias Perkams (Cambridge: Cambridge University Press, 2013), pp. 146–64.

[11] *ST* I-II, q. 100, a. 2, corpus.   [12] *ST* I-II, q. 100, a. 2, corpus.

[13] Aristotle, *Politics* IV,1, trans. Benjamin Jowett (New York: Random House, 1943), p. 170; Aquinas references this passage in *ST* I-II, q. 100, a. 2, corpus.

Aquinas also draws upon Aristotle in a. 5, which examines why the Decalogue commands that we honor our parents but says nothing about the love we owe to children and neighbors. In his *respondeo*, Aquinas states that the Decalogue includes only the "immediate dictate[s] of natural reason." The debt of a child to his or her parents is just such an "immediate dictate" because of what a child owes to parents for life, upbringing, and education; whereas parents are not indebted to children in a comparable way. In his reply to the fourth objection of a. 4, Aquinas cites Book VIII of the *Nicomachean Ethics*, where Aristotle holds that "parents love their children as themselves: offspring is, as it were, another self, 'other' because it exists separately."[14] On this basis, Aquinas comments that since the Decalogue does not specify the behavior that we owe to ourselves, it need not include a precept about what parents owe to children.

Article 7 raises the issue of why God, in his wisdom, framed the Decalogue largely but not entirely in negative precepts. The only two affirmative precepts in the Decalogue are "remember the sabbath day, to keep it holy" (Exod 20:8) and "honor your father and your mother" (Exod 20:12). Why did God not formulate more affirmative precepts, given the importance of acts of virtue? Furthermore, it seems that God should be consistent in explaining that a violation of the precept will incur punishment. But only twice in the Decalogue does God explicitly attach punishment to the violation of a precept, namely after commanding that God alone be worshipped (Exod 20:5, "for I the Lord your God am a jealous God, visiting the iniquity of the fathers upon the children to the third and the fourth generation of those who hate me") and after commanding that people not take his name in vain in swearing oaths (Exod 20:7, "the Lord will not hold him guiltless who takes his name in vain").

Aquinas benefits from Aristotle on both these issues. In his reply to the first objection of a. 7, Aquinas points out that the two affirmative precepts comprise the only two instances where the one who benefits *cannot* in any way repay what is due to the benefactor. As Aristotle says in the passage cited by Aquinas (from *Nicomachean Ethics* VII): "In some cases, in fact, it is impossible to make the kind of return which the giver deserves, for instance, in the honors we pay to the gods and to our parents. Here no one could ever make a worthy return, and we regard a man as good if he serves them to the best of his ability."[15]

Aquinas notes, too, that rather than requiring a good act, negative precepts simply command us not to do an evil act. In general, it is due in justice to other humans that we not harm them, but it is *not* due to them that we do specific good acts on their behalf.[16] By contrast, we always specifically owe service and devotion to God and parents. In his reply to the fourth objection of a. 7,

---

[14] Aristotle, *Nicomachean Ethics* VIII,12 (p. 237).
[15] Aristotle, *Nicomachean Ethics* VIII,14 (p. 244).   [16] *ST* I-II, q. 100, a. 7, ad 1.

regarding why only the first two precepts of the Decalogue contain threats of punishment, Aquinas refers to Aristotle's discussion in Book X of the *Nicomachean Ethics* about how to inculcate virtue. There Aristotle observes that although books about ethics can inspire some young people, nonetheless such books "do not have the capacity to turn the common run of people to goodness and nobility."[17] Most people live according to passions rather than according to reason. How then can people who are caught up in vice become virtuous? Books and theories cannot do it, because "a man whose life is guided by emotion will not listen to an argument that dissuades him, nor will he understand it."[18] On this basis, Aristotle defends the value of punishment (and threats of punishment) for making wayward people more virtuous.[19]

Agreeing with Aristotle about the value of punishment, Aquinas asks why God attaches the threat of punishment only to the first two commandments regarding idolatry and oaths, and not also to the other precepts which seem also to be quite frequently violated, such as the precepts against killing, adultery, stealing, lying, and coveting. Aquinas argues that not only individuals, but indeed whole nations were prone to regulating their affairs through idolatry and perjury. Idolatry was not merely committed by some wicked individuals but had become, by Moses's time, "the general custom of the nations."[20] Similarly the failure to keep oaths had become a problem that was no longer confined merely to some individuals. For this reason, then, God specially attached the warning of punishment to the first two commandments, in order to wean the people from these fundamental (anticovenantal) evils.

The Decalogue reveals what is due in justice to God and neighbor. As Aquinas points out in a. 8, however, it may appear that the precepts of the Decalogue do not always hold in every circumstance. For example, although the Decalogue commands that we should not kill, God sanctions war and capital punishment in certain instances, as can be seen from the very next chapter of Exodus (ch. 21). In fact, the precept has to do with the killing of the innocent.[21] But this does not solve the problem, because in Gen 22, for example, God commands Abraham to kill his son Isaac, an innocent child. I have elsewhere addressed how Aquinas resolves this question; suffice it to say that he denies that there are ever any true dispensations from the Decalogue, although God as lawgiver is able to accomplish his ends directly if he wishes.[22]

---

[17] Aristotle, *Nicomachean Ethics* X,9 (p. 295).

[18] Aristotle, *Nicomachean Ethics* X,9 (p. 296).

[19] In his commentary on Aristotle's *Nicomachean Ethics*, Aquinas gives various examples of such punishment. See Thomas Aquinas, *Commentary on Aristotle's Nicomachean Ethics*, trans. Charles I. Litzinger (Notre Dame, IN: Dumb Ox Books, 1993), pp. 641–2.

[20] *ST* I-II, q. 100, a. 7, ad 4.

[21] See Carol Meyers, *Exodus* (Cambridge: Cambridge University Press, 2005), p. 174.

[22] See Matthew Levering, "God and Natural Law: Reflections on Genesis 22," *Modern Theology* 24 (2008): pp. 151–77.

Aristotle, however, causes difficulties for Aquinas's position that the precepts of the Decalogue—which Aquinas considers to be precepts of natural
law—are never dispensable. In *Nicomachean Ethics* V, which comprises the
basis for the first objection of a. 8, Aristotle defines political justice as consisting of two kinds, natural and conventional. Natural justice "has the same force
everywhere and does not depend on what we regard or do not regard as
just."[23] Yet Aristotle goes on to say that "among us there are things which,
though naturally just, are nevertheless changeable, as are all things human."[24]
He might seem to mean that certain circumstances or conditions can make
idolatry, killing the innocent, adultery, and so forth to be just. In reply to the
objection, Aquinas argues that Aristotle is not here "speaking of the natural
law which contains the very order of justice."[25] Instead, as suggested by the
Latin translation that Aquinas uses, Aristotle is simply affirming that nothing
human is unchangeable, since humans are not unchanging like the heavenly
spheres or gods. What then is changeable as regards things that are "naturally
just"? In Aquinas's interpretation, the changeable element is the particular
punishment applied to violations of natural justice. Aquinas states that Aristotle
has in view the "fixed modes of observing justice, which fail to apply in certain
cases."[26] After all, Aristotle explicitly rejects the view that "everything just
exists only by convention," a view that some people hold because "they see
that notions of what is just change."[27]

Aristotle appears five times in the next article (a. 9) of q. 100. This article
examines what counts as obedience of the Mosaic law. If a person does not
have the virtue of justice but nonetheless acts in a just manner in a particular
case, has the person thereby actually *violated* the law by performing the good
act without the virtue of justice? In the second objection of a. 9, Aquinas cites
Book II of the *Nicomachean Ethics*, where Aristotle states: "Lawgivers make
the citizens good by inculcating [good] habits in them, and this is the aim of
every lawgiver; if he does not succeed in doing that, his legislation is a
failure."[28] If a person lacks the virtue of justice, then no matter what individual
acts of justice the person performs, he or she fails to attain the holiness sought
by the Mosaic law. It would seem, then, that for the Mosaic law, as Aquinas
puts it, "the mode of virtue falls under the precept,"[29] so that the precept will in
fact be violated unless one obeys it in holiness, that is to say, in possession of
the virtue.

---

[23] Aristotle, *Nicomachean Ethics* V,7 (p. 131).
[24] Aristotle, *Nicomachean Ethics* V,7 (p. 131).   [25] *ST* I-II, q. 100, a. 7, ad 1.
[26] *ST* I-II, q. 100, a. 7, ad 1. For a more extensive discussion in the same vein, see Aquinas,
Commentary on Aristotle's Nicomachean Ethics, pp. 327–8.
[27] Aristotle, *Nicomachean Ethics* V,7 (p. 131).
[28] Aristotle, *Nicomachean Ethics* II,1 (p. 34); referenced in *ST* I-II, q. 100, a. 9, arg. 2.
[29] *ST* I-II, q. 100, a. 9, arg. 2.

In his *sed contra* and *respondeo*, Aquinas denies that a person who obeys the precept without possessing the relevant virtue thereby violates the precept. In the *sed contra*, he cites Books II and V of the *Nicomachean Ethics*, where Aristotle states that to possess a virtue is not merely to do acts that belong to that virtue, but to have the habit of the virtue: "The just and self-controlled man is not he who performs these acts, but he who also performs them in the way just and self-controlled men do."[30] Aquinas points out, however, that the central purpose of law is to lead humans who are not yet virtuous to become virtuous, by habituating them to performing acts of the virtue. After all, as Aristotle goes on to say, "without performing them [acts of the virtue], nobody could even be on the way to becoming good."[31] What sort of law would punish the good acts of those who are "on the way to becoming good" but do not yet possess the virtue and so are not yet performing the acts virtuously? In the *sed contra*, therefore, Aquinas underscores that the divine lawgiver gave the Mosaic law in order to habituate his people to good works. No matter what one's interior disposition, so long as one refuses to steal, one thereby obeys the commandment not to steal.

Does God then ignore our inward disposition in assessing whether or not we have obeyed the Mosaic law? On the contrary, says Aquinas in the *respondeo* of a. 9, God "is competent to judge of the inward movements of wills."[32] What then constitutes a violation of the law for which we may be punished? Aquinas makes a threefold distinction, again drawing upon Book II of the *Nicomachean Ethics*. First, the "mode" of an act is important for both human and divine law, because someone cannot be punished if he does not act knowingly. Second, intention can be punished by divine law but not by human law, because God alone knows (for example) if we intended to commit adultery but simply failed to find the opportunity. A wicked intention merits punishment, but only God knows when such an intention exists. Third, the person who performs a good act may or may not be doing so out of a firm and stable habit (a virtue). In this sense, Aquinas specifies that the lack of a firm and stable virtuous habit is not in itself sinful or worthy of punishment. In his reply to the third objection, Aquinas gives the example of a good action that is performed sadly, an example indebted to Book II of the *Nicomachean Ethics*. If we honor our parents sadly—and thus unwillingly—this bad intention violates the precepts of love of God and of neighbor (Deut 6:5 and Lev 19:18). But our bad intention does not violate the precept regarding honoring our parents.

Of what value were the moral precepts of the Mosaic law?[33] In q. 100, a. 12, Aquinas argues that the moral precepts disposed the people of God toward

---

[30] Aristotle, *Nicomachean Ethics* II,4 (p. 39).

[31] Aristotle, *Nicomachean Ethics* II,4 (p. 40).   [32] *ST* I-II, q. 100, a. 9, corpus.

[33] In this regard John Hood argues: "Did the Law in fact make the Jews a uniquely virtuous people worthy of God's friendship, or did it lead them into sin? Torn between his loyalty to Paul

becoming just and signified their becoming just (through the Messiah who fulfills the law). But he does not think that the moral precepts of the Mosaic law *caused* the people of God to become just. To become just, the people needed the grace of God to heal them of sin; thus they needed "infused" virtues, which they were able to receive through implicit faith in Christ.[34] Viewed from another angle, however, the precepts of the Mosaic law (including the ceremonial and judicial precepts) certainly did prompt the people of God to become just, because these precepts in themselves were just. Here Aquinas again takes up Aristotle's distinction in *Nicomachean Ethics* V between general justice and special justice.[35]

To sum up: Aquinas's discussion of the Mosaic law's moral precepts is aided by Aristotle in three central ways. First, Aristotle's distinction between general and special justice helps Aquinas to explore why the Mosaic law contains not only the usual kinds of laws that regulate a just social order, but also laws that pertain to interior dispositions such as coveting one's neighbor's goods. Divine law requires that we be well ordered interiorly, not merely that we be just in the sense of what Aristotle calls special justice. A community's end or goal, inscribed in its constitution, determines its laws. Second, as would be expected, Aquinas is concerned with whether or not the laws that God commands are well expressed. In this regard, he draws upon Aristotle to defend the Decalogue's distinction between kinds of covetousness. Similarly, he uses Aristotle to help explain why the Decalogue contains a command to honor our parents but no command about what we owe to our children; why the only two affirmative precepts of the Decalogue have to do with God and parents; and why the only two threats of punishment in the Decalogue are attached to idolatry and oaths. Third, Aquinas uses Aristotle to take up particular problems that arise when one considers the moral precepts and especially the Decalogue itself. These problems include whether there are in fact any moral precepts that are unchangeable no matter what the circumstances; whether a person who lacks a fully formed virtue can actually violate the commandment even in obeying it; and whether the moral precepts of the Mosaic law (or the ceremonial and judicial precepts) have any real use, given that they do not justify human beings. In all these areas, Aristotle assists Aquinas in arriving at an answer that vindicates the validity and value of the Mosaic law precisely *as law*.

---

and his Aristotelian belief in the efficacy of practical reason and the virtues, Thomas raises the discussion to a purely abstract level—the predisposition to justice versus justice itself, justification with God versus performing just acts—and manages to avoid entirely the question of the Law's effectiveness in making Israel a holy people" (Hood, *Aquinas and the Jews*, p. 49). It seems to me that Hood is posing a false choice between the Law differentiating the Jewish people from pagan idolatry, and the Law exacerbating Israel's awareness of its sins.

[34] On implicit faith see *ST* II-II, q. 2, a. 7.   [35] *ST* I-II, q. 100, a. 12.

4.3. RATIONALITY OF THE JUDICIAL
PRECEPTS (*ST* I-II, Q. 105)

Does the Mosaic law provide a good structure of governance?[36] Aquinas certainly intends to answer yes. In the first article of q. 105, however, he acknowledges that the Mosaic law lacks the very thing that Aristotle considers to be most necessary for a well-constituted community, namely, the Mosaic law does not describe how the ruler should be chosen. As Aquinas states in the first objection of a. 1, this apparent omission contrasts with Aristotle's emphasis, in Book III of the *Politics*, on the importance of the ruler. Instead, the Mosaic law contains precepts regarding elders—Aquinas cites Exod 18:21, Num 11:16, and Deut 1:13—without providing a mode of choosing the ruler.

Aquinas is well aware that over the centuries the people of Israel ran into trouble with respect to the problem of choosing a ruler. Since in the Mosaic law God gave them no precept about choosing a king, they had no king at first. Later they chose a king, but this resulted relatively quickly in the devastating division of the kingdom under two kings—a division that God himself sanctioned as punishment for Solomon's excesses. In this regard, Aquinas references 1 Kgs 11:31-2, where Ahijah prophesies to Jeroboam, "thus says the Lord, the God of Israel, 'Behold, I am about to tear the kingdom from the hand of Solomon, and will give you ten tribes (but he shall have one tribe, for the sake of my servant David and for the sake of Jerusalem).'"[37] Does not this division simply underscore that God has given Israel insufficient laws about how to choose a ruler? Along the same lines Aquinas recalls that God himself, via the prophet Samuel, describes Israel's kingship as tyrannical (see 1 Sam 8:11-17). This is the form of government that Aristotle deems to be worst. It seems that if God had given Moses better laws with respect to the ruler, Israel would not have fallen into such a bad plight.

In his *respondeo*, Aquinas answers these concerns with the help of two points from Aristotle. First, Aquinas notes that Aristotle, in evaluating the Spartan constitution in Book II of the *Politics*, observes that "the people are contented when they have a share in the highest office" so that the government is sure to uphold the common interest.[38] From this Aquinas concludes that in the best constitutions, the whole people will "take some share in the government."[39] Second, Aquinas cites Book III of the *Politics*, where Aristotle holds that the best government is ruled by a king who serves the common interest.[40]

---

[36] It is important to recognize at the outset that although Aquinas defends the wisdom of the judicial precepts, he does not consider them to be perfect. The judicial precepts' imperfection (and pedagogical intention) can be seen in the precept that permits divorce, a precept that according to Aquinas is not "just absolutely speaking" (*ST* I-II, q. 105, a. 4, ad 8).
[37] *ST* I-II, q. 105, a. 1, arg. 3.   [38] Aristotle, *Politics* II,9 (p. 111); III,7 (p. 139).
[39] *ST* I-II, q. 105, a. 1, corpus.   [40] See Aristotle, *Politics* III,7 (p. 139).

Aquinas argues that a kingdom in which all citizens enjoy a share in the government is not only the best possible government, but is also what God instituted for Israel. Chosen by God, Moses occupied the role of the king. So as to ensure wide participation in his rule, Moses gave the elders of the tribes a share in the government as "commanders of thousands, commanders of hundreds, commanders of fifties, commanders of tens, and officers" (Deut 1:15). These elders were chosen by the tribes themselves. Moses instructed the people: "Choose wise, understanding, and experienced men, according to your tribes, and I will appoint them as your heads" (Deut 1:13). In this way Israel under Moses corresponded to the form of government most praised by Aristotle: part kingdom, part aristocracy, and part democracy—and the best of each.

In agreement with Book III of the *Politics*, Aquinas defines the best form of government as consisting "in a state or kingdom, wherein one is given the power to preside over all; while under him are others having governing powers: and yet a government of this kind is shared by all, both because all are eligible to govern, and because the rules are chosen by all."[41] Nonetheless, like Aristotle, Aquinas is all too aware that kingship easily degenerates into the worst form of government, tyranny, unless the king happens to be an exceptionally virtuous person. Complementing his discussion of tyranny in the *Politics*, Aristotle in Book IV of the *Nicomachean Ethics* observes that good fortune (such as noble birth, power, or wealth) makes many people "haughty and arrogant, for without virtue it is not easy to bear the gifts of fortune gracefully."[42] In his reply to the second objection of a. 2, Aquinas cites this text from the *Nicomachean Ethics* and argues that it helps to explain why the Mosaic law does not contain provisions for kingship. God, as a wise lawgiver, recognized how difficult it is for a man to be a good king and therefore chose not to "set up the kingly authority with full power."[43] As indicated by 1 Sam 8:7 (cited here by Aquinas), it was only as a punishment that God granted Israel's later request to have a fully empowered king rather than a judge/governor.

In his reply to the second objection of a. 1, Aquinas also points out that God did not in fact leave the Mosaic law bereft of instruction regarding the appointment and behavior of kings. Rather, in the Mosaic law God commanded Israel that if they eventually desired a king, they should appoint an Israelite "whom the Lord your God will choose" (Deut 17:15; cited here by Aquinas). In order to prevent the king from becoming a tyrant, the king should learn and

---

[41] *ST* I-II, q. 105, a. 1, corpus.

[42] Aristotle, *Nicomachean Ethics* IV,3 (p. 96); referenced in *ST* I-II, q. 105, a. 1, ad 2.

[43] *ST* I-II, q. 105, a. 1, ad 2. For Aquinas on kingship (which he addressed also in his *De regno, ad regem Cypri*), see Kries, "Thomas Aquinas and the Politics of Moses," pp. 91–3; James M. Blythe, "The Mixed Constitution and the Distinction between Regal and Political Power in the Work of Thomas Aquinas," *Journal of the History of Ideas* 47 (1986): pp. 547–65.

obey the law of Moses and should not be allowed to accumulate horses, wives, and wealth for himself (see Deut 17:16–20).[44] Again, Aquinas knows that the kings of Israel did not live up to this commandment; indeed Deut 17 well describes the faults of David's son Solomon. Given his concerns about tyranny, Aquinas's praise for human kingship is highly tempered, as befits the biblical witness.

Having addressed the concern that the Mosaic law's judicial precepts provided poorly for the rule of Israel, Aquinas next asks, in q. 105, a. 2, whether the judicial precepts provided well for the economic relations between citizens. Most troubling, the judicial precepts seem to undermine basic rules of property and credit. The result could be economic chaos bad for wealthy and poor alike. Among the laws that Aquinas pinpoints as potentially worrisome (in the objections of a. 2) are the following: Exod 22:10, "If a man delivers to his neighbor . . . any beast to keep, and it dies or is hurt or is driven away, without any one seeing it, an oath by the Lord shall be between them both to see whether he has put his hand to his neighbor's property; and the owner shall accept the oath"; Lev 25:28, "What he sold shall remain in the hand of him who bought it until the year of jubilee; in the jubilee it shall be released, and he shall return to his property"; Deut 15:2, "Every creditor shall release what he has lent to his neighbor; he shall not exact it of his neighbor, his brother, because the Lord's release has been proclaimed"; Deut 23:24, "When you go into your neighbor's vineyard, you may eat your fill of grapes, as many as you wish"; and Deut 24:10, "When you make your neighbor a loan of any sort, you shall not go into his house to fetch his pledge."[45]

In various ways, these laws appear to make it disadvantageous to loan something to one's neighbor or to buy something from one's neighbor. Why loan anything when the one who loans seems to bear all the risk? Why buy anything when it will be restored to the seller at the jubilee year, and when one can get food for free anyway by roaming the fields of one's neighbor? Indeed, without suitable rules for property and exchange, human societies will suffer. Thus, in the third objection of a. 2, Aquinas appeals to Book I of the *Politics*, where Aristotle describes the "natural art of acquisition which is practiced by managers of households and by statesmen."[46] Although he protests against such things as usury, the unlimited getting of wealth, and laws that allow for a few landowners to own all the land, Aristotle recognizes the validity of private property and of coinage as a means of exchange. As Aristotle says in Book II of the *Politics* (in a passage to which Aquinas refers in his *respondeo*), "Property

---

[44] As Kries observes, "Aristotle, on the other hand, does not emphasize piety as a requirement for kingship, but he does point out that it is advantageous for a tyrant to seem pious, for this calms the people and makes insurrection less likely; however, Aristotle adds, the tyrant should not overdo his pursuit of religion, for this would make him appear silly" (Kries, "Thomas Aquinas and the Politics of Moses," p. 93).

[45] See *ST* I-II, q. 100, a. 2, arg. 1, 3, 4, and 5.   [46] Aristotle, *Politics* I,8 (p. 66).

should be in a certain sense common, but, as a general rule, private; for, when every one has a distinct interest, men will not complain of one another, and they will make more progress, because every one will be attending to his own business."[47] Aristotle thinks that private property encourages the thrifty management of households that provides the foundation for the political order. He also points out in the same passage that private property offers the opportunity for the important virtue of liberality as regards wealth: "No one, when men have all things in common, will any longer set an example of liberality or of any liberal action; for liberality consists in the use which is made of property."[48] For Aristotle, a good life requires sufficient property not only to live temperately, but also to exercise liberality with one's wealth.

As Aquinas notes in the second objection of a. 2, Aristotle adds in Book II of the *Politics* that the holding of property by women led to the downfall of the political economy of Sparta. Aristotle comments that "nearly two-fifths of the whole country are held by women; this is owing to the number of heiresses and to the large dowries which are customary."[49] The result, he thinks, was fewer men who could afford to raise families, and (due to the land inequality) fewer opportunities for those children who were born. Aristotle blames this for Sparta's decrease in population and eventual loss of the ability to defend itself. Aquinas points out in the second objection, however, that the Mosaic law teaches in Num 27:8, "If a man dies, and has no son, then you shall cause his inheritance to pass to his daughter."[50] If Aristotle rightly understood the consequences of Sparta's inheritance laws, then Num 27:8 would seem to be unwise.

In the *respondeo* of a. 2, Aquinas sums up Aristotle's position in Book II of the *Politics* as in favor of private property but with the caveats that "the use thereof should be partly common, and partly granted to others by the will of the possessors."[51] Property should be "partly common" in the sense that all property ultimately serves the common good, and property should be "partly granted to others by the will of the possessors" through acts of liberality, selling, loaning, and so forth. Aquinas then argues that these three aspects of well-ordered economic life—private property, the relationship of property to the common good, and sharing one's property—are skillfully provided for and balanced by the Mosaic law.

First, with regard to private property, Aquinas points out in his *respondeo* that God commands that the Israelites divide the land among them by lot (Num 33:54). Lest the land be concentrated among only a few landowners,

---

[47] Aristotle, *Politics* II,5 (p. 88).
[48] Aristotle, *Politics* II,5 (p. 89). For the importance that Jews and Christians gave to almsgiving, see Gary A. Anderson, *Sin: A History* (New Haven, CT: Yale University Press, 2009).
[49] Aristotle, *Politics* II,9 (pp. 109–10).   [50] *ST* I-II, q. 105, a. 2, arg. 2.
[51] *ST* I-II, q. 105, a. 2, corpus.

God requires that the larger tribes receive a larger amount of land to divide, and the smaller tribes a smaller amount. Furthermore, recognizing that wealthier landowners can buy up the land around them, with the eventual result that poorer persons and young men will lack the resources to establish households of their own, God commands through the jubilee laws that "possessions could not be alienated for ever."[52] Aquinas here refers to Book II of the *Politics*, and, although he does not quote it explicitly, to Aristotle's warning about the faulty laws of Sparta: "While some of the Spartan citizens have quite small properties, others have very large ones; hence the land has passed into the hands of a few. And this is due also to faulty laws."[53] In his reply to the second objection, which concerned the right of women to inherit land (challenged by Aristotle in *Politics* II), Aquinas likewise emphasizes that the Mosaic law commands that the land be passed down through families rather than sold to wealthier landowners. When there are no male heirs, a daughter can inherit, but in order to preserve the distribution of land God commands that heiresses "shall marry within the family of the tribe of her father. The inheritance of the people of Israel shall not be transferred from one tribe to another" (Num 36:6–7, cited here by Aquinas).[54] The Mosaic law avoids the problem that afflicted Sparta. Similarly, in replying to the third objection (which as we saw was based upon *Politics* I), Aquinas suggests that Aristotle's own reflections on the regulation of possessions in Book II of the *Politics* help to confirm the wisdom of the jubilee year's purpose of fostering trade without allowing property to be consolidated in the hands of a few.

Second, with regard to property's relationship to the common good, Aquinas remarks in his *respondeo* that God mandates that if people find things that they know to belong to others, they should care for and return these things. The whole society should bear some responsibility for caring for the possessions of all. Lest private ownership cause people to forget that property should serve the good of the whole society, the Mosaic law commands that people can eat the fruits that they find on their neighbor's land, but they cannot carry these fruits away to eat them later. The loss will be minimal to the landowner, but the principle of the common good will be sustained. This principle is further strengthened by the commandment that fields, vineyards, and orchards should not be cultivated or harvested on the seventh year, so "that the poor of your people may eat; and what they leave the wild beasts may eat" (Exod 23:11, cited here by Aquinas).

Lastly, the third aspect of Aristotle's view—sharing, selling, and loaning one's property—also finds expression in the Mosaic law, according to Aquinas. In his *respondeo*, Aquinas refers to the commandment that people tithe their produce every four years, so that the Levite, "the sojourner, the fatherless,

---

[52] *ST* I-II, q. 105, a. 2, corpus.   [53] Aristotle, *Politics* II,9 (p. 109).
[54] Cited in *ST* I-II, q. 105, a. 2, corpus.

and the widow, who are within your towns, shall come and eat and be filled" (Deut 14:29).[55] The Mosaic law contains numerous commandments regulating selling and loaning one's property (and one's labor). Aquinas emphasizes that like the Mosaic law, Aristotle is concerned with "the equalization of property"—although Aristotle also recognizes that "the avarice of mankind is insatiable" and so, even were property equalized, citizens would still find ways to quarrel.[56] As Aristotle goes on to say in this passage from Book II of the *Politics*, "it is not the possessions but the desires of mankind which require to be equalized, and this is impossible, unless a sufficient education is provided by the laws."[57] Such an education, Aquinas makes clear, is provided in an excellent fashion by the Mosaic law. The Mosaic law's pedagogy, however, cannot suffice without grace to heal human nature.

What about the Mosaic law's precepts regarding relations with foreigners? Thus far Aquinas has argued that the Mosaic law's precepts about government and political economy are wise and beneficial, not least from the perspective of Aristotle's political philosophy. He generally assumes the wisdom of Aristotle's judgments and makes a fairly persuasive case that the Mosaic law accords with these judgments. Even when this is not so as regards the letter— for example, Moses is not a king—nonetheless the Mosaic law's precepts about government do seem to contain elements of monarchical, aristocratic, and democratic rule that are in accord, at least broadly speaking, with Aristotle's principles. The same can be said for the Mosaic law's economic precepts. Even though Aristotle does not envision things such as the jubilee year, he certainly does share the Mosaic law's central concern for the equitable distribution of property. The precepts of the Mosaic law take a balanced view of private property, as Aristotle does. Does the same pattern hold for relations with foreigners, what would now be called international relations?

In q. 105, a. 3, Aquinas addresses the Mosaic law's precepts about foreigners. In the objections, he is particularly concerned with the ways in which God seems to command Israel to exclude or mistreat people from other nations. In the first objection, Aquinas points out that on the one hand, God commands Israel through Moses, "You shall not abhor an Edomite, for he is your brother; you shall not abhor an Egyptian, because you were a sojourner in his land" (Deut 23:7). After two generations have passed, Edomite and Egyptian children can enter the assembly of God. But on the other hand, this relatively merciful view of Edomites and Egyptians does not extend to Ammonites and Moabites, among others. God bans these "even to the tenth generation" (Deut

---

[55] *ST* I-II, q. 105, a. 2, corpus. See also Kries, "Thomas Aquinas and the Politics of Moses," p. 97: "in Thomas's eyes, property in the Mosaic legislation is regulated not simply in accord with the directives that Aristotle laid down, but also in accord with a higher end."

[56] Aristotle, *Politics* II,7 (p. 98). In *ST* I-II, q. 105, a. 2, ad 3, Aquinas makes reference to the passage from which this quotation is taken.

[57] Aristotle, *Politics* II,7 (p. 99).

23:3), which appears to mean forever: "You shall not seek their peace or their prosperity all your days for ever" (Deut 23:6).[58] Similarly, the fourth objection notes that God requires his people to love their neighbor, but he also commands that Israel kill all the inhabitants of the cities "that the Lord your God gives you for an inheritance" (Deut 20:16). While commanding that these people die, God mandates that the Israelites spare the fruit trees in the land surrounding these cities. Again, the third objection observes that God instructs his people that "you shall not wrong a stranger or oppress him, for you were strangers in the land of Egypt" (Exod 22:21). Yet, after commanding that no Israelite lend money for interest to another Israelite, God permits his people to lend money for interest to foreigners. Is this not precisely to wrong and oppress strangers, which God forbids?

As one would expect, Aquinas's answers to these concerns do not all draw upon Aristotle. When he does use Aristotle in his *respondeo*, it is to move the discussion in the direction of citizenship. On this view, such commandments as "you shall not wrong a stranger" (Exod 22:21) have to do with newcomers or travelers. By contrast, the commandments regarding the Ammonites, Moabites, Egyptians, and Edomites have to do with full legal membership in the people of God. For this distinction Aquinas cites Book III of Aristotle's *Politics*, where Aristotle defines a citizen as one "who has the power to take part in the deliberative or judicial administration of [the] state."[59] In the passage referenced by Aquinas, Aristotle goes on to say that "in practice a citizen is defined to be one of whom both the parents are citizens; others insist on going further back; say to two or three more ancestors."[60] In his commentary on Aristotle's *Politics*, Aquinas observes that Aristotle mentions this definition of citizenship but excludes it, on the grounds that rooting citizenship in ancestry risks endless regress, because it forces the person not only (in Aquinas's words) to "trace his ancestry back to the third or fourth citizen ancestor," but also to answer questions regarding "how the third- or fourth-generation ancestor was a citizen."[61] But in the *Summa theologiae*'s question on the rationality of the judicial precepts, Aquinas simply observes that, as Aristotle testifies, "it was the law with some nations that no one was deemed a citizen except after two or three generations."[62] Inquiring into why nations would have understood citizenship in this way, Aquinas reasons that these nations must have been concerned that if foreigners were immediately accepted as citizens, they might not yet have at heart the common good of their adopted nation.

---

[58] Deut 23:3 and 7 are cited in *ST* I-II, q. 105, a. 3, arg. 1.
[59] Aristotle, *Politics* III,1 (p. 127).   [60] Aristotle, *Politics* III,2 (p. 127).
[61] Thomas Aquinas, *Commentary on Aristotle's* Politics, trans. Richard J. Regan (Indianapolis, IN: Hackett, 2007), pp. 184–5.
[62] *ST* I-II, q. 105, a. 3, corpus.

He then proposes that God's commandments regarding the Ammonites, Moabites, Egyptians, and Edomites can be understood in this light. God allowed the Israelites to welcome, after a waiting period of three generations, Egyptians and Edomites into full citizenship or full membership in the people of God. God did so because although the Egyptians and Edomites had been Israel's enemies, the Israelites had also enjoyed significant bonds with them in the past. But the Ammonites and Moabites had been nothing but enemies of Israel, and so God excluded them permanently from membership in his people. The Amalekites had been such bitter enemies of Israel that God commanded Israel not merely to exclude them from membership but indeed always to regard them as enemies (see Exod 17:16). In his *respondeo*, therefore, Aquinas sees in the citizenship practices of other nations, mentioned by Aristotle, a plausible way of understanding the precepts of the Mosaic law regarding membership in and exclusion from the assembly of Israel. In his reply to the first objection, Aquinas adds that the exceptions to the harsh laws regarding Ammonites and Moabites come about when members of these tribes show particular love for the people of God. Thus the Ammonite leader Achior, who had warned the Assyrian general Holofernes against attacking Israel and for his pains had been handed over by Holofernes to the Israelites, was gladly received into full membership in Israel (Jdt 14:10), as was Ruth the Moabite, who showed her devotion to Naomi (Ruth 3–4).[63]

Aquinas also uses Aristotle's reflections on citizenship to interpret God's commandment through Moses that "he whose testicles are crushed or whose male member is cut off shall not enter the assembly of the Lord" (Deut 23:1, cited by Aquinas in the second objection of a. 3). Why does God seem to punish these people for things that were beyond their control? In his reply to the second objection, Aquinas refers to Aristotle's position in Book III of the *Politics* that not all males in the city should be citizens in the full sense. Among those who should not be full citizens, Aristotle includes children, slaves, artisans, and laborers, although Aristotle grants that "under some governments the mechanic and the labourer will be citizens."[64]

Applying Aristotle's logic to the people of Israel, Aquinas notes that in the Israelite polity membership or "citizenship" was based on physical descent from Abraham, Isaac, and Jacob, and the purpose of membership was to offer divine worship as the chosen people of God. This purpose, Aquinas thinks, helps to explain why the Mosaic law excluded certain people from full citizenship without necessarily being unjust. Eunuchs and bastards were lacking in precisely the area—physical generation—that defined membership or citizenship in the people of God. Eunuchs "were not competent to receive

---

[63] See *ST* I-II, q. 105, a. 3, ad 1. Aquinas mentions with respect to Ruth that women "are not competent to be citizens absolutely speaking" (*ST* I-II, q. 105, a. 3, ad 1).

[64] Aristotle, *Politics* III,5 (p. 135).

the honor due to a father,"[65] and bastards were unable to represent the dignity of Israel's physical descent from Abraham, Isaac, and Jacob. At issue was the way in which the chosen people of God, descended from the patriarchs, offered communal worship to God. In this light, the Mosaic law was not unjust to correlate membership in the worshiping assembly with paternity. As Aquinas remarks in his reply to the second objection, according to Aristotle (in *Politics* II) the Spartans did something similar in encouraging "the citizens to have large families."[66] Aquinas adds, however, that "in matters pertaining to the grace of God, eunuchs were not discriminated from others, as neither were strangers."[67] He considers that Isa 56 makes this abundantly clear, by stating that "to the eunuchs who keep my Sabbaths, who choose the things that please me and hold fast my covenant, I will give in my house and within my walls a monument and a name better than sons and daughters; I will give them an everlasting name which shall not be cut off" (Isa 56:4–5).[68]

The first three articles of q. 105 treat the judicial laws about government, political economy, and foreign relations. The fourth and final article of q. 105 treats the judicial laws about the organization of households. The issues here involve three kinds of relationships: between husband and wife, between parents and children, and between master and servants (slaves). In thinking about the relationship of the second and third kinds of relationship, Aquinas refers to Books I and III of Aristotle's *Politics*. In the first objection of a. 4, Aquinas points out that for Aristotle the slave "wholly belongs to [the master]," and therefore is the master's property.[69] For this reason, as Aquinas states in the fourth objection, Aristotle finds that to be master of a slave differs, in terms of authority, from being a husband or a parent. Aristotle explains that "the rule of a master, although the slave by nature and the master by nature have in reality the same interests, is nevertheless exercised primarily with a view to the interest of the master," whereas "the government of a wife and children and of a household . . . is exercised in the first instance for the good of the governed or for the common good of both parties."[70] If Aristotle is right, says Aquinas, then it would seem that it was unfitting, at least, for the Mosaic law to command that "when you buy a Hebrew slave, he shall serve six years, and in the seventh he shall go out free, for nothing" (Exod 21:2). The master would thereby lose his property without receiving any recompense. The Mosaic law also appears to violate the principles established by Aristotle

---

[65] *ST* I-II, q. 105, a. 3, ad 2.

[66] Aristotle, *Politics* II,9 (p. 110). Aristotle disapproves of this Spartan law on the grounds that "it is obvious that, if there were many children, the land being distributed as it is, many of them must necessarily fall into poverty" (II,9; p. 110).

[67] *ST* I-II, q. 105, a. 3, ad 2.

[68] See *ST* I-II, q. 105, a. 3, ad 2. See Kries, "Thomas Aquinas and the Politics of Moses," p. 98.

[69] Aristotle, *Politics* I,4 (p. 58).   [70] Aristotle, *Politics* III,6 (p. 137).

when the law permits a father to sell "his daughter as a slave" (Exod 21:7). Surely it is unjust for a father to sell his daughter into slavery?

Aquinas's replies to these objections, as well as his *respondeo*, help us to understand his view of slavery. He interprets the Mosaic law to be fundamentally opposed to slavery, at least as regards the people of God. Thus the precept commanding the release of the Hebrew slave after six years shows a quite different perspective on slavery than that of Aristotle. The Hebrew slave is never a slave by nature or the mere property of his master.[71] Aristotle imagines slaves as mere property, but the Mosaic law does not regard them as such. At least this is the case with God's chosen people, because God himself redeemed them from (literal) slavery in Egypt. Aquinas explains in his reply to the first objection, "As the children of Israel had been delivered by the Lord from slavery, and for this reason were bound to the service of God, He did not wish them to be slaves in perpetuity." No person who has been redeemed by God in order that he or she might serve God can be truly a slave. In support of his interpretation, Aquinas quotes the Mosaic law's commandment that if one Israelite sells himself to another, the owner must treat him "as a hired servant and as a sojourner" and must release him at the jubilee year, on the grounds that "they [the chosen people] are my servants, whom I brought forth out of the land of Egypt; they shall not be sold as slaves" (Lev 25:40, 42).

The same point holds for the father who sells his daughter into slavery. Aquinas insists that the Mosaic law has a significantly different view of slavery than does Aristotle, because of God's redemptive work. An Israelite could sell himself or his child into slavery because it was not the form of slavery that Aristotle envisions. Rather, as Aquinas says in his reply to the fourth objection, "no Jew could own a Jew as a slave absolutely: but only in a restricted sense, as a hireling for a fixed time." The reason why an Israelite father would sell his daughter (or son) would not be for material gain, as in the selling of property, but simply because due to extreme poverty he could not afford to care for his child.

---

[71] See Kries, "Thomas Aquinas and the Politics of Moses," p. 98. Kries goes on to remark that "for the most part, Thomas argues that the *Torah* and the *Politics* are in agreement. However, time and again Thomas intimates that the judicial precepts, in the name of religion, go beyond what would seem to be required according to Aristotle. Consequently, the *Politics* is useful to Thomas only up to a certain point. The *Politics* provides reasonable explanations for many of the judicial precepts, but it cannot provide all the explanations" (pp. 98–9). Kries argues that this limitation comes from the fact that Aristotle's God, unlike Moses's, is uninterested in human affairs. Kries also points out, "The human law of the gentiles subordinated religion to the public good, but the Old Law worked in the opposite direction, first directing human beings to God through the ceremonial precepts and then, secondarily, through the judicial precepts, directing human beings to each other in a manner befitting the end of the divine law" (p. 100). The Mosaic law is thereby more, not less, reasonable than the laws of the *Politics*. See also Joseph E. Capizzi, "The Children of God: Natural Slavery in the Thought of Aquinas and Vitoria," *TS* 63 (2002): pp. 31–52; Hause, "Aquinas on Aristotelian Justice," pp. 160–1.

In the *respondeo* of a. 4, Aquinas places his discussion of the judicial precepts regarding households under the aegis of Aristotle's definition of the family (in Book I of the *Politics*) as "the association established by nature for the supply of men's everyday wants."[72] The family serves the preservation of our individual life, and for this purpose we need food, clothing, and other goods which may require servants to oversee. The preservation of life also has an extended sense, namely as regards the furtherance of the species by means of the procreation of children. Thus the family or household includes or can include husband, wife, children, and servants. Aquinas defends the Mosaic law's precepts about servants (slaves) as moderate and just—not a view that we could accept today—in terms of work and punishment. He focuses on the Mosaic law's insistence upon marriage as being for the purpose of continuing the twelve tribes for the sake of the worship of YHWH, and he argues that the Mosaic law provides well for the development of "conjugal love" (*dilectio inter coniuges*). He points out that the Mosaic law rightly emphasized the education of children in the faith and morality of Israel. With respect to children, he remarks in reply to the fifth objection that Aristotle, in Book X of the *Nicomachean Ethics*, is right that "a father's command does not have the power to enforce or compel," unlike the command of a ruler or a law.[73] For this reason, he approves of the Mosaic law's commandment that parents who have "a stubborn and rebellious son, who will not obey the voice of his father or the voice of his mother" should have recourse to the elders of the city[74]— although he interprets the death penalty given to the rebellious son (who is a "glutton and a drunkard" [Deut 21:20]) as due to the son not because of gluttony and drunkenness, but because the son sins against God not unwillingly through ignorance, nor even through malice, but because of deliberate rebellion against God's law.[75]

4.4. AQUINAS'S INTERPRETATION OF THE MOSAIC LAW: CONCLUDING REFLECTIONS

In an erudite essay on "Aquinas and the Children of Abraham," Edward Synan identifies both strengths and weaknesses of Aquinas's biblical interpretation. Among the weaknesses, he finds that Aquinas's "innocence of Hebrew made the Hebraic mindset of scriptural authors alien to him, as it was to his liberal arts training. This led him on occasion to bring biblical sources under a

---

[72] Aristotle, *Politics* I,2 (p. 53); see *ST* I-II, q. 105, a. 4, corpus.
[73] See Aristotle, *Nicomachean Ethics* X,9 (p. 297), cited in *ST* I-II, q. 105, a. 4, ad 5.
[74] See *ST* I-II, q. 105, a. 4, ad 5.   [75] See *ST* I-II, q. 105, a. 2, ad 9.

systematization in a spirit foreign to them."[76] Beryl Smalley suggests that this spirit of systematization was not only a weakness, but also a strength. By contrast to William of Auvergne, who sought to know what the original hearers of the Mosaic law would have understood by it and thereby "floundered in a quagmire" caused by medieval ignorance of ancient Near Eastern history, Aquinas "avoided rash speculation on its historical setting."[77] The drawback to Aquinas's approach, says Smalley, is that his discussion of the Mosaic law does not ask or answer the questions that historical-critical biblical scholars would ask today.

By bringing Aristotle so deeply into his interpretation of the Mosaic law's moral and judicial precepts, has Aquinas turned the Mosaic law into an ancient Greek law code that bears insufficient resemblance to the words of the living God given to Israel through Moses (or to ancient Near Eastern law codes stitched together by a later redactor, as many biblical scholars now think)?[78] On the one hand, it seems clear that his way of defending the Mosaic law's precepts about the kingship, the jubilee year, the division of the land, the rejection of the Ammonites and Moabites, the exclusion of eunuchs and bastards from the assembly of Israel, and slavery at times obscures the Torah's own concerns by replacing them with the worldview of Aristotle. Put another way, the framework for Aquinas's reflection on government, political economy, relations with foreigners, and citizenship often comes from Aristotle (and Maimonides) rather than from the Old Testament.[79] Likewise, his approach to the Mosaic law's moral precepts in terms of virtue theory and the dictates of natural reason, as well as his account of why the Decalogue is formulated as it is (with only two affirmative precepts, and so forth), seem more Aristotelian than the Old Testament actually is.

On the other hand, to criticize Aquinas in this way is to a significant degree to miss the point. After all, Aquinas is engaged in *sacra doctrina*, which is different from modern biblical interpretation. His use of Aristotle should be judged in terms of whether it leads us deeper into the realities delineated in the

---

[76] Edward A. Synan, "Aquinas and the Children of Abraham," in *Philosophy and the God of Abraham: Essays in Memory of James A. Weisheipl, OP*, edited by R. James Long (Toronto: Pontifical Institute of Mediaeval Studies, 1991), pp. 203–16, at 209.

[77] Smalley, "William of Auvergne," p. 68.

[78] See, e.g., Calum M. Carmichael, *The Laws of Deuteronomy* (Ithaca, NY: Cornell University Press, 1974).

[79] On Maimonides's influence see Amos Funkenstein, "Gesetz und Geschichte: Zur historisierenden Hermeneutik bei Moses Maimonides und Thomas von Aquin," *Viator* 1 (1970): pp. 147–78; David Novak, "Maimonides and Aquinas on Natural Law," in *St. Thomas Aquinas and the Natural Law Tradition: Contemporary Perspectives*, edited by John Goyette, Mark S. Latkovic, and Richard S. Myers (Washington, DC: The Catholic University of America Press, 2004), pp. 43–65; Idit Dobbs-Weinstein, *Maimonides and St. Thomas on the Limits of Reason* (Albany, NY: State University of New York Press, 1995).

Mosaic law.[80] With regard to the moral precepts, these realities are holiness, sin, punishment, and the law of God knowable (in principle) by created reason. In the judicial precepts, the realities at stake are government, the distribution of property and land, dealings with foreign peoples, slavery, and marriage and family. With regard to these realities of the biblical world, Aquinas's approach is often deeply penetrating. His discussion of the moral and judicial precepts certainly employs Aristotelian lenses, but he raises the issues that must be raised if the Mosaic law is to be taken seriously as the law of an actual people in concrete historical circumstances. For instance, how can a real law contain precepts about interior virtues and vices, as the Decalogue does? How is it that the Decalogue includes the commandment that we honor our parents but says nothing about other human relationships of similar import? Why are the precepts of the Decalogue not all negative ones, and why do only some contain threats of punishment? Can the precepts of the Decalogue be dispensed with in certain circumstances? Do we have to be interiorly virtuous in order to truly obey God in anything, or can we obey God's precepts without yet possessing the corresponding virtuous habit and interior disposition?

Aquinas's answers to these questions shed valuable light on the meaning of the Mosaic law. He helps us to see its particular status as divine law, rather than simply another human law. He points out the special place of God and of our parents in our relationships of debt and gratitude. He makes us aware of the fact that idolatry and perjury, for the Old Testament, are interrelated sins (and the most deadly sins for Israel), not least because of the covenantal nature of their relationship with God. He shows that a careful reading of the Old Testament need not and should not result in the view that the precepts of the Decalogue can be changed according to circumstances. He guides us to understand the Mosaic law as pedagogy rather than as presupposing interior virtue on the part of the people of Israel.

The same can be said for Aquinas's insight into the judicial precepts. Certainly he seeks to illumine these precepts by Aristotelian philosophical means. At the same time, he willingly confronts many of the most difficult texts of the Old Testament, including the diverse and seemingly conflicting statements about kingship, the fact that Israel's leadership declined so precipitously after Joshua's death because Joshua had no real successor, the problem of tyrannous kings, the strangeness of the jubilee laws in terms of

---

[80] In an essay that compares Maimonides and Aquinas on providence, Idit Dobbs-Weinstein comments that they "are heirs to traditions which understand the Torah to possess many faces and to speak in the language of the sons of men, and hence hold interpretation to be the very stuff of human existence"; Idit Dobbs-Weinstein, "Medieval Biblical Commentary and Philosophical Inquiry as Exemplified in the Thought of Moses Maimonides and St. Thomas Aquinas," in *Moses Maimonides and his Time*, edited by Eric L. Ormsby (Washington, DC: The Catholic University of America Press, 1989), pp. 101–20, at 104. Aquinas's interpretation of the Mosaic law is not only exegetical but also necessarily philosophical.

their economic impact, the apparently harsh commands about the death penalty, the divine rejection of whole peoples such as the Ammonites and Moabites, the exclusion of people such as eunuchs and bastards from the assembly of Israel, the acceptance of slavery, and so forth. In engaging these difficult texts, he enables us to appreciate the generally quite balanced approach of Israel's political and economic laws, which on the one hand allow for kingship and private property but on the other hand repeatedly undermine the supremacy of both. He shows that some of Israel's judicial laws, including those about exclusion from the assembly and those about slavery, can be better understood from within Israel's privileged status as God's chosen people. Even the laws about God's rejection of the Ammonites and Moabites make more sense when viewed in terms of the purpose and requirements of membership in God's people.

Although Aquinas also employs the spiritual sense as a way of interpreting the Mosaic law (especially with regard to the ceremonial precepts), his treatise values the Mosaic law as an actual law given to regulate the lives of God's people, Israel. He does not turn the Mosaic law into an Aristotelian document, because he is careful to quote widely and frequently from the Mosaic law. The Mosaic law that emerges from his treatise clearly retains its own distinctive voice, which speaks through the Decalogue, through the laws about idolatry and oaths, and through the jubilee laws and the rejection of any permanent or natural slavery for God's redeemed people. Instead of overwhelming the Mosaic law, his use of Aristotelian lenses such as virtue and citizenship presses the point that the Mosaic law was a wise law, even if an imperfect one.[81] To argue that a law is wise, and not merely arbitrary, inevitably requires philosophical tools for evaluating the goodness of laws. Aristotle's moral and political philosophy serves this purpose well for Aquinas.[82]

As a wise law, the Mosaic law was fitted to a particular people in a particular time and place, with a particular end or goal.[83] This end or goal was twofold: the right worship of God and the preparation for Christ. The people for whom this law was suited were the inheritors of God's covenant with Abraham: they dwelt in the promised land and descended from Abraham according to the flesh. Yet as regards the moral precepts of the Mosaic law, Aquinas emphasizes that these apply to every people. The Decalogue is the core of Israel's law, the only portion of the law written directly by God, because it reveals the unchangeable norms of natural law, knowable by reason but obscured, in

---

[81] *ST* I-II, q. 98, aa. 1 and 6; *ST* I-II, q. 105, a. 4, ad 8; *ST* I-II, q. 106, a. 3.

[82] The significance of Aristotle arises, of course, from Aquinas's view (in Jeffrey Hause's words) that "Aristotle, despite a few flaws, lacunae, and putative inconsistencies, succeeded brilliantly in articulating, without the aid of revelation, an ethical system that captured the truth about human ends and how to achieve them, about the sort of person worth becoming, about human action, and about the need for friendship" ("Aquinas on Aristotelian Justice," p. 163).

[83] On this point see *ST* I-II, q. 100, a. 2; Aristotle, *Politics* IV,1 (p. 170).

application at least, by sin. The moral precepts include the love of God and love of neighbor. The judicial precepts are applications of the moral precepts to the concrete relations of Israelites with one another and with their neighbors. As such, they do not possess universality, and Aquinas does not suggest in his treatise that we need to revive (for example) the jubilee laws or the particular ways in which Israel dealt with slavery. In defending their wisdom in their time and place, however, he does help us to see that the judicial laws are balanced and moderate in ways that we might not have otherwise observed. Aristotle's review of ancient laws helps Aquinas in this task. Not least in its use of Aristotle, therefore, Aquinas's treatise on the Mosaic law teaches us how and why Christians should gladly affirm that, as Paul says, "the law is holy, and the commandment is holy, and just, and good" (Rom 7:12).

5

Aristotle's Philosophy in Aquinas's
Theology of Grace in the
Summa Theologiae

Simon Francis Gaine, OP

Recent accounts of Aquinas's doctrine of grace have been principally shaped
by the realization of the importance to him of 2 Pet 1:4's "partakers of the
divine nature," together with his appropriation of the Fathers' teaching on
deification and the Platonic notion of participation;[1] by a perception of a
fundamentally personalist worldview driving his thought;[2] or by the appreciation of grace's link to further scriptural, patristic, or other philosophical
and theological themes found in his biblical and systematic works.[3] These
interpretations of Aquinas's teaching on grace generally pay comparatively
little attention to the influence of Aristotle. Daniel Keating writes approv-
ingly that recognition of the centrality for Aquinas of 2 Pet 1:4 "can help
to offset the tendency to view his doctrine of grace as the application of
Aristotelian categories to Christian theology."[4] According to Stephen Duffy,

---

[1] Anna N. Williams, *The Ground of Union: Deification in Aquinas and Palamas* (Oxford:
Oxford University Press, 1999), pp. 82–101; Daniel A. Keating, "Justification, Sanctification and
Divinization in Thomas Aquinas," in *Aquinas on Doctrine: A Critical Introduction*, edited by
Thomas G. Weinandy, Daniel A. Keating, and John P. Yocum (London: T. & T. Clark, 2004),
pp. 139–58, at 151–5; Rudi A. te Velde, *Aquinas on God: The "Divine Science" of the* Summa
Theologiae (Aldershot: Ashgate, 2006), pp. 147–69.

[2] Stephen J. Duffy, *The Dynamics of Grace: Perspectives in Theological Anthropology* (Collegeville, MN: Liturgical Press, 1993), pp. 121–70.

[3] Theo Kobusch, "Grace (Ia IIae, qq. 109–114)," in *The Ethics of Aquinas*, edited by Stephen
J. Pope (Washington, DC: Georgetown University Press, 2002), pp. 207–18; Keating, "Justifica-
tion," pp. 139–51; Joseph P. Wawrykow, "Grace," in *The Theology of Thomas Aquinas*, edited by
Rik van Nieuwenhove and Joseph P. Wawrykow (Notre Dame, IN: University of Notre Dame
Press, 2005), pp. 192–221.

[4] Keating, "Justification," p. 154. For an example of an older account, first published in 1948,
which is in fact more balanced, see Henri Rondet, *The Grace of Christ: A Brief History of the
Theology of Grace*, trans. Tad W. Guzie (Westminster, MD: Newman, 1966), pp. 198–248.

it had previously been the "Aristotelian elements that caught the eye of interpreters of Thomas."[5]

Where there has continued to be significant concentration on Aquinas's use of Aristotle, critical concerns about the latter's impact are often raised. Duffy holds that the basic personalist and anthropocentric "thought-form" (*Denkform*) he attributes to Aquinas is "obscured by the metaphysical categories of Aristotle that are so much to the fore in his work."[6] Roger Haight's slightly older study, which still treated Aquinas more straightforwardly as the apex of the medieval reception of Aristotle into Western theology, had expressed similar reservations from the perspective of the author's *own* personalism.[7] Sometimes one can gain the impression from such works that Aquinas's very purpose was the translation of his Christian inheritance into contemporary philosophical categories, in such a way that today's theological task is simply to attempt an analogous translation.[8] On this view, what might be worth reviving from Aquinas himself would be his personalist elements rather than the Aristotelian ones in his thought.[9] While affirming that deification (our participation in the divine nature) is indeed what is at the center of Aquinas's theology of grace, I shall instead treat his creative appropriation within it of certain Aristotelian concepts, which he held to correspond with the very truth of reality, as in fact undertaken in service of a genuine and lasting theological understanding of this mystery. While a proper philosophical vindication of the Aristotelian concepts Aquinas employs is beyond the scope of this chapter, I hope to clarify the theological advantages that this use may still bring to our quest for understanding of Christian faith.

As a pagan philosopher, Aristotle had nothing to teach about the Judeo-Christian doctrine of grace. Though Aquinas was generous in his assessment of Aristotle's intellectual achievement in regard to God as Creator of all things, he never supposed that Aristotle had ever postulated even the possibility of divine grace.[10] Both thinkers spent considerable effort exploring what contributed to human happiness, including *internal* principles of human action

---

[5] Duffy, *The Dynamics of Grace*, p. 126. For an older study, first published over 1941–1942, which engaged with the presence of Aristotle in Aquinas's theology of grace, see Bernard J. F. Lonergan, S.J., *Grace and Freedom: Operative Grace in the Thought of St. Thomas Aquinas*, ed. J. Patout Burns (London: Darton, Longman & Todd, 1971).

[6] Duffy, *The Dynamics of Grace*, p. 124. For both reservations about this position and agreement, see Kobusch, "Grace," pp. 212–14. This kind of criticism can be traced back to Adolf Harnack, *History of Dogma*, vol. 6, trans. Neil Buchanan (Boston: Little, Brown, and Company, 1899), pp. 184–5 and 279–80.

[7] Roger Haight, *The Experience and Language of Grace* (New York: Paulist Press, 1979), pp. 69–73.

[8] Haight, *The Experience and Language of Grace*, pp. 67–9. Precursors for this approach may possibly be traced in Henri Bouillard, *Conversion et grâce chez S. Thomas d'Aquin: Étude historique* (Paris: Aubier, 1944); and Rondet, *The Grace of Christ*, pp. 379–84.

[9] Duffy, *The Dynamics of Grace*, pp. 167–9.   [10] See *De veritate*, q. 27, a. 2, ad 7.

such as habits and virtues, where Aquinas was able to draw on Aristotle to considerable advantage. However, following his consideration of such internal principles in the *Summa theologiae*, Aquinas turned to the *external* principles of human action, namely, God and the devil.[11] As befits a member of an anti-Manichaean religious Order, which had been founded to preach the goodness of God's creation, Aquinas merely indicates that he has already briefly treated of the devil, a fallen angelic creature who inclines human beings to evil action, earlier in the *Summa*.[12] God, however, whom he has already treated of at great length in himself and in relation to creatures, especially as their source, he now treats of again at some length as the external principle of the good acts by which humans make their return to him as their end. God acts as this principle, Aquinas says, by instructing us through law and assisting us by grace.[13]

Aristotle of course knew something of human law, and Aquinas made use of him in his analysis of the Old Law given by God to the Jews.[14] When he came to the New Law, Aquinas identified its principal content as "the grace of the Holy Spirit," that is obtained through Christ,[15] and of this Aristotle had nothing to say. Yet, in pursuit of theological understanding of this mystery, Aquinas is able to draw on Aristotle to provide a kind of partial infrastructure for his account of grace, adapting to it Aristotle's notions of nature and end, change or motion, substance and accident, habit and virtue, causation and generation. These are drafted into service as Aquinas seeks answers to questions raised in the *Summa*'s treatise on grace concerning this datum of faith. Why is grace needed by us (its necessity)?[16] What exactly is it (its essence)?[17] What brings it about (its cause)?[18] And what does it do for us (its effects)?[19] Each of these questions I shall treat in turn, drawing attention to how in each case Aristotle occupies a place of no little importance in Aquinas's theology.[20]

What follows is hardly a complete account of Aquinas's treatise on grace in the *Summa*. Were it read as such, it would surely show Aquinas as narrowly Aristotelian in his sources, without his rich dependence on Dionysius and others. My purpose rather is simply to present his theological understanding of grace insofar as it manifests the service of Aristotle's philosophy, particularly in confirmation of two of Aquinas's chief theological priorities. These I label the "anti-Manichaean" and "anti-Pelagian" orientations of his

---

[11] *ST* I-II, q. 90, Prologue. Cf. *SCG* III, chs. 147–163 and *Compendium theologiae* I, ch. 143, where he had treated grace under the heading of divine providence, by which God directs us to himself.

[12] *ST* I, q. 114.   [13] *ST* I-II, q. 109, Prologue.

[14] See Chapter 4 in this work.   [15] *ST* I-II, q. 106.   [16] *ST* I-II, q. 109.

[17] *ST* I-II, q. 110.   [18] *ST* I-II, q. 112.   [19] *ST* I-II, qq. 113–114.

[20] I largely omit consideration of q. 111 on the divisions of grace, where Aristotle's influence is less evident. Aquinas does, however, appeal in a. 5, ad 1 to *Metaphysics* XII,10 (1075a11) on the character of the common good.

theological inheritance from Augustine, which are, respectively, the goodness of the created order and the nonnegotiable primacy of divine grace.

5.1. NATURE'S NEED OF GRACE

The theme of grace does not make its first appearance in the *Summa* only in the treatise on grace; rather it surfaces as a theme throughout the *Summa*. When treating of God the Holy Trinity, for example, Aquinas had told us that the divine persons are enjoyed by us through the gift of grace;[21] when he broke off writing the *Summa* he was telling of the sacrament of penance, through which grace, once lost, can be restored. It is a refrain of Aquinas's thinking, said or unsaid, and stated as early as the *Summa*'s first question, that grace perfects nature.[22] Nature and grace are thus correlative: grace presupposes nature,[23] and nature's ultimate perfection is only intelligible in terms of grace. Though Aristotle said nothing of grace, his works presented Aquinas with a solid account of *nature* on which he could build in service of the goodness and integrity of the created order, an account through which he was able to refine his understanding of the grace that presupposes and perfects nature. In the first place, Aristotle's account of nature helped him to specify precisely why human beings, even apart from their sinfulness, stand in need of the grace of God. To think of nature *as such* in this way, apart from sinfulness, could only confirm the basic anti-Manichaean thrust of Aquinas's Augustinian inheritance, liberating "human nature" from any possibility of thinking of it basically in terms of sinfulness, and thinking of it instead in terms of the goodness and integrity of creation.

Augustine's legacy had in fact referred the necessity for grace overwhelmingly to human sinfulness: on account of original sin and its effects sinners needed divine grace in order to be *healed* in terms of their willing and desiring. There was, however, one place in which Augustine mentioned a prelapsarian reliance on grace on Adam's part, intimating a need for grace prior to sin, a need for something other than healing.[24] It is such a need of grace independent of sin that Aquinas is able to establish with the help of Aristotle's approach to nature, which cannot be found in Augustine.[25] Augustine did indeed speak of human "nature" and its various conditions, such as its differing states before and after the Fall, but he did not benefit from Aristotle's philosophy in this respect. However, from such texts as *Physics* II,1 (192b8–193a8) and

---

[21] *ST* I, q. 43, a. 3.   [22] *ST* I, q. 1, a. 8, ad 2.   [23] *ST* I-II, q. 99, a. 2, ad 1.

[24] Augustine, *De correptione et gratia*, chs. 31–32.

[25] For Aquinas on the presence of grace in prelapsarian Adam, see *ST* I, q. 95. For grace in the angels, see q. 62.

Metaphysics V,4 (1014b16–1015a19) Aquinas learned of nature as an intrinsic principle of change and stability found in natural things such as animals and plants, earth, air, fire, and water. Each natural being was the kind of thing it was on account of its specific nature. Nature is the intrinsic principle that makes a thing what it is, and thus a human being is a human being on account of his or her human nature. Every natural being acts moreover in accordance with its nature, and so Aquinas was able, with Aristotle's help, to name acts of intellect and will proper to human nature. It is on this basis that he was able to argue for what God had constituted in humanity by nature, as distinct from what he gives to this humanity by grace.

For example, drawing on Aristotle's natural epistemology in *De anima* II and III, Aquinas could give an account of the human ability to know the world, as rooted in the natural light of the intellect. Though he hardly wants to rule out the possibility of miraculous assistance for human knowledge, he also wants to rule out any possible confusion of the intellectual light God has given in human nature with what God might grant by grace.[26] Likewise, human nature is the God-given principle whereby human beings can undertake the whole range of acts that are proper to them as human,[27] and Aquinas includes under this that human beings were naturally able to fulfill the commandments of the law in their substance before the arrival of sin.[28] He even goes so far as to say that, apart from the Fall, a human being can love God above all things with a natural love. Quoting *Physics* II,8 (199a10) for the principle that each thing acts according to what is proper to it by nature, he argues that each thing in some sense desires and loves an object according to what is proper to it by nature, and, given the principle that the good of the part is for the good of the whole, concludes that every creature, including humanity prior to the damaging of human nature by sin, naturally loves its own good for the sake of God, who is the common good of the whole.[29] This nature remained in all the conditions that Augustine had attributed to human nature, despite the damage done to nature by the Fall, which impeded what it had previously been able to achieve. So full an articulation of human nature enabled Aquinas to specify the need for grace apart from sin more precisely by building up a picture of what grace was *not* needed for, apart from sin, because it was provided by nature. Seeing the extent of what God had placed in nature, Aquinas was better able to discern nature's limitations.

Aquinas understood the limitations of nature and the consequent deepest need for grace in light of the *end* to which God had called human beings. In appropriating Aristotle's theory of nature, Aquinas was especially attentive to its teleological character. According to Aristotle, every natural being acts according to its nature in view of its proper end, its proper goal or

---

[26] *ST* I-II, q. 109, a. 1.   [27] *ST* I-II, q. 109, a. 2.
[28] *ST* I-II, q. 109, a. 4.   [29] *ST* I-II, q. 109, a. 3.

flourishing.[30] Each natural being is equipped by its nature with the possibility of attaining to its end through its activity. Aquinas was aware of Aristotle's account of the end of *human* nature, a kind of natural, philosophical contemplation of the cosmos,[31] and it was the teleological principle of nature that had guided Aquinas's whole account of the actions that were possible for human beings by nature. Aristotle knew nothing, however, of the higher end to which God had in fact ordained rational creatures, namely, that heavenly union with the Triune God that consists in the intellectual vision of his very essence,[32] where those blessed by this knowledge are said by Aquinas to be "deiform," that is, "like to God,"[33] and to enjoy a *full* participation in the divine nature.[34]

This end, the actual realization of which in the next life is proved by Scripture (1 John 3:2),[35] clearly outstrips the active capacities of human nature, even apart from sin.[36] In one way human beings do indeed have the potential for such knowledge. Unlike other creatures of the material world, they are intellectual and so free, able to know and love in a higher way than other animals. It is by way of their intellectual nature that Aquinas explains how human beings are by nature "in the image of God" with a certain capacity to become able to know and love him in a way that transcends their nature.[37] This does not mean, however, that they thereby have the natural power actively to attain such a union as the beatific vision. The infinite divine essence simply cannot be known by the kind of limited and empirical way of knowing that humans have by nature, which Aquinas had grasped with the help of Aristotle. Aquinas in fact argues that *no* created intellect, whether human or angelic, can know the infinite essence of God by its own finite, natural powers.[38] The upshot is that, while knowledge of the divine essence is natural to God, this end is beyond nature ("supernatural") for all rational creatures, human beings included.[39] The concept of the "supernatural" (what is added over and above created nature) is thus refined by the theologians of the thirteenth century, partly with the help of an Aristotelian account of nature with its notions of ends and natural capacities. For Aquinas, then, human beings are exceptional in that they have a twofold end to be pursued, one natural, proportionate to the active capacities of nature and pursued in this life, and one supernatural, which transcends such capacities, and is granted to us only in the next life.[40]

Aquinas holds that, as supernatural, this final end can only be reached in the journey of this life by proportionate, that is, supernatural means.[41] While human beings were able to fulfill the commandments of the law in their

---

[30] Aristotle, *Physics* II,8 (198b10–199b33).

[31] Aristotle, *Nicomachean Ethics* X,7–8 (1177a12–1179a32).

[32] *SCG* III, ch. 48.   [33] *ST* I, q. 12, a. 5, corpus. Cf. *ST* I-II, q. 3, a. 1, ad 1.

[34] *ST* III, q. 1, a. 2.   [35] *ST* I, q. 12, a. 1.   [36] *ST* I-II, q. 5, a. 5.

[37] *ST* I, q. 93, a. 4. Cf. *ST* I-II, q. 113, a. 10.   [38] *ST* I, q. 12, a. 4.

[39] *ST* I-II, q. 5, a. 7.   [40] E.g. *ST* I-II, q. 4, a. 5.   [41] *SCG* III, ch. 147.

substance by their undamaged natural powers, they are unable to fulfill these same commandments *by way of charity* through their natural powers, whatever their state of nature.[42] According to Aquinas, while nature loves God above all things as the source and end of natural good, charity so loves him insofar as he is the object and source of our supernatural end, and insofar as we already have by charity a kind of spiritual association with God.[43] Supernatural charity will be treated by Aquinas, with the help of Aristotle's theory of friendship in *Nicomachean Ethics* (Books VIII–IX), as a friendship with God that transcends the limitations of our human nature.[44] Fulfilling the commandments by way of charity is then impossible without supernatural aid or *grace*.

Aquinas thus contrasts the natural good that can be achieved through the endowment of nature with the good that can be achieved only through supernatural grace, that is, the supernatural good. It is the performance of the latter good that is meritorious of the final end of heaven.[45] It is for the performance of this supernatural good that supernatural grace is required in this life, the grace by which God directs us to our ultimate beatitude in him and so is the external principle of our acts. In contrast to the "full participation" in the divine nature that comes in heaven, Aquinas speaks in this earthly connection of "a certain participation."[46] He compares the glory of heaven to the grace of this life as a tree to its seed.[47] By this grace we can pursue a supernatural good that goes beyond the good that is possible for us by nature, and through such supernatural acts of grace we are directed to our glorious last end and the fullness of our participation in the divine nature.

In all this then Aquinas discerns a reason for the necessity of grace other than sin. It is the finite limitations that go with a created nature, even with the rational nature of an intellectual being. Even before the introduction of sin, human beings stood for this reason in need of grace, if they were to reach their heavenly, supernatural goal. Thus, according to Aquinas, grace had the role of *elevating* human beings above the limitations of their nature, before grace took on the further role of *healing* (which in this context is very much referred to the healing of our *nature* rather than simply to our willing and desiring). It is thus a twofold need for grace on the part of nature that Aquinas expounds in his question on necessity. Once sin arrives, grace is required for more things than before, for healing as well as elevation.[48] Insofar as Aquinas balances his account of the necessity for grace between these two needs, Wawrykow is right to say of grace's twofold function that "Neither seems for Aquinas to take

---

[42] *ST* I-II, q. 109, a. 3.   [43] *ST* I-II, q. 109, a. 3, ad 1.
[44] *ST* II-II, q. 23, a. 1.   [45] *ST* I-II, q. 109, a. 5.
[46] *ST* II-II, q. 19, a. 7, corpus. See also *ST* I-II, q. 62, a. 1, ad 1.
[47] *ST* I-II, q. 114, a. 3, ad 3.   [48] *ST* I, q. 95, a. 4, ad 1.

precedence; he views both with equal seriousness."[49] Nevertheless, in respect of the order of priority between them, elevation surely takes some kind of precedence. The need for elevation is attributed by Aquinas to humanity prior to the Fall and to its introduction of the need for healing from sin. Thus the need for elevation would appear to belong to human nature as such, however its historic condition might change. Though grace may be needed *for more things* after the Fall, it was not needed *more* than it was before the Fall.[50] Our natural dependence on grace to come to our supernatural goal is absolute. Without something like an Aristotelian account of human nature, placed in the context of a supernatural end, it is difficult to see how a theologian can successfully vindicate this more profound need for grace. In Aquinas's case, Aristotle's concept of nature has thus contributed not only to his treatment of the goodness and integrity of nature, but also to his account of the primacy of grace.

Nature is not, however, the only Aristotelian concept that plays a fundamental role in Aquinas's articulation of our need for grace. Another is *motus*— Aristotle's idea of motion or movement, especially his doctrine of the Prime Mover, to which all changes in the world are ultimately traced.[51] From the beginning of Aquinas's treatment of the twofold purpose for which grace is required, elevation and healing, we find that our need for grace is also twofold in another way. While Aquinas makes use of Aristotle's concept of nature to clarify his position on the purposes *for* which we need grace (elevation and healing), he makes use of the concept of *motus* to clarify what we need *from* grace. According to Aquinas, our need here is not only for some kind of stable "gift" (*donum*) from God by which we are healed and elevated, but also for God himself to move us to act in relation to this gift.[52] The stable or habitual gift we receive from God becomes the internal principle of our spontaneous action, and in the following question on the essence of grace Aquinas will define it in more detail with the help of Aristotelian categories. This gift, however, is not the whole story: by the time he wrote the *Summa* Aquinas had come to appreciate it very much in the context of the divine "assistance" (*auxilium*), which is required as much for our continuing action as for the presence of the internal gift. What Aquinas is aiming to do is to follow the trajectory set by Augustine against Pelagianism, especially against what scholars now call "Semipelagianism," by eliminating any way in which a loophole is left whereby some aspect of the need for grace is disregarded. For Aquinas, the supernatural *means* by which we are brought to our supernatural *goal* must similarly lie just as much beyond our natural capacities to obtain for ourselves.[53] To think that we do not need grace to obtain grace is a

---

[49] Wawrykow, "Grace," p. 196.   [50] *ST* I, q. 95, a. 4, ad 1.
[51] For the Prime Mover, see, e.g., *Physics* VIII,5–6 (256a4–260a19).
[52] E.g. *ST* I-II, q. 109, a. 9.   [53] *SCG* III, ch. 147.

mark of the doctrine of the Pelagians (that is, the "Semipelagians"). In pursuit of the goal of excluding Pelagianism, Aquinas establishes this second twofold dependence on divine grace—God's moving us to act *as well as* an internal gift—with the help of the Aristotelian ideas of *motus* and the Prime Mover.

Aquinas speaks for the first time of *motus* in the *Summa*'s treatise of grace in connection with *natural* human knowledge. "*Motus*" represents Aristotle's use of "movement," which includes not simply change of place but every kind of physical change.[54] On his Aristotelian account of the physical world, Aquinas holds that *motus* always requires not only a form or internal principle of motion or action in a body, but also the active motion of a higher, primary mover. One can sense already here the distinction Aquinas is to make between the internal *donum* of grace and the gracious motion of the divine *auxilium*. The example given by Aquinas from the perspective of his Aristotelian scientific worldview is fire being able to give heat not only on account of its intrinsic heat, but also through the actual motion of a heavenly body, which is the "prime mover" in this particular order of bodily realities.[55] What concerns us more than such examples is how Aquinas understands this twofold dependence to extend far beyond the physical world. He was encouraged in this by the discovery that Aristotle himself had also refused to limit the influence of the Prime Mover to the merely physical.[56]

Like Aristotle then, Aquinas also used the concept of *motus* to cover those rational, free acts that pertain to human nature, acts that are not the acts of any corporeal organ and transcend the merely physical.[57] In the treatise on grace, he first applies the twofold pattern of dependence to natural acts of the intellect.[58] He justifies this application by saying that, for Aristotle, *any* use or exercise, including acts of knowing and willing, implies some movement, taking the latter word in a broad sense.[59] Ultimately all created movements and changes in the natural order, whether physical or spiritual, are derived from God, who is the Prime Mover not just in some particular aspect of nature but without qualification. Every such movement thus depends on God's assistance in two ways, first by the fact that the internal form by which something acts has been established by God the "Prime Actuality" (*primus actus*), and secondly by the fact that that which acts is moved to action by God the Prime Mover (*primum movens*). In the case of natural human knowledge, the internal principle in question is the natural light of the human intellect that comes with the endowment of nature. The establishment of this internal principle by the Prime Actuality does not, however, exhaust

---

[54] Aristotle, *Physics* V,1–2 (224a21–226b17).   [55] *ST* I-II, q. 109, a. 1.
[56] Aristotle, *Eudemian Ethics* VII,14 (1248a18–29). A fragment of this work was known to Aquinas's age as the *Liber de bona fortuna*.
[57] Aristotle, *De anima* III,4 (429a25–27); Aquinas, *ST* I, q. 75, a. 2.
[58] *ST* I, q. 109, a. 1.   [59] See Aristotle, *De anima* III,4 (429b25) and III,7 (431a4).

natural dependence on God: the intellect is also dependent on the Prime Mover for its actual movement or act of knowing.[60]

This reliance on divine motion, as well as on an internal principle, holds for all free action in regard to natural good.[61] Aquinas had puzzled over the thought that, given that a human being is master of his or her acts, the question of whether or not to deliberate over some action would be subject to some preceding deliberation, and then so on back to infinity. An infinite chain of acts of deliberation was not something that could be thought reasonable, and Aquinas adopted Aristotle's solution: at some point in the chain one must reach not another act of deliberation but the motion of something higher than human reason, namely, the Prime Mover.[62] Aquinas, for whom creaturely freedom was established rather than removed by its dependence on God, concluded that even a human being with a nature undamaged by the Fall is not master of his or her acts so as not to need the motion of the Prime Mover for his or her action.[63] Thus, for any free act of will in the natural order, as for intellect, one depends not only on one's internal power, but on the divine motion also.

This twofold pattern of dependence Aquinas applies not just in Aristotelian fashion to the entire natural order, but to the supernatural order as well. Thus, where there is required to be the gift of some supernatural internal principle in order to widen the stable scope of human action beyond the limitations of nature, the twofold structure of dependence that Aquinas identifies in the natural order persists. For example, nature's range of knowledge is surpassed by the light of faith or prophecy as an internal light of grace given by God, and here too the act of faith or prophecy remains dependent on the intellect being moved by God, just as the intellect is dependent on God's motion for an act of knowledge in the natural order.[64] This need for gracious divine assistance so as to act well in regard to the supernatural good by way of charity runs throughout Aquinas's account of the need for grace. Such assistance in the supernatural order is needed for perseverance in grace to the very end of this life,[65] and will still be required for action even in the next life, where grace is brought to perfection in the heavenly state of glory.[66] In this context of human need for the supernatural, the divine *auxilium* is grace,[67] and Aquinas has offered a theological explanation for the work of this grace with the help of the principle of *motus*, which he had drawn from the philosophy of Aristotle.

This approach provides Aquinas with a way to deal more thoroughly with the challenge of Pelagianism, and its denial of the depth of our need of divine

---

[60] *ST* I-II, q. 109, a. 1.   [61] *ST* I-II, q. 109, a. 2.
[62] Aristotle, *Eudemian Ethics* VII,14 (1248a18–29).
[63] *ST* I-II, q. 109, a. 2, ad 1.   [64] *ST* I-II, q. 109, a. 1.
[65] *ST* I-II, q. 109, a. 10.   [66] *ST* I-II, q. 109, a. 9, ad 1.
[67] Te Velde, *Aquinas on God*, p. 152.

grace in the name of human freedom, than he had done in his previous writings.[68] In answer to the query as to whether a human being *needs grace* in order to prepare himself or herself for grace, following Augustine he wants to reply that it is *only by grace* that people can prepare themselves for grace. He puts against himself the objection that this must imply an unseemly regression: in preparation for each grace a previous grace is needed, and for that another is needed, and so on to infinity.[69] This he answers through his application of the Aristotelian concept of *motus* to the priority of grace. He definitely concedes that the objection would have a point, if one thought of grace only in terms of the internal gift, which itself prepares us to do the supernatural good.[70] On the principle that every form requires the recipient to be disposed for it, this gift does indeed require some kind of preparation of its own. However, this preparation is not another gift of the same type. Aquinas avoids the need for a regression to infinity by attributing the preparation for the gift not to yet another such gift but to the gracious motion of the Prime Mover.[71] Hence it is by *this* grace moving us interiorly that we prepare ourselves for the stable gift of grace, and so any Pelagian account of our preparation is ruled out. The life of grace begins with grace, but not every use of the word "grace" is the same. Without this distinction of graces, it is difficult to see how Aquinas could rule out Pelagianism so thoroughly, because without his doctrine of the divine motion, human beings would be able to move themselves to act in the supernatural order on the basis of the internal gift. In those circumstances, though this gift is a gift, it could more easily be misconceived in Pelagian style as something possessed over against God.

5.2. THE ESSENCE OF GRACE

What then is the essence of grace? From a broad picture of our need of grace, Aquinas now trains his focus on what exactly this grace is that we need so profoundly. Aquinas was aware that the word *gratia* had different, but related, uses, in both ordinary and theological speech. One distinction he makes in regard to the grace of God is between (1) God himself and (2) the gift God gives us that is not God himself but a participation in the divine. From God's general love by which he bestows natural being on all things, Aquinas distinguishes the special love by which God wills rational creatures to a supernatural

---

[68] Bouillard, *Conversion et grâce*, pp. 92–123, has argued influentially that the basic difference between Aquinas's account in the *Summa* and earlier accounts was based on increased knowledge of Augustine's rejection of Semipelagianism.

[69] *ST* I-II, q. 109, a. 6, arg. 3.   [70] *ST* I-II, q. 109, a. 6, ad 3.

[71] *ST* I-II, q. 109, a. 6, ad 3.

participation in his own good. The latter is one sense of grace: God's eternal love, *God himself* willing himself to the rational creature as its supernatural goal, God graciously predestining or choosing some to be his adopted children, and so on.[72] Under this heading would also fall *God himself* graciously moving us to act for the supernatural good, the divine motion. To define the very essence of *this* grace more precisely is not going to be a course open to Aquinas in his search to say what more precisely grace is: for Aquinas the essence of God just cannot be defined, as though God were a member of some wider class.[73] Rather God is no creature, but the Creator of all things.

With whatever is not God, however, matters are different. Here we are concerned with the differences that God's special love makes in the creature, the results of divine favor. Referring back to the twofold dependence on grace he established in the previous question, Aquinas mentions here two kinds of gracious effect, namely, where the soul is moved by God to an *action* in the supernatural order, and the stable, habitual *gift* given by God.[74] With reference to *Physics* III,3 (202a13) he declares the former to be movements of the soul.[75] The essence of the latter (what the theologians of Aquinas's day were driving at when they said that "grace places something in the soul"[76]) Aquinas sets out to explore at greater length. Elsewhere he had noted that in his own day the term *gratia* was usually used for this habitual gift.[77] The definition of this grace, since it is not God but a participation in God, Aquinas *can* set within his sights, and he does so with the help of Aristotle's *Categories*.

Aquinas's initial move is to locate this grace, that by which the recipient participates in the divine nature, in the Aristotelian category of *quality*.[78] According to Aristotle, quality is that in virtue of which something is said to be such-and-such.[79] Aquinas reads Aristotle as providing ten categories of being, of which quality is one. The first category overall is substance, and the other nine, of which quality is one, are accidents. Thus in declaring the gift of grace to be a quality, he was declaring it to be an accidental rather than a substantial mode of being. While a substance is a stand-alone being, so to speak, a subsisting thing in itself, the accidents have their being only *in* a substance and not in their own right. For example, the accident of whiteness has being only insofar as something, some substance, is white. Aquinas takes it from Aristotle that an accident is more properly said to be *of a being* than *a being*.[80] Thus it is substances that are properly said to exist, while accidents are said to "co-exist" in their substances.[81] Returning to the example of whiteness, it is the white substance that exists, strictly speaking, while the whiteness

---

[72] *ST* I-II, q. 110, a. 1.   [73] *ST* I, q. 3, a. 5.   [74] *ST* I-II, q. 110, a. 2.
[75] *ST* I-II, q. 110, a. 2.   [76] "Gratia ponat aliquid in anima." Cf. *ST* I-II, q. 110, a. 1.
[77] *De veritate*, q. 24, a. 14.   [78] *ST* I-II, q. 110, a. 2.
[79] Aristotle, *Categories* 8 (8b25).   [80] Aristotle, *Metaphysics* VII,1 (1028a18).
[81] *ST* I, q. 45, a. 4, corpus.

"co-exists" in it. Thus an accident comes into existence or goes out of existence only insofar as its substance begins or ceases to be in the mode of that accidental being: whiteness comes in and out of existence only insofar as some substance begins or ceases to be white.[82]

This then is what we also have with that accident which is the habitual gift of grace. By understanding it to be an accident rather than a substance, Aquinas avoids "reifying" it, as though it were some kind of stand-alone subsistent reality in its own right, which comes into existence or goes out of existence in its own right. In this sense grace is not some kind of "thing" intruded into the human being. Rather it exists only insofar as an intellectual creature, its recipient, is "graced," just as whiteness exists only insofar as something is white. Again, by understanding this gift as an accident, Aquinas avoids any sense in which the human recipient might be changed by it into something else, at the loss of the recipient's humanity. Instead, the human substance remains human substance.

In his theory of *motus*, Aristotle distinguished "accidental change," where the substance remains the same while gaining or losing some accident, from "substantial change" of one thing into something else, where the original substance ceases to be.[83] By placing the gift of grace in the category of accident, Aquinas avoids any sense that it removes our humanity, any sense that deification makes us no longer human, any sense that human nature is not of intrinsic worth in God's good creation. There is no substantial change of the human substance, nor even some kind of miraculous transubstantiation.[84] It is rather that a human substance begins to participate in the divine nature.

It is worth noting that, although it plays no formal part in the definition,[85] this accident is something *created* or rather "co-created." Indeed, it is the fact that this gift is *not* the uncreated God that opens up the possibility of the search for its definition. Setting Aristotle's categories within his own metaphysics of creation, Aquinas says that it is substances that are properly said to be "created" (*creatae*), while accidents are better said to be "co-created" (*concreata*) in their substances. This is of course because accidents have their existence only in substances. It is the white *substance* that is created and exists, strictly speaking, while the whiteness is "co-created" and "co-exists" with it, and comes in and out of existence only insofar as the substance begins or ceases to be white.[86] Though he never speaks explicitly of grace as "co-created," it is in this accidental sense that Aquinas must maintain that grace is created, not as a self-subsisting being, but as a co-created quality of its created recipient.

---

[82] *ST* I-II, q. 110, a. 2, ad 3.   [83] Aristotle, *Physics* I,7 (190a31–b9).
[84] See *ST* III, q. 75.   [85] *ST* I, q. 44, a. 1, ad 1.
[86] *ST* I, q. 45, a. 4; *ST* I-II, q. 110, a. 3, ad 3.

Aquinas deploys this understanding of grace as accidental being to interpret the Pauline Epistles' use of the language of creation with regard to grace. When Eph 2:10 says that we have been "created in Christ for good works," Aquinas argues from context (2:8–9) that this "creation" refers not to any creation *ex nihilo* (with no preceding matter) but to our constitution "in new being" (*in novo esse*), that is, with *no preceding merits on our part.*[87] In this light he interprets Paul's talk in Gal 6:15 of a "new creature," which he takes to refer to the gift of grace,[88] to mean that *humans* are "created" insofar as they are constituted in this new (co-created) accidental mode of being. This explains for him why the Epistles can speak of grace as "created."[89] He himself seems to prefer to speak of a "*re*-creation" (*recreatio*).[90] Of course in a more general sense of "creation," this gift is dependent on God for its very being, just as Aquinas holds every being *of whatever mode* so to depend on God.[91] In this sense he can say himself that it is "something created" (*quiddam creatum*).[92] Thus he had also spoken in an earlier work of "created grace" (*gratia creata*), though only rarely and in the context of distinguishing it in the soul of Christ from his unique grace of union, which Aquinas insists is *un*created.[93]

In firmly maintaining that the gift of grace was a quality, Aquinas prevented it from being confused with any other category of accident. It is not in the categories of quantity or position, for example. However, there is more work for Aquinas to do here, because in *Categories* 8 (8b26–10a25) Aristotle had further divided quality into habits and dispositions, natural capacities and incapacities, passions and passible qualities and affections, and shape. So which kind of quality is grace? Taking them in reverse order, Aquinas concedes that the gift of grace cannot be a shape, because it is not bodily. Likewise, Aquinas thinks it is not a matter of passion, because it is not a gift to the sensitive part of the soul, given that this is where Aristotle places passions in *Physics* VII,3 (245b3). Again, neither is it a matter of innate capacities and incapacities, because these refer to nature, while grace is supernatural, nor is it related to good and evil as a natural capacity is.[94] Finally this leaves habits and dispositions, and Aquinas takes grace to be in *this* division of quality. For Aristotle, habits are stable dispositions,[95] and, as we have already seen, Aquinas often speaks of the gift of grace as habitual. Understanding grace according to the Aristotelian concept of habit brings Aquinas a number of advantages: he can underline its stability as a gift, and explain how grace can

---

[87] *ST* I-II, q. 110, a. 2, ad 3. See also *In Ad Ephesios*, ch. 2, lect. 3.

[88] *ST* I-II, q. 110, a. 2, arg. 3; q. 112, a. 2, arg. 3. Cf. *In Ad Galatas*, ch. 6, lect. 4.

[89] Previously, when he had held there to be no instrumental causes of grace, Aquinas had explained this creation language with reference to the absence of instrumental causes in the divine act of creation. See *In IV Sent.*, dist. 5, q. 1, a. 2.

[90] *ST* I-II, q. 110, a. 4, corpus.   [91] See *ST* I, q. 44, a. 1.

[92] *ST* III, q. 7, a. 11, sed contra.   [93] *De veritate*, q. 29.

[94] *ST* I-II, q. 110, a. 3, arg. 3.   [95] Aristotle, *Categories* 8 (8b27–28).

be greater or less in different recipients in the manner that a habit can be greater or less in relation to its subject.[96] Just as someone can be more or less courageous, so he or she can be more or less graced.

Despite this move, however, Aquinas is careful not to reduce the habit of grace to a virtue, virtue and vice being further concepts for which he and his contemporaries were indebted to Aristotle. Aquinas knew that what was often said about virtues suited grace too,[97] and that many theologians thought grace and virtue ultimately identical.[98] It was easy to make a case against himself that grace was the same as virtue, since virtues are habits of the mind, and it is in the mind rather than the sensitive part of the soul that Aquinas wanted to locate the gift of grace.[99] Aquinas manages to distinguish grace from virtue, however, by appealing to what Aristotle had to say about virtue in relation to nature. He quotes *Physics* VII,3 (246a13) to the effect that a virtue disposes something *in accordance with its nature*. Aquinas draws the conclusion that to speak of something's virtue is to do so *in reference to* its pre-existing nature.[100] He now looks back to his treatment of virtues earlier in the *Summa* as internal principles by which we make our way to happiness.[101] He says that when he covered those virtues that can be naturally acquired by people, he was speaking of what disposed them in accordance with their nature, by which they were already human.

Aquinas also spoke, however, of what Aristotle did not, namely, *infused* virtues as habitual dispositions that could not be naturally acquired.[102] We have already mentioned two virtues that cannot be naturally acquired but that are infused, namely, faith and charity.[103] The infused virtues, Aquinas says, dispose us not in accordance with our nature, but in accordance with our higher, supernatural end, and hence with a higher nature. Aristotle's principle that virtue perfects in accordance with a nature is thus crucial: it is just that in the case of the infused virtues, it is not our human nature that is at stake. Here he quotes 2 Pet 1:4, saying that by participation in the divine nature we are regenerated as sons of God. The infused virtues thus dispose us in accordance with a participation in the divine nature, such that grace differs from virtue as this prior participation.[104] The habit of grace is then a sort of "new nature" that we have *by participation* in the nature of God. Though it belongs among the habits within Aristotle's category of quality, it does not do so as a virtue but as a habitual state that the infused virtues presuppose as their "principle and root."[105] Without Aristotle's distinction between virtue and nature, it is

---

[96] *ST* I-II, q. 112, a. 4. Cf. q. 114, a. 8.   [97] *ST* I-II, q. 110, a. 3, arg. 2.
[98] *ST* I-II, q. 110, a. 3.   [99] *ST* I-II, q. 110, a. 3, arg. 3.
[100] *ST* I-II, q. 110, a. 3.   [101] *ST* I-II, qq. 55–67.   [102] *ST* I-II, q. 63.
[103] *ST* II-II, q. 6, a. 1; q. 24, a. 2.   [104] *ST* I-II, q. 100, a. 3.
[105] *ST* I-II, q. 110, a. 3, ad 3.

difficult to see how Aquinas could have made a case against his contemporaries for a distinction between grace and virtue.

Aquinas fills out this picture by asking where grace is to be located within the human being. Virtues as concerned with operation have their subject, according to Aquinas, in the capacities or powers of the soul: they dispose these powers to their proper activity.[106] Faith, for example, is in the power of the intellect, disposing us to acts of belief, and charity in the power of the will, disposing us to acts of love. For Aquinas, to locate the habit of grace in a power of the soul would be to treat it precisely as such a virtue.[107] Instead, for the very root of the virtues he has another subject, namely, the root of the powers themselves. In his treatment of the soul as such, Aquinas had distinguished the soul from its capacities by speaking of the soul in terms of its own nature or essence,[108] a distinction he had supported through an application of Aristotle's distinction between first and second actuality.[109] The distinction between the essence and powers of the soul was itself not uncontroversial at the time, but it had brought advantage to Aquinas in dealing with the relationship between the subsistent soul and the body of which it was a form in the context of his appropriation of Aristotle's teaching in the *De anima*. Now it was to bring him the advantage of being able to locate the root of the virtues in the root of the powers:

> For just as through the intellectual power a human being participates in the divine knowledge through the virtue of faith, and according to the power of will participates in the divine love through the virtue of charity, so also through the "nature of the soul" he participates in the divine nature according to a certain similitude, through a certain regeneration or recreation.[110]

What this means is that, at bottom, the impact of grace is not merely at the level of the powers of knowing and willing but is a yet more profound transformation: Aquinas's personalism is rooted in a deeper metaphysics, a recreation across the soul that goes from its action right down to the depths of its being. Given his distinction between the essence of the soul and its capacities, Aquinas's doctrine of recreation by grace would have neglected a key aspect of the soul, had the gift of grace not been distinguished from virtue and placed "deeper" than it. Instead his doctrine of grace is truly wholistic—no depth of the soul is left untouched—and it is on the basis of Aristotle's understanding of the relationship between nature and virtue that Aquinas argues to this conclusion.

---

[106] *ST* I-II, q. 56, a. 1.   [107] *ST* I-II, q. 110, a. 4.   [108] *ST* I, q. 77, a. 1.

[109] Aristotle, *De anima* II,1 (412a22–28).

[110] *ST* I-II, q. 110, a. 4, corpus: "Sicut enim per potentiam intellectivam homo participat cognitionem divinam per virtutem fidei, et secundum potentiam voluntatis amorem divinum per virtutem caritatis, ita etiam per naturam animae participat secundum quamdam similitudinem naturam divinam per quamdam regenerationem, sive recreationem." See also q. 50, a. 2.

Having focused on the essence of grace, Aquinas then begins to broaden the picture once more, eventually coming to place it in the context of its cause and then of its effects. Now Aquinas cannot be concerned with any cause of grace insofar as grace is God himself, since the First Cause is in every way *un-caused*.[111] Rather his concern is mainly to seek to explain how the habit of grace comes to be in its recipient. To perform this and other such theological inquiries, Aquinas's theological work draws inter alia on Aristotle's fourfold explanatory scheme as found in *Physics* II,3 (194b16–195b29) and *Metaphysics* V,2 (1013a24–1014a25). Aristotle had used his scheme flexibly of both natural and artificial realities. Aquinas used it more flexibly still, putting to fresh use Aristotle's material, formal, efficient, and final causes of realities, their changes and stability. He begins by asking whether God alone is the *efficient* cause of habitual grace. Aristotle had spoken of the original source of some change of rest as a cause, giving the examples of someone making a plan or fathering a child, a doer or maker of something.[112] In this case then Aquinas is seeking to explain how the habit of grace comes to be in its recipient with reference to the agent that produces it. His starting point is that this habit is "a certain participation in the divine nature" (*quaedam participatio divinae naturae*), and the divine nature of course surpasses every other (created) nature. He thus concludes that no creature has the power to cause grace, or else that creature would be acting beyond the capacities of its nature by causing an effect of greater power than itself. With every creature ruled out, it is clear that only God can "deify" (*deificare*) the rational creature, that is, bestow on it a share in the divine nature through his being the efficient cause of some participated likeness given to it.[113]

What is important to note, however, is that Aquinas takes this conclusion to count only for the *principal* efficient cause, leaving open the possibility of the subordinate involvement of creaturely causes in the efficient causation of grace.[114] Both Christ and the sacraments he instituted for the New Law play an important role for Aquinas in the communication of grace to its recipients.[115] The habit of grace is found in the soul of Christ, who is the Head of the Body, and his members receive grace by a share in the grace of the Head.[116] Scripture, moreover, suggested to Aquinas a role for the sacraments in the causation of grace when it spoke of such things as our being saved "through the bath of regeneration" (Titus 3:5).[117] Aquinas knew and retrieved the patristic doctrine of Christ's humanity as an "instrument" (*organum*) of the divinity. It has often been supposed that Aquinas also applied a concept of "instrumental causality" from Aristotle to Christ's humanity and the

---

[111] See *ST* I, q. 2, a. 3.   [112] Aristotle, *Physics* II,3 (194b29–31).
[113] *ST* I-II, q. 112, a. 1, corpus.   [114] Cf. *De veritate*, q. 27, aa. 3–4.
[115] See Chapters 9 and 10 in this work.   [116] *ST* III, q. 8.   [117] *ST* III, q. 62, a. 1.

sacraments,[118] but the extent of Aristotle's contribution has been called into question.[119] When speaking of the final cause, the end or goal that something is for, Aristotle had spoken also of drugs and tools used for an end,[120] and his commentators had developed from this and other texts the notion of an instrumental cause employed by the agent to attain its goal.[121]

Aquinas refined his own notion of instrumental causality, where the instrument does its work through the motion of the principal cause, and he applies this systematically to Christ's humanity and the sacraments later in the *Summa*.[122] Thus, while God is the principal cause of grace, Christ's humanity and the sacraments are its instrumental causes. Whereas in earlier works Aquinas had limited their instrumental causation to producing a disposition for grace, he now thinks of them as instrumentally causing grace itself. Thus what Aquinas has to make clear in the treatise on grace is why Christ's humanity and the sacraments can cause grace instrumentally but not principally: the deifying power by which they perform their action is not one that belongs to Christ's humanity or the sacramental signs in their own right, but is rather the power of the divinity, the principal agent, that deploys them as instruments.[123] While Aristotle hardly has anything like so advanced an account of instrumental causality, there is no doubt that Aquinas, in developing his very own account of the instrumental causation of grace, did so within the matrix of the philosophical tradition stemming from Aristotle and the latter's wider explanatory scheme. It is this that in part enabled him both to deny that a creature could be the principal efficient cause of grace *and* to recognize a true instrumental role for the sacraments in grace's causation. Aquinas thus satisfied his anti-Manichaean desire to uphold the intrinsic goodness of material realities, which God uses in the sacraments to communicate spiritual realities, while at the same time reserving the primacy in the causation of grace to the gracious motion of God himself.

---

[118] Hyacinthe-François Dondaine, OP, "À propos d'Avicenne et de S. Thomas: De la causalité dispositive à la causalité instrumentale," *RThom* 51 (1951): pp. 441–53; Louis-Marie Chauvet, *Symbol and Sacrament: A Sacramental Reinterpretation of Christian Existence*, trans. Patrick Madigan and Madeleine Beaumont (Collegeville, MN: Liturgical Press, 1995), pp. 15–21.

[119] Mark D. Jordan, "Theology and Philosophy," in *The Cambridge Companion to Aquinas*, edited by Norman Kretzmann and Eleonore Stump (Cambridge: Cambridge University Press, 1993), pp. 232–51, at 241–7; Bernhard Blankenhorn, OP, "The Instrumental Causality of the Sacraments: Thomas Aquinas and Louis-Marie Chauvet," *Nova et Vetera* 4 (2006): pp. 255–93.

[120] Aristotle, *Physics* II,3 (195a1); *Metaphysics* V,2 (1013b3).

[121] Aristotle, *Physics* II,7 (198a24–30); *Generation of Animals* I,22 (730b9–24); *Parts of Animals* I,1 and I,5 (642a11 and 645b14); *Metaphysics* IV,3 (381a10); *De anima* II,1 (412b11) and III,8 (432a2); *Meteorologica* IV,3 (381a10).

[122] *ST* III, q. 8, a. 1, ad 1; q. 62, a. 1.   [123] *ST* I-II, q. 112, a. 2, ad 1.

5.3. GRACE'S MATERIAL, FORMAL,
AND FINAL CAUSES

After the efficient cause of grace, Aquinas turned to the material and formal causes. On Aristotle's scheme, the matter is that out of which something is made: he gives the example from artifice of the bronze of a statue.[124] The form in this case would be the statue's shape, that by which the bronze was a statue rather than just a lump of bronze. As we noted above (in section 5.2), Aristotle applied his scheme flexibly, and Aquinas was to apply it more flexibly still. In the case of the habit of grace, we do not have a form by which the recipient is what he or she is substantially—grace does not form the recipient to be human out of a mass of flesh and bones. On Aquinas's Aristotelian scheme it is the *soul* that is the "substantial form" of a human being.[125] The medievals, however, distinguished "accidental forms" from "substantial forms." As we saw above (in section 5.2), Aquinas had placed the habit of grace in the category of accident, and grace is thus the "accidental form" by which a human being is now made a participant in the divine nature. However, given the principle that no form can exist in matter unless that matter is disposed for it, Aquinas says its human recipient must in some way be disposed for this form of grace. Hence Aquinas has to raise a query about the disposition for grace required in its recipient.

In his response Aquinas is able to draw on what he had already established in the treatise on grace with the help of the Aristotelian concept of *motus*. The first thing he does is to recall the distinction between grace as habit and grace as divine assistance moving the soul to good. Taking grace in the former sense, it of course requires a disposition in the matter, as we have just seen. But what is this disposition? Aquinas notes that Scripture speaks of people being told to prepare to meet God, to prepare their hearts for him, and so on.[126] In anti-Manichaean fashion Aquinas is absolutely committed to the reality and role of free will. Now to explain this preparation for grace on the part of human free will, Aquinas turns to the other basic meaning of "grace" he has distinguished. Here he finds an answer to the question of how matter comes to be perfected by its new form, given the principle that matter does not move itself to perfection: it is moved by the divine motion.[127] Now taking "grace" as meaning the divine *auxilium* that moves the soul to act in regard to the good, Aquinas recalls that there can be no preparation *for this assistance* on the part of the recipient's free will. Rather, God principally and graciously moves the free will towards the good.[128] But in this movement of the free will,

---

[124] Aristotle, *Physics* II,3 (194b23–25); *Metaphysics* V,2 (1013a24–26).
[125] Aristotle, *De anima* II,1 (412b4). See Chapter 3 in this work.
[126] *ST* I-II, q. 112, a. 2, sed contra.   [127] See *SCG* III, ch. 149.
[128] *ST* I-II, q. 112, a. 2.

which depends on the grace of God the Prime Mover, we have the ultimate preparation required *for the habit of grace*. Thus God as an agent of infinite power causes instantaneously *both* the form of grace *and* the disposition of the matter for the form.[129] Aquinas has again, with the help of Aristotelian concepts, more thoroughly ruled out any Pelagian role for free will at the expense of grace. Even the will's preparation for (habitual) grace is the fruit of grace (the assistance of the Prime Mover). Insofar as the preparation arises from free will, it can have no necessary claim on habitual grace, which exceeds any preparation of human virtue, but insofar as it arises from divine motion it will be unfailingly accompanied by habitual grace.[130]

Aquinas does not have a separate article to treat the final cause of grace, but the purpose and end of grace has been in view throughout the treatise: grace heals and elevates us so that God can bring us to himself; it grants us a certain participation in the divine nature, which is the seed of a full participation in the divine nature in heaven. As we saw above (in section 5.1), this broader perspective was established before Aquinas focused on defining the essence of grace. Moreover, in the midst of his treatise he has already summarized a pathway of effects of grace in the following manner:

> There are five effects of grace in us, the first of which is that the soul be healed, the second that good be willed, the third that the good willed be efficaciously performed, the fourth that there be perseverance in the good, and the fifth that there be arrival at glory.[131]

In his scriptural commentaries especially, he is also cognizant of the need to relate the biblical categories of justification, sanctification, regeneration, and so on.[132] What Aquinas does at the conclusion of his question on the cause of grace in the *Summa* is not to ask about the final cause, but to look in another way at the immediate purposes fulfilled by grace under the heading of its "effects" in this life.

The immediate effect of grace in this life is indicated in one way by Aquinas's preferred term for the habit of grace: *gratia gratum faciens*, which is conventionally translated as "sanctifying grace." This grace makes us graced, united to God: through this accidental form God makes us pleasing and acceptable to himself, sanctified and holy.[133] What Aquinas now does in two questions is to give a basic division of two immediate effects of grace by a creative use of Augustine's distinction between operative and cooperative

---

[129] *ST* I-II, q. 112, a. 2, ad 3.   [130] *ST* I-II, q. 112, a. 3.

[131] *ST* I-II, q. 111, a. 3, corpus: "Sunt autem quinque effectus gratiae in nobis: quorum primus est, ut anima sanetur; secundus, ut bonum velit; tertius est, ut bonum quod vult, efficaciter operetur; quartus est, ut in bono perseveret; quintus est, ut ad gloriam perveniat."

[132] For Aquinas on the relationship between adoption, regeneration, sanctification, justification, and so on, see Keating, "Justification."

[133] *ST* I-II, q. 111, a. 1.

grace, which he had already applied across the more Aristotelian distinction between habit and motion from the Prime Mover.[134] In the case of cooperative grace, we shall have the effect of merit, where the mind is not only moved by God but also itself actively moves in such a way that the operation is attributed to the soul as well as to God. From operative grace, however, we have the prior effect of justification, where God alone is the mover and the operation attributed to him only.[135] Thus Aquinas speaks of *gratia gratum faciens* in this context as "the gift of justifying grace" (*donum gratiae iustificantis*).[136] In this way he continues his plan, having focused on the essence of grace, of viewing it in the wider perspective not only of its cause but also of its effects in this life, namely, justification, where sin is forgiven, and merit, whereby the justified deserve the final reward of heaven. As we shall see, he is accompanied in all this by the same Aristotelian aids to theological understanding, especially the divine *motus*, which have proved so useful up till now, but also by Aristotelian notions of justice.

Following Augustine, medieval theologians interpreted the Pauline language of justification as involving the *making just* of the sinner. Aquinas's choice of putting this language at the center of his account of the effect of operative grace continues the "wholistic" character of his thinking that we noted in connection with his location of the habitual gift in the essence of the soul. His explanation for the forgiveness of sins being named from "justice" (as "justification") rather than from faith or charity, despite the involvement of these latter in forgiveness, is that faith and charity only refer to a *particular ordering to God* in terms of intellect and will. Though he does not make the point, the same might be said in this context of the deification that is the habit of grace in the essence of the soul. Justice, in contrast, implies "the whole rectitude of order in general" (*generaliter totam rectitudinem ordinis*).[137] This rightness of order he specifies by calling on the various senses attributed to "justice" by Aristotle: the justice with which we are concerned here is not the virtue of justice that gives a certain order to human actions,[138] but rectitude of order in someone's entire interior disposition, which he says Aristotle calls "metaphorical justice."[139] This disposition involves the subjection of the lower powers to the higher, and the higher to God, and this whole process is what is brought about when one is justified by the habit of grace being present in the essence of the soul. Though Aquinas allows for the gift of justice to be given by God to one who had never sinned, referring to Adam in "original justice" before the Fall, the "justification of the ungodly" of which Paul speaks in Rom 4:5 he takes to refer to the justification of sinners, where there is a transformation of

---

[134] *ST* I-II, q. 111, a. 2.   [135] *ST* I-II, q. 113, Prologue.
[136] *ST* I-II, q. 113, a. 3, corpus.   [137] *ST* I-II, q. 113, a. 1, ad 2.
[138] Aristotle, *Nicomachean Ethics* V,1 and V,2 (1129b13 and 1130a14).
[139] Aristotle, *Nicomachean Ethics* V,11 (1138b5).

the sinner from a fallen "state of injustice" to a "state of justice."[140] And in the latter we meet a third state or condition in which human nature has existed.

To give a further theological explanation of this "being made just," Aquinas draws once again on Aristotle's idea of *motus*. Justification in its passive sense thus implies for Aquinas a "movement of the soul" towards justice, as heating by analogy implies a physical movement towards heat. Theologians had become accustomed by Aquinas's time to think of justification as a "process" of being made just, a process that involved various elements. These were normally listed in such a way as to include a reference in one way or another to the infusion of habitual grace, as well as to an act of free will, such as faith or contrition, and the forgiveness of sins. In the *Summa* Aquinas enumerates these elements as: firstly, the infusion of grace; secondly, a movement of the free will directed towards God through faith; thirdly, a movement of free will in regard to sin; and finally, the forgiveness of guilt.[141] These four elements are what is required for the complete process of justification. It is Aquinas's purpose to seek understanding of this whole process and its constituent elements with the assistance of, among other things, Aristotle's idea of motion.

Thus Aquinas takes any movement in which something is moved by something else to involve three things. The first of these is the motion given by the mover, the *motio moventis*; the second is the movement itself of what is moved, the *motus mobilis*; and the third is the consummation of the movement, that is, arrival at the movement's end term. The last of these in the movement of justification Aquinas identifies as the forgiveness of sins.[142] Without the presence of this last requirement, the whole movement of justification would be left incomplete and would not be the movement of justification at all. This identification of the forgiveness of sins with the end term had enabled him to explain why the justification of the ungodly was spoken of *as* the forgiveness of sins, though it is only one of its elements. Thinking of a movement as being defined from its end point rather than with regard to its wider content, Aquinas had already explained that justification is said to be the forgiveness of sins precisely because the latter is the end point of the whole movement.[143]

One basic question is why this overall movement from injustice to justice by grace should include a movement of human free will. As we have seen (in the present section 5.3), it is part of Aquinas's anti-Manichaean tendency to maintain the role of free will, but in such a way that by his anti-Pelagian tendency the door is closed to exaggerating its role at the expense of divine grace. Now one can easily perceive the presence of both Aristotle's notions of movement and nature in how Aquinas tackles the question. He works from the principle that God moves each thing according to its own nature. One can

---

[140] *ST* I-II, q. 113, a. 1, corpus.   [141] *ST* I-II, q. 113, a. 6.
[142] *ST* I-II, q. 113, a. 6.   [143] *ST* I-II, q. 113, a. 1; a. 6, ad 1.

observe this, he says, in the physical world, where heavy things are moved by God in one way and light things in another. The implication is that he moves human beings according to their nature too, and since by nature they have free will, he moves them according to their free will. Aquinas can then conclude that, where someone is able to exercise free will, God will not give the motion towards justice without moving the free will at the same time. At the same time as he gives the habit of justifying grace, he moves the free will to accept this gift.[144] As one can see, Aquinas is working here to exclude Pelagianism according to the same Aristotelian principles he had already applied to our preparation for grace when treating our need of grace and its cause.

So what is the act of free will that constitutes the *motus mobilis* in the case of justification? As we have already seen, Aquinas's account of the process of justification specifies two *motus*. One is the movement towards God by faith, and the other is the movement with regard to sin. There is no doubt for him that an act of faith in God must be required. In order to arrive at the forgiveness of sins, a sinner must be turned to God through divine motion, and according to Scripture the first turning or conversion happens through faith informed by charity.[145] However, in this movement of mind from one state to another there must be reference to both of its terms, the starting point as well as the end point, the state of sin as well as the state of justice. Aquinas takes up the analogy of local movement of a physical body from one place to another: the body both leaves its starting point and approaches its end point. The upshot is that in justification there is a "twofold movement of free will" (*motus liberi arbitrii duplex*), renunciation of sin and desire for God's justice.[146] Thus these two movements correspond to the *motus mobilis*.[147] Aquinas can treat them as undertaken simultaneously, because he sees no problem in willing two things at once where there is a certain unity between them. By analogy with understanding two things together at once, where subject and predicate are understood together in a single affirmation, free will can be moved simultaneously in regard to two things where there is an order of one to the other. In this case there is such a unity of order because sin is contrary to God, such that the movement of desiring union with God and the movement of renouncing sin can exist simultaneously.[148] Aquinas relates them most neatly by looking into their natural order with reference to *Physics* II,9 (200a19): in movements of the mind, the movement to the end of action comes first. This means that, according to the order of nature, the free will moves first to God as its end and consequently to remove the impediment of sin.[149]

With his typically anti-Pelagian stance, supported by the Aristotelian idea of *motus*, Aquinas rules out either of these acts taking place without grace. What

[144] *ST* I-II, q. 113, a. 5.   [145] *ST* I-II, q. 113, a. 4.
[146] *ST* I-II, q. 113, a. 5.   [147] *ST* I-II, q. 113, a. 6.
[148] *ST* I-II, q. 113, a. 7, ad 2.   [149] *ST* I-II, q. 113, a. 8, ad 3.

most definitely comes first by natural order in the overall *motus* of justification is the "pouring in" (*infusio*) of the habit of justifying grace. It is this "infusion" that leads (in a non-temporal sense) to the acts of free will and the forgiveness of sins. Aquinas explains that in any movement the motion of the mover (*motio moventis*) must come first, after which comes the *motus mobilis* or disposition of the matter, and then finally the end point of the movement where the *motio moventis* terminates. It is the *infusion* of habitual grace that comes by the primary divine motion, and so it is this infusion of grace that leads to the movements of free will by which the recipient is prepared for grace, and the forgiveness of sins.[150] To the objection that the disposition for grace, namely the movement of free will, must precede that for which it disposes, Aquinas replies that while the disposition of the recipient of grace indeed precedes the *receiving* of this form according to natural order, this disposition must itself follow the action of the agent to dispose it.

So what we have is this: according to natural order, the movement of the free will precedes the *attaining* of grace on the part of the recipient, but follows the *infusion* of grace on the part of God.[151] All of this happens simultaneously, however. God needs no period of time over which to prepare the recipient by his final disposition for the habit of grace.[152] That is not to say that there is no history of remote preparation of the sinner by the divine *auxilium*, though in cases such as Paul's conversion God can dispense even with this.[153] But it is to say that, given that God himself provides the ultimate disposition for habitual grace, his infinite power to do so cannot be hindered by any difficulty on the part of matter. Rather, he gives at the same time both grace *and* the disposition for grace. Justification, for Aquinas, is in all its elements an entirely instantaneous movement.[154] His use of Aristotle's philosophy helps him to affirm both this simultaneity and the natural priority of grace in justification.

5.4. GRACE AND MERIT

Finally, at the conclusion of his treatise on grace, and indeed on the whole moral life by which God brings us to himself, Aquinas places grace within its broadest setting as the principle of meriting the vision of God in heaven. The ultimate effect of grace in this life is the merit of heaven. Aquinas seems to have less direct use for Aristotle here as he considers the very cusp of this life. That is not to say that there is not some use that is implicit. For example, he teaches that grace is the principle of merit through charity,[155] and, as we

---

[150] *ST* I-II, q. 113, a. 8.
[152] *ST* I-II, q. 113, a. 7.
[154] *ST* I-II, q. 113, a. 7.

[151] *ST* I-II, q. 113, a. 8, ad 2.
[153] *ST* I-II, q. 112, a. 2, ad 2.
[155] *ST* I-II, q. 114, a. 4.

pointed out above (in section 5.1), Aquinas will explain charity as friendship with God with the help of Aristotle's theory of friendship. However, what Aquinas receives from authority about merit comes more through Scripture as interpreted by Augustine: heaven is a reward merited through the justifying gift of grace.[156] This doctrine he had earlier on in the *Summa* supported with Aristotle's teaching in *Nicomachean Ethics* I,9 (1099b16) that (natural) happiness is a reward for acts of (natural) goodness.[157] So, just as in the order of nature the doing of the good is rewarded by natural beatitude, by analogy the doing of the supernatural good by cooperative grace merits the supernatural beatitude of seeing God in heaven.

One place in which Aquinas does explicitly call on Aristotle in the treatise on grace is where he sets the scene for everything that will follow by establishing the very possibility of meriting something from God. His appeal to Aristotle arises from the fact that the payment of any reward for work done is an act of *justice*.[158] What kind of justice can be at work in the case of meriting heaven? As he had already drawn on Aristotle for his definitions of justice when treating justification, so Aquinas turns once again to the same place to reply to this new query. He says that, according to Aristotle, justice is a certain equality.[159] Where parties who are strictly equal are at issue, we have a quite straightforward notion of justice. Between God and human beings, however, there is the greatest inequality on account of the infinite distance between them. Hence there can be no justice between them in the straightforward sense that implies absolute equality. Aquinas saves the notion of merit from this problem by deploying a more restricted sense of justice, where each party operates according to its own different mode.[160] Aristotle provides Aquinas with analogies from the merely human sphere: a father and his son and a master and his slave are not equals, as fellow citizens are, but justice in some kind of restricted sense nevertheless prevails in these relationships.[161] On this basis, Aquinas can conclude that a son can merit from his father and a slave from his master in a restricted sense. The solution is thus that God ordains that human beings may merit from him according to a certain proportion, inasmuch as each operates according to his own mode. Again Aquinas employs an analogy Aristotelian in character: just as physical bodies obtain through their movements and operations that for which they are ordained by God, so rational creatures by their meritorious actions obtain from God a reward according to his ordination.[162]

---

[156] On Aquinas's authorities for the question of merit, see Joseph P. Wawrykow, *God's Grace and Human Action: "Merit" in the Theology of Thomas Aquinas* (Notre Dame, IN: University of Notre Dame Press, 1995), pp. 260–84.

[157] *ST* I-II, q. 5, a. 7.   [158] *ST* I-II, q. 114, a. 1.

[159] Aristotle, *Nicomachean Ethics* V,3 (1131a12).   [160] *ST* I-II, q. 114, a. 1.

[161] Aristotle, *Nicomachean Ethics* V,6 (1134a25).   [162] *ST* I-II, q. 114, a. 1.

Finally, on this basis Aquinas can turn to the issue of what may or may not be merited from God. Here one encounters the same Aristotelian principles and concepts that have served Aquinas well from the very beginning of the treatise on grace, and Aquinas continues to build on what has gone before. When asking whether someone could merit eternal life without grace, Aquinas's idea of nature, so indebted to Aristotle, appears. He answers that eternal life surpasses the proportionate order of created nature, and so no created nature is a sufficient principle of an act that merits eternal life. For this the supernatural gift of grace is required, and this applies even before the appearance of sin, which adds a second reason why humans may not merit without grace.[163]

When enquiring further into merit by grace, he yet again employs the Aristotelian concept of *motus*. For example, our merit of eternal life by grace is considered to be merit in the sense of equivalence, not in virtue of our free will, but in virtue of the power of the Holy Spirit *moving us* to eternal life: what falls under this merit is that to which the motion of his grace extends.[164] Again, the movement of the human mind in this life towards the enjoyment of God in heaven is said to be the act proper to charity.[165] When asking whether a human being can merit growth in habitual grace or charity, he says that the motion of any mover extends not only to the end point of the movement but to the entire progress of that movement. Thus one can merit not only the end of eternal life, but also the growth in grace that takes place along the way.[166] As far as perseverance on the way is concerned, it cannot be merited, because it depends only on the divine motion as the source and principle of merit.[167]

5.5. ARISTOTLE AND AQUINAS'S THEOLOGY OF GRACE: CONCLUDING REFLECTIONS

In such ways as these, Aquinas pursued theological understanding of the goodness of creation and the primacy of grace by putting philosophical concepts drawn from Aristotle into theological service. It is clear that not all of his uses of Aristotle are of the same value: his employment of Aristotelian notions of justice seems weak in the light of research into biblical notions of justice, and yet, while priority lies always with the authority of Scripture, the two sources of insight can hardly be considered by any theologian broadly favorable to Aquinas to be incompatible in principle. Again there are evident lacunae in his account, such as the role of grace in the psychology of the remote preparation for justification.[168] Of course not all of Aquinas's explicit

---

[163] *ST* I-II, q. 114, a. 2.   [164] *ST* I-II, q. 114, a. 3; cf. a. 8.
[165] *ST* I-II, q. 114, a. 4.   [166] *ST* I-II, q. 114, a. 8.
[167] *ST* I-II, q. 114, a. 9.   [168] Rondet, *The Grace of Christ*, pp. 224–36 and 244–8.

positions were always accepted throughout scholasticism, whether medieval or early modern, though some were the common currency of the schools. However, even to engage in such particular debates, such as over the distinction between grace and virtue, is to presuppose a broader framework of theological understanding informed by a certain approach to philosophy, to be guided by concepts such as natural and supernatural.

What, however, has this to do with the quest for theological understanding today? So long as it is supposed that Aquinas's philosophy and theology are serviceable only for a past era, when they draw on Aristotle and even when they do not, we cannot even properly ask whether his teaching continues to have insights for us today. Until fairly recently the theology of grace was largely pursued along the lines of a personalism, possessed of its own insights, but that had nevertheless tried to jettison the metaphysical theology of an older age, together with concepts such as the "supernatural."[169] It now seems doubtful on the basis of this experiment whether a purely personalist theology of grace can deliver everything that a theology of grace needs to deliver, and so a more metaphysical grounding is required after all. The renewal of debate over the character and function of the natural desire for the supernatural bears witness to this fact.[170] Of course the philosophical question of the validity of the concepts drawn from Aristotle cannot ultimately be avoided. What this chapter has done is to examine the presence of Aristotle's philosophy in Aquinas's theology of grace in the conviction that it contains enduring insights about the dependence of a good creation on a loving and gracious God, which contemporary theology cannot afford to ignore.

---

[169] See Piet F. Fransen, *The New Life of Grace*, trans. Georges Dupont (London: Chapman, 1969); Francis Colborn, "The Theology of Grace: Present Trends and Future Directions," *TS* 31 (1970): pp. 692–711; Haight, *The Experience and Language of Grace*.

[170] See, for instance, Lawrence Feingold, *The Natural Desire to See God according to St. Thomas Aquinas and his Interpreters*, 2nd ed. (Naples, FL: Sapientia Press, 2010).

6

Aristotle and Aquinas's Theology of Charity in the *Summa Theologiae*

Guy Mansini, OSB

In what follows, an introduction (first section) establishes a platform for understanding charity in Aquinas and lays down some main planks of his theological anthropology.[1] The second section explains how charity meets the definition of Aristotelian *philia*. According to the third section, it meets it strictly. According to the fourth section, it meets it analogically. There follows some further contrast with Aristotle in the fifth section. The sixth section rounds out St. Thomas's understanding of charity with a word about its objects and acts, and entertains two questions about how well he integrates Aristotle into his account of charity. Lastly, in the seventh section, there is a word about friendship as a necessarily created reality, not to be found in the Trinity.

6.1. NATURE AND WHAT IS BEYOND NATURE

St. Thomas thinks that it is entirely natural for man to love God above all things.[2] Why then does he think we need an infused habit, charity, in virtue of which we

---

[1] Good introductory studies include: Joseph Bobik, "Aquinas on Friendship with God," *The New Scholasticism* 60 (1986): pp. 257–71; Jordan Aumann, OP, "Thomistic Evaluation of Love and Charity," *Ang.* 55 (1978): pp. 534–56; David M. Gallagher, "Desire for Beatitude and Love of Friendship in Thomas Aquinas," *Mediaeval Studies* 58 (1996): pp. 1–47; Eberhard Schockenhoff, "The Theological Virtue of Charity (IIa IIae, qq. 23–46)," in *The Ethics of Aquinas*, edited by Stephen J. Pope (Washington, DC: Georgetown University Press, 2002), pp. 244–58; Joseph P. Wawrykow, *The Westminster Handbook to Thomas Aquinas* (Louisville, KY: Westminster John Knox Press, 2005), pp. 22–5: "Charity." More extensive treatment can be found in Michael S. Sherwin, OP, *By Knowledge and by Love: Charity and Knowledge in the Moral Theology of St. Thomas Aquinas* (Washington, DC: The Catholic University of America Press, 2005).

[2] *ST* I-II, q. 109, a. 3; for the angels, see *ST* I, q. 60, a. 5. On natural love in Aquinas, see Marie-Rosaire Gagnebet, OP, "L'amour naturel de Dieu chez saint Thomas et ses contemporains," *RThom* 48 (1948): pp. 394–446 and 49 (1949): pp. 31–102.

are to love God and fulfill the gospel precept? Is it that sin, especially the sin of Adam which enfeebles human nature itself, makes us require special help to do what nature could do before the Fall? Sin does make us need special help.[3] But that is not the fundamental reason for charity, which was given to Adam and Eve even in the first and sinless economy of salvation before the Fall.[4]

St. Thomas asks about the need for charity and the other theological virtues in the *Prima Secundae*. Man's actions direct him to happiness. But happiness is twofold. There is a natural happiness proportioned to the principles of our nature, a happiness projected by what we can naturally know and then naturally love according as we know it. It was of this happiness that Aristotle wrote in the *Nicomachean Ethics* and *Politics*. This natural happiness, however, is imperfect when compared to the happiness to which we are actually called by God, a happiness beyond the proportion of our nature, since that happiness is God's *own* happiness, the beatitude natural to divinity. Since beatitude is something proper to God alone and to the divine nature, it must be that our real ordination to that happiness presupposes a share in the divine nature itself, and that, of course, is what habitual grace is.[5] In the phrase of 2 Pet 1:4, it makes us *divinae consortes naturae* (*theias koinōnoi physeōs*).

The principles of our created nature, however, are by no means sufficient for us to attain this happiness to which we are de facto oriented by the gift of grace. "Whence it is necessary that there be divinely superadded to man principles through which he is ordered to supernatural beatitude just as he is ordered by his natural principles to his connatural end."[6] These principles are the theological virtues, which have God as their object and are infused by him into our soul.[7] They are dispositions relative to our *new* nature, are similarly supernatural and indeed derived from grace,[8] and enable a passage from grace, which conforms us to God, to our final end, when we know God even as he knows himself.[9]

Grace and the theological virtues are both required to enable us effectively to move to eternal life by meriting it, since eternal life exceeds both our natural desire and our natural ability even to know that it is our end: "Eye hath not seen nor ear heard what God has prepared for those who love him" (1 Cor 2:9), St. Thomas will repeat.[10] Faith lets us know what we cannot naturally know about our true end and the divine economy in which it is attained through those supernatural principles of knowledge that are the articles of the creed.[11] Hope emboldens us with the surety of God's power to

---

[3] *ST* I-II, q. 109, a. 3; cf. *ST* I-II, q. 85, a. 1.   [4] *ST* I, q. 95, aa. 1 and 3.

[5] *ST* I-II, q. 110, a. 3.   [6] *ST* I-II, q. 62, a. 1, corpus.

[7] *ST* I-II, q. 62, a. 1.   [8] *ST* I-II, q. 110, a. 3.

[9] Robert Sokolowski, *The God of Faith and Reason: Foundations of Christian Theology* (Notre Dame, IN: University of Notre Dame Press, 1982), pp. 79–80, remarks that the infused virtues are in some ways more like an Aristotelian power than a habit.

[10] *ST* I-II, q. 114, a. 2, corpus.   [11] *ST* I-II, q. 62, a. 3; *ST* II-II, q. 1, a. 6, ad 1, and a. 8.

help us on our way in attaining our end.[12] And charity lets us enjoy spiritual union with God even now, for the love that it empowers unites us and conforms us to him.[13]

It follows from the foregoing that the love of God above all things naturally possible to us in virtue of the sheer capacity of our created nature is by no means a love that moves us to union of life and love with God in heaven. The natural love of God is a love of God as the greatest good, who therefore ought by right and by the nature of things acting in accord with their nature to be loved just as such above all other things, as our first cause and last end.[14] This love of our first cause and last end, however, is something we share with every created thing.[15] It is not the love of God as our Father. It is not the love of Christ as our brother. It is not the love in virtue of which the Holy Spirit dwells within us as in a temple.

None of this goes without saying, of course, since so brilliant a mind as that of John Duns Scotus can suppose that the love of God above all things, fulfilling the gospel precept, is something substantially natural.[16] For Thomas it is not. And it is precisely already at this foundational point that the role of Aristotle in St. Thomas's theology of charity is to be appreciated. It consists in the firm correlation between end and nature, the understanding that a nature just is a finality to a determinate end, that one cannot define a nature without speaking of its end, and that different natures must have different ends on pain of ceasing to be different natures. Here is how he puts it in his commentary on the *Physics*:

> These things are said to be according to nature, that is to say, whatever things are moved by some intrinsic principle until they attain to some end, not to something they just happen to reach, nor by whatever principle unto whatever end you please, but by a determinate principle unto a determinate end.[17]

Nature is "a principle of motion and rest in that to which it belongs essentially and not accidentally."[18] Thus, the "motion" of which human nature is the seat cannot land a man in a beatitude that belongs to another "nature"—and here one infinitely superior, God's. If by nature we could love God's goodness just

---

[12] *ST* I-II, q. 62, a. 3, and *ST* II-II, q. 17, aa. 1–2.

[13] *ST* I-II, q. 62, a. 3, corpus and ad 3.   [14] *ST* I-II, q. 62, a. 1, ad 3.

[15] See *SCG* III, chs. 17–20; *ST* I, q. 44, a. 4, ad 3; q. 103, a. 2.

[16] John Duns Scotus, *Ordinatio* III, dist. 27, a. un., nos. 53 and 63, in John Duns Scotus, *Opera omnia*, vol. 10, *Ordinatio: Liber tertius, a distinctione vigesima sexta ad quadragesimam*, ed. Commissio Scotistica (Vatican City: Typis Vaticanis, 2007), pp. 72 and 77.

[17] *In Physic.* II, lect. 14 (no. 267): "Haec enim dicuntur esse secundum naturam, quaecumque ab aliquo principio intrinseco moventur continue, quousque perveniant ad aliquem finem; non in quodcumque contingens, neque a quocumque principio in quemcumque finem, sed a determinato principio in determinatum finem."

[18] In the Latin St. Thomas worked with: "principium motus et quietis in eo in quo est primo et per se et non secundum accidens" (*Physics* II,1 [192b22–23]).

as he does and as our own fulfillment, then we would be God. On the other hand, if our end by God's will unexpectedly and unpredictably really *is* God's end—his beatitude—then we are not proportioned to it, ordered to it, by our nature. We must have superadded principles of operation really to incline us to it and really to enable us to place those acts that direct us to it, step by step, and merit for us its last bestowal.

Now, this underlying *basso sostenuto* of Aristotle's grasp of what a nature is, and how it is known according to its operations, and how it cannot be understood without seeing its finality unto its own discrete and determinate end, an end distinct from the ends of whatever other natures there may be, supports a brighter, more richly enjoyable melody when Thomas comes around to saying what charity is.[19]

6.2. WHAT CHARITY IS

When St. Thomas treats the theological virtue of charity in *ST* II-II, the initial question he poses is whether charity is a kind of friendship.[20] He means friendship as Aristotle understands it in the *Nicomachean Ethics*, and indicates this from the three arguments to the contrary, all of which appeal to the authority of Book VIII of the *Nicomachean Ethics*. He answers by reconstituting the definition of true friendship in that same book. First, friendly love must be for the sake of the friend, for his or her good; it must be a benevolent love. In this way, it is not like the love of wine, which does not terminate in the wine, but in the one who drinks it. *Amor amicitiae* is not *amor concupiscentiae*.[21] Second, the benevolence must be mutual. Both of these things are specified in chapter 2 of Book VIII. In order to count charity as an instance of friendship, St. Thomas then recalls the ninth chapter of the same book, where Aristotle observes that the presupposition of friendship is some sort of

---

[19] This Aristotelian base line itself is quite indispensable to St. Thomas's view of the relation of the creature to creator, however much it is modified by the Neoplatonism he receives from St. Augustine, Dionysius the Areopagite, the *Book of Causes*, and so on. This metaphysical enrichment does not abolish the fact that divine and human natures are really natures, really distinct as natures, and no matter that created natures must now be understood to be created participations of the divine nature. Among many good studies of the intersections involved in producing St. Thomas's view of the world, see Jan A. Aertsen, *Nature and Creature: Thomas Aquinas's Way of Thought* (Leiden: Brill, 1988) and the last chapter of Edward Booth, OP, *Aristotelian Aporetic Ontology in Islamic and Christian Thinkers* (Cambridge: Cambridge University Press, 1983): "Thomas Aquinas: The 'Aufhebung' of Radical Aristotelian Ontology into a Pseudodionysian-Proclean Ontology of 'Esse.'"

[20] *ST* II-II, q. 23, a. 1.

[21] On this distinction, see Guy Mansini, OSB, "*Duplex Amor* and the Structure of Love in Aquinas," in *Thomistica*, edited by Eugene Manning (Leuven: Peeters, 1995), pp. 137–96.

common possession, a common possession that makes a community (*koinō-nia*) between friends, whether this be family ties, the same citizenship, or the bonds that unite travelers or soldiers together.[22] Mutual benevolence, Aquinas says, is founded on some commonality or sharing (*fundatur super aliqua communicatione*). Then he observes that there is just such a community between Christians and God, namely, his sharing with us his happiness or beatitude, of which sharing St. Paul speaks to the Corinthians when he says: "God is faithful, through whom you have been called into the society (*societas*) of the love of God" (1 Cor 1:9). (*Societas* and *communicatio* both translate *koinōnia*.) The mutual benevolence between God and the Christian founded on this sharing is charity. Charity itself is a created form, a created *habitus* ordered to the love of God, as Thomas explains in the second article of the question; it is a form superadded to our natural powers, since its exercise merits for us the very beatitude of God, the promise of which founds our friendship.[23] It is a *habitus* infused into the Christian by God, as Thomas explains in the next question.[24]

St. Thomas's identification of charity as friendship with God, and as Aristotle understands friendship, is his own contribution to the understanding of graced life.[25] In St. Bonaventure's commentary on distinction 27 of the third book of the *Sentences*, by contrast, charity is a created habit, distinct from the other virtues (a. 1, q. 1), whose act is to will the eternal and highest good for the one whom it loves (a. 1, q. 2), but it is not styled friendship with God. Nor is there any reference to Aristotle in any of the four questions on charity as a habit,[26] while references to Aristotle in Aquinas are abundant.[27]

---

[22] St. Thomas does not list Aristotle's examples here but he does in q. 23, a. 5, corpus.

[23] See also *ST* I-II, q. 51, a. 4, and q. 62, aa. 1 and 3.   [24] *ST* II-II, q. 24, a. 2.

[25] For factors governing the possibility of conceiving charity as friendship, see Gilles G. Meersseman, OP, "Pourquoi le Lombard n'a-t-il pas conçu la charité comme amitié?," in *Miscellanea Lombardiana*, edited by Pontificio Ateneo Salesiano di Torino (Novara: Istituto Geografico de Agostini, 1957), pp. 165–74.

[26] In a. 2 of Bonaventure's *In III Sent.*, dist. 27, on the act of and mode of charity, there are some four references to the *Physics* and the *Topics*, and at the end of dist. 27, a reference to the *De anima* at Dubium I. Replying to an objection at a. 2, q. 2, ad 2, Bonaventure employs the distinction between *amor amicitiae* and *amor concupiscentiae*, both of which are acts of charity. Still, he does not call charity friendship. The editors send us to the *Rhetoric* II,4 and to the *Nicomachean Ethics* VIII,3.

[27] Of course not all these references have the same importance or even indicate a concerted "Aristotelianism," as we would say today. Still, for what it is worth, in the questions on charity as a habit, qq. 23–26, there are forty references (explicit or understood) to Books VIII and IX of the *Nicomachean Ethics*; another eight to the rest of the *Nicomachean Ethics*; and another eight to other works. The *sed contra*'s of qq. 23–26 invoke the authority of Scripture or the Fathers, with two exceptions: q. 24, a. 5, appealing to the *Physics*; and q. 26, a. 12, appealing to the *Nicomachean Ethics*. In the same questions, there are thirty-nine citations of Augustine. Where is the Pseudo-Denys? Mostly in the *Prima Secundae*, the questions on love, qq. 26–28. For the difficulty in assessing Aquinas's citations of Aristotle, see Mark D. Jordan, *The Alleged Aristotelianism of Thomas Aquinas* (Toronto: Pontifical Institute of Mediaeval Studies, 1992).

Thomas's position, moreover, is early, but not as complete as the treatment in the *Summa*. In his own commentary on distinction 27 of the third book of the *Sentences*, St. Thomas begins by reminding us that love, like appetite, is found in the sensitive and intellective parts of the soul. The subsequent tour de force proceeds: (1) from concupiscent love for the presence of what perfects the lover; (2) to the love of this perfection for the beloved, one's other self; (3) to bestowing these things by beneficence; (4) to the concord this works with the beloved, which pertains to friendship (with reference to *Nicomachean Ethics* IX,6). In addition to the four previous things (5) love (*amor*) imports the note of appetite resting in the beloved. Next, (6) the passion of love (*amatio*) in turn bespeaks a certain intensity of love, a kind of fervor. Last, (7) *amicitia* adds two things: a kind of community (*societas*) of lover and beloved, such that they mutually love and are mutually cognizant of this love; and second, the choice (*electio*) by which they love, such that it is not only from passion but involves intellect. "Thus therefore it is evident that friendship is the most perfect among all the things that pertain to love, including all the foregoing." Therefore further, charity is to be placed precisely here, in friendship, for charity "is a kind of friendship of man to God through which man loves God and God loves man, and thus is brought about an association of God and man, as St. John speaks of it: 'If we walk in the light, just as he is in the light, we have community (*societas*) with one another' (1 John 1:7)."[28] Friendship is the most perfect kind of love, including all its partial aspects, and therefore charity too must be some form of friendship.

This early treatment has us reaching up to charity from the many lesser forms of love, and does not manifest so well the supernatural character of charity, although that shows up directly in the next article. Further, the *societas* or *associatio* he speaks of is not that on which charity is founded, but *is* charity. There is no contradiction to be recorded here. But the more developed position of the *Summa* should guide our reading.[29] *Convivere amico* is the most salient property of friendship, and the *conversatio* friends engage in with one another is the most excellent part of friendly living together.[30] But the

[28] Aquinas, *In III Sent.*, dist. 27, q. 2, a. 1, corpus.

[29] See Schockenhoff, "The Theological Virtue of Charity," p. 246. Schockenhoff notes that the *communicatio* of beatitude as the foundation of charity is first expressed in *Quodlibet* I, q. 4, a. 3, ad 1. Weisheipl dates the first *Quodlibet* and *ST* II-II to 1269–1272. These are also the same years for dating the *Quaestio disputata de caritate*. Charity is friendship, here, too, but Thomas devotes no article to showing this. He seems rather to take it as obvious. In a. 2, "Whether charity is a virtue," the corpus insists that we love the good of the celestial city not for ourselves, concupiscently, but for its own sake, and that this love makes us fit for the society of the blessed. Charity is expressly "friendship" in the reply to the eighth argument to the contrary, and those animated by charity are "friends" in the reply to the sixth argument to the contrary.

[30] Bobik, "Aquinas on Friendship," pp. 260–1. See St. Thomas, *Sent. Ethic.* VIII, lect. 5, esp. no. 1598: "neque etiam senes, neque severi, idest homines austeri in verbis et convictu, videntur esse amativi."

communicatio on which charity is based according to the *Summa* is something prior to charity; it makes the likeness between friends which is presupposed to the mutual choice friends make of one another, and is as it were the material cause of friendship.[31]

6.3. CHARITY IS FRIENDSHIP STRICTLY SPEAKING

Notwithstanding the supernatural character of charity, St. Thomas means that charity meets Aristotle's definition strictly but analogically.[32] It meets it strictly, for as has already been mentioned (in section 6.2), all the arguments to the contrary in the *Summa* (*ST* II-II, q. 23, a. 1) are taken from Aristotle and answering them ensures that we stay within his understanding of friendship. The first objection observes that according to Aristotle, nothing is more proper to friends than a common life.[33] Is this property of friendship verified in the friendship between the invisible God and corporeal men? Yes, but now only spiritually, Thomas answers. Our *conversatio* with God is imperfect in this life, as St. Paul acknowledges (Phil 3:20) but will be perfected when we shall see him face to face (Rev 22:4). Later, when he treats the sacraments, Thomas observes that the Eucharist in its visibility is ordained to fulfill the demand that friends live with one another—the visible sacrament of Christ ensures a common and corporeal *conversatio*, and is a sign of supreme charity.[34] The second objection recalls that friendship requires a return of love, as was said in the corpus of the article. But charity extends to one's enemies, who do not love us. How can they be our friends in charity? Aquinas answers by saying that, for love of a friend, we may also love what belongs to him, his sons or servants, even if they offend us. In this way, loving God, we love what belongs to him, and we love our enemies *in ordine ad Deum*.[35]

---

[31] Bobik, "Aquinas on Friendship," pp. 263–4 and 267: "these *communicationes* [of blood, of military life, of travelling together] are the disposing relational contexts not only for friendship, but prior to that, for justice." See also Louis-Bertrand Gillon, OP, "À propos de la théorie thomiste de l'amitié: 'Fundatur super aliqua communicatione' (II-II, q. 23, a. 1)," *Ang.* 25 (1948): pp. 3–17, esp. 10, where the genesis of friendship for St. Thomas is from some likeness of potential friends, to an association based on this likeness (an actual sharing or *communicatio*) to the choice that makes friendship actual.

[32] Schockenhoff, "The Theological Virtue of Charity," p. 247, also insists on this.

[33] Aristotle, *Nicomachean Ethics* VIII,5 (1157b18–19); IX,12.

[34] See *ST* III, q. 75, a. 1.

[35] Though St. Thomas does not say so, this approaches Aristotle's observation that a parent loves his children as being a part of him, as a sort of other self: *Nicomachean Ethics* VIII,14 (1161b18–19 and 27–28); see the transitivity of friendship in *Rhetoric* II,4 (1381a14–15). If we love a man, we love his dog. In his *Quaestio disputata de caritate*, Thomas observes that Aristotle holds that from nature we love all men, and concludes that in loving our enemies, charity perfects nature (a. 8, ad 7).

Third, the authority of St. Jerome is invoked to the effect that charity is neither pleasant nor useful, and so cannot be a friendship based on those goods. Neither can it be an instance of the third kind of friendship that Aristotle lists in the *Nicomachean Ethics*, friendship among the virtuous, who intend the true good of human nature for one another, since by charity we are to love even sinners, who do not act virtuously.[36] Charity therefore cannot find a place in Aristotle's analysis of friendship. St. Thomas grants that in the strict sense, the highest friendship bears only on the virtuous, but counters that we can love sinners *propter Deum*. We love them, not as sinners, but as we love our enemies *in ordine ad Deum*. Later, he will point out that Aristotle acknowledges that we love morally imperfect friends as long as there is hope of their healing.[37]

The objections increase in seriousness. First, it is alleged that charity lacks a property of friendship, a common life; second, that it lacks one of its internal essential elements, the return of love; and last that it altogether is outside of whatever Aristotle could count as friendship. Certainly, it extends Aristotle's friendship beyond itself. Does it break the mold? Thomas's answers insist that we are speaking of what Aristotle teaches us to recognize as friendship. This is crucial if we want to maintain that grace presupposes and perfects but does not abolish nature.

The question of friendship with God arises in St. Thomas's commentary on the *Nicomachean Ethics*, written about the same time as the *Secunda Pars*, for Aristotle raises it himself. In discussing friendships between unequal partners, Aristotle says the friendship of children to parents is like that of men to the gods, for both parents and the gods confer being and nutrition and discipline on us.[38] Thomas does not demur, although he speaks of God and not of gods, and lists the same benefits as grounding the friendship. But this does not gainsay for Thomas Aristotle's earlier denial that there is friendship with the gods, for there, the question is of friendship between equals.[39] Thomas makes no correction, but observes merely that "if the parties are very distant, for instance as men are from God, there no longer remains such friendship about which we are now speaking."[40] "Such friendship" as is here in question is wholly natural. The calculation changes for St. Thomas when we are conformed to God by grace and made to share in his nature.

The calculation changes also granted that God becomes man in Christ in order to save us from sin.[41] Given that frame, the equality of perfect friends points to one of the *convenientiae* of the Incarnation:

---

[36] Aristotle, *Nicomachean Ethics* VIII,2 and VIII,4.
[37] *ST* II-II, q. 25, a. 6, ad 2; cf. Aristotle, *Nicomachean Ethics* IX,3 (1165b13–20).
[38] Aristotle, *Nicomachean Ethics* VIII,12 (1162a4–7).
[39] Aristotle, *Nicomachean Ethics* VIII,7 (1159a4–5).
[40] *Sent. Ethic.* VIII, lect. 7 (no. 1635).   [41] *ST* III, q. 1, a. 3.

Since friendship consists in a kind of equality (*Nicomachean Ethics* VIII,5 [1157b36]), things that are very unequal seem not to be able to be joined in friendship. For this reason, therefore, that there might be a more familiar friendship between men and God, it was suitable for man that God become man, because man is even naturally a friend to man (*Nicomachean Ethics* VIII,1 [1155a17]): so that in this way, "while knowing God visibly, we may be enraptured to the love of invisible things" [Preface for Christmas].[42]

In this remarkable text, Aristotle (the equality of friends), Augustine (the passage from the visible to the invisible), and Dionysius the Areopagite (rapture, the ecstasy of love) all come together.

It is noteworthy, then, that St. Thomas never raises an objection to considering charity as friendship from the disproportion of the excellence or the inequality of the friends, neither in the *Summa* nor in the commentary on the *Sentences*, in the articles where charity is defined. It is not that the difference between God and man is obliterated. But grace really does make natural for us what is proper to God. John Duns Scotus raises the objection of the inequality of God and man in considering charity as friendship, and he answers that "friendship" cannot be taken here in the strict sense, precisely in Aristotle's sense. The habit of charity is "similar to or more perfect than friendship."[43] But charity is not really in the same line as friendship, as it is for St. Thomas.

6.4. CHARITY IS FRIENDSHIP ANALOGICALLY SPEAKING

Robert Sokolowski has pointed out that Aristotle's *Nicomachean Ethics* comes to three peaks or crests in its treatment of moral virtue. First is the treatment of *megalopsychia* in Book IV, which perfects the individual. Second is the treatment of justice in Book V, which governs our relations to others. But last is the treatment of friendship in Books VIII and IX, which is by no means an afterthought. Rather, friendship "completes justice and the other moral virtues" and "is the finest way in which we exercise practical reason."[44] In this context, to think of charity as the supernatural instance of friendship magnifies our appreciation of it. It is not just that charity commands the other virtues and so crowns whatever possible good we may strive for in the practical

---

[42] *SCG* IV, ch. 54, fifth argument. It would be a mistake, however, to say that the Incarnation is absolutely necessary for establishing the friendship of charity.

[43] John Duns Scotus, *Ordinatio* III, dist. 27, a. un., nos. 68–69 (pp. 79–80).

[44] Robert Sokolowski, "Phenomenology of Friendship," *The Review of Metaphysics* 55 (2002): pp. 451–70, at 452.

order, and in a way beyond our natural ken or capacity to acquire.[45] In addition, the finest thing Aristotle knows of what makes a life good is matched in the supernatural order by a friendship than which no greater could be conceived.

For St. Thomas, charity is not beyond friendship, but rather true friendship, and even truest friendship: it is founded on the surest *communicatio* of the best foundation of what potentially unites God and the angels and men, the divine beatitude; its first act is an act of divine love, where God estimates us as worthy of himself, and so makes us to share his nature; and its answering act is our own love of God above all things, and in the power of the love proper to him, and so, supernaturally. To maintain that it is the best friendship, the friendship which directs all the others, the others founded on some natural sharing of a natural, created good, and is the friendship according to which all other should be measured, is perfectly in line with Thomas's usual course: the infused moral virtues are truly and properly virtues, and the acquired virtues only virtues *secundum quid*; the science of theology is the true and highest science, since it is a share in God's science, and so judges all other disciplines.[46] The other sciences do not really measure up to it as *science*. Thus, of charity St. Thomas will say: "Since the good upon which whatever other true friendship is founded is ordered as to its end to the good on which charity is founded, it follows that charity commands the act of whatever other friendship there is."[47]

Relative to all other friendships, charity is the architectonic friendship.[48] Since it most surely brings us to our supernatural end in God and in company with all the saints, charity is *friendlier* than all other friendships. We ought not to say that charity is friendship "only analogically." It is supereminently analogically friendship.

6.5. FURTHER CONTRAST WITH ARISTOTLE

For Aristotle, happiness such as befits men and that we can hope for consists in the philosophic contemplation especially of divine things in the company of friends who likewise recognize the excellence and know the joy of such an exercise of intellect. Happiness does not consist in the exercise of moral virtue, but moral virtue is a prerequisite for its attainment, and is necessary for constituting the company of like-minded friends. Most men, to be sure, are not suited either by circumstance or by the acquisition of virtue realistically to

---

[45] See Sherwin, *By Knowledge and by Love*, pp. 170–202.   [46] *ST* I, q. 1, aa. 5–6.
[47] *ST* II-II, q. 26, a. 7, corpus.
[48] See Thomas M. Osborne, Jr., "Perfect and Imperfect Virtues in Aquinas," *Thom.* 71 (2007): pp. 39–64.

aim at the happiness discussed in the last book of the *Nicomachean Ethics*. After all, most people are poor, and most people are bad.[49]

In the Christian universe of Aquinas, however, there are important shifts in the above picture of human prospects. In the first place, we are called to the perfect beatitude of God, a participation in his own knowledge of himself, and pursuant to this, there are the gifts of grace and charity, by which we might merit to be admitted to the company of God and the blessed, even as the exercise and acquisition of moral virtue prepares an Athenian gentleman for the company of philosophers. But while few can hope for the happiness limned by Aristotle, all can hope for the happiness of heaven. And while few can manage to acquire moral virtue in Aristotle's world, charity is infused into all the baptized. All Christians, therefore, have the hope of sharing in a beatitude infinitely beyond that known by Aristotle. And just as Christian blessedness is a created participation in infinite understanding, so Christian friendship is a created participation in divine love, where we love God in a way conformed to his own love of the infinite good he is.[50]

The above view of Aquinas does not predict how many Christians so practice charity as to merit inclusion in the company of heaven, but it is a declaration that the playing field, so to speak, has been leveled. If our chances for earthly but imperfect happiness remain regrettably unequal and liable to chance, as they did in Aristotle's day as in Aquinas's, the chance for heavenly and perfect happiness is really and truly given to all. And if sin in fact limits our growth in charity or even snuffs it out, and if our share in the contemplative anticipation of perfect happiness is likewise similarly limited by our own moral choices, those choices, which, as limiting our happiness are rejections of God and his grace, are our own affair and in nowise able to be imputed to God.

6.6. THE OBJECTS, THE ORDER, THE ACTS, AND THE *CONVERSATIO* OF CHARITY

6.6.1. The Objects and Order of Charity

While the friendship that is charity has as its first and controlling object God himself,[51] it is nonetheless stretched beyond itself to all those who belong to

---

[49] Aristotle, *Rhetoric* II,5 (1382b4).

[50] For an extended comparison between and contrast of Aristotle and Aquinas on happiness, see Joseph Owens, C.Ss.R., *Human Destiny: Some Problems for Catholic Philosophy* (Washington, DC: The Catholic University of America Press, 1985), chs. 1–2: "Human Destiny in Aristotle" and "Human Destiny in Aquinas."

[51] *ST* II-II, q. 25, a. 1.

God, and that is everyone, including sinners and those who hate us.[52] For God wills all men to be saved, as the Apostle says (1 Tim 2:4).[53] Therefore, the scope of charity is the entire Church, which means humanity in its entirety, since all men pertain to the Church, either actually or potentially.[54]

That God is loved first and above all by charity is, perhaps, obvious, since he is the greatest good and the source of charity.[55] And that those who are better in charity ought to be loved more is also perhaps obvious enough.[56] But St. Thomas carefully modulates this second principle according to the closeness of our neighbor to us, especially by familial bond: we will in justice want a better good for those who are better, but our affection may be more intense for those closest to us.[57]

When we love our neighbor *ex caritate*, the *ratio* of the love, its why and wherefore, is God, and we love him "so that he may be in God."[58] Because of the presence of God behind every act of charity directed to the neighbor, Marko Fuchs wonders whether Aquinas can really have it that we love the neighbor by charity "for himself," and so in that way maintain the Aristotelian form of virtuous friendship. He writes that, for Aquinas, we "love our neighbor not because of himself but because of God," and that charitable love "still requires us to refer our neighbor's intrinsic goodness . . . to God as the ultimate end."[59] I am not quite sure I understand this objection. Of course, it is true that love of neighbor *ex caritate* means referring the neighbor's goodness to God as the ultimate end, since I am loving God above all things, and all things have to fit in to that; but it also means that I want the neighbor to possess God's beatitude, and that I want this because it is his, the neighbor's, ultimate good. So I cannot love the neighbor "for himself" unless I want him to possess that ultimate and supernatural perfection of his person, the vision of God, which entails that I, too, love God in the same sense, as the subsistent good and to possess which in vision would be my own best good. The Neoplatonic and Christian commitments of St. Thomas here weigh on, but (I think) do not break, the Aristotelian form of friendship. One virtuous friend in Aristotle's world is not a participation in another, or in an infinite One and Good who creates them both. But the virtuous Christian, in both the created and

---

[52] *ST* II-II, q. 25, aa. 6 and 8.   [53] Cf. *ST* I, q. 19, a. 6, ad 1.

[54] *ST* III, q. 8, a. 3. As St. Thomas says in *In III Sent.*, dist. 29, a. 6, corpus, beyond the *communicationes* Aristotle recognizes, those of nature or of economics, or of politics, there is a divine *communicatio*, "according to which all men share in the one body of the Church, either in act or in potency; and this is the friendship of charity which extends to all men, even to enemies."

[55] *ST* II-II, q. 25, aa. 2–3.   [56] *ST* II-II, q. 26, a. 6.

[57] *ST* II-II, q. 26, aa. 7–8.   [58] *ST* II-II, q. 25, a. 1; q. 44, a. 2.

[59] Marko Fuchs, "*Philia* and *Caritas*: Some Aspects of Aquinas's Reception of Aristotle's Theory of Friendship," in *Aquinas and the* Nicomachean Ethics, edited by Tobias Hoffmann, Jörn Müller, and Matthias Perkams (Cambridge: Cambridge University Press, 2013), pp. 203–19, at 218.

supernatural orders, is indeed a participation in God, and so he cannot love the neighbor "in himself" without loving God.[60]

6.6.2. Acts of Friendship

That friends do good to one another is part of the definition of friendship, as we saw above (in section 6.2), and St. Thomas devotes a question to the beneficence of charity. What, more specifically, are the goods those united in charity will for and effect for one another? For his part, God gives to us the goods by which we are enabled to reach our final end, beatitude, his sharing of which with us is the foundation of charity. So, the best gift he gives us is the increase of charity itself, the principle of merit, by which we come to him, as St. Thomas makes clear in the question on the subject of charity and its increase.[61]

For our part, there is the noteworthy objection that we cannot really benefit God. St. Thomas grants in reply that we cannot properly benefit God, but that by charity we honor and obey him.[62] Fuchs thinks that here too charity fails to meet the Aristotelian pattern, likened as it is to the friendship between parent and child.[63] A pattern of charity more faithful to the Aristotelian pattern can be located if we think not of the Trinity in the divine nature but of the Son of God in his human nature. For here, real service is possible, as St. Thomas makes plain in his commentary on the gospel according to John. Commenting on John 15:14, "No longer do I call you servants, but friends," he distinguishes service that is forced and service that springs from freedom:

> It happens sometimes that some servant does something for the sake of an-other . . . but that he does so from himself, insofar as he moves himself to the work: and this is good servitude, because he is moved from charity to do good works; but he does not work on his own account, because charity does not seek the things that are its own but the things that belong to Jesus Christ and the salvation of the neighbor. . . . Therefore it is evident that the disciples are good servants, but by the good servitude, which proceeds from charity.[64]

In this way, it is easier to see that from friendship in charity with Christ as man, we can do the good things that he, as man, cannot accomplish through

---

[60] In n. 32 on p. 219 of "*Philia* and *Caritas*," Fuchs says that the friend must be loved "only" for himself. If this is the requirement, then Aquinas cannot meet it. But I think the participationist metaphysics of St. Thomas means that he cannot and also that he does not need to meet it in maintaining the Aristotelian form of *philia* in *caritas*. See further Guy Mansini, OSB, "*Similitudo, Communicatio,* and the Friendship of Charity in Aquinas," in *Thomistica*, edited by Eugene Manning (Leuven: Peeters, 1995), pp. 1–26.

[61] *ST* II-II, q. 24, aa. 4 and 6–7.   [62] *ST* II-II, q. 31, a. 1, arg. 1 and ad 1.

[63] Fuchs, "*Philia* and *Caritas*," pp. 213–14.

[64] *Lectura super Ioannem*, ch. 15, lect. 3 (no. 2015).

his human agency. And yet, in doing such things, such as preaching the gospel to the ends of the earth, we are benefiting a divine person loved *ex caritate* in the fulfillment of his own mission, his own work. He prepares the disciples for this work, moreover, by treating them as friends, making known to them whatever he has known from the Father (John 15:15), for, as St. Thomas observes, the Lord makes us his friends by making us to share in his wisdom.[65]

As to our neighbor, our exchanges of goods founded on charity likewise aim ultimately at our mutual growth in the love of God and neighbor.[66] But we most love each other when by prayer or word or example we help one another to increase in the friendship of the God who is love. The spiritual works of mercy, whereby we pray for, instruct, counsel, comfort, reprove, pardon, and forbear one another, are therefore of greater moment than corporeal works.[67] There is also fraternal correction, the act of charity by which we drive out evil in our brothers and sisters.[68]

6.6.3. The *Conversatio* of Friends United in Charity

The spiritual works of mercy already anticipate the *conversatio* between friends united in charity. Just as the virtuous friends of Aristotle will, according to their circumstances and abilities, help each other know divine things, so is this true in its own way for those united in charity, which means that evangelizing, catechizing, and teaching theology count as preeminent acts of charity: those who belong to the Order of Preachers and any who share their life are, as it were, placed in such a position as to enact charity of the most direct and highest order one human being can have for another. To hand on to others what has been learned in contemplation is an act of charity than which only martyrdom is more perfect.[69]

As for our direct converse with God, this leads us on the one hand to St. Thomas's estimation of Scripture as the word of God, hearing which is hearing him, and on the other to the praise of God in choir and at mass.[70]

---

[65] *Lectura super Ioannem*, ch. 15, lect. 3 (no. 2016).   [66] *ST* II-II, q. 32, a. 4.
[67] *ST* II-II, q. 32, aa. 2–3.   [68] *ST* II-II, q. 33.
[69] See *ST* II-II, q. 188, a. 6, on the excellence of the Dominican life. At *ST* II-II, q. 124, a. 3, St. Thomas says of martyrdom that "it most greatly manifests the perfection of charity," and that, considered in its genus, as preferring God and his truth to one's life, "it is the sign of the greatest charity." Which is not to say, as Cajetan points out, that the Virgin's charity is less than Peter's in his martyrdom; see the note to "secundum suum genus" in the Marietti edition at q. 124, a. 3 in Thomas Aquinas, *Summa theologiae: Pars II^a II^ae*, ed. Pietro Caramello (Turin: Marietti, 1962), p. 882.
[70] Bobik, "Aquinas on Friendship," p. 270. For the role of the Psalms in this *conversatio*, see Martin Morard, "Sacerdoce du Christ et sacerdoce des chrétiens dans le *Commentaire des Psaumes* de saint Thomas d'Aquin," *RThom* 99 (1999): pp. 119–42.

6.7. CHARITY, THE GIFT OF WISDOM, AND THE TRINITY

When St. Thomas treats the cardinal and theological virtues in the *Secunda Secundae*, he treats each virtue itself as a habit, determining its definition, where it is located in one who possesses it, and its object. He considers also the acts and effects of the virtue, the vices opposed to it, the precepts of the revealed law that direct it, and the gifts of the Holy Spirit corresponding to it. In this way, the *Secunda Pars* brings order into the riot of Christian moral discourse for the perfection of the theological consideration of our return to God and for the service of the ministry of confessors, for the accuracy of their judgment of sin, and the right direction of their compassion for sinners.[71] So, at the end of his treatment of charity, St. Thomas considers the corresponding gift of the Holy Spirit, the gift of wisdom. To the most excellent of the theological virtues corresponds the most excellent of the gifts.[72] The gifts, in St. Thomas's view, render us docile to the promptings of the Holy Spirit, beyond what reason itself might discern as the right thing to do,[73] for the right thing to do, remember, is what leads us to a happiness beyond the proportion of our nature by ways beyond the capacity of our nature naturally to posit.

Naturally acquired wisdom, as Aristotle teaches, gives us knowledge of the highest causes, even God, and so is by right directive of all other sciences. The gift of wisdom also enables us to judge according to the highest cause, God, but in a higher way. Charity unites us to God, and therefore enables a connatural knowledge of divine things, the exercise of which knowledge is through the gift of wisdom.[74] The gift of wisdom judges rightly both about divine things themselves and about the ordering of our actions to God in the light of the divine precepts.[75] We just recalled that, in the *Prima Secundae*, the gifts are necessary because, in order to progress to our supernatural end, we need to be moved and led by the Holy Spirit. The judgments that spring from the gift of wisdom, judgments about divine things and about the practical order insofar as it leads to God, these are the promptings of the Spirit, the motion he imparts to us as pilgrims.

Now the gift of wisdom, St. Thomas says, is a created likeness of the Son, the Word of God, who is the expression and image of the entire intelligibility of the divine essence, and including all that the divine power, which is that

---

[71] See Leonard E. Boyle, OP, *The Setting of the* Summa Theologiae *of Saint Thomas* (Toronto: Pontifical Institute of Mediaeval Studies, 1982), esp. pp. 20ff.

[72] For charity as the most excellent of the theological virtues, see *ST* I-II, q. 68, a. 7.

[73] *ST* I-II, q. 68, a. 2.

[74] *ST* II-II, q. 45, a. 2: as a chaste man judges rightly about matters pertaining to chastity, so the gift of wisdom, conforming us to God.

[75] *ST* II-II, q. 45, a. 5. Suitably strengthened, this gift enables prelates to discharge their work of teaching and governance.

essence, extends to. It is because of this that the seventh beatitude—"Blessed are the peacemakers, for they shall be called children of God"—is associated with wisdom (and so with charity).[76] For it is the office of wisdom to order things (Aristotle), and the right order of things makes for peace, for "peace is the tranquility of order" (Augustine).[77] Rightly therefore does the reward of peacemaking establish us as the children of God, according to the beatitude, and the gift of wisdom just is a created likeness of the naturally begotten Son of God. In this light, because of the gift, we are like the Son and are sons.[78]

If the gift of wisdom likens us to the Son, the virtue of charity itself likens us to the Holy Spirit; it is a created likeness of the Holy Spirit.[79] "Charity exists in us . . . by the infusion of the Holy Spirit, who is the Love of Father and Son, whose participation in us is created charity itself."[80] *Amor*, which names the interior act of friendship,[81] is a name proper to the Holy Spirit, properly understood,[82] who is also the nexus or bond between Father and Son.[83] It becomes friends to give gifts,[84] and "Gift" (*Donum*) is another name proper to the Spirit.[85] As Gilles Emery puts it, "the Communion of Father and Son, their mutual Bond or their love-Knot is the Holy Spirit who proceeds as their mutual Love."[86]

If the name of the principal *act* of the friendship of charity, love, is a name proper to the Holy Spirit, and if the name of one of the *effects* of the friendship of charity, a gift given, is another name proper to the Spirit, and if the Holy Spirit can be called the communion (or *societas* or *koinōnia*) of Father and Son, why should we not also call the Spirit *Caritas*, or *Amicitia*? Correlatively, should not Father and Son be called Friends? This question arises in part because of the modern proclivity to find the things that belong to the divine Persons according as we behold them in the economy of salvation as already always present eternal realities that have been constituted before the foundation of the world in their relations to one another.[87]

Naming the Spirit "Friendship" and supposing that Father and Son are eternally "Friends" one to another has consequences for how we think of our

---

[76] *ST* II-II, q. 45, a. 6.

[77] Concord and peace are effects of charity according to *ST* II-II, q. 29.

[78] Which does not gainsay the fact that, for St. Thomas, we are adopted children of God relative to the whole Trinity, not just relative to the Father; see *ST* III, q. 23, a. 2.

[79] *ST* II-II, q. 23, a. 3, ad 3; q. 24, a. 5, ad 3.   [80] *ST* II-II, q. 24, a. 2, corpus.

[81] *ST* II-II, q. 27.   [82] *ST* I, q. 37, a. 1.   [83] *ST* I, q. 37, a. 1, ad 3.

[84] *ST* II-II, q. 31, a. 1, ad 2.   [85] *ST* I, q. 38.

[86] Gilles Emery, OP, *The Trinitarian Theology of Saint Thomas Aquinas*, trans. Francesca A. Murphy (Oxford: Oxford University Press, 2007), p. 241. Moreover, concord, an effect of charity (*ST* II-II, q. 29, a. 1), is appropriated to the Holy Spirit (*ST* I, q. 39, a. 8).

[87] See Bruce D. Marshall, "The Unity of the Triune God: Reviving an Ancient Question," *Thom.* 74 (2010): pp. 1–32, where at 25 he says: "the urge to suppose that everything which belongs to the persons of the Trinity in the economy goes all the way down in their immanent divine life . . . regularly threatens to make the unity of God unintelligible."

own relation to God, consequences that some might welcome. First, if it were fitting to call the Holy Spirit "Friendship," we could say that the friendship of our own charity was something whose archetype is something eternal and absolute. It would be a created participation of an uncreated reality, and entering into friendship with God would be entering into a sort of absolute reality, whose formality is exactly the same in both its eternal and temporal, uncreated and created instances. Second, entering into friendship with God would mean entering quite particularly into friendship with an eternal friend-Son, who is already distinctly a friend (with the Father) before the foundation of the world. We would be picking up on what he already always must be.

Neither of these proposals, however, is acceptable. That is, they are not acceptable if we stick to Aristotle's understanding of friendship, for which an independent exercise of individually and really distinct agencies is required. Friendship consists in mutual benevolence and love, as we saw at the beginning of this chapter. But "mutual love involves choice," Aristotle says.[88] In St. Thomas's more developed anthropology, friendship depends on the exercise of two individually and really distinct wills. Thus, friendship can be verified in God only if Father and Son have distinct wills. Just as tritheism is implied when theologians impute an intradivine obedience to the Son, so is it also just one step—one ineluctable step—away if we think of the Holy Spirit as "Friendship."

To think there is friendship in the strict sense between Father and Son, moreover, is tantamount to holding that the Son proceeds from the will of the Father, as Arius thought. But if the divine will is common to the three, there is no friendship in God, but rather that unity upon which, in the created order, our own friendships are founded but which is not itself "friendship" in the strict sense.[89]

For the same reason, that of the unity of the divine will, our friendship with Christ as depending on his own personally distinct exercise of freedom, an exercise not at one with that of the Father and the Holy Spirit, depends on his assumption of a human nature, another way of exercising rational agency, and a way distinct from that of the divine nature itself. When the Lord tells the disciples that he no longer calls them servants, but friends (John 15:14–15), that is something he does as a man, insofar as he shares the revelation of the Father through his humanity with them, and there is therefore something distinctive about this friendship, which our friendship with Father and Spirit does not share. When St. Thomas explains what it means to say that they have

---

[88] Aristotle, *Nicomachean Ethics* VIII,5 (1157b30). This is the Ross translation.

[89] The foundational character of our relation to ourselves relative to our friendships is noted by Aristotle (*Nicomachean Ethics* IX,4) to which St. Thomas appeals (*ST* II-II, q. 25, a. 4) in explaining that we love ourselves out of charity. And we are to love ourselves more than our neighbor, for unity is more powerful than union, St. Thomas explains (*ST* II-II, q. 26, a. 4). For the power of unity, of the One, see Dionysius, *The Divine Names* XIII (*PG* 3, col. 980B–981B).

not chosen him, but he has chosen them (John 15:16), he adverts to the eternal election by which, prior to any merits real or foreseen, God chooses those who are to be saved.[90] This eternal choice, of course, is communicated to them through his assumed humanity, his assumed human freedom. The salient point, however, is that the friendship in question depends on a choice, something that has no place in the divine processions. Moreover, the divine choice requires an answering choice, an answering act of freedom on our part. That he first chooses us does not mean we must not subsequently and on the basis of grace choose him. "He infuses the gift of the grace of justification in such a way that also with it and by it he moves free will to accept the gift of grace."[91]

Charity is friendship with God. And God is love. But God is not friendship. For there to be friendship with God there must be created persons, and, in the actual order of redemption, a created humanity assumed by a divine Person. Charity names the abundance of divine love for what is beyond God. It is in that way the *ecstasis* of divine love.[92]

---

[90] *Lectura super Ioannem*, ch. 15, lect. 3 (nos. 2021–2023).
[91] *ST* I-II, q. 113, a. 3, corpus.
[92] See *ST* I-II, q. 28, a. 3, and Dionysius, *The Divine Names* IV,13.

7

Aristotelian Doctrines in Aquinas's Treatment of Justice

Christopher A. Franks

No treatment of a particular virtue in the *Secunda Secundae Pars* of the *Summa theologiae* manifests more clearly Aquinas's well-known affirmation of "nature" than the treatment of justice. Yet it is my contention in this chapter that the justice Aquinas discusses is as "graced" and Christian as it is "natural." The virtue of justice stands in Aquinas's ethics at the intersection of what is knowable by reason and what requires the illumination of faith. The peculiar situation of this virtue can be seen especially through careful study of Aquinas's use of and revision of Aristotle's account of justice.

7.1. AQUINAS'S USE OF ARISTOTLE ON JUSTICE: PRELIMINARY OBSERVATIONS

Aquinas's use of Aristotle on justice is often seen as an affirmation of nature over against the truths accessible only by faith. Michel Villey has argued that Aquinas stepped away from an earlier Augustinian tendency to derive law and the claims of justice connected with it from the Scriptures, and that, in doing so, Aquinas arrived at a different basis for law derived from Aristotle and from Roman law.[1] What Aquinas achieved by taking Aristotle so seriously in his account of justice is "a rehabilitation of nature and natural reason as the

---

[1] See Michel Villey, *La formation de la pensée juridique moderne* (Paris: PUF, 2003), pp. 133–8; Michel Villey, "Saint Thomas et l'immobilisme," in *Seize essais de philosophie du droit: Dont un sur la crise universitaire* (Paris: Dalloz, 1969), pp. 94–106, esp. 97–100; and Jean-Marie Aubert, *Le droit romain dans l'œuvre de saint Thomas* (Paris: Vrin, 1955), cited in John R. T. Lamont, "Conscience, Freedom, Rights: Idols of the Enlightenment Religion," *Thom.* 73 (2009): pp. 169–239, here at 203, nn. 38 and 39.

deciding factors in the determining and identification of justice."[2] In the wake of Vatican II's promulgation of *Dignitatis Humanae*, Yves Congar sought the roots of that document's positive account of the justice of natural rights and claimed to find those roots in the fact that Thomas (and Albert) "had disengaged and established a consistency of nature independent of its condition of supernatural justice or of sin, and consequently, a validity of the natural order independent of faith and charity."[3]

Such readings of Aquinas seem appealing both for exegetical and apologetic reasons. Exegetically, such a reading takes seriously Aquinas's distinction between justice and charity, and between moral and theological virtues. Apologetically, such a reading seems to give a theological grounding for an attention to "autonomous nature" in keeping with the spirit of our times. But I suggest on the contrary that recovering the role of revealed wisdom in Aquinas's account of justice reflects more faithful exegesis of Aquinas and better shows how Aquinas's thought answers to what is best in the spirit of our times.

The "natural" elements of virtue certainly come to the fore in the discussion of justice. Yet what Aquinas achieves by his use of Aristotle here is not a "disengagement" of nature from the context of faith that illumines it,[4] but rather an account of the shape of the virtue of justice in Christian life that pays close attention to the concrete, temporal, embodied character of life in this world. Thus, while Aquinas can expect many of his conclusions to be affirmed by, and even discoverable by, natural reason, he is far from holding an immanent natural teleology at arm's length from Christian eschatology. On the contrary, Aquinas weaves the two together, "correcting" Aristotle's view of life in this world by taking equally seriously its providential ordering toward its maker.[5]

The treatise on justice fits into the *Secunda Pars*, which is Aquinas's account of the Christian life, of the human return to God through the way opened up by Jesus Christ. As elsewhere, Aquinas's arguments often engage the arguments of philosophers, sometimes even beginning from premises Aquinas

[2] Lamont, "Conscience, Freedom, Rights," p. 204.

[3] Yves M.-J. Congar, OP, "Avertissement," in *La liberté religieuse: Déclaration "Dignitatis humanae personae*," edited by Jérôme Hamer and Yves M.-J. Congar (Paris: Cerf, 1967), pp. 11–14, at 12, cited in Jean-Pierre Torrell, OP, *Saint Thomas Aquinas*, vol. 2, Spiritual Master, trans. Robert Royal (Washington, DC: The Catholic University of America Press, 2003), p. 300, n. 77.

[4] The very image of "disengaging" nature from an illumining context suggests in a manner quite alien to Aquinas that there could be a "bare nature" and a corresponding "justice" that is timeless and contextless.

[5] As Thomas Hibbs keeps reminding us, in Aquinas theology engages philosophy dialectically. See Thomas S. Hibbs, *Virtue's Splendor: Wisdom, Prudence, and the Human Good* (New York: Fordham University Press, 2001), p. 19.

attributes to natural reason, but Aquinas unfailingly appropriates those arguments for his own theological purposes. As Thomas Hibbs comments:

> The quintessentially Thomistic thesis on nature and grace implies that Christianity cannot confect an entirely new moral vocabulary. It must embrace and transform the available discourses. The complexity of Thomas's thought and the nuanced form in which he couches his arguments have too often proven impediments to the comprehension of the christocentric nature of his moral thought. The role of Christ is approached indirectly, as befits the order of human learning.[6]

When discussing justice, Aquinas makes much use of Aristotle's moral vocabulary, but he also stretches it and puts it to new uses. In a sense, the Christian narrative context is important for understanding Aquinas on justice exactly because he is so Aristotelian. For both Aristotle and Aquinas justice is about rendering what is due, and for both what is due depends on a multitude of considerations about goods, about what human life is for, about the differentiations that relate persons to one another in various ways, about the concrete situation of a particular time and place, and about one's own place in one's community. In short, knowing what is just requires careful judgments that get better the more attentive they are to the particularities of one's context. Aquinas's Christian account of justice does "embrace and transform the available discourses": it embraces Aristotle's attention to the concrete particular and to the need for practical judgments sensitive to context, and it transforms Aristotle by attending not to the context of the ancient Greek *polis*, but to the context of the Christian people *in via*.

I will not be able in this short span to address all aspects of Aquinas's use of Aristotle on justice. Nor will I give a general overview of Aquinas's account of justice, as many fine treatments already exist.[7] My goal here is simply to highlight what seem to me the major lessons to be learned from a study of Aquinas's use of Aristotle on justice. I divide the discussion into four parts. First (in section 7.2), I establish the Aristotelian character of Aquinas's account of justice by distinguishing it from a more Platonic view on the one hand and a modern inherent rights view on the other. Both Aristotle and Aquinas, I argue, maintain a keener attention than either of these alternatives to the concrete contours of human distinctness and relationality. The next three sections explore how Aquinas moves beyond Aristotle while retaining

---

[6] Thomas S. Hibbs, "*Imitatio Christi* and the Foundation of Aquinas's Ethics," *Communio* 18 (1991): pp. 556–73, at 572.

[7] See, for example, Josef Pieper, "Justice," in *The Four Cardinal Virtues: Prudence, Justice, Fortitude, Temperance*, trans. Richard and Clara Winston, Lawrence E. Lynch, and Daniel F. Coogan (Notre Dame, IN: University of Notre Dame Press, 1966), pp. 41–113; and Jean Porter, "The Virtue of Justice (IIa IIae, qq. 58–122)," in *The Ethics of Aquinas*, edited by Stephen J. Pope (Washington, DC: Georgetown University Press, 2002), pp. 272–86.

Aristotle's grasp of human particularity and finitude. Section 7.3 investigates slavery to display how Aquinas extends moral standing beyond Aristotle's limits. Section 7.4 treats property conventions in order to display how Aquinas more forcefully than Aristotle puts them at the service of the sustenance of all people. Section 7.5 discusses the relation of justice to particular political communities, and elucidates how Aquinas envisions arenas of justice that are more than political. The last three sections together constitute an argument that Aquinas overcomes certain limitations in Aristotle's account, but never by the abstractions by which modern thinkers are often tempted; instead, he overcomes those limitations by retaining Aristotle's attention to the concrete character of life in this world, while attending simultaneously to the ordering of that life toward its end in God. In short, I argue in what follows that Aquinas learns from Aristotle while reworking justice around God's intention to form a charitable community.

Although we cannot examine it in detail, there is one move Aquinas makes that gives structural insight into Aquinas's use of Aristotle on justice, namely, the association of certain other virtues with justice as its "potential parts." In *ST* II-II, q. 80, Aquinas explains the connection of these other virtues with justice. Aquinas's main template for his list of such virtues comes from Cicero and Macrobius. But Aristotle helps Aquinas explain the connection in two ways. First, Aquinas makes much of Aristotle's claim that some friendships are unequal to such a degree that "it is impossible to make the kind of return which the giver deserves, for instance, in the honors we pay to the gods and to our parents."[8] Aquinas sees a similar logic concerning the honor owed to superiors when Aristotle describes the magnanimous man who takes only moderate pleasure in honor, because he knows that no honor is an adequate return for perfect virtue.[9] Aquinas takes both these statements to support his view that we have some debts of justice we can never fully repay. For Aquinas, virtues that aim at paying such debts have an aspect of justice, but are distinct from justice itself since they have the note of inequality.

Second, Aquinas picks up Aristotle's distinction between the aspects of justice in two different kinds of business friendship and puts it to quite different use. Aristotle distinguishes business friendships built on written contracts (legal) from those entered into without any fixed terms (moral).[10] Aquinas makes this distinction do much more systematic work, establishing a "moral due" (*debitum morale*) that is less strictly due than debts of justice proper. This notion allows Aquinas to mark how the remaining virtues on the list are similar to justice, but different in having a "due" that is not legally obligatory. Aquinas also uses a good deal of Aristotle in describing many of

---

[8] Aristotle, *Nicomachean Ethics* VIII,15. All quotations from the *Nicomachean Ethics* are cited from Martin Ostwald's translation (Englewood Cliffs, NJ: Prentice Hall, 1962).
[9] Aristotle, *Nicomachean Ethics* IV,3.   [10] Aristotle, *Nicomachean Ethics* VIII,13.

these particular "parts of justice," especially piety, observance, gratitude, truth, affability, and liberality. Even there he often transforms Aristotle's view, and some of those transformations we will have opportunity to examine. And of course, it is a transformation of Aristotle simply to identify some of these as virtues (piety and observance), and to link all of them so closely to the virtue of justice. Aquinas thereby makes the notion of the "due" of justice even more supple and differentiated than in Aristotle, so that "at the heart of the Thomistic account of justice is the paradox of debts that cannot be fully repaid, the virtuous response to which is gratitude, liberality, and hospitality."[11] This conceptualization is one way Aquinas gives voice to his understanding that part of what we "owe" one another is to give beyond what is strictly owed. As we will see, at a number of points where Aquinas adopts Aristotle's ideas, he also breaks open the implied self-sufficiency of the just agent who is the term of Aristotle's immanent natural teleology. Aquinas thereby constructs a Christian view of justice that he nevertheless takes to reflect what is truly natural.

7.2. THE EXTERNAL AND RELATIONAL CHARACTER OF ARISTOTELIAN JUSTICE

One of the most prominent distinguishing marks of justice, according to Aquinas, is that it concerns actions "toward another." Justice is distinguished by being about "operations in which there is an element of something due or undue to another."[12] Justice is thus set apart from the other moral virtues which are judged with reference to the agent rather than to something external to her.[13]

Aristotle did not say it in quite the same way, but the point goes back to Aristotle. For Plato, of course, justice was primarily internal, a harmony of the soul. Aristotle distanced himself from Plato's definition, saying the proper rule of the higher powers of the soul is only justice metaphorically.[14] Aquinas quotes this text of Aristotle and extends its reasoning. Since justice rectifies actions and actions belong to supposits and wholes, "justice properly speaking demands a distinction of supposits."[15] This is the most fundamental move from Aristotle's discussion that Aquinas adopts and extends. This distinction is implied, Aquinas says, in the very notion of equality that is so central to justice, and thus in the very notion of *ius*, which is the object of justice. *Ius*, or "right," Aquinas says,

---

[11] Hibbs, *Virtue's Splendor*, p. 126.
[12] *ST* I-II, q. 60, a. 2, corpus. Quotations from the *Summa theologiae* are taken from the translation by the Fathers of the English Dominican Province.
[13] *ST* II-II, q. 57, a. 1; q. 58, a. 3, ad 3.   [14] Aristotle, *Nicomachean Ethics* V,11.
[15] *ST* II-II, q. 58, a. 2, corpus.

must be a relation,[16] for justice (*iustitia*) denotes a certain equality, "since it is commonly said that things that are made equal are adjusted (*iustari*)."[17] Such "adjustment" of one thing and another presupposes their distinctness.

To clarify the significance of Aquinas's use of Aristotle here, it is helpful to recall Aristotle's objection to the lack of precision he felt marred Plato's account of justice in the city. On Aristotle's interpretation of the *Republic*, Plato calls for a city in which everything that can be shared is shared, including wives, children, and property. Plato's concern, apparently, is unity. Aristotle agrees that political unity is good, and even that a political community should be as united as possible. But Aristotle claims that if a political community becomes as unified as Plato proposes, it will cease to be a political community. Too much blurring of the human distinctness signified by the terms "mine" and "yours" changes the nature of an association in the direction of a household, and then in the direction of a single person. That degree of unity would destroy the political community, for the political community "is composed both of many human beings and different kinds of human beings."[18]

Aristotle departed from Plato on justice largely because of Aristotle's concern to attend to the embodied particularity of the human being. Aristotle found Plato's vision of political unity psychologically implausible,[19] and he found no good reason to consider the body any less integral to human nature than the rational element.[20] In Aristotle's view, Plato neglected the concrete realities of life in this world, effacing the significance of bodies and blurring the line between the "yours" and "mine" of one soul and another. Bodies, Plato contended, are of limited significance in determining what is just, since the body, after all, is "only the outer shell" (*Republic*, 588d). A related concern of Aristotle was Plato's view that souls should not be thought of as overly separate. Plato proposed that, while reason should rule the appetites, for most people such rule requires obedience to someone else's reason. Thus, for Plato, what is significant is the good of the unified whole, the city.[21] Later, in the *Laws*, Plato even suggests that the ruler's reason is not in the most important sense "someone else's," since what is better and higher and suited to rule one is properly considered "one's own" (*Laws*, 726a); what stands in the way of this sort of unity is the "vulgar sort of self-love that considers each person as a separate unit (of any sort, bodily or psychic)."[22]

---

[16] Michel Villey has, quite rightly, made much of the difference between "right" in Aristotle and Aquinas as an objective relation and modern "rights" as subjective properties of individuals.

[17] *ST* II-II, q. 57, a. 1, corpus.   [18] Aristotle, *Politics* II,1.

[19] Aristotle, *Politics* II,4.   [20] Aristotle, *De anima* II,1.

[21] This emphasis on unity over separateness presumably contributes to Plato's motivation for defining justice as a harmony among the parts of the soul.

[22] Martha Craven Nussbaum, "Shame, Separateness, and Political Unity: Aristotle's Criticism of Plato," in *Essays on Aristotle's Ethics*, edited by Amélie Oksenberg Rorty (Berkeley: University of California Press, 1980), pp. 395–435, at 413.

In contrast to Plato, Aquinas follows Aristotle in emphasizing the concrete realities of individual difference and distinctness, and this is clear in the way he makes the language of "one's own" fundamental to his discussion of every act of justice and injustice.[23] But if Aristotle and Aquinas avoid a Platonic view of justice, it is important to distinguish them also from modern views of justice grounded in inherent rights. In our day, we might be inclined to think that emphasizing the distinctness of the individual person leads in the direction of modern doctrines of inherent rights. Indeed, as we will see in the following sections of this chapter, Aquinas extends this distinctness to more subjects than Aristotle does, and some have seen in that move an incipient development toward modern notions of rights. After all, do we not pay the most attention to individual difference and distinctness when we consider justice as a response to something inherent in the individual considered in isolation? For Aquinas as much as for Aristotle, though, when we take the concrete reality of the individual seriously, we recognize that the individual is constituted by its relations—to consider the individual in isolation is to abstract from the real contours of things. The modern inherent rights tradition tends to assume that people are rights-bearers first, so that people only have obligations because of the rights of others and not vice versa, and so that there are social bonds because of these obligations and not vice versa. That is, it is assumed that relations are secondary to, rather than given with, the nature of individuals, and that debts of justice are grounded in qualities of those individuals. For Aquinas and Aristotle, though, individuals are not ontologically prior to the bonds and relations proper to and constitutive of them; debts of justice depend on the proper shape of these relations, which cannot be "got behind."[24]

Thus, when Aquinas speaks of rendering "to each his *ius*,"[25] he does not mean rendering him something that is his inherently or prior to relation. Since the term "rights" in our day tends to imply that justice is a response to some prior quality of isolated individuals, it is not helpful to think of Aquinas's account of justice in such terms.[26] I do not mean that Aristotle and Aquinas

---

[23] It is perhaps evident as well in Aquinas's determination to analyze the contours of the various acts of justice and injustice, as if in answer to Aristotle's unfulfilled promise to give "an examination of the various kinds of acts of justice and of injustice" (*Nicomachean Ethics* V,7). Of course, Aquinas's concern with specific acts could also reflect the psychological and phenomenological expertise required of confessors.

[24] This is why a "due" is never merely one's possession. Cf. Pieper's account of distributive justice, in which the "due" is not the individual's exclusively: Pieper, "Justice," p. 82.

[25] *ST* II-II, q. 58, a. 1.

[26] Fred Miller has claimed that there are "rights" in Aristotle and that they are crucial to understanding Aristotle on justice. Yet, a number of scholars have argued convincingly otherwise. See in particular Richard Kraut, who points out that even if the term "right" may be applicable to Aristotle's thought in some sense, it plays no significant role. See Richard Kraut, "Are There Natural Rights in Aristotle?," *The Review of Metaphysics* 49 (1996): pp. 755–74. Cf. Fred D. Miller, Jr., *Nature, Justice, and Rights in Aristotle's* Politics (Oxford: Clarendon Press, 1995).

deny that certain people should always be treated in certain ways as a matter of justice and because of their (and our) nature. But for neither Aristotle nor Aquinas would such rules of justice arise because of anyone's inherent rights. Instead, they arise partly because human beings, by their social and teleological nature, are aimed at forms of personal and social flourishing that would be undermined by certain types of action. This difference marks a wide gap between ancient eudaemonist and typically modern conceptions of the human being. In a recent defense of inherent rights, for example, Nicholas Wolterstorff has suggested that justice must be grounded in inherent rights, which are conceived as prior to any ordering or membership, in order to avoid placing the standards of justice outside the human being.[27] This view assumes that neither relations nor inclinations toward the flourishing of those relations can be constitutive of the human being. Such a view stands squarely on the modern side of the nominalist break with ancient thought of which Servais Pinckaers has written. It sets the human being's directedness and belonging in opposition to the human's freedom and identity, instead of seeing natural inclination and sociality as constitutive of human identity and the source of human freedom.[28]

Aquinas's (and Aristotle's) conception of justice as external, and of human life in this world as involving the real distinctness of individuals, does not mean that justice is grounded in the qualities of isolated individuals. On the contrary, both approach justice in a way that attends to concrete reality without abstractions. Thus, they recognize that justice belongs where there are social bonds, the flourishing of which is the constitutional aim of society's members.

We can see the assumption of a shared teleological context in the very notion of *ius*. *Ius* presupposes not only the distinctness of the supposits, but also their mutual relation. After all, the notion of *ius*, something that is "right-in-relation" or "due," "depends on some reflective sense of what it means to live in a community, what one's place in that community is, and what kinds of claims others can make on oneself."[29] So specific *iura* reflect a particular shared social context. Justice is present, for example, when two human beings are both subjects in the same political community.[30]

Aristotle elaborates on the need for such a context for justice in his discussion of friendship. For Aristotle the term *philia* has wider range than

---

[27] Nicholas Wolterstorff, *Justice: Rights and Wrongs* (Princeton, NJ: Princeton University Press, 2008), p. 37.

[28] See, for example, Servais Pinckaers, OP, *The Pinckaers Reader: Renewing Thomistic Moral Theology*, ed. John Berkman and Craig S. Titus (Washington, DC: The Catholic University of America Press, 2005), pp. 139 and 365.

[29] Jean Porter, *Nature as Reason: A Thomistic Theory of the Natural Law* (Grand Rapids, MI: Eerdmans, 2005), p. 217.

[30] *ST* II-II, q. 57, a. 4, corpus, citing *Nicomachean Ethics* V,6.

"friendship" has for us, since it includes not only intimate attachments but also relationships between family members, between certain business associates, between members of social clubs, and between fellow citizens. We might say that the central idea in *philia* is an affection correlative to some common interest through which the interests of the individuals bound by *philia* merge in certain respects.[31] Justice belongs in such contexts. According to Aristotle, "friendship is present to the extent that men share something in common, for that is also the extent to which they share a view of what is just." He goes on to assert that the intensity of the debts of justice varies with the intensity of the bonds of *philia*. Thus, it is a more brazen and shocking injustice to strike one's father than to strike someone else, or to refuse to help a brother than to refuse to help a stranger. "It is natural that the element of justice increases with the closeness of the friendship, since friendship and what is just exist in the same relationship and are coextensive in range."[32] It is the structure and aims of the friendship that determine what people owe one another. Among these friendships, the *philia* of citizenship plays a leading role since the *polis* is so important for the flourishing at which human beings are aimed.

Aquinas agrees with Aristotle that justice presupposes distinct supposits who share a bond that has specific aims. But in a number of ways Aquinas distinguishes his view of justice from Aristotle's by transforming the latter's preoccupation with the good of citizens in a *polis* in light of his own understanding of how God providentially directs the human being toward his or her end in God. In the next three sections, I will consider how and why Aquinas does so, specifically with regard to slavery, to property conventions, and to the relation of justice to particular political communities.

7.3. JUSTICE AND THE HOUSEHOLD

Aquinas follows Aristotle's external account of justice and his criticisms of Plato's account largely, I think, to affirm Aristotle's attention to the concrete, embodied realities of human life. But that externality, and the distinction of supposits it assumes, is quite restricted when it comes to Aristotle's account of the subordinate members of the household. For Aristotle, of course, the citizens of a *polis* are the free adult men. Others—slaves, children, wives—are

---

[31] John Cooper explains why *philia* is crucial to human flourishing by showing that one's own good can only be secured "by merging one's activities and interests with those of others." See John M. Cooper, "Aristotle on Friendship," in *Essays on Aristotle's Ethics*, edited by Amélie Oksenberg Rorty (Berkeley: University of California Press, 1980), pp. 301–40, at 329.

[32] Aristotle, *Nicomachean Ethics* VIII,9.

not fully distinct from the male head of household to whom they are attached, and so relations of justice do not apply in the proper sense. Thus, for example, the slave is as it were a part of his master, as a living but separate part of his body,[33] and therefore "there is nothing just in the relation of a craftsman to his tool, of the soul to the body, and of a master to his slave."[34] Notice that households are thus practically as unified for Aristotle as the ideal political community is for Plato.

We moderns will quarrel with Aristotle here, but it is important to be careful where we locate this quarrel. Aristotle denies the political distinctness of women and slaves primarily on the grounds of their constitutional incapacity for it, which he proposes as an observation of the concrete reality of human differences. A promising way forward is to accuse Aristotle of insufficient attention to the concrete realities of human particularity. But much modern political philosophy has instead resorted to abstraction, ignoring the specific shape of bodily and psychic differences and diversities. Rawls's original position, for example, assumes everyone has the capacity for political participation despite differences in the degree to which such capacities are actually realized from person to person. Or consider Kant, whose notion of universal moral rationality as the basis of equal dignity requires us to consider bodily and psychic differences between relatively healthy and sane persons, not to mention differences of habit or knowledge, to be morally and politically irrelevant. As such examples show, it is quite possible to extend distinction to more subjects than Aristotle did by getting more abstract rather than more concrete.

The way of abstraction is not Aquinas's approach. His difficulty, though, is that the more concrete his doctrine becomes, the more the possibilities for error in judgment arise, i.e. for making generalizations inadequate to the specificity of the phenomena. And Aquinas has frequently been charged, along with Aristotle, of faulty generalizations in his judgments about the best household authority structures.[35] I cannot examine such charges here. Instead, I want to stress the fact that Aquinas's accounts of these phenomena represent an attempt, partly inspired by Aristotle, to attend to the concrete shape of human life and the particular differentiations, bodily and psychic, that are part of human communities. For example, Aquinas attends to such differentiations to argue that the possibility of political authority arises from

---

[33] Aristotle, *Politics* I,4.   [34] Aristotle, *Nicomachean Ethics* VIII,11.

[35] John Finnis, for example, gives a very sympathetic account of Aquinas on husbands and wives, but faults Aquinas for his generalization that women are more likely to have their rational judgment deflected by emotion. I wonder if perhaps an even more important caveat would question Aquinas's neglect of the possibility that whoever is in a position of authority might be likely to truncate the function of reason by starving it of the proper influence of emotion. See John Finnis, *Aquinas: Moral, Political, and Legal Theory* (Oxford: Oxford University Press, 1998), pp. 173–4.

the complementarity of differently constituted persons.[36] Something similar goes on at the household level, so that Aquinas believes that a certain complementarity makes it natural for wives to be subject to their husbands.[37]

Slavery is a more complicated case on which I want to spend a little more time, because it provides especially clear examples of how and why, without abstraction, Aquinas extends the bonds of justice beyond Aristotle's assumptions. It is not clear that Aquinas's acceptance of slavery is an attempt to attend to concrete human differences, for Aquinas holds that no human differences could have legitimated the practice of slavery in the state of innocence. Only in man's fallen state could slavery appear acceptable, since it involves a pain implying punishment. As Aquinas writes, "Every man's proper good is desirable to himself, and consequently it is a grievous matter to anyone to yield to another what ought to be one's own."[38] This view is quite at odds with Aristotle, who holds that the limited capacity for self-direction among some men shows that they are meant by nature to be slaves for their own benefit.[39] Aquinas here quotes not the *Politics*, where Aristotle speaks of natural slaves, but the *Metaphysics*, where Aristotle simply provides a distinction between free men, who can dispose of themselves, and slaves, who are ordered to another. Aquinas uses the distinction to argue that slavery cannot be natural in the sense Aristotle says elsewhere that it is.

Presumably Aquinas accepts slavery not so much due to a belief that natural human differences legitimate it but due to its apparent ubiquity among the nations (the *ius gentium* is an expression of natural reason) and the acceptance of slavery in the Bible. But he also echoes some of Aristotle's ideas about slavery. For example, he adopts the Philosopher's classification whereby justice between a husband and wife is not quite justice in the same sense that exists between men of the same political community, and whereby the relation between a man and his slave or his children is even further from proper justice.[40] And interestingly, he holds together his rejection of natural slavery with his acceptance that it has the naturalness of the *ius gentium* by appealing to Aristotle. There is nothing about a particular man considered absolutely that makes him destined for slavery, he says, but according to some "resultant utility" we find "it is useful to this man to be ruled by a wiser man."[41] The conclusion is most curious, since it seems to mean that, although concrete differences in virtue or psychic ability do not legitimate slavery in the

---

[36] *ST* I, q. 96, a. 4. Cf. Paul J. Weithman, "Complementarity and Equality in the Political Thought of Thomas Aquinas," *TS* 59 (1998): pp. 277–96.

[37] *ST* I, q. 92, a. 1. The effort to revise Aquinas's view of women is beyond my purposes here, but see Jean Porter, "At the Limits of Liberalism: Thomas Aquinas and the Prospects for a Catholic Feminism," *Theology Digest* 41 (1994): pp. 315–30.

[38] *ST* I, q. 96, a. 4, corpus.   [39] Aristotle, *Politics* I,3–5.

[40] *ST* II-II, q. 57, a. 4; Aristotle, *Nicomachean Ethics* V,6.

[41] *ST* II-II, q. 57, a. 3, ad 2; Aristotle, *Politics* I,2.

state of innocence, they do legitimate it the way the world is now. One might presume to explain this curiosity by suggesting either that on account of sin the differences now are not the same kinds of differences, or that after sin the sting of punishment entailed in the practice of slavery can serve God's providential intent. Either explanation goes beyond what Aquinas explicitly says, but the example in any case shows Aquinas's sympathy for Aristotle's ostensible commitment to take human differences seriously, even if the conclusion sits uneasily with Aquinas's clear determination to qualify Aristotle's view of slavery in significant ways.

If Aquinas qualifies Aristotle but not by way of abstraction, how does he do it? He does it by setting what he adopts from Aristotle within the drama of the Christian life. For Aristotle, as we have seen (in section 7.2 and in the present section), justice takes its shape from the structure and aims of the relations in which people are members. Those with subordinate roles in the household are not fully distinct supposits and so do not participate fully in relations of proper justice. For Aristotle, there is no more-than-immanent horizon that would qualify the ordering of slave to master. It is true that household relations are ordered to the good of the *polis*, but the *polis* itself is built on slavery and aims at securing for its citizens the good life, to which the enslavement of some conduces. For Aquinas, on the other hand, those with subordinate roles in the household may be less than fully distinct supposits in one sense, but the relations that subordinate them to the head of household are themselves subordinate to the true ordering of all human beings to their end in God.

Consider Aquinas's account of the origins of justice in the doctrine of creation. When discussing God's justice, Aquinas addresses the objection that justice does not apply to God since God owes no one anything.[42] Something is one's due (*debitum*) as a matter of justice if it is his own (*suum*). Something is one's own if it is ordered (*ordinatur*) to him. There is a debt of justice, therefore, as long as something is ordered to someone. Aquinas argues that a thing is "due" to human beings in the following secondary sense. God wills to create human beings. Since God wills it, it is something God "owes" Godself. In "owing" Godself the making of human beings, God "owes" giving them the qualities, capacities, and contexts constitutive of humanity. In that way these qualities, capacities, and contexts become "due" to human beings. This creative ordering is the origin of the idea that certain relations between human beings, such as the relation between parent and child, are "right" by nature (natural *ius*).[43] And the "dues" that correspond

---

[42] *ST* I, q. 21, a. 1, ad 3.

[43] *ST* II-II, q. 57, a. 3. This discussion, combined with the discussion of law, would seem to be Aquinas's account of how people come to have a *ius*. Wolterstorff claims that Aquinas never explains *ius*, presumably because he is looking for an account of *ius* as an inherent possession. See Wolterstorff, *Justice*, p. 42.

to such ordering belong (though not "inalienably" since they depend on God's will), of course, to every human being.

Notice how this drama of the human being's origin and end in God shifts the terrain of justice from what we see in Aristotle. Aristotle acknowledges that insofar as the slave is a man, friendship with him is possible and thus also some sort of justice and legal obligation obtains.[44] It would seem that even for Aristotle any act toward the slave that would harm the qualities, capacities, and contexts that are the slave's *qua* human being would be unjust. But what would count as such harm depends on what a slave is for, and with no more-than-immanent horizon beyond the goods of citizens in a *polis* to determine that, Aristotle has no reason to consider that slaves may be ordered to the good in any other way than as instruments of the good of others. For Aquinas, in contrast, what slaves are for is the same as what everyone is for, beatitude in God. And that shapes Aquinas's account of what capacities a slave has *qua* human being. If reaching beatitude involves becoming good through God's grace, and becoming good means "freely and rightly (choosing) the means that are in accordance with reason,"[45] then no one can be constitutionally excluded from the capacity for real self-direction.

This providential drama is, I suggest, a large part of the reason Aquinas rejects Aristotle's notion of natural slaves. To be ordered to God rather than to another human being and to have the capacity for self-direction are linked. This link is exactly why Aquinas rejects Aristotle's notion that the slave is ordered completely to his master.[46]

It is true that the slave's capacity for self-direction does not negate the master's authority; part of a slave's self-direction is to submit to the proper authority of his master in those things to which the master's authority extends.[47] But Aquinas limits the master's authority by extending the range of the slave's self-direction with respect to a number of bodily actions. This extension, particularly in the case of disposing one's own procreative activity, has frequently been recognized. But it is often thought that here Aquinas is taking steps toward a modern account of human equality, especially since he justifies this self-direction by saying that "by nature all men are equal (*pares*)."[48] But if it were true that Aquinas has at least incipient civic equality in mind, it would be hard to account for the specific choice of actions in which the slave's self-direction is to be unobstructed. I suggest that Aquinas is not

---

[44] Aristotle, *Nicomachean Ethics* VIII,11.

[45] Nicholas M. Healy, *Thomas Aquinas: Theologian of the Christian Life* (Aldershot: Ashgate, 2003), p. 142.

[46] *ST* I-II, q. 104, a. 1, ad 3; cf. *ST* II-II, q. 58, a. 9, ad 3.

[47] *ST* II-II, q. 104, a. 5, corpus.

[48] *ST* II-II, q. 104, a. 5, corpus. See, for example, Porter, *Nature as Reason*, pp. 356–7 and 393–4.

here taking steps toward civic equality. Rather, he is subordinating civic difference to the ordering of all persons toward their fulfillment in God. If that fulfillment is made possible by God's grace and aimed at *in via* through the life of the Church, then no household or civic relationship can lawfully restrain anyone from making his or her own contribution to the life of the Church. That explains why "servants are not bound to obey their masters, nor children their parents, in the question of contracting marriage or of remaining in the state of virginity or the like."[49] Everyone is *by nature* the peer of everyone else not in some civic sense that abstracts from human particularity and difference, but in being naturally ordered to beatitude in God. That ordering is worked out *in via* through the providence that calls all to participate freely in the life of the Church, here either by partaking of the sacrament of marriage or by following the counsel of chastity.[50] A similar logic accounts for another limitation of the master's authority: no one can lawfully restrain anyone from participating in the proper worship and reverence for God, and thus slaves can and should refuse to perform on the Sabbath any task imposed on them as slaves.[51]

Thus, household and political arrangements, no matter how natural in view of human diversities and differences, are subordinate to God's intention to create a redemptive, charitable community. And that intention can have politically radical implications. For the ordering of all things to God means, among other things, that the whole institution of slavery is subject to the will of God. After all, the Old Law precept to let slaves go free reflects the fact that Israelites were never intended to be slaves in perpetuity since God had freed them from slavery in Egypt; thus, slavery is subject to God's intent, which sometimes includes freeing slaves.[52]

Aquinas's use of Aristotle on the subordinate members of households is not without its difficulties. But the major lesson to be drawn from it is that Aquinas seeks to adopt an Aristotelian attention to the concrete particularities and differences of human beings while also attending, in a way Aristotle could not, to the ordering of human beings toward beatitude in God, an ordering that qualifies the sorts of subordinations that seem so natural to the shape of households and political communities.

---

[49] *ST* II-II, q. 104, a. 5, corpus.

[50] Thus, Aquinas also holds that laws to promote marriage, which would seem to be for the common good of the political community, may not prevent one from a commitment to virginity (*ST* II-II, q. 152, a. 4, ad 3). Notice the similarity to Aquinas's argument that young people past the age of puberty cannot be restrained by their parents from entering a religious order. Slaves, though, can be restrained by their masters from entering a religious order (*ST* II-II, q. 189, a. 5). I presume Aquinas has pragmatic considerations in mind.

[51] *ST* II-II, q. 122, a. 4, ad 3.   [52] *ST* I-II, q. 105, a. 4, ad 1.

7.4. JUSTICE AND PROPERTY

For Aristotle and Aquinas justice presupposes both the distinction of the supposits between whom something is "due"—the distinction of "yours" from "mine"—and a common membership in structured forms of relation— a shared "us." Conventions of property are one of the most prominent ways in which human societies give expression to such distinctiveness within commonality. In fact, Aquinas suggests the language of justice is most at home in situations involving exchanges of property ("to each his own"), although the notion is readily transferred to other settings.[53]

Both Aristotle and Aquinas take very seriously conventions of property, and the distinctions of "yours" from "mine" they articulate. But they both take the common membership such conventions serve and hold together very seriously as well, so seriously that the ends of the whole qualify the practice of the conventions of property. Yet here again Aquinas goes beyond Aristotle. For Aristotle, the end that qualifies conventions of property is the good of the *polis*, which is especially realized in the good of its citizens (most of whom Aristotle assumes are fairly well served by existing property relations). For Aquinas, on the other hand, the "yours" and "mine" of conventional property relations are more susceptible to being countered by alternative distribution obligations and even suspended altogether in light of God's goal of succoring the poor and creating an interdependent community of charitable exchange.

Yet, although Aquinas goes beyond Aristotle in qualifying the "yours" and "mine" of property conventions, nevertheless he does not take less seriously than Aristotle the distinction of supposits those conventions articulate. Indeed, he takes those distinctions and those conventions seriously enough that he seems to leave open the door to the idea that property conventions might have existed "naturally" even in Eden. Some interpreters have suggested from a Christian perspective that Aquinas is *too* Aristotelian at this point—they worry that Aquinas's appreciation for Aristotle leaves him allowing an immanent natural teleology, rather than the eschatological determination of the human's fulfillment, to determine what is truly natural. Joan Lockwood O'Donovan, for example, has charged Aquinas with opting for Aristotle over against a more Augustinian (and Christian) conviction that the regime of "mine" and "yours" is necessary only in light of human sin. Aquinas thus allegedly moves away from the idea that a unity of spiritual participation is natural, replacing it with a sense of distributed proprietorship.[54]

---

[53] *ST* II-II, q. 58, a. 11, ad 3.
[54] Joan L. O'Donovan, "Christian Platonism and Non-Proprietary Community," in Oliver O'Donovan and Joan L. O'Donovan, *Bonds of Imperfection: Christian Politics, Past and Present* (Grand Rapids, MI: Eerdmans, 2004), pp. 73–96, at 94, n. 77.

To understand Aquinas's position on this question, it is helpful to recall some aspects of his historical setting, especially since O'Donovan identifies more with what she calls a Franciscan-Wycliffite view. As a Dominican, Aquinas of course had much in common with the Franciscans.[55] But he resisted a tendency among some Franciscans to idealize poverty so much that they considered property as such to be a mark of imperfection.[56] And he was especially wary of those committed to a Joachimite eschatology, who saw the Franciscan movement as the harbinger of the dawning of a new, more "spiritual" age, an age in which no one claims anything as "mine" or "yours." Aquinas sought to combat such notions by, for example, insisting that poverty is not to be identified with perfection, but is merely instrumental to it.[57]

The basic grammar of Aquinas's view on the justification of property is worked out over the course of the first two questions on theft in *ST* II-II, q. 66, aa. 1–2. The two articles mark a distinction between an indeterminate dominion belonging to all human beings (a. 1) and the convention of individual property (a. 2). A number of Aristotelian arguments appear here, including the idea that humans may use external goods since the imperfect is for the sake of the perfect,[58] as well as some reasons an individual property regime works better than a common property regime.[59] But the very distinction between an indeterminate dominion in a. 1 and possessing as "one's own" (*proprium*) in a. 2 marks an important difference from Aristotle. For Aristotle property per se is natural. Property is natural because separate households are natural, and households cannot exist without appropriating the belongings they require.[60] For Aquinas what is straightforwardly natural is human dominion, which is not necessarily distributed as individual property, while a regime of property is a *ius gentium* convention instituted as "an addition (to the natural law) devised by human reason,"[61] and thus natural in a secondary sense. As we will see in the present section, Aquinas employs this distinction to subordinate individual property to the intention of God for the sustenance of all.

If O'Donovan is right, these two articles establish that property is "natural in its distributive aspect"[62] in a way that fails to account for the difference

---

[55] The classic treatment of the "vita apostolica" movements in general is Herbert Grundmann, *Religious Movements in the Middle Ages: The Historical Links between Heresy, the Mendicant Orders, and the Women's Religious Movement in the Twelfth and Thirteenth Century, with the Historical Foundations of German Mysticism*, trans. Steven Rowan (Notre Dame, IN: University of Notre Dame Press, 1995).

[56] See Malcolm D. Lambert, *Franciscan Poverty: The Doctrine of the Absolute Poverty of Christ and the Apostles in the Franciscan Order, 1210–1323* (London: SPCK, 1961).

[57] Jean-Pierre Torrell, OP, sees an attempt to address certain Franciscans on this issue in the *SCG*. See Torrell, *Saint Thomas Aquinas*, vol. 2, pp. 88–9.

[58] *ST* II-II, q. 66, a. 1; Aristotle, *Politics* I,3.

[59] *ST* II-II, q. 66, a. 2; Aristotle, *Politics* II,2.

[60] Aristotle, *Politics* I,1.   [61] *ST* II-II, q. 66, a. 2, ad 1.

[62] O'Donovan, "Christian Platonism," p. 94.

between what is "natural" in paradise and what is "natural" in light of human sin. O'Donovan's concern is important. In effect, she sees Aquinas's use of Aristotle here as anticipating the modern assumption that what Christians call the contingent effects of sin in human life are instead inescapable aspects of the human condition. After all, Aquinas borrows from Aristotle reasons for an individual property regime that clearly presuppose human wickedness (to promote care rather than laziness and to avoid quarrels), but he does not specify that under sinless conditions such reasons would not apply. Aquinas's distinction between q. 66, a. 1 and q. 66, a. 2 does not obviously map onto a chronological distinction between innocence and sin. The distinction is between God's intent that humans have the goods they need and a particular convention for facilitating God's intent. These two articles can appear to reflect something like an Aristotelian natural teleology with "God" playing the role of "nature."

But I contend that Aquinas intentionally omits reference to innocence and sin here in order to leave open the possibility that an individual property regime may have been compatible with life in the state of innocence. And in doing so, he does not, I suggest, let a non-Christian narrative control the story; rather, he builds into his account of property an attention to the concrete and embodied character of human existence, whether in the state of innocence or not. Notice that in addition to the two reasons for property that have been mentioned, Aquinas also includes a reason not found in Aristotle (to avoid confusion and disorder over who is to care for what). This novel reason of Aquinas's does not presuppose human sin in his view, as is clear from his discussion of dominion in the state of innocence. There he mentions the inequalities and differences that would exist among people even in a state of innocence, different degrees of advancement in virtue, or differences of bodily strength and disposition.[63] And he suggests that there would have been rule among such people, both to employ the gifts of those more knowledgeable or virtuous and because a common life requires a presidency to order it, "for many, as such, seek many things, whereas one attends only to one."[64] Even in the state of innocence, in other words, there could be confusion and disorder if there were no leader.

Aquinas does not definitively say there would be individual property in the state of innocence. When discussing the state of innocence, he never raises the question. His silence may reflect an Augustinian presumption that there would be none. But Aquinas's novel reason for individual property suggests he can imagine that an individual property regime, which among sinful humanity

---

[63] *ST* I, q. 96, a. 3.

[64] *ST* I, q. 96, a. 4, corpus; Aquinas nods to Aristotle's *Politics* here. See Paul J. Weithman, "Augustine and Aquinas on Original Sin and the Function of Political Authority," *Journal of the History of Philosophy* 30 (1992): pp. 353–76.

better facilitates God's intent that humans have the goods they need, may have done the same even in a state of innocence. He is not thereby reading sin back into the very nature of the human being. On the contrary, he is affirming that even sinless people would be temporal people, developing over time, so that some would be more advanced than others, and that even sinless people would be separate people, unable to read one another's minds. Thus, even sinless people would need order in the form of a leader (and maybe in the form of conventions of individual property). This is not to deny "the unity of spiritual participation," but to envision a unity of real, embodied human beings. And this Aristotelian emphasis serves other interests of Aquinas that are ecclesiological and biblical. Aquinas wants to resist the implication of some Franciscans that perfection requires non-ownership, because of ecclesiastical traditions suggesting that bishops (who own goods) are in a state of perfection at least as great as religious (who take vows of poverty). Those traditions are supported by biblical texts that seem to suggest that riches under certain circumstances can be compatible with perfection.[65]

Aquinas also follows Aristotle in distinguishing ownership (which is individual) from use (which is common), but here Aquinas employs his un-Aristotelian distinction between indeterminate dominion and the convention of property to reconfigure quite radically the rationale for and implications of the ownership–use distinction. For Aristotle, as we have seen in the present section, property is perfectly natural. The rationale for commonality of use is that without it, the practice of individual ownership would undermine the unity of the *polis*.[66] Thus, the friendship of citizens is fostered if one may use the property of another (his slave, his dog, his horse) when there is need. The goal of political unity shapes the range of application of common use. Common use clearly does not extend, for example, to a slave using what he needs that belongs to another. And it is more about a friendship of equals than about caring for the poor. Aristotle does not mention common use as relevant to alleviating poverty at all. Caring for the poor is not really a concern of his, except insofar as civil strife is avoided by regulating property so as to limit poverty,[67] and insofar as patronage friendships between persons of unequal means[68] allow the virtuous to practice their liberality.

For Aquinas, on the other hand, the rationale for common use is the intention of God to succor the needy, which corresponds to the indeterminate dominion God grants humanity by nature. Consider Aquinas's acceptance of what is commonly called the "right of need" (*ius necessitatis*), that if the poor are in dire enough straits, their need makes all property common so that whatever they take to meet their need is not theft.[69] Whereas for Aristotle,

---

[65] *ST* II-II, q. 184, a. 7; q. 185, a. 6, ad 1.   [66] Aristotle, *Politics* II,4.
[67] Aristotle, *Politics* II,8.   [68] Aristotle, *Nicomachean Ethics* VIII,14.
[69] *ST* II-II, q. 66, a. 7.

ownership should be conditioned by common use for the sake of political unity, for Aquinas the convention of property is subordinate to the intention of God, which can under certain circumstances completely negate the convention. Even when need falls short of a mortal threat to survival, Aquinas sees common use as aimed at succoring the needy, so that excessive possession amounts not only to a lack of liberality, but to injustice. Aristotle faults those who fail in liberality, but his concern is not meeting the needs of the poor so much as fostering the liberal man's achievement of human freedom and initiative.[70] For Aquinas, on the other hand, to have more than others is no sin if one is willing to share it, but one sins "if he excludes others indiscriminately from using it."[71] Moreover, Aquinas exegetes Ambrose's statement, "Let no man call his own that which is common," as supporting his own defense of individual possession by interpreting "that which is common" as referring to one's excess that could be used by others, and he confirms that reading of Ambrose by continuing the quote: "He who spends too much is a robber."[72]

Whereas for Aristotle, the covetous are a nuisance who should be kept from having too much power,[73] for Aquinas the covetous, insofar as they keep what others may need, offend against justice; it is "a sin directly against one's neighbor, since one man cannot overabound in external riches, without another man lacking them."[74] The complexity of Aquinas's account of "one's own" is evident here, for the rich man's excess is in one sense *not* "his own," but neither is it strictly someone else's, as though the poor man would be justified in taking it even aside from the case of an emergency. Aside from the emergency case, the rich man's claim is not completely suspended, although it is overwritten by the claims of divine justice. Discerning these complex and overlapping "dues" requires divinely bestowed prudence, but in Aquinas's view they are clearly configured both to press God's goal of succoring the needy and to encourage such succor to be done not against the will of the rich man, but by the virtue of God's people.[75]

Notice how Aquinas transforms Aristotle. For both, property is natural in a sense. But Aquinas reads the origin of property not in terms of the immanent teleology of the *polis* but in light of the intention of the Maker. And for Aquinas the Maker aims primarily not at a civic community that has the

---

[70] Terence H. Irwin, "Generosity and Property in Aristotle's *Politics*," *Social Philosophy and Policy* 4 (1987): pp. 37–54.

[71] *ST* II-II, q. 66, a. 2, ad 2.   [72] *ST* II-II, q. 66, a. 2, ad 3.

[73] Aristotle, *Politics* II,9.   [74] *ST* II-II, q. 118, a. 1, ad 2.

[75] Thus, Old Law precepts allowing the poor to take what they needed from the fields of a neighbor were intended to bring into being a people capable of living out the charity that characterizes the life of God (cf. *ST* I-II, q. 105, a. 2, ad 1). See Matthew Levering, *Christ's Fulfillment of Torah and Temple: Salvation according to Thomas Aquinas* (Notre Dame, IN: University of Notre Dame Press, 2002), pp. 115–16. See section 3 of Chapter 4 in this work.

proper stability, civic bonds, and rewards for virtue, but at caring for the needs of all alike and at creating a charitable community in which needs are cared for voluntarily. These divine intentions determine what property is for, and thus what counts as justice in possession. So justice, in all its "naturalness," aims at an object that would not have the shape it does except for the charity of God. And a *polis* aimed at the nobility and self-sufficiency so prominent in Aristotle would be in Aquinas's view a *polis* inadequately aimed at its own good, even failing of justice and failing to recognize its failure of justice. These aspects of Aquinas's account of property have been called a fundamental "humanism."[76] If that is the right word for it, it is a humanism of the Gospel.

7.5. JUSTICE AND THE POLITICAL COMMUNITY

As we have seen in sections 7.2 and 7.4, justice presupposes the distinction of "mine" and "yours" in the context of a shared "us." For Aristotle, the "us" that provides that context is primarily the *polis*. So the laws of a *polis* are the primary reference points for determining the standards of justice, and justice only obtains between members of the same *polis*. Aquinas goes beyond Aristotle here, by appealing to a transcendent standard of law and by assuming that relations of justice exist between any persons. But, as on slavery and on possessions, it is easy to misconstrue how Aquinas goes beyond Aristotle. Particularly, it is easy to assume that Aquinas takes less seriously than Aristotle how conventional and how particular human political life is.

Aquinas's account of justice seems to stretch Aristotle's account in Stoic directions. Of course, he offers a multilayered account of law, in which human law is rooted in natural law, which stems from eternal law in the mind of the universal lawgiver. Further, Aquinas considers humanity not only naturally political, but social (*sociale*), using the Latin translation of *koinōnikon*, the Stoic term meaning that a man is a citizen not just of some city, but of the whole inhabited world of his time.[77] Justice, Aquinas says, pertains not only to actions toward one's fellow citizens, but to actions "towards all persons in general," a class Aquinas equates with "our neighbor."[78]

The contrast between Aristotle's view and Aquinas's on these matters is sometimes construed as a shift from Aristotelian attention to the particularities of the *polis* and the adaptability of practical wisdom to those particularities in

---

[76] Anthony Parel, "Aquinas' Theory of Property," in *Theories of Property: Aristotle to the Present*, edited by Anthony Parel and Thomas Flanagan (Waterloo, ON: Wilfrid Laurier University Press, 1979), pp. 89–111, at 89.

[77] Torrell, *Saint Thomas Aquinas*, vol. 2, p. 279.

[78] *ST* II-II, q. 122, a. 6, ad 1.

the direction of a more abstract or inflexible natural universalism. But Aquinas is more Aristotelian than that. Here we touch on a tangle of issues much too large to address adequately here, namely the proper understanding of natural right, natural law, positive law, and politics in Aristotle and Aquinas. Scholarly discussion has been especially intense in this area, and the major problems are by no means settled.[79] But the advances made by that scholarly discussion allow some brief remarks to be made here in order to suggest that, when it comes to the relation of justice to particular political communities, Aquinas continues to adopt Aristotle's attention to the concrete shape of life in this world, while continuing to "correct" Aristotle in light of the ordering of human beings toward their beatitude in God.

Concerning the relation of justice to the laws of a particular political community, it is important to notice that Aquinas's teaching on natural law is not about humans having some sort of unconditioned access to universal moral truth. Rather, natural law is the name for the activity by which humans identify and act on the precepts, accessible to natural reason but requiring more and more wisdom as one descends further into concrete particulars, in accord with which a life of virtue may be lived out. One of the primary venues for such activity is the framing of civil laws, which is always undertaken in specific historical and political contexts. Thus, we should not be surprised that Aquinas agrees with Aristotle (and Augustine) on the importance of heeding written laws.[80] Of course, the notion of natural law gives Aquinas a more straightforward way than Aristotle had to name the fact that some so-called laws are really perversions of law, but it does not provide any shortcut to discerning which laws those are.[81]

---

[79] Scholars continue to discuss, for example, Harry Jaffa's argument in *Thomism and Aristotelianism* that Aquinas teaches a natural law doctrine less flexible and accessible than Aristotle's teaching on natural right, and that Aquinas distorts our understanding of Aristotle by reading his natural law teaching back into Aristotle. Pamela Hall has successfully, in my view, refuted the notion that Aquinas's natural law teaching is inflexible or in any way ahistorical, yet questions remain about the relation of natural and divine law. More recently, Mary Keys has made a compelling case that Aquinas does not read his own teaching back into Aristotle and that insofar as Aquinas's teaching differs from Aristotle's, it is an improvement more than a loss; yet here questions remain about the character of this improvement. I will address some of those questions in what follows. These examples only scratch the surface of scholarly interest in issues of natural right, natural law, and politics in Aristotle and Aquinas. And that is to say nothing of the scholarly interest in Aquinas's ecclesiology, which is also relevant here. Harry V. Jaffa, *Thomism and Aristotelianism: A Study of the Commentary by Thomas Aquinas on the Nicomachean Ethics* (Chicago: University of Chicago Press, 1952); Pamela M. Hall, *Narrative and the Natural Law: An Interpretation of Thomistic Ethics* (Notre Dame, IN: University of Notre Dame Press, 1994); Mary M. Keys, *Aquinas, Aristotle, and the Promise of the Common Good* (Cambridge: Cambridge University Press, 2006).

[80] *ST* II-II, q. 60, a. 5.

[81] Aristotle's respect for civil laws does not keep him from declaring popularly enacted laws to be unjust. For example, in the *Politics*, he makes clear his view that laws allowing one class to plunder the possessions of the others are unjust laws, whether they favor the poor or the rich

For Aquinas, as much as for Aristotle, there is no escaping the need for virtue here. It requires virtue even to determine in particular circumstances what the laws promulgate more generally. Aquinas makes this clearest in his account of the judgment of a judge, where he expands on Aristotle's claim that the judge is a "personification of justice"[82] to say that judgment must belong to the virtue of justice since "to decide rightly about virtuous deeds proceeds, properly speaking, from the virtuous habit."[83] To make a right judgment about justice, a judge requires prudence.[84]

The same contrast between the generality of laws and the specificity of the just act can be seen in Aquinas's general and specific accounts of *iura*. *Iura* at first sound quite simple, mathematical even, but it becomes clear that much virtue is required to identify them in detail. Consider the first example of justice Aquinas uses, that of paying a wage for services rendered.[85] On the face of it, hitting the mean in such cases is not difficult. But when Aquinas elaborates on such exchanges in a later question, he makes clear that discerning the right amount of money to exchange for a thing calls for virtue. For achieving the appropriate equality is not merely a matter of the worker and hirer each getting what they can bargain for. Rather, both must try for a real equality in what is exchanged. That is, they must have the determination (perhaps even the perpetual and constant will) to achieve a just result. Trying to buy low and sell high is a threat to the achievement of justice.[86] Any lack of virtue can undermine the possibility of achieving justice, but some dispositions are especially hazardous, such as the "prudence of the flesh" or being oversolicitous about temporal matters.[87] Behind the mathematical simplicity of the initial account of *ius*, therefore, is the messier truth that *iura*, or rules of right relation, call for a fine-tuned prudence to discern their precise contours.

(*Politics* III,10). Apparently laws allowing adultery, theft, or murder would be equally unacceptable (*Nicomachean Ethics* II,6). Such statements clarify what Aristotle means when he speaks of the "naturally just," for as he says, the naturally just "has the same force everywhere and does not depend on what we regard or do not regard as just" (*Nicomachean Ethics* V,7). For a thought-provoking but exaggerated argument that nature functions as no standard of justice at all in Aristotle, see Bernard Yack, "Natural Right and Aristotle's Understanding of Justice," *Political Theory* 18 (1990): pp. 216–37.

[82] Aristotle, *Nicomachean Ethics* V,4.   [83] *ST* II-II, q. 60, a. 1, corpus.

[84] *ST* II-II, q. 60, a. 2, corpus.   [85] *ST* II-II, q. 57, a. 1, corpus.

[86] *ST* II-II, q. 77. Aquinas appeals to Aristotle for the principle that buying and selling are undertaken for mutual advantage (*Politics* I,3), from which he argues that exchange should burden neither party and so the price should reflect the equality of justice. Then Aquinas goes beyond Aristotle to introduce the idea that in certain circumstances what a thing is worth to seller and buyer may be different (say the seller was ready to part with the thing and the buyer needed it with unusual urgency). In such cases, a seller may not sell above its worth to him despite the buyer's willingness, and the buyer is encouraged, though not required by justice, to pay an additional amount on account of his great advantage from the sale out of honesty.

[87] See Hibbs, *Virtue's Splendor*, p. 107; Pieper, "Justice," p. 41, quoting Aquinas on Job 8:1: "Justice is destroyed in twofold fashion: by the false prudence of the sage and by the violent act of the man who possesses power."

Laws can only establish them in very general terms. This distinction helps to account for the fact that for both Aristotle and Aquinas a part of justice is *epikeia*, the virtue of enacting the true will of the legislator even when the relevant law does not adequately cover the case at hand.[88]

If one needs virtue to judge what laws require, it demands great virtue to discern what the laws should be. Aristotle assumes lawgivers can improve at their task, thereby moving in the direction of real justice, which he says in *Politics* VII is determined by the laws of the best *polis*.[89] Aquinas concurs about the possibility of improving laws over time. Although human law expresses natural law, human law can be changed to fit the condition of a people, particularly in light of advances in practical wisdom among law-givers.[90] In this way, natural law is gradually discovered, and its discovery has a narrative shape that responds to the situation and history of a particular people.[91] Thus, the laws God gave to the ancient Israelites to help them recover the knowledge of the natural law were not all timeless moral general-izations; rather, they "represent a prudent disposition in view of the character and historical situation of the Jewish people."[92]

The primary difference between Aristotle and Aquinas here is not that natural law gives Aquinas criteria unavailable to Aristotle for judging laws, but that for Aquinas the *telos* toward which the improvement of human laws aims is seen more clearly because of the guidance toward that *telos* provided by the textured dispensation of divine law. Thus, Aquinas makes the fallibility of the lawmaker even more evident than Aristotle does by comparing existing laws not to the hypothetical laws of the best *polis*, but to the revealed standards of divine justice: if lawmakers are not intent on the common good regulated by divine justice, their laws only make people good in the sense that someone who does well what robbery requires may be called a "good" robber.[93] Consider that apart from the revelation of divine justice, many might errone-ously assume that a starving man taking food from another man's house is committing a theft that must be punished, and so they might pass laws that would rob the needy of what they should have by divine intent. One of the reasons God gives divine law is that, on account of the uncertainty of human judgments in particular matters, we need a law that can show us what is to be

---

[88] Aristotle, *Nicomachean Ethics* V,10; Aquinas, *ST* II-II, q. 120. It seems that Aquinas shifted his understanding of justice in Aristotelian directions over time, since in his commentary on the *Sentences*, he contrasted legal justice with *epikeia*, but in the *ST* he defines legal justice so as to harmonize better with the latter. See Weithman, "Augustine and Aquinas on Original Sin," pp. 370–1.

[89] Cf. Aristotle, *Nicomachean Ethics* V,7.

[90] *ST* I-II, q. 97, a. 1; cf. *ST* I-II, q. 94, aa. 4–5.

[91] Hall, *Narrative and the Natural Law*.

[92] Mark D. Jordan, *Rewritten Theology: Aquinas after his Readers* (Malden, MA: Blackwell, 2006), p. 57.

[93] *ST* I-II, q. 92, a. 1; cf. q. 95, a. 2.

done and what is to be avoided with certainty.[94] Divine law is thus not only a boon to the Church. It helps to clarify standards of justice for society as a whole. Perhaps it is Aquinas's familiarity with the New Testament's guidelines for Church life, for example, that prompts him to notice that even thinking ill of another without sufficient reason is an injury,[95] or that speaking ill of another is injustice.[96] Surely it is biblical commands to care for the poor and love the neighbor that teach Aquinas that judges should, without undoing the equality of justice, seek to succor the poor,[97] and that in certain circumstances lawyers are obliged to work *pro bono* for those who cannot pay.[98] In sum, it is the quite specific laws given to the particular body of the Church that offer Aquinas his transcendent reference for judging human standards of justice.

Concerning the extension of justice beyond the bounds of the particular political community, it is important to notice that Aquinas does not use the term "common good" for the arrangement of temporal goods that might be required to maintain the civil peace of a community coextensive with all humanity. Aquinas certainly uses the term "common good" to go beyond Aristotle. For Aristotle, the common good is simply the good of the particular political community organized for the good of its citizens. For Aquinas, the term "common good" has much more importance, and much wider reference. It has more importance because Aquinas clarifies that general justice takes its cue not from law but from the common good which is the end of law and because Aquinas uses it to distinguish how general justice can be a specific virtue that gives shape to other virtues.[99] It has wider reference because Aquinas uses the term "common good" analogously for a number of ends of human action, so that not only can it refer to those sets of goods in a political community that are required to nurture virtue and civic peace, but also it can refer to God as the end of the human being[100] or to the created enjoyment of God in which human beings can share.[101]

---

[94] *ST* I-II, q. 91, a. 4. Even divine law is not an inflexible standard. The Old Law commands were adapted to their time and place, and the New Law brings those subject to it not under a rigid set of precepts but into the freedom of life in the Spirit, which instills law in human hearts in a way that not only indicates what to do but helps accomplish it (*ST* I-II, q. 106, a. 1, ad 2).

[95] *ST* II-II, q. 60, a. 3, ad 2.   [96] *ST* II-II, qq. 72–76.

[97] *ST* II-II, q. 63, a. 4, ad 3.   [98] *ST* II-II, q. 71, a. 1.

[99] *ST* II-II, q. 58, aa. 5–6. See the careful discussion of how Aquinas clarifies Aristotle here in Keys, *Aquinas, Aristotle, and the Promise of the Common Good*, pp. 178–9. Paul Weithman argues that the fundamental difference between Augustine and Aquinas on government is that Aquinas believes human governments have a positive role to play, perhaps even in the state of innocence, since being subject to political authority can help foster attachment to the common good. See Weithman, "Augustine and Aquinas on Original Sin."

[100] *ST* I-II, q. 109, a. 3; *ST* III, q. 46, a. 2, ad 3; q. 65, a. 3, ad 1.

[101] *ST* I-II, q. 3, a. 1; q. 3, a. 2, ad 2. See Michael S. Sherwin, OP, "St. Thomas and the Common Good: The Theological Perspective: An Invitation to Dialogue," *Ang.* 70 (1993): pp. 307–28.

Aquinas's complexly layered use of the term "common good" surely has something to do with his assumption that justice is found not only within relations in the same particular political community. The "all persons" who are "neighbors" are such partly because they all share in a single "us," the community of those whose end is God. But Aquinas is not moving in Stoic or cosmopolitan directions here. Despite his evocation of Stoic language in calling man a "social" animal, Aquinas is as convinced as Aristotle that the human being is a citizen not of the whole world but of his or her own particular political community. *Pace* Mary Keys, who claims that for Aquinas the human being is "not simply or unproblematically a part of any concrete political community, not even by nature,"[102] Aquinas is quite fond of repeating that human beings—concrete, finite, temporal human beings—are precisely parts of concrete, limited, particular political communities.[103] They are, of course, members of the community of the universe of which God is governor, but they are so *by* and not in spite of their membership in particular political communities (not to mention the fact that the good of such a universal community is apprehended only by God[104]).

Aquinas's justice does transcend the bounds of particular political communities in a way Aristotle's justice does not. But it does so not by abstracting from the concreteness of human political membership and gesturing toward a hypothetical cosmopolis, but rather by holding onto that concreteness while setting it in the context of the Christian drama of the two cities. Neither city is cosmopolis, but the household of God provides a vision of how God creates unity across cultural boundaries.[105] It is thus the divine law given to the household of God that teaches that it accords with the common good for us to "treat every man as our neighbor and brother."[106] Aquinas's universalism is not a version of cosmopolitanism but rather an entailment of commitment to the *civitas Dei*.[107]

---

[102] Keys, *Aquinas, Aristotle, and the Promise of the Common Good*, p. 131.

[103] *ST* II-II, q. 58, aa. 5, 6, and 12; q. 61, a. 1, ad 2; q. 64, aa. 2 and 5; q. 65, a. 1; cf. *ST* I-II, q. 90, a. 3, ad 3; *ST* II-II, q. 26, a. 3.

[104] Cf. *ST* I-II, q. 19, a. 10.

[105] For Aquinas's account of the Church, see Torrell, *Saint Thomas Aquinas*, vol. 2, pp. 291–4.

[106] *ST* II-II, q. 78, a. 1, ad 2. The temptation to read Aquinas as cosmopolitan seems related to the assumption that Aquinas must have had a social or political theory. But as Mark Jordan has argued, it does not seem Aquinas desired to construct a political theory. Thus he breaks up his theoretical comments on political questions and puts them at the service of a moral and salvific pedagogy shaped by Christian theology. See Jordan, *Rewritten Theology*, esp. ch. 3.

[107] Alasdair MacIntyre, *Whose Justice? Which Rationality?* (Notre Dame, IN: University of Notre Dame Press, 1988), p. 153.

7.6. ACQUIRED AND INFUSED JUSTICE:
CONCLUDING REFLECTIONS

There is no doubt that the "natural" stays more consistently close to the surface in Aquinas's discussion of justice than in any other virtue treated in *ST* II-II. Aquinas makes a great deal of use of Aristotle on justice, and Aristotle's account of a virtue often stands as a sort of template representing the acquired version of the virtue. So it is perhaps not surprising that the most common way of dealing with the "naturalness" of justice among Aquinas's interpreters is to assume that it is the acquired version that determines the shape of justice.[108]

But as we have seen in this chapter, Aquinas transforms Aristotle in dramatic ways, and he makes no attempt to hide the fact that he is discussing justice as it appears to the Christian in light of divine law. Could it be that Aquinas has in mind infused rather than acquired justice? But if so, why does he place such emphasis on the naturalness of the precepts of justice? I suggest that the difficulties here arise from the unique character of justice as a virtue whose mean is external to the agent.[109] For that reason, although acquired and infused justice would have distinct aims, the former aiming at a civic good and the latter at the good of the household of God,[110] the mean of these two virtues cannot in practice differ. Consider the mean of temperance. Acquired temperance urges only that eating should not harm the health of the body or hinder the use of reason, while infused temperance calls one to a more severe abstinence in accord with the commands of the Scriptures.[111] The two means can differ since the virtue is a matter of adjustment within oneself, and what counts as a proper adjustment can depend on the agent's circumstances. But in the case of justice, the mean is an adjustment of thing and thing, of person and person. What counts as such an adjustment or equalization could not be different between infused and acquired justice any more than there could be a difference between what counts as theft according to divine law and what counts as theft according to natural law.

Justice is therefore different from the other cardinal virtues for Aquinas not because it is a merely natural virtue, but because it uniquely operates at the intersection of what is knowable by reason and what requires the illumination

---

[108] Even Thomas Hibbs, who is typically very attentive to the theological character of Aquinas's writings, has written of justice as though it were a natural, not an infused virtue. See Thomas S. Hibbs, "Divine Irony and the Natural Law: Speculation and Edification in Aquinas," *International Philosophical Quarterly* 30 (1990): pp. 419–29, at 423.

[109] *ST* II-II, q. 58, a. 10; Aristotle, *Nicomachean Ethics* II,6 and V,4.

[110] *ST* I-II, q. 63, a. 4.   [111] *ST* I-II, q. 63, a. 4.

of faith. Consider how Aquinas identifies the precepts of justice with the Decalogue, which are first principles of law, to which "natural reason assents...at once."[112] We cannot make sense of that move by supposing that the operation of natural reason can never depend for illumination on the theological virtues. After all, while many of the precepts of the Decalogue are easily recognized by most people, the Decalogue includes, for example, a precept against worshipping a graven image. Natural law precepts proceed from principles known naturally, such as that the good to be done includes the worship of God. But as reason seeks to judge on such a matter in particular circumstances, it may need the aid of the wise, or in this case even the aid of divine instruction.[113] That is, this precept may be out of natural reason's range without divine intervention, but it still accords with natural reason since its reasonableness is evident once the precept is presented.[114]

Operating within the knowledge of the divine law, Aquinas is able to give a more certain account of the *iura* that natural reason recognizes as just. So here as elsewhere, the Christian life, illuminated by the teaching of Holy Scripture, is in view, and the characterization of justice reflects teachings of Scripture not commonly held, and in some cases not even available, apart from a people who have received divine law. Yet these *iura* remain the *iura* of justice per se, whether acquired or infused. And this correspondence, too, is written in the Scriptures, for the Gentiles "do by nature those things that are of the Law."[115]

In his treatment of the virtue of justice, we see that Aquinas does not reduce the "natural" merely to what might arise within an immanent natural teleology like that of Aristotle, nor does he posit a more perfect but still "purely natural" teleology by beginning with the life of charity and subtracting grace to imagine what would remain. Rather, he holds together an Aristotelian attentiveness to the concrete shape of human life and the temporal character of human knowledge with a conviction of the naturalness of God's providential action to assist human beings toward their true end. I have tried to show at every turn how Aquinas weaves the Aristotelian attentiveness and the Christian conviction together, assured that humanity's divine destiny does not efface our created concreteness and that neither does humanity's embodied and

---

[112] *ST* II-II, q. 122, a. 1, corpus.   [113] *ST* I-II, q. 100, a. 1.

[114] This sort of benign dependence of natural reason on divine intervention is taken even further in *ST* I-II, q. 104, a. 1, ad 3: "Even in those precepts which direct us to God, some are moral precepts, which the reason itself dictates when it is quickened by faith; such as that God is to be loved and worshipped."

[115] Rom 2:14, cited in *ST* I-II, q. 100, a. 1, sed contra. Aquinas's point here is not that unbelievers ("the Gentiles") worship the true God or in any other way fulfill the Law, but that what the Law requires is accessible to them "by nature."

temporal particularity limit the glorious heights of our supernatural end. Of course, much of what God's action achieves in human life Aquinas sees as beyond the capacities of human nature, but God's action also fulfills human nature in a way that clarifies what the teleological orientation of human nature was aiming at from the beginning.[116]

---

[116] In the words of Thomas Hibbs, "the aspirations of natural law, which are identical to the goals of human nature, are realized only in divine law." See Hibbs, "Divine Irony," p. 423. Cf. Hibbs, "*Imitatio Christi*," p. 562: "the needs, capacities, and defects of human nature become fathomable only under the tutelage of divine instruction."

8

Contemplation and Action
in Aristotle and Aquinas

Mary Catherine Sommers

Both Aristotle and Thomas Aquinas begin their ethical masterpieces, the *Nicomachean Ethics* and the *Secunda Pars*, respectively, with a consideration of the end of human life and end them with arguments about which kind of human life is the best life. This concern for the "form" that a whole life can take may seem archaic, but even in the postmodern era there remains an intuition that there should be something more to human existence than a set of discrete acts, a shape that is not merely chronological or spatial.

8.1. CONTEMPLATION AND THE QUESTION OF THE "BEST LIFE": PRELIMINARY OBSERVATIONS

There are certainly commonalities in Aristotle's and Aquinas's understandings of the terms "contemplation" or "contemplative life." For Aquinas, as for Aristotle, contemplation is both an act and a way of life; it is both the means to happiness or blessedness and happiness itself. However, for Aquinas, contemplation is also freedom for God, making time for which is required by the moral law and designated as Sabbath by the laws of the Church and synagogue.[1] It is the Holy Spirit who, making us lovers of God, also makes us contemplators of God, as it is in contemplation that our *conversation* with God takes place.[2] It is the means of welcoming the indwelling of the Trinity.[3] Contemplation is the reward of labor, able to be shared not only by those whose temporal activities have fitted them for this, as for Aristotle, but by

---

[1] See *In III Sent.*, dist. 37, q. 1, a. 5, quaestiuncula 1, ad 2.
[2] See *SCG* IV, ch. 22 (no. 2).   [3] See *Super Ieremiam*, ch. 7, lect. 4.

those whose lives are characterized by toil.[4] It is an intrinsic cause of devotion despite the fact that the most devout, those who are simple people and women, seem defective in the ability to contemplate.[5] Contemplation, for Aquinas, is of necessity more "democratic" than for Aristotle.

The influence of Aristotle on Aquinas's teaching on contemplation, nevertheless, is profound. It seems reasonable to credit Aristotle for the fact that there is "nothing of anti-intellectualism" in Aquinas's notion of contemplation, even in that type that is a gift of the Holy Spirit. For, although Aquinas roots the motivation for contemplation in love, his doctrine "concedes to the intellect its apprehensive function."[6]

The purpose of this chapter will be to look at Thomas Aquinas's consideration of the meaning of contemplation in conjunction with the problem of the "best life." I will first engage Aquinas's reflections on the "eight reasons by which the Philosopher proves" that "the contemplative life is unconditionally better than the active life."[7] Next, I examine Aquinas's argument explaining why Christ did not choose to live a contemplative life, but rather an active life that "gives to others the fruits of contemplation."[8] I then set forth a hierarchy of the types of contemplation according to Aquinas, in order to show what type of contemplation can be given to others. Finally, the question of whether and to what extent Aquinas has repudiated Aristotle's reasoning about the "best life" will be addressed.

8.2. AQUINAS AND ARISTOTLE'S EIGHT REASONS FOR THE EXCELLENCE OF THE CONTEMPLATIVE LIFE

Although he occasionally uses the threefold division of "lives"—the contemplative, civil, and pleasure-seeking—from the beginning of the *Nicomachean Ethics*,[9] Thomas Aquinas consistently defends a twofold division, demoting

---

[4] See *Catena in Lucam*, ch. 17, lect. 4.   [5] See *ST* II-II, q. 82, a. 3, corpus.

[6] Paul Philippe, OP, "Contemplation, VI.7: Saint Thomas, † 1274," in *Dictionnaire de spiritualité*, vol. II/2, edited by Charles Baumgartner (Paris: Beauchesne, 1953), col. 1983–8, at 1986: "La doctrine mystique de saint Thomas n'a rien de l'anti-intellectualisme d'un Thomas Gallus ou d'un Hugues de Balma. Quoiqu'elle ne le cède en rien à ceux-ci pour le rôle primordial assigné à l'amour, elle reconnaît à l'intelligence sa fonction appréhensive."

[7] *ST* II-II, q. 182, a. 1, corpus.   [8] *ST* III, q. 40, a. 1 (cf. ad 2).

[9] See *Compendium theologiae* I, ch. 163: "Necesse est enim cuiuslibet viventis esse aliquam operationem cui principaliter intendit, et in hoc dicitur vita eius consistere: sicut qui voluptatibus principaliter vacant, dicuntur vitam voluptuosam agere; qui vero contemplationi, contemplativam; qui vero civitatibus gubernandis, civilem." Cf. *Sent. Ethic.* I, lect. 5, no. 5 (Leonine ed., vol. 47/1, p. 18, line 76 to p. 19, line 82): "Vita igitur voluptuosa dicitur quae finem constituit in voluptate sensus, vita vero civilis dicitur quae finem constituit in bono practicae rationis, puta in

the *vita voluptuosa* to a less-than-human existence.[10] According to Jean Leclercq, this makes him a defender of the Christian tradition.[11] It is unlikely, however, that Aquinas understood his position as opposed to that of Aristotle. He appears to think that the Philosopher agrees with him that the *vita activa* and the *vita contemplativa* are the only distinctly human lives.[12]

The twofold division is mirrored, for Aquinas, in the Old and New Testaments, in the two love-commandments[13] and, thus, in the differing perfections of the religious and episcopal "states." It is symbolized by the contrasting pairs: Rachel and Leah, Mary and Martha, Peter and John, male and female, the Peripatetics and the Stoics.[14]

While God's blessedness is fully active and contemplative[15] and angels are able to teach and carry out divine business in the temporal order without defecting from the vision of God that has been granted to them,[16] for human beings action and contemplation present themselves as distinct life choices. Indeed, even Christ is confronted with this choice. Although in the fourteenth century Christine de Pizan will make a plea for the "mixed life" for those lacking the moral stamina to embrace one in exclusion of the other,[17] Aquinas rejects the "mixed life" as a distinct alternative, since in any mix, some one element will predominate, in this instance, either contemplative or active.[18] In *ST* II-II, q. 182, a. 1, Thomas Aquinas offers eight arguments from Aristotle that "the contemplative life is unconditionally better than the active life." This is hardly surprising, since he had already used some of them in demonstrating that some sort of contemplation forms human beatitude.[19] These arguments are vetted as well in his commentary on Book X of the *Nicomachean Ethics*.[20] Indeed, they appear individually in works of Aquinas of

exercitio virtuosorum operum, vita autem contemplativa quae constituit finem in bono rationis speculativae, scilicet in contemplatione veritatis."

[10] See *In III Sent.*, dist. 35, q. 1, a. 1, ad 5; *ST* II-II, q. 179, a. 1, corpus; *De veritate*, q. 11, a. 4, corpus (Leonine ed., vol. 22, p. 362, lines 42–50).

[11] Jean Leclercq, "La vie contemplative dans S. Thomas et dans la tradition," *Recherches de théologie ancienne et médiévale* 28 (1961): pp. 251–68, at 253–4.

[12] Nor is it clear that, even if Aristotle does uphold a threefold division, that the twofold version is exclusively Christian, since this seems to be a Stoic position as well.

[13] See Sermon XVII, *Lux orta* (Leonine ed., vol. 44/1, p. 271, lines 404–413); *Catena in Matthaeum*, ch. 19, lect. 5.

[14] See *Catena in Marcum*, ch. 1, lect. 7; *Catena in Lucam*, ch. 22, lect. 3; *Catena in Ioannem*, ch. 21, lect. 5; *Lectura super Ioannem*, Prologue (no. 1); *Lectura super Ioannem*, ch. 20, lect. 1; *ST* II-II, q. 182, a. 1, corpus; *Super Psalmo* 32 (nos. 11–12); *In I Ad Corinthios*, ch. 11, lect. 3.

[15] See *ST* I, q. 26, a. 4, corpus.

[16] See, e.g., *In II Sent.*, dist. 10, q. 1, a. 4, ad 1.

[17] Christine de Pizan, *The Treasure of the City of Ladies: Or the Book of the Three Virtues*, trans. Sarah Lawson, rev. ed. (London: Penguin, 2003), chs. 6–7 and 14–18.

[18] See *ST* II-II, q. 179, a. 2, ad 2.   [19] See *ST* I-II, q. 3, a. 2, ad 4.

[20] See *Sent. Ethic.* X, lect. 10, no. 18 (Leonine ed., vol. 47/2, p. 585, lines 186–197); lect. 10, no. 16 (p. 584, lines 167–171); lect. 11, no. 7 (p. 587, lines 73–78); lect. 11, no. 8 (p. 587, lines 83–90); lect. 11, no. 9 (p. 588, lines 95–104); lect. 12, no. 14 (p. 592, lines 161–168).

almost every sort: systematic theology, apologetic writings, disputed questions, biblical commentaries and from the beginning to the conclusion of his teaching career. Here are the arguments:

[1] "The contemplative life belongs to a man according to what is best in him, namely according to the intellect . . . while the active life is occupied with exterior things."[21] Therefore, while angels and saints are "in no way" impeded in contemplation through engagement in exterior occupations, for other human beings the "purity of contemplation" will be "blocked" or "slowed."[22]

[2] "The contemplative life is more continuous."[23] While the "summit" of contemplation, which "approaches the uniformity of divine contemplation,"[24] cannot last a long time, other acts of contemplation do, because, in themselves, they are concerned with the incorruptible and unchanging, have no contrariety, no push-pull factor, attached to them, except what is owing to our weaknesses.[25] As human acts they are "intellectual" and so the products of the part of us that lasts beyond this life and, as unconnected with corporeal labor, we are able to persist in them. Indeed, the greater "durability" of the active life does not come from "any property of either life considered in itself, but from our weakness, we who retreat from the height of contemplation through heaviness of body."[26]

[3] "The pleasure of the contemplative life is greater than that of the active."[27] Contemplation is more productive of delight than any corporeal pleasures, owing both to (1) the pleasure that comes from appropriate operations, since contemplation belongs to humans because they are by nature "rational animals," and (2) on account of the object of contemplation, which is God, who is more desirable and lovable than any other object of sense or intellect.[28] Therefore, even though the contemplation of God that is had in this life is imperfect, "it is nevertheless sweeter than any other contemplation, however perfect, because of the excellence of

---

[21] *ST* II-II, q. 182, a. 1, corpus. For the first argument, see Aristotle, *Nicomachean Ethics* X,7 (1177a19–21).

[22] *In IV Sent.*, dist. 44, q. 2, a. 1, quaestiuncula 3, ad 4; *ST* I, q. 112, a. 1, ad 3.

[23] *ST* II-II, q. 182, a. 1, corpus. For the second argument, see Aristotle, *Nicomachean Ethics* X,7 (1177a21–22).

[24] *ST* II-II, q. 180, a. 8, ad 2.

[25] *ST* II-II, q. 180, a. 7, ad 2. Cf. *De veritate*, q. 24, a. 9, corpus (Leonine ed., vol. 22, p. 702, lines 79–104).

[26] *ST* II-II, q. 181, a. 4, ad 3.

[27] *ST* II-II, q. 182, a. 1, corpus. For the third argument, see Aristotle, *Nicomachean Ethics* X,7 (1177a22–27).

[28] *ST* II-II, q. 180, a. 7, corpus.

the thing contemplated."[29] Its "wonderful pleasures," which are not subject to a calculus, are owing to its stability and purity, that is, its "unmixed" character.[30] It is productive of joy and can be compared to "play."[31] Bodily pain or sadness, however, can impede it.[32]

[4] "A man is more self-sufficient when living the contemplative life."[33] This is because contemplation is an interior activity, which not only can be accomplished without "the help of many," but is increased in efficiency by increasing solitariness.[34] Indeed, the "wedding wine" must be put away if one is serious about contemplation.[35]

[5] "The contemplative life is loved more for itself, while the active life is ordered to something else."[36] Indeed, "peace is the end with respect to utility of the active life, and peace is ordered to contemplation."[37] So, while those who wish to devote their lives to contemplation must sometimes put this aside for the needs of the world,[38] or the Church, as with bishops,[39] this is only a *secundum quid et in casu* priority.[40] However, there is a second and more significant sense in which the active life can be said to have a priority over the contemplative. Adam and Eve before the Fall were capable of "a clear and firm contemplation of the intelligible effects [of God], which they perceived through an irradiation of the First Truth, whether by natural or gratuitous cognition."[41] This contemplation was not impeded by any disordered passion from tending towards God.[42] After the Fall, "certain sins will

---

[29] *ST* II-II, q. 180, a. 7, ad 3.

[30] *Sent. Ethic.* VII, lect. 13, no. 14 (Leonine ed., vol. 47/2, p. 433, lines 155–168). Cf. lect. 14, no. 4 (p. 436, lines 39–53); lect. 14, no. 19 (p. 438, lines 252–259); lect. 14, no. 20 (p. 438, line 268 to p. 439, line 276); *Sent. Ethic.* X, lect. 3, no. 7 (Leonine ed., vol. 47/2, p. 559, line 74 to p. 560, line 88); lect. 10, no. 11 (p. 584, lines 116–122); *Expositio libri Boetii De ebdomadibus*, lect. 1 (Leonine ed., vol. 50, p. 268, lines 36–46).

[31] *Expositio libri Boetii De ebdomadibus*, lect. 1 (Leonine ed., vol. 50, p. 267, line 22 to p. 268, line 32); Sermon XX, *Beata gens* (Leonine ed., vol. 44/1, p. 321, lines 320–326).

[32] *Expositio super Iob ad litteram*, ch. 17 (Leonine ed., vol. 26, p. 108, lines 154–170).

[33] *ST* II-II, q. 182, a. 1, corpus. For the fourth argument, see Aristotle, *Nicomachean Ethics* X,7 (1177a27–b1).

[34] *Expositio libri Boetii De ebdomadibus*, lect. 1 (Leonine ed., vol. 50, p. 267, lines 3–8). See also *ST* II-II, q. 188, a. 8, corpus; *Super Threnos*, ch. 3, lect. 10.

[35] *Lectura super Ioannem*, Expositio in Prologum S. Hieronymi (Marietti ed., no. 18).

[36] *ST* II-II, q. 182, a. 1, corpus. For argument 5, see Aristotle, *Nicomachean Ethics* X,7 (1177b1–4).

[37] *Super Psalmo* 45 (no. 8).

[38] See *Contra impugnantes*, ch. 19 (Leonine ed., vol. 41, p. A 152, lines 79–93); *Quaestio disputata de caritate*, a. 11, ad 6; *In I Ad Corinthios*, ch. 12, lect. 3 (no. 746).

[39] See *De perfectione*, ch. 21 (Leonine ed., vol. 41, p. B 93, lines 21–39); ch. 27 (p. 105, lines 136–163).

[40] See *ST* II-II, q. 182, a. 1, corpus.

[41] *ST* I, q. 94, a. 1, corpus; cf. *ST* II-II, q. 5, a. 1, ad 1; *De malo*, q. 5, a. 1, corpus (Leonine ed., vol. 23, p. 131, lines 173–184).

[42] See *In II Sent.*, dist. 30, q. 1, a. 1, corpus.

darken the intellect's contemplative act" because they disturb and disorder the passions.[43] This is not falsified by the fact that some "on account of their natural genius" can perform feats of subtle reasoning despite their uncleanness.[44] In the end, however, only "the pure of heart" will see God. Therefore, the active life in pursuit of the moral virtues is propaedeutic to contemplation and has precedence in that regard.[45] Contemplation, however, can impede incontinence.[46] And, of course, the blessed, who continuously contemplate God, have their wills totally conformed to his.[47]

[6] "The contemplative life consists in a certain freedom and quiet."[48] Despite its stillness,[49] however, contemplation because of its very intensity is not to be confused with "sloth."[50] And, if philosophers are not condemned for withdrawing from mundane activities in order to contemplate, then neither should those be condemned who do so for religious reasons.[51] The same *a fortiori* argument applies to those living on alms or begging in order to be free for contemplation.[52] Indeed, those "who leave everything" in order to be free for contemplation are following a "counsel of Christ."[53]

[7] "The contemplative life is lived divinely, but the active life is lived humanly."[54] Its exercise admits the human person into a life common to God and the angels: "Consequently, for God as well as for the angels and even for man, the supreme happiness and blessedness is the contemplation of God—this is the view not only of the saints, but also of the philosophers."[55] And again:

Thus the Philosopher in the tenth Book of the *Ethics* rejects the position of those who say that man ought not to intrude himself into divine things, but only human ones, saying: "But we must not follow those who advise us, being men, to think of

---

[43] *In II Sent.*, dist. 39, q. 3, a. 3, expositio textus. Cf. *De veritate*, q. 18, a. 1, ad 4.

[44] *ST* II-II, q. 15, a. 3, ad 1.

[45] See *Contra retrahentes*, ch. 7 (Leonine ed., vol. 41, p. C 51, lines 239–258); *Super Psalmo* 54 (no. 5).

[46] See *De perfectione*, ch. 10 (Leonine ed., vol. 41, p. B 76, lines 82–94); *Primae redactiones Summae contra Gentiles*, liber 3*; *De veritate*, q. 26, a. 10, corpus (Leonine ed., vol. 22, p. 784, lines 178–191), ad 2, and ad 5.

[47] See *De veritate*, q. 23, a. 8, corpus (Leonine ed., vol. 22, p. 674, lines 115–125).

[48] *ST* II-II, q. 182, a. 1, corpus. For argument 6, see Aristotle, *Nicomachean Ethics* X,7 (1177b4–26).

[49] See *Quodlibet* IV, q. 12, a. 1, ad 16.

[50] See *Quodlibet* VII, q. 7, a. 2, corpus (Leonine ed., vol. 25/1, p. 44, line 250 to p. 45, line 277).

[51] See *Contra impugnantes*, ch. 6 (Leonine ed., vol. 41, p. A 98, lines 412–426).

[52] See *Contra impugnantes*, ch. 7 (Leonine ed., vol. 41, p. A 111, lines 533–543).

[53] *Contra impugnantes*, ch. 5 (Leonine ed., vol. 41, p. A 92, lines 570–576).

[54] *ST* II-II, q. 182, a. 1, corpus. For argument 7, see Aristotle, *Nicomachean Ethics* X,7 (1177b26–1178a2).

[55] *In II Sent.*, dist. 4, q. 1, a. 1, corpus.

human things, and, being mortal, of mortal things, but must, so far as we can, make ourselves immortal, and do all we can to live in accordance with the best thing in us."[56]

[8] "The contemplative life is [lived] according to that which is most proper to man, i.e. the intellect, while in the operations of the active life, the inferior powers, which are common to us and to brute animals, are also involved."[57]

8.3. *SED CONTRA*: THE LIFE CHRIST CHOSE

It would seem that the conclusion that the contemplative life is "unconditionally better" than the active life is firmly established in the *Summa theologiae* and throughout Thomas Aquinas's works by means of Aristotle's eight arguments. Indeed, when Aquinas recites a ninth argument, which "the Lord appends," it is not to bolster up a weak edifice, but to complete with gospel testimony an edifice secure through reason: "Mary has chosen the better part." Nevertheless, writing his "life of Jesus" in the *Tertia Pars*, Aquinas firmly recants this reasoning. An argument that it would have been appropriate for Christ to live as a "solitary," because solitude is characteristic of the contemplative life, which is the "most perfect life,"[58] is answered with a qualification:

> As it is said in the Second Part, the contemplative life is unconditionally better than the active [life] which concerns itself with bodily acts; but the [type of] active life in which someone gives to others the products of contemplation through preaching and teaching is *more perfect* than the life which is devoted solely to contemplation, because such a life presupposes an abundance of contemplation. And thus Christ chose this kind of life.[59]

Aquinas here refers back to *ST* II-II, q. 188, a. 6 where he argues for a hierarchy of religious orders based on the type of "life" enjoined by the end for which the order exists: the active life of teaching and preaching, e.g. that of the Order of Preachers, is the highest, and is shared by bishops; contemplative orders are next; and they are followed by those that deal with the corporal works of mercy, e.g. ransoming captives, visiting the sick. It cannot be accidental that Aquinas makes the argument *for* the solitary life here (in *ST* III, q. 40, a. 1) from the conclusion of the eight arguments of Aristotle (in *ST* II-II, q. 182, a. 1) only to frame the argument *against* it from the

---

[56] *Super Boetium De Trinitate*, q. 2, a. 1, corpus (Leonine ed., vol. 50, p. 93, lines 72–86).

[57] *ST* II-II, q. 182, a. 1, corpus. For argument 8, see Aristotle, *Nicomachean Ethics* X,7 (1178a2–8). See also *ST* I-II, q. 3, a. 5, corpus.

[58] *ST* III, q. 40, a. 1, arg. 2.   [59] *ST* III, q. 40, a. 1, ad 2 (my emphasis).

conclusion of *ST* II-II, q. 188, a. 6. He is letting us know that he has changed his mind.[60] This change is sudden and, in some sense, unprecedented. Aquinas never hints at the existence of two types of active life until q. 188, a. 6. His defection from the priority of the contemplative life has caused a good deal of confusion among his commentators. Jean Leclercq, for example, says he posits "another [and likely novel] category of contemplatives," those that can be called "the active contemplatives."[61] How does this defection come about?

Thomas Aquinas assumes that there was a moment when Christ chose the form his life would take. Aquinas organizes his teaching on Christ in the *Tertia Pars* into two parts: the "mystery of the Incarnation" and those things that the incarnate God did and suffered for our salvation.[62] The deeds and sufferings are organized according to Christ's life-cycle—*ingressus, progressus, exitus*, and *exaltatio*.[63] Aquinas locates the moment of choice in the *progressus* subsequent to the baptism by John at the initiation of Christ's public life. Aquinas uses the expression *Christus elegit* sparingly: "Christ chose" for himself a virgin mother, poor parents, twelve apostles, a Church, voluntary poverty, sorrow, and a certain type of life, an active life that gives to others the fruits of one's contemplation through teaching and preaching. He chose to "rub shoulders" with his fellow human beings (*inter homines conversando*) despite the more godlike character of the solitary life when embraced "in order to contemplate the truth," as Aristotle says.[64]

To identify the type of life chosen by Christ is clearly important. In an age concerned with the *imitatio Christi* it establishes an ideal, a "first." However, this identification is the end, not the beginning, of Aquinas's attempts to determine the best type of life and, correlatively, to understand religious orders in terms of action and contemplation. In the *Contra impugnantes*, Aquinas had defended various practices of mendicant orders, e.g. teaching, preaching, hearing confessions, begging, while assuming (at least for the sake of the argument) that all religious orders, mendicants included, live lives ordered to contemplation. In the *De perfectione spiritualis vitae* Aquinas

---

[60] Torrell does not understand this as a shift in Thomas's thinking. He describes the first treatment of the relative perfection of the two lives (*ST* II-II, q. 182, aa. 1–2) as pertaining "to the treatise on religious life," which, apart from *ST* II-II, q. 188, a. 6, corpus, "is not only incomplete, it is truncated, and its perspective is completely distorted." However, the treatment of the "lives" (*ST* II-II, qq. 179–182) is *not* part of a "treatise on religious life"; it is, as is clear from the Prologue preceding *ST* II-II, qq. 171–189, part of a treatise on "habits and acts of the rational soul" insofar as these differentiate human beings, the preceding questions (qq. 1–170) having covered "the virtues and vices which pertain to human beings of all conditions and states." The differences are caused by gratuitous graces, forms of life, states (among which is the "religious state"), and duties. For arguments that there is a shift in Aquinas's thinking and for the stages of his thinking on the "best life," see Mary Catherine Sommers, "Thomas Aquinas' Polemic of Perfection," in *Atti del IX Congresso tomistico internazionale*, vol. 5, Problemi teologici alla luce dell'Aquinate, edited by Antonio Piolanti (Città del Vaticano: Libreria Editrice Vaticana, 1991), pp. 362–73.

[61] See Leclercq, "La vie contemplative," p. 263.   [62] *ST* III, Prologue.

[63] *ST* III, q. 27–59; cf. *ST* III, q. 27, Prologue.   [64] *ST* III, q. 40, a. 1, arg. 1.

identified religious perfection with the contemplative life and the first love precept ("thou shalt love the Lord thy God"), and episcopal perfection with the active life and the love of neighbor. The priority of the contemplative life is assumed, indeed, its priority is an argument *against* ranking of bishops higher than religious in the ecclesiastical hierarchy, which Aquinas must address.

Since there is a novel sense of the active life—insofar as it is concerned not solely with "external acts" but also with teaching and preaching, which have both interior and exterior components—one wonders whether there is an altered sense of "contemplation" as well. Have both components been changed in order to be integrated into a single life? In discussing what Aquinas means by "contemplation" in the questions on the life of Christ in the *Tertia Pars*, Jean-Pierre Torrell says:

> Here it is not a question of infused contemplation of the kind that later John of the Cross and the Carmelite mystics will speak of. Thomas certainly understands what this type involves, but he also knows that one cannot identify it as the source of preaching or teaching. For his part, Thomas is speaking of something very lofty, to be sure, but he is thinking rather of a contemplation acquired by human means through the practice of various exercises within a whole life driven by this dominant activity—and which is called on that account "contemplative." A contemplation of the sort he conceives is the act of the habit of acquired wisdom which is built on a foundation of the faith. In the realized act, [this contemplation] certainly culminates in a simple grasp of truth (*simplex intuitus veritatis*), but it is preceded by a search where hearing the Word of God, prayer and study normally lead to this accomplishment.[65]

The contemplation that may overflow into action has several characteristics: (1) it is an acquired, not an infused habit; (2) while acquired, it is founded on faith; (3) it is constituted by practices that in-form a complete life that can be called "contemplative," including the *lectio divina*, prayer, and study; (4) it comes to fruition in a vision of the truth; (5) it is a means to teaching and preaching.

What Torrell describes as "theological contemplation" has this major difference from "the contemplation of mystics," namely "that it lives on the human level, it remains an expressible reality; the *contemplata*, the truths being contemplated, could then become the object of a communication," i.e., teaching or preaching.[66] How does this "theological contemplation" fit into Aquinas's schema of contemplative acts and is it the only candidate for a contemplation that could form the basis of the kind of active life lived by mendicant friars?

---

[65] Jean-Pierre Torrell, OP, *Le Christ en ses mystères: La vie et l'œuvre de Jésus selon saint Thomas d'Aquin*, vol. 1 (Paris: Desclée, 1999), p. 218.
[66] Torrell, *Le Christ en ses mystères*, p. 219.

8.4. THE PRIMARY AND SECONDARY
SENSES OF "CONTEMPLATION"

It may be appropriate to understand "contemplation" in Aquinas as a *pros hen* equivocal. It denominates an activity that is carried out by God, angels,[67] and human beings; and, human beings carry it out both *in via* and *in patria*. What becomes very clear from Aquinas's way of speaking is that in thinking about contemplation we have to consider both what it is in itself and how it differs among the different classes of practitioners. A list of the contemplative activities possible to human agents in descending order of perfection would look something like what follows.

8.4.1. Contemplation of God *per essentiam in patria*

From his earliest writing, Aquinas distinguishes between the contemplation of the *viator* and the contemplation of the blessed *in patria*, one imperfect, the other perfect:

> All who have thought correctly have posited the end of human life to be the contemplation of God. However, contemplation of God happens in two ways: one through creatures, which is imperfect . . . in which sort of contemplation the Philosopher posits contemplative happiness, which nevertheless is a happiness of this life. There is another sort of contemplation of God, by which he is seen immediately through his essence; and this is perfect contemplation, which will take place in heaven and is possible to man on the basis of faith.[68]

In the *Summa theologiae* Aquinas again distinguishes two primary senses of contemplation, whose object is God, one "which will be perfect in the future life when we see Him face to face" and another that we have now, "imperfect, namely through a glass darkly."[69] These two primary types of contemplation are coordinate with two senses of final end:

> The human being is proportioned according to his nature to a certain end for which he has a natural appetite and which he is able to pursue through the use of his natural powers, which end is a type of contemplation of the divine, the kind which is possible to the human being according to the faculty of nature, in which [activity] the philosophers identified the highest human happiness. However, there is an end for which the human being is prepared by God, which exceeds any proportion to human nature, namely eternal life, which consists in a vision of

---

[67] See *ST* I, q. 62, a. 1, corpus; *Expositio super librum Dionysii De divinis nominibus*, ch. 5, lect. 2 (no. 656).

[68] *In I Sent.*, Prologue, q. 1, a. 1, corpus. Cf. *Super Boetium De Trinitate*, q. 6, a. 4, ad 3; *ST* I-II, q. 3, a. 5, corpus.

[69] *ST* II-II, q. 180, a. 4, corpus.

God's essence, which exceeds any proportion to any created nature whatsoever, and is connatural to God alone.[70]

8.4.2. Contemplation of God *per essentiam in raptu*

Because the vision of God *per essentiam* requires that the human mind be "totally loosened" from bodily things, it can only happen "through death or through some sort of rapture."[71] Any vision that is had *ante mortem* does not bestow perfect happiness because it does not last and it does not arise from a disposition existing in the intellect, but only through divine power.[72] The vision of God that the saints have through contemplation must be distinguished from this.[73] The highest contemplative experience cannot be had in this state or life, except *potentialiter*, "insofar as someone's soul joined as form to a mortal body, such that he or she may not use the bodily senses or even the imagination, as happens in rapture."[74] The norm, however, is that "according to the state of our present life, human contemplation is not able to occur without phantasms, because it is connatural to humans that they see the intelligible species in the phantasm."[75] Nevertheless, "intellectual knowledge is not found in the phantasms themselves, but in them it contemplates the purity of intelligible truth. And this is not only the case in natural cognition, but also in those things we know through revelation." Between knowledge that begins in phantasms and knowledge of God *per essentiam*, however, the road is "impassable" (*in via*). The contemplation of God *in raptu*, then, occupies the middle ground between contemplation *in patria* and that *in via*.

8.4.3. Contemplation of God *ex infusione*

In commenting on the Gospel of John, Aquinas identifies four progressively higher ways of "seeing" God, none of which "attain to a vision of the divine essence": (1) "through a creature present to *bodily sight*," as Abraham saw the three strangers; (2) "through an image present in the *imagination*," as Isaiah saw the Lord seated above the height of the sun; (3) "through an *intelligible species* abstracted from sensible things," i.e. from creatures to creator; (4) "through a certain *spiritual light infused* by God into spiritual minds in

---

[70] *De veritate*, q. 27, a. 2, corpus (Leonine ed., vol. 22, p. 794, lines 121–135).
[71] *SCG* III, ch. 47 (no. 2).   [72] See *In IV Sent.*, dist. 49, q. 2, a. 7, ad 4 and ad 5.
[73] Cf. *Super Psalmo* 26 (no. 3).
[74] *ST* II-II, q. 180, a. 5, corpus. Cf. *De veritate*, q. 10, a. 11, ad 2; *Expositio super librum Dionysii De divinis nominibus*, ch. 1, lect. 1 (nos. 31–32).
[75] *ST* II-II, q. 180, a. 5, ad 2. Cf. *Compendium theologiae* I, ch. 167 (Leonine ed., vol. 42, p. 145, lines 7–20).

contemplation . . . as Jacob saw God face to face."[76] This "new illumination" strengthens the natural light of reason with "the light of faith, the gifts of wisdom and understanding," and produces an "elevated" and "intimate" contemplation of God as "above everything which can be naturally known."[77]

8.4.4. Contemplation of God *secundum vires naturales*, Which Produces *felicitas contemplativa*

In this life, there is "nothing that more closely resembles the highest and perfect happiness than the life of those who contemplate the truth" and, so, the philosophers who cannot fully know that happiness "posit the highest happiness in the contemplation which is possible in this life." The contemplation of truth begins in this life, but is "consummated in the future," unlike the "active or civil life, which cannot reach beyond the boundaries of this life."[78]

Philippe remarks that "St. Thomas is not very interested in the degrees of contemplation," although "he enumerates as degrees the six kinds distinguished by Richard of St. Victor"[79] as a sequence of acts rising to the "consideration of intelligible which reason cannot discover or grasp, which pertain to the sublime contemplation of divine truth in which contemplation is perfected as through its end."[80] This is not the only text that suggests that a hierarchy of contemplative acts with God as their object is a hierarchy of abstractedness from the sensory origins of our knowledge.[81] "The manifestation of divine truth which occurs in the naked contemplation of truth itself is stronger than that which occurs under the appearance of corporeal things, for it more closely approaches the vision of heaven through which truth is seen in the essence of God."[82]

---

[76] *Lectura super Ioannem*, ch. 1, lect. 11 (no. 211). Cf. *De veritate*, q. 10, a. 11, ad 14; *De veritate*, q. 12, a. 6, sed contra 2; *Super Boetium De Trinitate*, q. 1, a. 2, corpus (Leonine ed., vol. 50, p. 85, lines 118–131); *In IV Sent.*, dist. 49, q. 2, a. 7, ad 3; *ST* I-II, q. 98, a. 3, ad 2.

[77] This infused contemplation is termed "mystical" by commentators—including Philippe, Maurer, and Torrell—although this is not Aquinas's term. He most commonly uses the term "mystical" to refer to levels of scriptural interpretation and to the Church as "mystical body."

[78] *SCG* III, ch. 63 (no. 7). Cf. *ST* I, q. 62, a. 1, corpus.

[79] Philippe, "Contemplation," col. 1987: "Saint Thomas s'est peu intéressé aux degrés de la contemplation. . . . Il énumère comme degrés les six genres discernés par Richard de Saint-Victor."

[80] *ST* II-II, q. 180, a. 4, ad 3. Cf. *Super Psalmo* 26 (no. 6) and 54 (no. 5).

[81] *Lectura super Ioannem*, ch. 1, lect. 11 (no. 213); *De veritate*, q. 13, a. 4, corpus (Leonine ed., vol. 22, p. 429, lines 172–187); *Expositio super librum Dionysii De divinis nominibus*, ch. 4, lect. 9 (nos. 414–415).

[82] *ST* II-II, q. 174, a. 2, corpus.

8.4.5. Secondary Senses of Contemplation

Two of the primary senses of contemplation, *in via* and *in patria*, are also attached to activities that, as a consequence, are called "contemplation" in some secondary sense. Howsoever different the existential planes of their consummation, each must have beginnings and developmental stages that occur *in via*. Just as "the contemplation of wisdom" as an end requires the natural inherence of the "*per se nota*" principles of demonstration, so "supernatural cognition" requires a temporal, though non-natural beginning in us, that is, "through faith, which grasps through an infused light those things which exceed natural cognition."[83] Some secondary senses of "contemplation," therefore, will be in service of the natural human end and some of the supernatural end. Aquinas states, "Thus, therefore, while the contemplative life has one act in which, as through an end, it is perfected, namely the contemplation of truth, from which it has unity, it has many acts by which it arrives at this final act," i.e. the grasp of principles and deductive reasoning, which are not "contemplation itself."[84] In addition, while signifying "that principal act by which someone contemplates God in himself," "contemplation" is extended secondarily to "that act by which someone examines the divine in created things" (although this is perhaps better named "speculation"), since "we are led to the contemplation of God through the divine effects."[85] The term "contemplation," then, can include the process of attaining truth, although this process of attainment is better called "cogitation," since "contemplation" proper ensues when truth is perfectly possessed.[86]

Much of the contemplative life could be spent in the process of attaining truth. Aquinas puts it this way: "the contemplative happiness, which philosophers treat of, consists in the contemplation of God because, according to the Philosopher it consists in the act of the highest power which is in us, namely intellect, and in the most noble habit, which is wisdom, and also concerns the most worthy object, which is God." This is why "they reserve the end of life, it is said, for contemplating the divine, spending the preceding time in other studies, in order that they might become through them more able to consider divine things."[87]

In the same way, there must be means proportioned to the end of contemplation *in patria*. This will not be *inquisitio* or *speculatio* beginning in creatures, but "through knowledge . . . directly inspired through the divine light,"

---

[83] *De veritate*, q. 14, a. 2, corpus (Leonine ed., vol. 22, p. 441, lines 165–187).

[84] *ST* II-II, q. 180, a. 3, corpus.   [85] *ST* II-II, q. 180, a. 4, corpus.

[86] *ST* I, q. 34, a. 1, ad 2.

[87] *In III Sent.*, dist. 35, q. 1, a. 2, quaestiuncula 3, corpus. Cf. *ST* II-II, q. 9, a. 4, ad 3; *Sent. Ethic.* X, lect. 10, no. 13 (Leonine ed., vol. 47/2, p. 584, lines 134–138).

i.e. the *doctrina theologiae*.[88] "The ultimate end of this teaching is the contemplation of the First Truth *in patria*."[89]

This is why it is appropriate to have a religious order whose purpose is study because (1) study is a means to contemplation "by illuminating the intellect"; and (2) "by removing the dangers to contemplation, namely the errors which occur frequently in the contemplation of divine things to those who do not know Scripture."[90]

While Aquinas distinguishes between acts secondarily called "contemplation" based on whether they are means to the "imperfect contemplation" that may be attained *in via* or to the "perfect contemplation" only achieved *in patria*, the two types are related when he discusses contemplative acts insofar as some are perfected through virtues and others through the gifts of the Holy Spirit.[91] There are contemplative acts that are conducted *secundum humanum modum*, some of which are concerned with "the necessary and eternal," and another, "which judges and orders" inferior things in the light of those first principles and causes. Both classes of contemplative acts are perfected by the intellectual and theological virtues: the inquiry into first principles by *intellectus*, the following of these principles to conclusions by *scientia*; the examination of those divine things above reason "through a glass darkly" by *fides*; the ordering of inferiors by *sapientia*. "However, that spiritual things may be captured as if in their naked truth is *supra humanum modum* and requires the *donum intellectus*." Similarly, that a human being transformed by his union with "those highest causes . . . may, from what is deepest in him, judge and order other things, not only knowable things, but also human actions and passions, this is *supra humanum modum*, and is accomplished through the *donum sapientiae*."[92]

This interesting text distinguishes not between acquired and infused virtues, but between both of these on the one hand and the gifts of the Spirit on the other. Aquinas makes a similar distinction in the commentary on Isaiah between types of "intellectual vision" or contemplation: (1) those for which the "natural light of the intellect" suffices; (2) those for which the "light of faith" suffices; (3) those (*in patria*) for which only the "light of glory" suffices (although sometimes this vision is had before death in a rapture); (4) those which are made possible through the "light of grace freely given," e.g. the "gift of prophecy." (1) and (2) are "insufficient" for (4); and, in turn, (4) has not "attained" (3).[93] The contemplation achieved through reason or faith, on this

---

[88] *In I Sent.*, Prologue, q. 1, a. 1, corpus.

[89] *In I Sent.*, Prologue, q. 1, a. 3, quaestiuncula 1, corpus.

[90] *ST* II-II, q. 188, a. 5, corpus.

[91] *In III Sent.*, dist. 34, q. 1, a. 2, corpus; dist. 35, q. 2, a. 2, quaestiuncula 2, corpus; *Expositio super Isaiam ad litteram*, ch. 11 (Leonine ed., vol. 28, p. 79, line 154 to p. 80, line 169).

[92] *In III Sent.*, dist. 34, q. 1, a. 2, corpus.

[93] *Expositio super Isaiam ad litteram*, ch. 1 (Leonine ed., vol. 28, p. 9, lines 74–99).

analysis, becomes "ordinary" in comparison with extraordinary gifts, such as prophecy.

This distinction between faith and gifts is consistent with Aquinas's position that the gifts make possible a more perfect operation of the imperfectly possessed theological virtues. While human reason is a do-it-yourself operation, the movement towards a supernatural end requires the "gifts," so-called "not only because they are infused by God but because through them a person is so disposed that she is rendered 'moveable' by the divine in-spiration," so that the movement towards God becomes not only possible, but irresistible.[94] The gifts are the common endowment of adult Christians, but the movements they make possible are clearly diverse.

While Torrell does not cite any particular texts of Aquinas in direct support of his claim that the "contemplation" that overflows into the active life of teaching and preaching is "a contemplation acquired by human means through the practice of various exercises within a whole life driven by this dominant activity . . . the act of the habit of acquired wisdom which is built on a foundation of the faith," these texts nevertheless support the existence, if not of such a "type," at least of an affinity between two types, one based in reason, the other in faith, which operate "in a human way." At the very root of the baptized Christian, faith has taken up residence with reason and each operates alongside the other *per humanum modum*, the new "base" from which human nature's orientation towards contemplative truth becomes capable of the beatific vision.

Just as the practice of the secondary acts of contemplation, which lead to the vision of truth that is possible through natural reason and towards which a philosopher may dedicate the bulk of his life, is sufficient to designate a life as "contemplative," so the practice of secondary acts of contemplation that prepare one for the contemplation of God *per essentiam et in patria* is sufficiently contemplative to facilitate teaching and preaching. The alignment is, nevertheless, asymmetrical. While the philosopher may hope that, at the end of his life, he will master the act of bringing the highest power to bear upon the highest objects, the *theologus* knows, rather, that his life will end before that is accomplished and that it will be not earned, but gratuitous.

But is Torrell correct in arguing that *only* this secondary kind of contemplation is integrable into an active life of teaching and preaching? Or, would it be more accurate to say that "theological contemplation" is *sufficient* to sustain the type of active life that requires a "fullness of contemplation"—that it does not require a mystic's storehouse?[95] In any case, mystics, prophets, and

---

[94] *ST* I-II, q. 68, a. 1, corpus.

[95] Philippe, "Contemplation," col. 1984: "Il revient à saint Thomas d'avoir discerné deux sagesses acquises, et par conséquent deux contemplations acquises, la sagesse philosophique et la sagesse théologique (1 *Sent*, prol. q. 1 a. 1; In 1 *Isaiam* c. 3 §1). A-t-il admis, entre la

philosophers often teach or preach. The preacher "emerges from the hidden-
ness of contemplation into the openness of preaching," drinking deep and
then pouring out. Christ emerges from concealment in the Father to the
publication of his Incarnation,[96] from the desert into his public life, a journey
consistent with the "life" that aims to give to others the fruits of one's
contemplation.[97] The quotation of Gregory the Great that Aquinas uses to
frame his introduction of this new kind of active life (in *ST* II-II, q. 188, a. 6)
describes the contemplative as driven "to publish the memory of your sweet-
ness." Surely this language of inebriation, joy, and release points to something
beyond the exercise of an "acquired habit" or the expression of "acquired
wisdom" and may indicate the operation of the "gifts" or "the spirits," even
those that are not generally but particularly bestowed.

At this point we are knocking on the door of infused contemplation,
which strengthens the natural light of reason with "the light of faith, the
gifts of wisdom and understanding," but does not extend to the vision of God
per essentiam, and might, in its humbler forms, represent some relative
closure to the pursuit of truths available through natural reason, if we
grant that the experience of infused contemplation need not make its subject
a mystic.

8.5. AQUINAS, ARISTOTLE, AND THE "BEST LIFE"

We are left, then, with the question of whether Aquinas's "eleventh hour"
discovery of a type of active life that is not constituted *totaliter* by exterior
activity represents an abandonment of what he understands to be Aristotle's
position on the "best life."

There are four possible alternatives. (1) One could hold, like Leclercq, that
the fused life is still primarily contemplative and, therefore, that Aristotle is
right in holding that both the highest *act* and the highest *life* are contemplative. Tempting as this might be, it cannot be supported by the text of
St. Thomas,[98] who clearly states that the best *life* is a kind of active life. (2)
Or, one might say that Aquinas never repudiates Aristotle's eight reasons

---

contemplation théologique, de finalité spéculative, et la contemplation infuse, l'existence d'une
contemplation acquise de type plus affectif et moins savant? Il semble bien que la q. 180 de la
2ᵃ 2ᵃᵉ règle le statut d'une contemplation qui englobe à la fois la contemplation infuse et une telle
contemplation affective, sans d'ailleurs exclure complètement la contemplation théologique
quand celle-ci est recherchée par amour pour Dieu. Cette *contemplatio* répond parfaitement
au type 'Western Mysticism.' "

[96] See Sermon IX, *Exiit qui seminat* (Leonine ed., vol. 44/1, p. 124, lines 340–351).
[97] See *ST* III, q. 40, a. 2, ad 3.   [98] *ST* II-II, q. 188, a. 6 and *ST* III, q. 40, a. 1.

insofar as they pertain to the *act* of contemplation, but that these uncondi-
tional priorities do not carry over into a whole *life* when measured against a
life that fuses together contemplation and action, although they still hold when
measured against a life that is centered around exterior actions. (3) Thirdly,
one could argue that, taking into account the asymmetrical trajectories of
contemplation through the light of natural reason alone and contemplation
supported by the light of faith and the gifts of understanding and wisdom,
Aquinas never repudiates Aristotle with respect to the priority of contemplation *or* the contemplative life. This is because the culmination of the latter is
beyond *status iste* and the experience of the blessed *in patria* is a contemplative *life*. (4) Finally, it could be argued that Aquinas repudiates Aristotle both
with respect to the priority of the *act* and *life* of contemplation, although this
possibility is only arguable *pro statu isto*, given Aquinas's clear position on the
life of the blessed. Since (1) is untenable, I will advance arguments for (2),
showing, at the same time, its superiority to (4); then arguments for (3), which
is, in the end, compatible with (2).

In support of the second view one might argue that, for Aquinas, the
determination of the "best life" begins not with conflicting testimonies
within the *polis*,[99] but with the uncontested testimony of Scripture and the
Church: the life of Christ is best, then the life led by his apostles and their
successors, the bishops, in imitation of him, then whatever type of religious
life might most resemble these. But what type of life is this? Aquinas's clear
determination is that it is an active life: Christ did not choose the life of a
solitary contemplative and *omnis Christi actio nostra est instructio*.[100]

The subtle change in the description of *doctrina* that takes place from *ST* II-
II, q. 181, a. 3 to q. 188, a. 6, and is echoed in *ST* III, q. 40, a. 1, reveals the
machinery of Aquinas's response to this "instruction." At *ST* II-II, q. 181, a. 3,
he answers the question of whether teaching is a work of the active or
contemplative life with a split decision. This is because the act of teaching,
which is carried out in speech, has a double object: one, the interior concept,
which can be the stuff of either the contemplative life (if it is an intelligible
truth "in whose consideration and love one takes delight" alone) or the active
(if it is conceived "in order that one may be directed through it in an exterior
action"); and the other, the hearer of the word, "the audible sign of the
concept," which object places teaching in "the active life to which pertain
exterior actions." Aquinas does not abandon these distinctions in *ST* II-II,
q. 188, a. 6. Rather, he specifies a third way in which the interior concept may
be disposed. Not only may it (1) originate and remain as the secret delight of
the contemplative or (2) originate and remain as an operational principle, but

---

[99] See Aristotle, *Nicomachean Ethics* I,4 (1095a14–28); I,5 (1095b14–1096a10).
[100] *ST* III, q. 37, a. 1, arg. 2. Cf. Torrell, *Le Christ en ses mystères*, p. 211.

it may also (3) originate in delight and then flow over, owing to its fullness, into operation.[101] While in his polemical works aimed at the antimendicants Aquinas emphasizes the connection between teaching and contemplation to argue the appropriateness of religious, traditionally identified as contemplatives, engaging in university teaching, it is in the *Secunda Pars* that teaching as a work of the active life and, finally, of a newly conceived type of active life, emerges. This "life" is the life chosen by Christ, lived by his apostles and their successors, the bishops, and adopted by the mendicant orders, particularly the Order of Preachers.

Nevertheless, this "life" retains a priority for contemplation: as the moral virtues of the active life must precede the practice of contemplation, so an abundance of contemplation must precede this sort of teaching. The *act* of contemplation, therefore, provides the material of the "best life," even though the best life is an active life.

In support of the third possibility, that Aquinas never repudiates Aristotle with respect to the priority of contemplation, whether considered as *act* or *life*, one can argue that, since human life *in via* is for the sake of human life *in patria*, therefore the active life devoted to "giving to others the fruits of one's contemplation" through teaching and preaching is for the sake of the contemplation to be enjoyed *in patria*. On this account, any priority of the active life is only *secundum quid et in casu*. However, the "necessity of the present life" takes on a meaning far removed from falling on "hard times," which Aristotle suggests as a reason for a person choosing the active life over the contemplative; it signifies the "infirmity" of the whole course of human life *in via*. As Aquinas says in the *Contra impugnantes* in defense of religious who leave the cloister to teach:

> Holy men seek something for themselves and something for others. For themselves they seek to inhere always in Christ either in this world, insofar as the infirmity of this present life will allow, or in the future life, where they will contemplate Him to the full. But for the sake of others they are forced sometimes to turn away from the desired contemplation and involve themselves in the hustle and bustle of the active life. Thus, therefore they both desire the quiet of contemplation and yet patiently endure the labor of action for the salvation of their neighbors.[102]

What has changed in the *Summa theologiae* from Aquinas's earlier apologetical writing is the disappearance of the "sting"; there is no backward glance towards the solitary chamber or the desert, no sense of strapping on one's

---

[101] This may be construed as minimally as "connecting the dots," but it remains the case that in *ST* II-II, q. 181 the two lives are described as *diversa studia hominum intendentium ad diversos fines* (a. 1, corpus) and the article on *docere* never identifies any fusion between contemplation and action.

[102] *Contra impugnantes*, ch. 19 (Leonine ed., vol. 41, p. A 152, lines 80–90).

pack.[103] There is instead a fluid, irresistible motion that leads from interior delight to exterior expression. Aristotle's "unconditionally better" life is not denied, but it is deferred and, in the interval, the "best life" will be structured dynamically, with one foot slogging through the infirmity of the "wayfaring" world, steadied by the other that is planted in the antechamber of divine rest and delight.

---

[103] See Augustine, *De civitate Dei* XIX,XIX: "Quam sarcinam si nullus inponit, percipiendae atque intuendae uacandum est ueritati; si autem inponitur, suscipienda est propter caritatis necessitatem; sed nec sic omni modo ueritatis delectatio deserenda est, ne subtrahatur illa suauitas et opprimat ista necessitas."

9

Aristotle in the *Summa Theologiae*'s Christology

Corey L. Barnes

Confronted with the question of whether Christ's resurrection causes the general resurrection (*ST* III, q. 56, a. 1), Thomas Aquinas responds with a telling combination of Aristotle and Paul. His response begins with a quotation from the *Metaphysics*: "what is first in a given genus is the cause of everything subsequent [in that genus]." Based upon his earlier affirmation that Christ's resurrection was first in the genus of resurrection,[1] Thomas concludes, "Christ's resurrection is the cause of our resurrection."[2] It comes as little surprise that Aquinas employs argumentation, and specifically deductive syllogism, within theology or *sacra doctrina*, but it is what immediately follows that reveals precisely how he uses this argumentation in the *Summa theologiae*. After completing the syllogism, Thomas confirms its conclusion through appeal to 1 Cor 15:20, and this confirmation illustrates his regular theological methodology of philosophical (Aristotelian) argumentation in accord with and at the service of Scripture. *ST* III, q. 56, a. 1, far from being a minor example of Aristotle's role in the *Summa theologiae*, provides an exemplar of the type of theological argumentation sketched in *ST* I, q. 1, a. 8.

Early in the *Prima Pars* (*ST* I, q. 1, a. 8), when defending the use of argumentation in theology, Thomas cites Paul on the causality of Christ's resurrection:

> It should be said that just as other sciences do not argue in order to prove their principles but argue from their principles in order to show other things within those very sciences, so also this doctrine does not argue in order to prove its principles, which are the articles of faith. Rather, it proceeds from those [principles]

---

[1] *ST* III, q. 53, a. 3.
[2] *ST* III, q. 56, a. 1, corpus. Citations are from *Summa theologiae*, ed. Institutum Studiorum Medievalium Ottaviense (Commissio Piana), 5 vols. (Ottawa: Harpell, 1941–1945).

in order to show something, as the Apostle, 1 Cor. 15:12, argued from the
resurrection of Christ in order to prove the common resurrection.[3]

Aquinas continues by noting that *sacra doctrina* properly disputes regarding
its principles only against those who deny them and only by refuting their
challenges. *ST* I, q. 1, a. 8 thus sets out compactly a theological procedure
based, at least to some degree, on Aristotelian *scientia* and takes Paul's
reasoning from Christ's resurrection to the general resurrection as the para-
digmatic case of appropriate argumentation *from* rather than *about* the
fundamental principles of theology.[4]

The article continues by emphasizing the propriety of two types of argumentation in theology, arguments from authority and arguments from reason:

> It should be said that arguing from authority is maximally proper to this doctrine
> from the very fact that the principles of this doctrine are had through revelation,
> and thus it is necessary that [the doctrine] be believed on the authority of those to
> whom revelation was made. This does not derogate from the dignity of this
> doctrine, for although the position from authority founded on human reason is
> weakest, the position from authority founded on divine revelation is most
> efficacious.
>
> Sacred doctrine also uses human reason, not indeed in order to prove faith,
> because through this the merit of faith would be removed, but in order to make
> manifest some other things which are handed down in this doctrine. Since
> therefore grace does not destroy nature but perfects it, it is necessary that natural
> reason is subservient to faith as the natural inclination of the will obeys charity.
> Whence even the Apostle says, 2 Cor. 10:5 . . . And thence it is that *sacra doctrina*
> even uses the authorities of the philosophers, where they were able to know the
> truth through natural reason, just as Paul, Act. 27:28.[5]

Throughout *ST* I, q. 1, a. 8, Thomas defends the use of arguments from various
authorities and from reason for the teaching and exploration of theology. The
authorities include Scripture (as internal or proper to *sacra doctrina* and
certain), doctors of the Church (as internal and probable), and philosophers
(as external and probable), and the rational arguments build upon established
principles. Aristotle's model for a *scientia* in the *Posterior Analytics* and
particularly the notion of subaltern sciences shaped Aquinas's approach in
the *Summa theologiae*, but this shaping falls far short of overly determining
Aquinas's approach. Thomas employs Aristotle and Aristotelian principles to
justify a specific scientific procedure in which Aristotle may function as an

---

[3] *ST* I, q. 1, a. 8, corpus.
[4] For appraisals of Aristotelian *scientia* in Aquinas's thought, see Marie-Dominique Chenu,
OP, *La théologie comme science au XIIIe siècle*, 3rd ed. (Paris: Vrin, 1957); John I. Jenkins, C.S.C.,
Knowledge and Faith in Thomas Aquinas (Cambridge: Cambridge University Press, 1997).
[5] *ST* I, q. 1, a. 8, ad 2.

authority, though only as an external and probable authority. This procedure is on full display in the *Summa*'s presentation of Christ's resurrection.

Though of paramount significance, the resurrection offers but one indication of the role Aristotle plays in the *Summa theologiae*'s Christology (*ST* III, qq. 1–59). Thomas does make explicit reference to Aristotle when treating Christological questions, but the implicit use of Aristotle's doctrines and procedures are just as significant and interesting. Consideration will be given here to Aristotle's explicit and implicit roles in the *Summa theologiae*'s Christology with a focus on four central ideas or topics: (1) fittingness, (2) *actiones sunt suppositorum*, (3) instrumentality, and (4) resurrection. The first three of these develop Aristotelian conceptual tools in a specifically theological arena and for specifically theological ends; they together reveal much about how Aquinas borrows from the Stagirite and how he alters what he borrows. These conceptual tools lead to theological and Christological gains in the *Tertia Pars* and all contribute to how Thomas presents Christ's resurrection as causing the general resurrection.

Aquinas's use of fittingness arguments relates to his practice of teaching theology along the basic lines of an Aristotelian *scientia*, a practice that requires its own justification insofar as *sacra doctrina* treats of particular and contingent realities. Arguments from fittingness provide a means for navigating the narrow passage between the constraint of necessity and the purposelessness of pure chance or contingency. The principle *actiones sunt suppositorum* (actions pertain to supposits) rests on a solidly Aristotelian foundation even as it represents a targeted specification of Aristotle's thought. Thomas is judged to have developed the principle *actiones sunt suppositorum*, and his motivation for this terminological specificity grew out of Christological concerns, concerns that also inspired the Angelic Doctor to develop Aristotle's understanding of instruments and instrumental causality in a bold new direction. Thomas crafts a notion of instrumental efficient causality that uses Aristotelian insights to rehabilitate a traditional affirmation of Christ's humanity as an instrument of the divinity (*instrumentum divinitatis*). The instrumental efficient causality of Christ's humanity itself helps to explain the fittingness of causing the general resurrection through Christ's resurrection.

All this is to indicate that Aristotle serves several crucial functions within the *Summa theologiae*'s Christology, functions that might appear far less obvious than with respect to other and more straightforwardly philosophical topics. Aquinas's engagement with Aristotle's thought was sufficiently deep and sufficiently critical to foster theological uses that were simultaneously enthusiastic and cautious. In the hands of such a skilled theologian as Thomas Aquinas, Aristotle's philosophical advancements become subtle tools for unexpected tasks, including reflections on the mystery of human salvation through the Incarnation of the Word.

9.1. FITTINGNESS

Arguments from fittingness (*convenientia*) appear throughout the *Summa theologiae* and play a particularly important role in the *Summa*'s Christology.[6] The details of these fittingness arguments are crucial for appreciating their larger function, but it is best to begin with a general sense of that larger function in order to draw out the Aristotelian implications of fittingness arguments. This larger function relates to how Aquinas develops theology and Christology along the lines of an Aristotelian *scientia*. One difficulty of recognizing theology as an Aristotelian *scientia* lies in the specification that a *scientia* concerns necessary knowledge.[7] Theology or *sacra doctrina* treats of individual and contingent realities, with the Incarnation serving as a prime example. How can there be necessary knowledge of contingent realities? Thomas's answer utilizes fittingness as a means to express a certain sapiential necessity without implying any constraint or limitation. This is not to suggest that fittingness arguments in the *Summa theologiae* answer solely Aristotelian or philosophical problems; rather fittingness arguments address many concerns, including concerns regarding the criteria for *scientia*.

Aristotle's *Metaphysics* begins by assigning the knowledge of causes or explanations to wisdom.[8] Aquinas supports this in his Christology while also recognizing human intellectual limitations with respect to the divine will as cause. Fittingness represents the appropriate noetic lens for understanding the divine will. Arguments from fittingness thus represent an Aristotelian inflection of pursuing Christian wisdom. Gilbert Narcisse has helpfully described fittingness in Aquinas as a theological form of necessity.[9] This intriguing observation conveys much about how fittingness arguments

---

[6] Joseph P. Wawrykow, "Wisdom in the Christology of Thomas Aquinas," in *Christ among the Medieval Dominicans: Representations of Christ in the Texts and Images of the Order of Preachers*, edited by Kent Emery, Jr., and Joseph P. Wawrykow (Notre Dame, IN: University of Notre Dame Press, 1998), pp. 175–96, provides an excellent introduction to how Aquinas uses fittingness arguments in the *Summa theologiae*'s Christology.

[7] *ST* I-II, q. 57, a. 5, ad 3: "It should be said that truth according to the practical intellect is accepted otherwise than truth according to the speculative intellect, as said in *Nicomachean Ethics* II,3, for truth according to the speculative intellect is accepted through conformity of the intellect to the reality. Because the intellect cannot be infallibly conformed to the realities in contingent matters, but only in necessary matters, no speculative habit of contingent matters is an intellectual virtue, but it is only [an intellectual virtue] concerning necessary matters."

[8] Aristotle, *Metaphysics* I,2 in *The Complete Works of Aristotle: The Revised Oxford Translation*, vol. 2, ed. Jonathan Barnes (Princeton, NJ: Princeton University Press, 1984; repr. 1985), p. 1553. See also Aristotle, *Metaphysica, Lib. I–X, XII–XIV: Translatio Anonyma sive "Media*," ed. Gudrun Vuillemin-Diem, "Aristoteles Latinus XXV.2" (Leiden: Brill, 1976), p. 9; *Metaphysica: Recensio et Translatio Guillelmi De Moerbeka*, ed. Gudrun Vuillemin-Diem, "Aristoteles Latinus XXV.3,2" (Leiden: Brill, 1995), p. 14; and Aquinas, *Sent. Metaph.* I, lect. 2 (nos. 36–44).

[9] Gilbert Narcisse, OP, *Les raisons de Dieu: Argument de convenance et esthétique théologique selon saint Thomas d'Aquin et Hans Urs von Balthasar* (Fribourg: Éditions Universitaires, 1997), pp. 146–7, 281, 292, and 318.

function within Christology as a *scientia*. The *Summa*'s Christology frequently pairs questions of necessity and fittingness, a pairing that serves both to unite fittingness with necessity over and against the connotations of contingency (such as meaninglessness, lack of order, purposelessness) and to distinguish fittingness from the connotations of constraint often implied with necessity.

The first article in the *Summa theologiae*'s Christology addresses the fittingness of the Incarnation. Something is fitting if it corresponds or "fits" with the very nature of a thing. Based upon this understanding of fittingness, Thomas employs two ideas from Pseudo-Dionysius's *De divinis nominibus* to support the Incarnation's fittingness. First, the divine nature is identified with the very essence of goodness. Second, the essence of goodness is construed in terms of communicating itself to others. The conclusion recognizes the fittingness of God as the supreme good supremely communicating Godself to others and acknowledges the Incarnation as God's supreme self-communication to creation.[10] Though Thomas here stresses fittingness, the force of his arguments could be mistaken to imply necessity. The next article tempers the risk of such a mistaken implication.

Whereas *ST* III, q. 1, a. 1 questions whether it was fitting for God to become incarnate, a. 2 questions whether the Incarnation was necessary for human reparation. The shift here concerns a change not only from fittingness to necessity but also from a frame of reference founded on the divine nature to one encompassing human reparation as the Incarnation's purpose or end.[11] Thomas responds by parsing two ways something can be necessary for an end, either as a *sine qua non* or as the most suitable means. He denies the Incarnation's necessity in the first sense on account of divine omnipotence but affirms the Incarnation's necessity as the most suitable means for achieving human salvation.[12] Aquinas further tempers any imposition of necessity in querying whether God would have become incarnate had human beings not sinned. After duly noting the diversity of opinions on this vexing topic, Thomas exercises epistemological restraint in maintaining that whatever

---

[10] *ST* III, q. 1, a. 1, corpus: "It should be said that what is fitting to any given thing is what corresponds to it according to the very definition of its proper nature . . . The very nature of God, moreover, is the essence of goodness, as stands through Dionysius, *De divinis nominibus* I. Thus, whatever pertains to the definition of good is fitting to God. It pertains to the definition of good that it communicate itself to others, as stands through Dionysius, *De divinis nominibus* IV. Thus, it pertains to the definition of the highest good that it communicate itself to creatures in the highest way."

[11] Gelber investigates the various meanings of internal and external senses of necessity in Hester G. Gelber, *It Could Have Been Otherwise: Contingency and Necessity in Dominican Theology at Oxford, 1300–1350* (Leiden: Brill, 2004), pp. 115–16.

[12] *ST* III, q. 1, a. 2, corpus: "In the first way [i.e. as a *sine qua non*] it was not necessary for the reparation of human nature that God become incarnate, for through God's omnipotent power God could repair human nature through many other means. In the second way it was necessary for the reparation of human nature that God became incarnate."

depends solely upon the divine will can only be known through revelation. Since Scripture throughout assigns sin as the reason for the Incarnation, it is "most fitting to say the work of the Incarnation was ordered by God to be a remedy for sin such that had there been no sin there would have been no Incarnation."[13] God would remain free and able to become incarnate apart from sin, but human knowledge does not extend to plumbing the depths of the divine will in such hypothetical scenarios.[14] Articles 2 and 3 thus undermine any suggestion that the Incarnation's fittingness implies its necessity. Even God's most fitting self-communication following the divine nature as the essence of goodness involves no natural obligation but relies instead on the divine will. In pursuit of a *scientia Dei*, Aquinas escorts his readers to the cusp of necessity and then pulls them safely back from a dangerous precipice over which an incautious reader could perilously tumble while grasping at knowledge transcending human reason. None of this is simply or straightforwardly Aristotelian, but it is suffused with Aristotelian concerns and principles. As Narcisse shows, fittingness is a theological form of necessity, and its theological particularity eliminates constraint and inevitability as well as the ability of human beings to employ it predictively with respect to hypothetical or counterfactual proposals. The pairing of necessity and fittingness arises in many other Christological questions, notably in Thomas's treatment of the *acta et passa Christi in carne* (*ST* III, qq. 27–59).

Another important type of fittingness in the *Summa*'s Christology focuses on purposefulness, and Aristotle provides the explicit warrant for this type of fittingness. Citing Aristotle's *De caelo*, Thomas affirms, "God and nature do nothing uselessly."[15] This formulation appears repeatedly in the *Tertia Pars*, serving as an explanatory principle for the fittingness of the Incarnation according to the revealed order. Even before he reflects on the gospel portrayals of Jesus in treating the *acta et passa Christi in carne* (*ST* III, qq. 27–59), Aquinas reflects upon the Incarnation's fittingness according to the purpose or utility of those things "co-assumed."[16] Christ's acquired knowledge (discussed below in section 9.3) provides one specific example of fittingness as opposed to futility. In that case, as in other cases related to what the Word assumed or co-assumed, Thomas emphasizes the proper functioning of Christ's humanity as well as the dignity of humanity.

---

[13] *ST* III, q. 1, a. 3, corpus.

[14] Aquinas certainly does allow for some reflection on hypothetical and counterfactual scenarios in Christology, but this allowance only concerns what God *could* do rather than what God *would* do.

[15] *ST* III, q. 5, a. 3, arg. 2: "Deus autem et natura nihil frustra faciunt." Cf. Aristotle, *De caelo* I,4.

[16] On the purpose or utility of Christ's assumption of defects, see Paul Gondreau, *The Passions of Christ's Soul in the Theology of St. Thomas Aquinas* (Scranton, PA: University of Scranton Press, 2009).

On a more general level, Thomas's arguments from utility or purposefulness depend upon the Aristotelian notion of final causality.[17] The final cause or cause for the sake of which has explanatory priority insofar as it accounts for the causality of an efficient cause. Aquinas makes perfectly clear that the final cause of the Incarnation was human reparation,[18] and that goal helps explain the fittingness of the Incarnation according to the details of the revealed order. Many of those detailed arguments depend upon the fittingness of the Word becoming incarnate, and Thomas's adherence to the principle *actiones sunt suppositorum* highlights the significance of the Word as the one actor in Christ.

9.2. *ACTIONES SUNT SUPPOSITORUM*

Alain de Libera's archaeology of the principle *actiones sunt suppositorum* (actions pertain to supposits) traced it through Leibniz back to the Christology of Thomas Aquinas.[19] Though de Libera acknowledged Aristotelian inspiration for Thomas's use, he argued the principle could most accurately be regarded as a Thomistic innovation devised precisely to answer Christological concerns. Without disputing de Libera's findings, this principle can still be regarded as fundamentally Aristotelian, though it is beyond dispute that Aquinas builds upon that Aristotelian foundation in myriad ways. Thomas found inspiration for his innovation in the *Metaphysics*, where Aristotle affirms, "actions and productions are all concerned with the individual."[20] While commenting on the *Metaphysics*, Aquinas notes that "actions concern singulars, and all generations pertain to singulars, because universals are not generated or moved except through accidents, in as much as this accords to singulars."[21] Substituting "supposit" for "individual" or "singular" might seem a slight alteration and hardly an innovation, but the consequences of this

---

[17] On final causality, see Aristotle, *Physics* II,8 (*The Complete Works of Aristotle*, vol. 1, pp. 339–41); Monte R. Johnson, *Aristotle on Teleology* (Oxford: Clarendon Press, 2005).

[18] *ST* III, q. 1, aa. 2–3.

[19] Alain de Libera, "Les actions appartiennent aux sujets: Petite archéologie d'un principe leibnizien," in *"Ad ingenii acuitionem," Studies in Honour of Alfonso Maierù*, edited by Stefano Caroti, Ruedi Imbach, Zénon Kaluza, Giorgio Stabile, and Loris Sturlese (Louvain-la-Neuve: Fédération internationale des Instituts d'Études Médiévales, 2006), pp. 199–219.

[20] Aristotle, *Metaphysics* I,1 (*The Complete Works of Aristotle*, vol. 2, p. 1552); *Metaphysica: Recensio et Translatio Guillelmi De Moerbeka* I,1 (p. 12): "Causa autem est QUIA experientia quidem singularium est cognitio, ars uero universalium, actus autem et omnes generationes circa singulare sunt." *Metaphysica: Translatio Anonyma sive "Media"* I.1 (p. 8): "actus autem et omnes generationes circa singulare sunt."

[21] *Sent. Metaph.* I, lect. 1 (no. 21): "Cujus causa est, quia actiones sunt circa singularia, et singularium sunt omnes generationes. Universalia enim non generantur nec moventur nisi per accidens, inquantum hoc singularibus competit."

substitution shape major conclusions within Aquinas's Christology. The significance rests in part on Thomas's terminological precision with respect to various names for primary substance and for names of first intention.[22] Hypostasis and supposit are names of first intention (i.e. names of real things rather than abstractions) that designate primary substances of whatever nature. In cases of rational nature, the primary substance receives the special designation of person. Stated otherwise, a person is a hypostasis or supposit of rational nature. The strict identification of person, hypostasis, and supposit in rational natures distinguished Aquinas from his immediate predecessors while also becoming a hallmark of his single-subject Christology.

Aquinas's later presentations of Christology share knowledge of patristic and conciliar sources unparalleled in the thirteenth century.[23] Among other things, these sources granted Thomas a privileged awareness of early Christological controversies and led him to suspect that some medieval approaches to Christology veered toward Nestorianism. Combating this unintended but nonetheless pernicious tendency required eliminating the imprecisions through which error could enter. The root Nestorian error, according to *ST* III, q. 2, a. 6, lies in positing an accidental union in Christ, against which Thomas affirms a substantial union, though Nestorius also erred in allowing two hypostases in Christ. Terminological imprecision had, in Aquinas's own age, led some to allow a duality of hypostases or supposits in Christ.[24] Thomas arrests this drift toward Nestorianism by specifying the relationship between supposits, hypostases, and persons and through the principle *actiones sunt suppositorum*. With such dangers controlled, the *Summa*'s Christology continues to utilize the Aristotelian principle *actiones sunt suppositorum* in order to explain how all of Christ's actions and passions were salvific.

Only existing individuals (supposits, hypostases, or persons) act or operate. The importance of this Aristotelian insight for Christology emerges from Thomas's stress on a single-subject Christology. Granting that *actiones sunt suppositorum*, affirming only one supposit in Christ, the supposit of the Word, yields the conclusion that all of Christ's actions and passions pertain to the supposit of the Word as the one subject in Christ. This conclusion achieves two noteworthy gains. First, it excludes the possibility of introducing a second and purely human actor in Christ under the guise of individual natures as operative. Aquinas maintains that Christ's individual human nature never acted but that the supposit of the Word acted through its human nature.

---

[22] See Henk J. M. Schoot, *Christ the "Name" of God: Thomas Aquinas on Naming Christ* (Leuven: Peeters, 1993).

[23] See Ignaz Backes, *Die Christologie des hl. Thomas v. Aquin und die griechischen Kirchenväter* (Paderborn: Schöningh, 1931); Martin Morard, "Thomas d'Aquin lecteur des conciles," *Archivum Franciscanum Historicum* 98 (2005): pp. 211–365.

[24] See Corey L. Barnes, "Albert the Great and Thomas Aquinas on Person, Hypostasis, and Hypostatic Union," *Thom.* 72 (2008): pp. 107–46.

Natures provide determinate principles according to which a supposit can act, but it is the supposit rather than the nature that acts. All actions or operations originate in a supposit, and all passions terminate in a supposit. This, according to Thomas, justifies the predication of all Christ's actions and passions to the Word and so to God. Second, Thomas's conclusion clarifies that all of Christ's human actions pertain to the supposit of the Word and work for human salvation through instrumental efficient causation. Aquinas presents Christ's human actions and passions as salvific because they cause a divine effect. This radical soteriological claim depends in part on the Aristotelian principle *actiones sunt suppositorum* and in part on Thomas's development and extension of an Aristotelian scheme of instrumental causation.

The principle *actiones sunt suppositorum* also reflects a particular interest in primary substance as the underlying metaphysical substrate for accidents. Following basic Aristotelian ideas, Thomas locates *esse* in the person, hypostasis, or supposit. Together with his defense of the unicity of substantial form, the association of primary substance with *esse* led Aquinas to limit *esse* or substantial *esse* in Christ to the one *esse* of the Word and to acknowledge multiple *esse secundum quid* or accidental *esse* in Christ (*ST* III, q. 17, a. 2).[25] This vexed question was the subject of heated scholastic debates, but Thomas's approach extended the initial arguments of Philip the Chancellor and Albert the Great, which were based upon broadly Aristotelian approaches

---

[25] On debates regarding the unicity or plurality of substantial form, see Roberto Zavalloni, *Richard de Mediavilla et la controverse sur la pluralité des formes: Textes inédits et étude critique* (Louvain: Éditions de l'Institut Supérieur de Philosophie, 1951). The literature covering Aquinas on Christ's *esse* is extensive and encompasses vastly divergent assessments. See Victor Salas, Jr., "Thomas Aquinas on Christ's *Esse*: A Metaphysics of the Incarnation," *Thom.* 70 (2006): pp. 577–603; Thomas G. Weinandy, O.F.M. Cap., "Aquinas: God *is* Man, The Marvel of the Incarnation," in *Aquinas on Doctrine: A Critical Introduction*, edited by Thomas G. Weinandy, Daniel A. Keating, and John P. Yocum (London: T. & T. Clark, 2004), pp. 67–89; Richard Cross, *The Metaphysics of the Incarnation: Thomas Aquinas to Duns Scotus* (Oxford: Oxford University Press, 2002), pp. 54–8, 62–4, and 254–6; Jason L. A. West, "Aquinas on the Metaphysics of *Esse* in Christ," *Thom.* 66 (2002): pp. 231–50; Stephen F. Brown, "Thomas Aquinas and his Contemporaries on the Unique Existence in Christ," in *Christ among the Medieval Dominicans: Representations of Christ in the Texts and Images of the Order of Preachers*, edited by Kent Emery, Jr., and Joseph P. Wawrykow (Notre Dame, IN: University of Notre Dame Press, 1998), pp. 220–37; Richard Cross, "Aquinas on Nature, Hypostasis, and the Metaphysics of the Incarnation," *Thom.* 60 (1996): pp. 171–202; Thomas V. Morris, "St. Thomas on the Identity and Unity of the Person of Christ: A Problem of Reference in Christological Discourse," *Scottish Journal of Theology* 35 (1982): pp. 419–30; Étienne Gilson, "L'*esse* du Verbe incarné selon saint Thomas d'Aquin," *Archives d'histoire doctrinale et littéraire du moyen âge* 35 (1968): pp. 23–37; Jean-Hervé Nicolas, OP, "L'unité d'être dans le Christ d'après saint Thomas," *RThom* 65 (1965): pp. 229–60; Albert Patfoort, OP, *L'unité d'être dans le Christ d'après S. Thomas: À la croisée de l'ontologie et de la christologie* (Paris: Desclée, 1964); Herman Diepen, "L'existence humaine du Christ en métaphysique thomiste," *RThom* 58 (1958): pp. 197–213; Maurice Corvez, OP, "L'unicité d'existence dans le Christ," *RThom* 56 (1956): pp. 413–26; Adrian Hastings, "Christ's Act of Existence," *Downside Review* 73 (1955): pp. 139–59; Paul Bayerschmidt, *Die Seins- und Formmetaphysik des Heinrich von Gent in ihrer Anwendung auf die Christologie: Eine philosophie- und dogmengeschichtliche Studie* (Münster: Aschendorff, 1941), pp. 43–67.

to metaphysical categories.[26] Aquinas's own use of Aristotle owed much to what and how he learned from his teacher Albert, and this is evident in Christology, where an emphasis on primary substances leads to vastly important soteriological consequences. In many ways, Thomas's understanding of the hypostatic union offers one of the most profound theological uses of Aristotle or Aristotelian philosophical principles because it joins together in a seamless whole arguments from the Stagirite and from patristic and conciliar sources.

9.3. INSTRUMENTALITY

A text widely known and frequently cited in scholastic theology, John Damascene's *De fide orthodoxa*, contains a curious phrase collectively ignored until Thomas Aquinas seized upon it. The phrase in question, *instrumentum divinitatis* (instrument of divinity), enjoys a pedigree both prestigious and unknown in the Middle Ages.[27] No conclusive argument can be offered based upon the collective silence among the scholastics regarding this phrase, but it seems reasonable that the phrase *instrumentum divinitatis* would have struck scholastic ears as problematic in two possible ways, to both of which Aquinas responds. One unsettling interpretation would read Christ's instrumentality in an Apollinarian fashion such that the Word took the place of a rational soul or intellect and will in Christ. Thomas combats this by regularly defending the integrity of Christ's human nature in soul and body,[28] in intellect,[29] in will,[30] and in operation.[31] Another worrisome understanding of instrumentality weds the concept to Nestorian reckonings of union in Christ. Aquinas acknowledges this understanding when he characterizes the varieties of accidental union posited by Nestorius to include a union "according to operation,

---

[26] On Philip the Chancellor, see Walter H. Principe, C.S.B., *The Theology of the Hypostatic Union in the Early Thirteenth Century*, vol. 4, Philip the Chancellor's Theology of the Hypostatic Union (Toronto: Pontifical Institute of Mediaeval Studies, 1975). On Albert, see Stephen A. Hipp, *"Person" in Christian Tradition and in the Conception of Saint Albert the Great: A Systematic Study of its Concept as Illuminated by the Mysteries of the Trinity and the Incarnation* (Münster: Aschendorff, 2001); Vincent-Marie Pollet, OP, "Le Christ d'après S. Albert le Grand," *La vie spirituelle* 34 (1933): pp. 78–108; Vincent-Marie Pollet, OP, "L'union hypostatique d'après saint Albert-le-Grand," *RThom* 38 (1933): pp. 505–32 and 689–724; Marie Lamy de la Chapelle, "L'unité ontologique du Christ selon saint Albert le Grand," *RThom* 70 (1970): pp. 181–226 and 533–59. Related themes are treated in Corey L. Barnes, "Christological Composition in Thirteenth-Century Debates," *Thom.* 75 (2011): pp. 173–206.

[27] Various patristic thinkers described Christ's human nature as an *instrumentum divinitatis* or *organon tēs theotētos*. For patristic and medieval uses, see Theophil Tschipke, OP, *L'humanité du Christ comme instrument de salut de la divinité*, trans. Philibert Secrétan (Fribourg: Academic Press, 2003).

[28] *ST* III, qq. 5–6.   [29] *ST* III, qq. 9–12.
[30] *ST* III, q. 18.   [31] *ST* III, q. 19.

namely inasmuch as they say that human being was the Word of God's instrument."[32]

Combating what Aquinas regarded as misinterpretations of *instrumentum divinitatis* and instrumentality required constructing a competing interpretation, and he found the essential framework for his own conception in Aristotle.[33] Thomas quotes Aristotle's *Politics* while presenting a taxonomy of instruments, including inanimate, animate, and rational.[34] All instruments share the defining feature of being moved by a principle agent, but instruments also all contribute their own distinctive causality insofar as the principal agent acts through an instrument according to that instrument's proper nature. An agent moves inanimate instruments through corporeal motion, animate instruments through sensitive appetite, and rational instruments through will. The Aristotelian category of rational instrument bears directly on Thomas's desire to articulate an orthodox conception of Christ's humanity as an *instrumentum divinitatis* and depends upon the Christological application of an Aristotelian anthropology. As a rational nature, the specific operation of a human instrumental cause depends upon intellect and will. Aquinas develops this theme in line with increasing medieval attention to Christ's humanity and in line with his own interpretation of Aristotle on intellect and will.[35] Since the Word assumed a perfect, integral human nature, all that applies to Thomas's Aristotelian anthropology applies, *mutatis mutandis*, to the *Summa*'s Christology.

The *Summa*'s presentation of Christ's knowledge garners attention insofar as it grants acquired knowledge in Christ (in contrast to Aquinas's assessment in the *Scriptum*), and Thomas's discussion of Christ's acquired knowledge highlights well the role of Aristotle in the *Summa*'s Christology.[36] The first

---

[32] *ST* III, q. 2, a. 6, corpus.

[33] *ST* III, q. 18, a. 1, ad 2. For a more extensive discussion of themes treated here, see Corey L. Barnes, *Christ's Two Wills in Scholastic Thought: The Christology of Aquinas and its Historical Contexts* (Toronto: Pontifical Institute of Mediaeval Studies, 2012).

[34] Aristotle, *Politics* I,4 (*The Complete Works of Aristotle*, vol. 2, p. 1989): "Now instruments are of various sorts; some are living, others lifeless; for in the arts a servant is a kind of instrument."

[35] Accounts of the increasing attention to Christ's humanity in the Middle Ages are provided in Giles Constable, "The Ideal of the Imitation of Christ," in *Three Studies in Medieval Religious and Social Thought: The Interpretation of Mary and Martha, The Ideal of the Imitation of Christ, The Orders of Society* (Cambridge: Cambridge University Press, 1995), pp. 143–248; and Richard W. Southern, *The Making of the Middle Ages* (New Haven, CT: Yale University Press, 1959), pp. 231–40.

[36] On Christ's knowledge in the *Summa*, see Guy Mansini, OSB, "Understanding St. Thomas on Christ's Immediate Knowledge of God," *Thom.* 59 (1995): pp. 91–124; Jean-Pierre Torrell, OP, "S. Thomas d'Aquin et la science du Christ: Une relecture des questions 9–12 de la 'Tertia Pars' de la Somme de théologie," in *Saint Thomas au XXᵉ siècle: Colloque du centenaire de la "Revue thomiste" (1893–1992)*, edited by Serge-Thomas Bonino (Paris: Éditions Saint-Paul, 1994), pp. 394–409. For Thomas's earlier denials of any acquired knowledge in Christ, see *In III Sent.*, dist. 14, a. 3, quaestiuncula 5, ad 3; dist. 18, a. 3, ad 5.

three articles of *ST* III, q. 9 establish that Christ possessed human knowledge, beatific knowledge, and infused knowledge, following which Aquinas raises the question of acquired knowledge. Nothing relevant to the perfection of human nature was lacking to Christ's assumed humanity, so Christ necessarily possessed an agent intellect in addition to a possible intellect. Thomas then appeals to an Aristotelian principle of fittingness (discussed above in section 9.1) by noting that "God and nature do nothing uselessly."[37] If Christ's agent intellect lacked its proper operation, it would have been assumed uselessly or in vain. "Thus," Aquinas concludes, "it is necessary to say that there were in Christ some intelligible species received in his possible intellect through the action of his agent intellect and that there was in him acquired knowledge, which some name experiential."[38] Thomas adds detail to this basic affirmation in the remainder of q. 9, a. 4, and throughout q. 12, but the larger point suffices to reinforce Aristotle's import. Combining an Aristotelian anthropology with an Aristotelian commitment to natural and divine utility or purposefulness leads Aquinas to defend Christ's possession and use of an agent intellect according to which he acquired knowledge.[39]

The same basic combination of Aristotelian anthropology and commitment to utility or purposefulness is equally evident in the *Summa*'s presentation of Christ's wills and operations. Thomas places his discussion of Christ's knowledge within a section on what the Word "co-assumed" and investigates Christ's wills and operations under the heading of the consequences of the union, but the operative principle in these diverse placements remains consistent.[40] In the earlier questions on the nature assumed, Aquinas clearly established the Word's assumption of a perfect, integral human nature, and this nature necessarily included an intellect and will. Together with this human intellect, the Word "co-assumed" certain types of knowledge for specific purposes. In parallel fashion, the consequence of the Word's assumption of a human will is a certain type of instrumental causality exercised for human salvation.

ST I, qq. 82–83 establish a fundamentally Aristotelian understanding of the human will, and Thomas employs this very understanding in investigating Christ's unity of will. Aristotle plays a crucial role with respect to two

[37] *ST* III, q. 9, a. 4, corpus, quoting *De caelo* I,4; Aristotle, *On the Heavens* I,4 (*The Complete Works of Aristotle*, vol. 1, p. 452): "But God and nature create nothing that is pointless."

[38] *ST* III, q. 9, a. 4, corpus.

[39] Christ's progress in acquired knowledge did not imply any deficiency in his human knowledge but only a new way of knowing what he already knew through infused knowledge (*ST* III, q. 12, a. 2).

[40] Gondreau, *The Passions of Christ's Soul*, discusses both what Christ "co-assumed" and the consequences of the union. Other useful sources on the consequences of the union include Louis-Bertrand Gillon, OP, "La notion de conséquence de l'union hypostatique dans le cadre de III^a, qq. 2–26," *Ang.* 15 (1938): pp. 17–34; Ghislain Lafont, OSB, *Structures et méthode dans la Somme théologique de saint Thomas d'Aquin* (Paris: Desclée de Brouwer, 1961).

particular questions on Christ's will. The first concerns a so-called "will of sensuality." Based upon Christ's assumption of a perfect, integral human nature, Thomas insists on Christ's possession of sensuality, but the question remains whether or how one can speak of a will of sensuality, as did many twelfth-century theologians. Aristotle helps Aquinas with an answer:

> It should also be known that sensuality or the sensual appetite, in as much as it is intended to obey reason, is called rational through participation, as stands through the Philosopher in I *Ethics*. And because the will is in reason, as was said, on the same grounds it can be said that sensuality is a will through participation.[41]

The second question where Aquinas makes significant and explicit use of Aristotle concerns the presence of free choice (*liberum arbitrium*) in Christ.[42] A previous article[43] had distinguished the will in regards to means (*voluntas ut ratio*) from the will in regards to ends (*voluntas ut natura*).[44] Thomas weaves together that previous distinction with a citation of *Nicomachean Ethics* III,2 to the effect that, properly speaking, the will concerns ends while election (*electio*) concerns means. Election is nothing other than the proper act of free choice. Since Christ possessed a will in regard to means, it follows that Christ possessed free choice and election as the proper act of free choice. Aristotle also factors into Thomas's reasoning that election need not require any doubt or deliberation,[45] which simultaneously eliminates certain worries regarding election in Christ and serves to distinguish the perfection of Christ's human intellect and will from sinful human intellect and will.

Based upon this fundamentally Aristotelian understanding of intellect and will, Thomas constructs an elegant and powerful approach to Christ's operations and instrumental causality. In the course of defending two united operations in Christ, Thomas explains the twofold action of an instrument. Instruments have a certain action according to their proper form and a certain action as moved by a principal agent.[46] The instrument's action is conditioned both by its nature and by its participation in the operation of the principal agent. Aquinas illustrates this through a carpenter wielding a hatchet. By its

---

[41] *ST* III, q. 18, a. 2, corpus. The Aristotelian reference is to *Nicomachean Ethics* I,13 (*The Complete Works of Aristotle*, vol. 2, p. 1742), where Aristotle writes: "Therefore the irrational element also appears to be two-fold. For the vegetative element in no way shares in reason, but the appetitive and in general the desiring element in a sense shares in it."

[42] Questions regarding Christ's possession of free choice were ignited largely through the translation and expanding use of John Damascene's *De fide orthodoxa*. The Damascene, building upon Maximus the Confessor, denied *gnōmē* in Christ, and *gnōmē* was rendered into Latin as *electio*, which sparked the question of free choice.

[43] *ST* III, q. 18, a. 3.

[44] On this distinction, see Tomás Alvira, *Naturaleza y libertad: Estudio de los conceptos tomistas de voluntas ut natura y voluntas ut ratio* (Pamplona: Ediciones Universidad de Navarra, 1985).

[45] *ST* III, q. 18, a. 4, ad 2.   [46] *ST* III, q. 19, a. 1.

nature, the proper operation of a hatchet is cutting. By its instrumental use in the hands of a skilled craftsperson, the operation of a hatchet is to make a bench. Applying this twofold action to the case of Christ yields intriguing results with profound implications. This model interprets Christ's humanity as an *instrumentum divinitatis* to preserve the integral operation of Christ's humanity according to its proper form and to elevate that operation as it participates in the operation of the divine nature. More specifically, this elevation means that Christ's humanity instrumentally participates in the divine efficient causality of the principal agent. The significance of this becomes clear when Thomas considers the passion's causality:

> It should be said that the efficient [cause] is twofold: principal and instrumental. The principal efficient [cause] of human salvation is God, but because Christ's humanity is an instrument of the divinity . . . it follows that all Christ's actions and passions operated instrumentally in virtue of [his] divinity for human salvation. According to this, Christ's passion efficiently causes human salvation.[47]

Aquinas construes the efficacy of Christ's passion through the novel category of instrumental efficient causality. Aristotle's writings do not recognize instrumental efficient causality, but such causality would be unrecognizable without Aristotle. Thomas's articulation of instrumental efficient causality demonstrates clearly that Aristotle's thought in no way functions as a governing principle for the *Summa*'s theology but rather serves as a rich source that lends itself well to creative reworkings in the service of theological aims. The larger shape of Thomas's Christology depends not upon Aristotle but rather upon Ephesus, Chalcedon, Constantinople III, Cyril of Alexandria, Augustine, Pseudo-Dionysius, John Damascene, and many other patristic and medieval sources. Within the parameters of that larger shape, Aristotle provides philosophical tools for organizing, exploring, and explaining particular Christological claims.

9.4. RESURRECTION

Aristotle plays an unexpectedly prominent role in the *Summa theologiae*'s presentation of the resurrection.[48] Aquinas develops individual arguments and general principles of argumentation from the Stagirite in describing the

---

[47] *ST* III, q. 48, a. 6, corpus.
[48] On the causality of Christ's resurrection in Aquinas, see Jean-Pierre Torrell, OP, "La causalité salvifique de la résurrection du Christ selon saint Thomas," *RThom* 96 (1996): pp. 179–208; Nicholas Crotty, C.P., "The Redemptive Role of Christ's Resurrection," *Thom.* 25 (1962): pp. 54–106; Ferdinand Holtz, "La valeur sotériologique de la résurrection du Christ selon saint Thomas," *Ephemerides theologicae Lovanienses* 29 (1953): pp. 609–45.

necessity, fittingness, manner, and causality of Christ's resurrection. The four questions on Christ's resurrection (*ST* III, qq. 53–56) thus exemplify Thomas's use of Aristotle in the *Summa*'s Christology and, even more significantly, in the *Summa*'s general approach to theology.

Treatment of the resurrection begins with the familiar pairing of necessity and fittingness, with a. 1 of q. 53 defending the necessity of Christ's resurrection on five grounds, a defense that reprises the five ways the Incarnation "promotes humanity in the good" listed in the *Summa*'s consideration of the Incarnation's necessity (*ST* III, q. 1, a. 2). Thomas concentrates on the fitting details of Christ's resurrection in q. 53, a. 2 and includes an unexpected citation to frame the fittingness of rising on the third day. Rising on the third day, Aquinas holds, "commends the perfection of the number three, 'which is the number of every thing, since it has a beginning, middle, and end,' as is said in *De caelo* I,1."[49] Aristotle exercises a greater, though implicit, role in a. 3, where Thomas explains the primacy of Christ's resurrection by distinguishing resurrection as a rescue "from death only in act" and as a freedom "not only from death, but from the necessity, and what is more, from the possibility of dying."[50] The primacy of Christ's resurrection functions as a premise in question 56's Aristotelian portrayal of the resurrection's causality, but the important thing to note here is that Thomas's articulation of that primacy depends upon a careful distinction rooted in the basic difference between act and potency. Aquinas's frequent deployment of this difference can instill a familiarity that leads to forgetfulness of the Aristotelian foundation for this difference and for Thomas's diverse uses of it.

On two further topics related to Christ's resurrection Aristotle plays a vital role in the *Summa*'s analysis. The topics concern the use of argumentation and the causality of Christ's resurrection. When considering the propriety of declaring the truth of Christ's resurrection through arguments, Aquinas begins with two competing understandings of argument. The first understanding affirms an argument as "a convincing reason of a doubtful thing" (*ratio rei dubiae faciens fidem*), and according to this understanding "Christ did not prove his resurrection to his disciples through arguments."[51] Thomas elaborates the deficiencies of such argumentation, reasoning that it would proceed

---

[49] *ST* III, q. 53, a. 2: "Per hoc etiam quod tertia die resurrexit, commendatur perfectio ternarii, 'qui est numerus omnis rei, utpote habens principium, medium et finem,' ut dicitur in I *De caelo*." See Aristotle, *De caelo* I,1 (*The Complete Works of Aristotle*, vol. 1, p. 447): "For, as the Pythagoreans say, the universe and all that is in it is determined by the number three, since beginning and middle and end give the number of the universe, and the number they give is the triad."

[50] *ST* III, q. 53, a. 3, corpus.

[51] *ST* III, q. 55, a. 5, corpus: "Primo igitur modo accipiendo argumentum, Christus non probavit discipulis suam resurrectionem per argumenta." This understanding seems to derive from Cicero's *Topics*, ch. 2 and from Boethius's commentary thereon, *In Ciceronis Topica*, lib. I.

from unknown principles and so achieve nothing or would proceed from wholly known principles that, by the very fact of being known, do not transcend human reason and correspondingly lack any persuasive force with respect to a reality transcending human reason.[52] The second conception, derived from Aristotle, regards an argument as "some sensible sign that leads to the manifestation of some truth."[53] According to this conception Christ did declare his resurrection through arguments, and Thomas provides scriptural citations why Christ did so. The provision of scriptural citations is hardly noteworthy in and of itself, but in conjunction with rational argumentation it bears directly on the *Summa's* typical use of Aristotle. That typical use is on most obvious display regarding the causality of Christ's resurrection.

Thomas devotes q. 56 to the causality of Christ's resurrection but investigates relevant topics in earlier questions. *ST* III, q. 53, a. 4 explains how Christ caused his own resurrection and implicitly relies upon the principle *actiones sunt suppositorum* and upon previous treatments of instrumental causality and Christ's unity of operation. These rational arguments are confirmed by a quotation of 2 Cor 13:4, foreshadowing what is to come in q. 56. Explaining the glory of Christ's resurrected body (*ST* III, q. 54, a. 2) provides additional foreshadowing, for there Aquinas describes Christ's resurrection as "the exemplar and cause of our resurrection, as is had in 1 Cor 15:12."[54] Thomas's explanation and defense of this description come later in q. 56, which presents Christ's resurrection as the cause of the resurrection of bodies and of souls.

ST III, q. 56, a. 1, corpus, begins with a quotation from the *Metaphysics*: "what is first in a given genus is the cause of everything subsequent [in that genus]," which functions as a major premise. Aquinas has already established the primacy of Christ's resurrection (q. 53, a. 3) and can here rely on that primacy as the minor premise in a deductive syllogism. Thomas completes the syllogism by arguing: "it is necessary that Christ's resurrection is the cause of our resurrection."[55] A quotation from Paul ("Christ rose from the dead as the first of those sleeping, because death [came] through man and resurrection from death [came] through man") confirms the rational argumentation.[56] Rather than simply following the typical pattern of Thomas's theological methodology by confirming a rational argument and citation of an external and merely probable authority with citation of an internal and certain authority, this response actually establishes that typical pattern initially mentioned in *ST* I, q. 1, a. 8. When defending the use of arguments in *sacra doctrina* (*ST* I, q. 1, a. 8), Thomas cited 1 Cor 15:20 as a scriptural example of such use,

---

[52] See *ST* III, q. 55, a. 5, corpus.
[53] *ST* III, q. 55, a. 5, corpus. The Aristotelian texts on which this sense of argument is based seemingly include the *Prior Analytics* II,27 and *Rhetoric* I,2.
[54] *ST* III, q. 54, a. 2, corpus.   [55] *ST* III, q. 56, a. 1, corpus.
[56] *ST* III, q. 56, a. 1, corpus.

and *ST* III, q. 56, a. 1 again cites 1 Cor 15:20 in conjunction with a quotation from Aristotle and a rational explanation of the conclusion.

The rational elaboration of the conclusion resumes many of the themes discussed so far. Thomas first identifies the Word as the principle of human vivification and develops that vivifying activity according to a divinely instituted natural order of first causes operating in what is nearest to them and through what is proximate operating on what is remote. The replies to objections develop this argument by making careful use of the Aristotelian notions and distinctions charted earlier in the *Tertia Pars*. Based upon the fundamental principle of *actiones sunt suppositorum*, Aquinas can note that Christ's resurrection exercises causality by virtue of the Word as the one actor operating as both an exemplar cause and as an instrumental efficient cause of resurrection. Divine justice functions as the primary cause of the general resurrection, but Christ's resurrection functions as a "secondary and quasi instrumental cause. For although the power (*virtus*) of the principal agent is not determined to this determinate instrument, nevertheless from that fact that it operates through this instrument, that instrument is an efficient cause."[57] Christ's humanity as an *instrumentum divinitatis* in no way limits divine efficacy according to the creaturely determination of the instrument but rather enjoys a causal elevation such that it instrumentally participates in divine efficiency. Aquinas further elaborates that since divine power extends to all times and places, this allows for a "virtual contact" of all, both the evil and the just, to Christ's resurrection, and such virtual contact suffices for Christ's resurrection to exercise instrumental efficient causality on all bodies in all times.

While this instrumental efficient causality extends to the good and the bad, the exemplar causality of Christ's resurrection properly extends only to the good. As a general principle of exemplarity, Aquinas argues, "what is most perfect is the exemplar of what is less perfect according to its mode."[58] This principle suffices to identify Christ's resurrection as an exemplar cause, but what is more interesting here is how Thomas extends the argument with respect to necessity and fittingness. Christ's exemplarity is necessary "not on the part of the one resuscitating, who did not need an exemplar, but on the part of those resuscitated, who must be conformed to that resurrection."[59] Only the just are conformed to Christ's filiation in the resurrection, and so Christ's resurrection only functions as exemplar cause of their resurrection. Aquinas develops many of the same arguments when discussing the resurrection of souls,[60] but the main points are sufficiently evident already from a. 1.

Thomas's rational elaboration of the causality of Christ's resurrection builds upon the vital importance assigned to supposits as source of action, upon the

---

[57] *ST* III, q. 56, a. 1, ad 2.   [58] *ST* III, q. 56, a. 1, ad 3.
[59] *ST* III, q. 56, a. 1, ad 3.   [60] *ST* III, q. 56, a. 2.

intricate workings of instrumental efficient causality, and upon the interplay of fittingness and necessity. The necessity of Christ's exemplar causality in the resurrection matches the necessity of the Incarnation. In both cases, the necessity depends entirely on the purpose of the action and amounts to the most fitting means for achieving that end. The very nature of Thomas's rational elaboration in terms of fittingness or the necessity of fittingness follows his approach throughout the Christological questions of the *Tertia Pars* in formulating rational appreciations of divinely revealed mysteries in order to praise divine wisdom rather than to constrain divine power.

9.5. ARISTOTLE IN AQUINAS'S CHRISTOLOGY: CONCLUDING REFLECTIONS

While composing the *Summa theologiae*, Thomas Aquinas was also engaged in another ambitious project, commenting on many texts from the Aristotelian corpus. Thomas approached Aristotle's thought with excitement for its remarkable utility and with caution for its potential to mislead those who misread or misuse it. As has long been noted, Aquinas's aim in his Aristotelian commentaries is not to reconstruct Aristotle's meaning within its original context but rather to interpret the texts in concert with the larger structures and themes of Aristotle's thought and as reoriented toward the exposition of truth informed by the Christian tradition. Jean-Pierre Torrell has summarized the manner well in writing:

> We will appreciate his work more equitably if we remember that he undertook these commentaries in an apostolic perspective in order better to carry out his job as a theologian, and better to accomplish his labor of wisdom such as he would understand it in the double school of Saint Paul and Aristotle: to proclaim the truth and refute error.[61]

Torrell's judgment of the Aristotelian commentaries applies as well to Thomas's use of Aristotle in the *Summa theologiae*. The *Tertia Pars* resorts often to the "double school of Saint Paul and Aristotle," with one particularly important example being *ST* III, q. 56, a. 1, where Aquinas defends the causality of Christ's resurrection through appeal to Aristotle and Paul. The Pauline text cited there appears far earlier in the *Summa* when Thomas explains the proper use of argumentation in theology (*ST* I, q. 1, a. 8). The double school of Paul and Aristotle guides the *Summa*'s Christology and its attention to proclaiming truth and refuting error.

---

[61] Jean-Pierre Torrell, OP, *Saint Thomas Aquinas*, vol. 1, The Person and his Work, trans. Robert Royal, rev. ed. (Washington, DC: The Catholic University of America Press, 2005), p. 239.

Aristotle assists Thomas in the dual task principally through various conceptual tools, many of which inform and enrich all aspects of Aquinas's theology. Beyond these aspects with broad applicability, Aristotle also provides specific philosophical ideas and principles that shape the *Summa theologiae*'s Christology. Three such ideas and principles are fittingness, *actiones sunt suppositorum*, and instrumentality. To be sure, Thomas uses these for purposes Aristotle could not have imagined and in ways he might never countenance, but this does not render Aquinas's use un-Aristotelian. Rather, it is Aristotelian in novel ways and manages to produce Christological reflections of astounding intricacy and beauty. The Aristotelian elements in the *Summa*'s Christology never set the agenda for Thomas but do grant him the means to address succinctly and effectively a host of perennially discussed and debated questions. This is not to suggest that Aquinas simply reproduces conciliar or patristic Christologies with an Aristotelian veneer; his profound engagement with Aristotle afforded Thomas the opportunity and ability to integrate diverse strains of thought and even diverse conceptual worlds into a coherent whole with well-managed internal stresses.

10

Aristotle in Aquinas's Sacramental Theology

John P. Yocum

When we ask about the influence of Aristotle on Aquinas's thought regarding the sacraments, we face a number of challenges. Aquinas's mature thought is found preeminently in the final, unfinished part of the *Summa theologiae*, which is an original work, written in Aquinas's own voice. In it he marshals his immense learning for the sake of an exposition of sacred doctrine. Though he makes use of authorities, the use he makes of them is original, and so is bound up with his own interpretation of those authorities, as well as with his own view of the issues he is addressing. We cannot, for example, find a "pure" Augustine, about whom all interpreters agree, abstracted from Aquinas's reading of Augustine.

If this is the case with Augustine, it is even more pronounced in the case of Aristotle. In general, Aquinas is laconic in the *Summa* in his citations of non-Christian authors; often Aquinas shares assumptions with Aristotle, but he does not always point them out. Moreover, that he shares them with Aristotle does not necessarily mean that he derived them from Aristotle. When he agrees with Aristotle it is because he thinks the position they hold in common accords with the truth of things.[1] In addition, Aquinas does not normally tell us whether or not he learned this or that view of things from Aristotle. Indeed, as Wayne Hankey, following Mark Jordan, says, "It seems that for Aquinas, belonging to a philosophical school was not appropriate for Christians."[2] Thus, we have to discern the "influence of Aristotle" somewhat cautiously,

---

[1] *Sententia libri De caelo* I, lect. 22 (Marietti ed., no. 228).

[2] Wayne J. Hankey, "Why Philosophy Abides for Aquinas," *Heythrop Journal* 42 (2001): pp. 329–48, at 336; cf. Mark D. Jordan, "The Alleged Aristotelianism of Thomas Aquinas," in *The Gilson Lectures on Thomas Aquinas*, introduced by James P. Reilly (Toronto: Pontifical Institute of Mediaeval Studies, 2008), pp. 73–106. On the other hand, it seems undeniable that Aquinas did, and valued, what we would call "philosophy" (as Hankey would agree). The interest his thought has aroused in philosophers as widely divergent as Martha Nussbaum, Alasdair

and our conclusions about the genesis of Aquinas's thought have to be held somewhat loosely, especially when he is not relying on an authoritative source of Christian doctrine.

10.1. AQUINAS AS AN "ARISTOTELIAN" IN HIS SACRAMENTOLOGY: PRELIMINARY OBSERVATIONS

There is prima facie evidence for taking Aquinas to be, in some loose sense, an "Aristotelian." He probably began the study of Aristotle's natural philosophy and metaphysics in Naples.[3] He seems to have studied Aristotle at Paris, and intensively at Cologne under Albert the Great, whose work he continued to follow for a long time.[4] He made a huge investment in commenting upon Aristotle at a point in his life when he was under severe pressure to produce other works.[5] The commentaries on Aristotle amount to something around 13 percent of his total literary output.[6] His motive and manner of exposition are strongly debated, but his attention to Aristotle and his depth and breadth of acquaintance with him are beyond question.[7]

How "Aristotelian" is Aquinas's theology of the sacraments? Mark Jordan points out that in the two crucial questions on sacramental effects (*ST* III, qq. 62–63) Aristotle is cited only five times among sixty citations, and two of those five citations have nothing to do with the central issue of sacramental causality.[8] In the thirty-one questions devoted to the sacraments (*ST* III, qq. 60–90) citations of Aristotle are not frequent, and occur most often in objections and replies. In dealing with the sacraments of the New Law, Aquinas stands firmly

MacIntyre, Anthony Kenny, and Elizabeth Anscombe is evidence of the power of his philosophical thought.

[3] Jean-Pierre Torrell, OP, *Saint Thomas Aquinas*, vol. 1, The Person and his Work, trans. Robert Royal, rev. ed. (Washington, DC: The Catholic University of America Press, 2005), p. 7.

[4] Torrell, *Saint Thomas Aquinas*, vol. 1, pp. 19–27.

[5] Torrell, *Saint Thomas Aquinas*, vol. 1, pp. 224–46.

[6] Robert Busa, *Index Thomisticus*, quoted in Jason L. A. West, "Aristotle through the Looking Glass: Aquinas as a Historian of Philosophy," in *Literary Form, Philosophical Content: Historical Studies of Philosophical Genres*, edited by Jonathan A. Lavery and Louis Groarke (Madison, NJ: Farleigh Dickinson University Press, 2010), pp. 104–14, at 113, n. 9.

[7] For a survey of views on Aquinas's motive and manner of exposition, see West, "Aristotle through the Looking Glass," pp. 104–6; John F. Wippel, *Metaphysical Themes in Thomas Aquinas II* (Washington, DC: The Catholic University of America Press, 2007), pp. 240–4. Both of these essays also offer their own analysis of Aquinas's approach, with some case studies of Aquinas's interaction with Aristotelian texts.

[8] Mark D. Jordan, "Theology and Philosophy," in *The Cambridge Companion to Aquinas*, edited by Norman Kretzmann and Eleonore Stump (Cambridge: Cambridge University Press, 1993), pp. 232–51, at 243.

on the ground of *sacra doctrina*, and in the realm of faith. Bernhard Blankenhorn has recently shown that Aquinas's mature sacramental theology is the fruit of deep reflection on Scripture, read particularly through the eyes of the Greek Fathers, especially John Damascene and Cyril of Alexandria,[9] as well as through Augustine. Thomas is also guided by the liturgical tradition of the Church as practiced in his time. Liam Walsh observes, "Thomas tells more in this part of his theology about what people were doing in their Christian life than anywhere else in his theology."[10]

While Aquinas affirms the superiority of *sacra doctrina* over other sciences, he also seems to assume that those other sciences can serve the articulation of truth known on the basis of revelation. Both sacred doctrine and human sciences are concerned with the truth of things, and though they approach the truth from different directions, ultimately truth known by natural reason and by revelation must cohere.[11] Perhaps this accounts for the fact that of the explicit citations to Aristotle in the section of the *Summa* directly devoted to the sacraments of the New Law, two thirds appear in objections and replies to objections. If the explication of sacred doctrine in which Aquinas is engaged is to prove convincing, it must at least be shown not to contradict what seems to be demonstrable by natural reason, even if its assertions ultimately rest not on what is demonstrable by human reason, but on supernatural revelation.[12]

Another aspect of Thomas's use of Aristotelian notions in his sacramental theology is that it generally involves analogical application of terms. Aristotle's object was to deal with the natural world, whereas Thomas is dealing with sacramental acts that, while symbolic, are spiritually effective. There is something in every sacrament that exceeds what can be analyzed by the methods of natural sciences. Faith is required, which exceeds the limits of the sense-based knowledge of unaided human reason.

Having accepted the tenets of faith with regard to the sacraments, however, Aquinas proceeds to use Aristotelian concepts to explicate (not to justify or explain by natural demonstration but to make intelligible to the light of faith)

---

[9] Bernhard Blankenhorn, OP, "The Instrumental Causality of the Sacraments: Thomas Aquinas and Louis-Marie Chauvet," *Nova et Vetera* 4 (2006): pp. 255–93; and, with some slight adjustment of his view of the most central biblical texts for Aquinas, Bernhard Blankenhorn, OP, "The Place of Romans 6 in Aquinas's Doctrine of Sacramental Causality: A Balance of History and Metaphysics," in *Ressourcement Thomism: Sacred Doctrine, the Sacraments, and the Moral Life: Essays in Honor of Romanus Cessario, OP*, edited by Reinhard Hütter and Matthew Levering (Washington, DC: The Catholic University of America Press, 2010), pp. 136–49.

[10] Liam G. Walsh, OP, "Liturgy in the Theology of St. Thomas," *Thom.* 38 (1974): pp. 557–83.

[11] Aquinas makes extended use of an analogy of ascent from what is knowable by reason and descent by means of revelation, so that the way of truth is one, even though the direction is different. See *SCG* IV, ch. 1.

[12] "Truth cannot be truth's contrary" (*SCG* IV, ch. 8, no. 1); "One must show that [those things proved from Scripture, rather than from natural reason] are not opposed to natural reason" (*SCG* IV, ch. 1, no. 10).

what goes on in the sacraments. In so doing he often "stretches" the concepts, applying them to a range of realities that far exceed the bounds of Aristotelian natural philosophy and metaphysics.

This is clearest, perhaps, in the case of the Eucharist. Beginning with the term that he held to have been authoritatively applied to the Eucharist at Lateran IV, "transubstantiation," Thomas explicates through Aristotle's distinction between substance and accidents the way in which the mysterious presence of Christ comes to occur under the species of bread and wine. For an unbelieving Aristotelian philosopher, of course, this is nonsensical: how does one posit a change in substance without a change in accidents? None of Aristotle's examples, such as the change of wood to ash, parallels this unique occurrence. Thomas's elaboration of Eucharistic doctrine demands faith as its premise; he is not seeking to demonstrate the possibility of the conversion of the elements on natural grounds, a conversion that in one instance he describes as a "miracle."

The same holds true for the use of other Aristotelian categories of thought in Thomas's mature view of the sacraments. My study will attempt to show a certain concordance between elements of Aristotle's thought and aspects of Aquinas's thought about sacraments in the *Summa*. In these questions, some positions Aquinas holds in common with Aristotle appear as assumptions with no reference to the Philosopher. Those assumptions are sometimes treated elsewhere in the *Summa*,[13] with explicit reference to Aristotle.[14] Aristotle's concepts do not, of course, set limits on what can be affirmed in Aquinas's sacramental theology; in fact, a good deal of what is interesting in *ST* III, qq. 60–90 is the way that Aquinas extends Aristotelian forms of thought or goes beyond Aristotle's insight even into matters accessible to natural reason. Nevertheless, there is a significant concordance evident between Aquinas and Aristotle on anthropology and causality in these questions.

Aquinas shares with Aristotle an understanding of man as a rational, social animal, a union of body and intellectual soul. Since the sacraments are instituted by God for the perfection of men, we would expect convictions about anthropology and causality to play a crucial role in sacramental theology, and this is indeed the case. I will examine the role of assumptions that Aquinas shares with Aristotle as they figure in his sacramental theology in two areas of anthropology. First, the sacraments as signs function as a kind of language. As well, the function of human language as communicative sign-making, which Aquinas discerns in Aristotle's *Peri hermeneias*, is critical to

---

[13] The *Summa* requires a holistic reading, though the long customary division of the work into "treatises" has often obscured this. Alasdair MacIntyre, *Three Rival Versions of Moral Enquiry: Encyclopaedia, Genealogy, and Tradition* (Notre Dame, IN: University of Notre Dame Press, 1990), pp. 134–5.

[14] E.g. *ST* I, qq. 75–88, where a great deal of explicit attention is given to Aristotle, especially in dialogue with "Plato."

the account of sacraments as signs. To root sacraments firmly in the history of salvation as their significative context, Aquinas uses Augustine's theory of signs as essentially intentional. Secondly, I will deal with the way in which Aquinas grounds, in part, the necessity of sacraments as sensible signs in the principle that man learns through the senses, an epistemological conviction that he shares with Aristotle. I will, finally, examine the analogous use Aquinas makes of the Aristotelian causal scheme to account for the way sacraments can be channels of grace, bringing human beings to their divinely appointed end as partakers of the divine nature. In this causal account he is building squarely on revelation and offers an account of causality that far exceeds what can be found in Aristotle.

10.2. SACRAMENTS AS COMPOUND SIGNS

For Aquinas, building on Aristotle and Augustine, language is a kind of sign-making, and words are the preeminent type of signs.[15] Sacraments, as complex signs, are thus a kind of language; therefore, some of the properties of language as sign-making that lie beneath Aquinas's theology of the sacraments are important points of concordance between Aquinas and Aristotle. For both Aquinas and Aristotle, language is rooted in the nature of the human being as a rational, social animal. Sacraments build on this, since "divine wisdom provides for each thing according to its mode."[16]

Aquinas divides his treatment of the sacraments of the New Law in *ST* III, qq. 60–65 into five parts: What is a sacrament? (q. 60); the necessity of the sacraments (q. 61); the effects of the sacraments (qq. 62–63); the causes of the sacraments (q. 64); and their number (q. 65). He begins by asking whether a sacrament is a kind of sign.

In the first question Aquinas determines the basic genus of a sacrament, which he takes to be a sign. The first article asks whether a sacrament is a kind of sign, and in the very first objection, Thomas confronts the chief alternative to this categorization: "a sacrament is a kind of cause rather than a kind of sign."[17] Thomas replies: "a sacrament need not always imply causality."[18] Rather, the general category under which the sacraments fall is that of a sign of a holy thing. This represents an important choice, which allows him to

---

[15] Mark D. Jordan, *Ordering Wisdom: The Hierarchy of Philosophical Discourses in Aquinas* (Notre Dame, IN: University of Notre Dame Press, 1986), p. 19.

[16] *ST* III, q. 60, a. 4, corpus. This is in keeping with the axiom that grace does not destroy, but perfects nature (see *ST* I, q. 1, a. 8).

[17] *ST* III, q. 60, a. 1, arg. 1.   [18] *ST* III, q. 60, a. 1, ad 1.

include certain old covenant rites within the category of sacraments.[19] It allows him also to include in this category other acts of worship as the central act of the virtue of religion.[20] This brings under the category of sacrament as sign the first of the two aspects of sacraments that Aquinas picks out as essential to the economy of the New Law: worship and sanctification.[21] While Aquinas acknowledges that, in a certain sense, every sign of a sacred thing is a sacrament, his concern is with sacraments as signs particularly of Christ as the cause of our holiness.[22] These two aspects of sacraments bear an intrinsic relation to one another, since the self-offering of Christ on the cross by which Christ sanctifies human beings is also the inauguration of the rites of Christian religion.[23] Both as acts of worship and as means of perfection for worship, then, sacraments are signs.

Aristotle's *Peri hermeneias* belongs to his *Organon*, which is concerned with methodology. He is concerned in the work with the kinds of utterance in which truth and falsity may be contained, and therefore with the basic units of enunciation that enable statements that affirm or deny something. For medieval Aristotelians, the occasion for discussing questions of linguistic meaning arose when expounding Aristotle's *Peri hermeneias*.[24] Such a theory in Aristotle himself would have to be gleaned from what he seems to presuppose here, especially in relation to what he says elsewhere. This is one effect of his participation in a tradition of commentary, an effect evident in his *Prœmium*. As Mark Jordan says:

---

[19] Aimon-Marie Roguet, OP, "Notes explicatives," in Thomas Aquinas, *Somme théologique: Les sacrements, 3ª, Questions 60–65* (Paris: Desclée, 1945), pp. 201–54, at 202; Hyacinthe-François Dondaine, OP, "La définition des sacrements dans la 'Somme théologique,'" *RSPhTh* 31 (1947): pp. 213–28; John F. Gallagher, C.M., *Significando Causant: A Study of Sacramental Efficiency* (Fribourg: Fribourg University Press, 1965).

[20] *ST* II-II, q. 81, a. 7, corpus: "In the Divine worship it is necessary to make use of corporeal things, that man's mind may be aroused thereby, as by signs, to the spiritual acts by means of which he is united to God. Therefore the internal acts of religion take precedence of the others and belong to religion essentially, while its external acts are secondary, and subordinate to the internal acts." For a careful discussion of the importance of this broad definition of sacraments for a Christian theology of religions, see Benoît-Dominique de La Soujeole, OP, "The Importance of the Definition of Sacraments as Signs," in *Ressourcement Thomism: Sacred Doctrine, the Sacraments, and the Moral Life: Essays in Honor of Romanus Cessario, OP*, edited by Reinhard Hütter and Matthew Levering (Washington, DC: The Catholic University of America Press, 2010), pp. 127–35.

[21] *ST* III, q. 62, a. 5, corpus: "Now sacramental grace seems to be ordained principally to two things: namely, to take away the defects consequent on past sins, in so far as they are transitory in act, but endure in guilt; and, further, to perfect the soul in things pertaining to Divine Worship in regard to the Christian Religion."

[22] *ST* III, q. 60, a. 2.

[23] For a fine presentation of the way in which Christ's life is a fulfillment of the Old Testament acts of worship and the source of sanctification for human beings, in which the two are intrinsically united, see Matthew Levering, *Christ's Fulfillment of Torah and Temple: Salvation according to Thomas Aquinas* (Notre Dame, IN: University of Notre Dame Press, 2002).

[24] Jordan, *Ordering Wisdom*, p. 9.

The constant rereading of Aristotle after the "recovery" of his pedagogical treatises by Andronicus was a rereading of a *corpus* of writings. The more obscure treatises, among which the *Peri hermeneias* must surely be included, begin to gather sense from the more discursive treatises. Thus the doctrine on signs in the *Peri hermeneias* is supplemented, not only by the context of the augmented *Organon*, which includes the *Poetics* and the *Rhetoric*, but also by the context of such works as the *De anima*, the *Politics*, and the *Ethics*. This ... result of the commentary tradition can be seen in Aquinas's readiness to read the concerns of the human community into Aristotle's elliptical discussion of word-types.[25]

In the first chapters of his commentary on *Peri hermeneias*, Aquinas takes up Aristotle's distinction between natural and conventional vocal signification. Aristotle establishes here three elements of linguistic signification (words, understandings, and things):

> Now those [enunciations] that are in vocal sound are signs of passions in the soul, and those that are written are signs of those in vocal sound. And just as letters are not the same for all men so neither are vocal sounds the same; but the passions of the soul, of which vocal sounds are the first signs are the same for all; and the things of which passions of the soul are likenesses are also the same. This has been discussed, however, in our study of the soul for it belongs to another subject of inquiry.[26]

This is the famous "semantic triangle" that establishes a relation between vocal sounds, passions of the soul, and things existing outside the mind.[27] Names— the general term that Aristotle uses to indicate a basic linguistic unit from which affirmations and denials are formed[28]—are not the same for all. Pointing ahead to what Aristotle will say later, Aquinas tells us that Aristotle means that names signify by convention, not by nature.[29]

---

[25] Jordan, *Ordering Wisdom*, p. 9. Aristotle himself makes the connection between this work and his larger corpus by referring rather generally to his treatment of "the passions of the soul" (παθήματα τῆς ψυχῆς), in his study of the soul; *Peri hermeneias* I (16a8).

[26] Aristotle, *Peri hermeneias* I (16a3–9): "Ἔστι μὲν οὖν τὰ ἐν τῇ φωνῇ τῶν ἐν τῇ ψυχῇ παθημάτων σύμβολα, καὶ τὰ γραφόμενα τῶν ἐν τῇ φωνῇ. καὶ ὥσπερ οὐδὲ γράμματα πᾶσι τὰ αὐτά, οὐδὲ φωναὶ αἱ αὐταί· ὧν μέντοι ταῦτα σημεῖα πρώτων, ταῦτα πᾶσι παθήματα τῆς ψυχῆς, καὶ ὧν ταῦτα ὁμοιώματα πράγματα ἤδη ταὐτά. περὶ μὲν οὖν τούτων εἴρηται ἐν τοῖς περὶ ψυχῆς, –ἄλλης γὰρ πραγματείας·" The translation is from Thomas Aquinas, *Aristotle On Interpretation: Commentary by Thomas Aquinas Finished by Cardinal Cajetan*, trans. Jean T. Oesterle (Milwaukee: Marquette University Press, 1962).

[27] "Things" here is not limited to physical objects, and Thomas does not take it to be so limited.

[28] In the opening lines of the *Peri hermeneias*, Aristotle says: "Πρῶτον δεῖ θέσθαι τί ὄνομα καὶ τί ῥῆμα, ἔπειτα τί ἐστιν ἀπόφασις καὶ κατάφασις καὶ ἀπόφανσις καὶ λόγος" (16a1–2). The list of terms often leads to an unwarranted assumption that Aristotle means "nouns" as opposed to "verbs." Later in his text, however, he will say that verbs are themselves names (16b19).

[29] Aristotle, *Peri hermeneias* I (16a26–29): "τὸ δὲ κατὰ συνθήκην, ὅτι φύσει τῶν ὀνομάτων οὐδέν ἐστιν, ἀλλ' ὅταν γένηται σύμβολον· ἐπεὶ δηλοῦσί γέ τι καὶ οἱ ἀγράμματοι ψόφοι, οἷον θηρίων, ὧν οὐδέν ἐστιν ὄνομα."

What the names signify is "passions of the soul," by which Aquinas understands Aristotle to be referring to "conceptions of the intellect," as opposed to affections of the sensitive appetite, such as anger and joy. Passions in the latter sense, Aquinas says, can be expressed naturally in, for example, the groans of the sick. He points to Aristotle's contrast between human and other animal sounds in *Politics* I,2 (1253a10–14) in order to support this contrast.[30] In that passage, Aristotle explicitly contrasts the vocal sounds other animals make in order to signify sense experiences, with human speech that is capable of expressing what is useful, harmful, just, unjust. Following the same line of thought here, Aquinas says:

> Now if man were by nature a solitary animal the passions of the soul by which he was conformed to things so as to have knowledge of them would be sufficient for him; but since he is by nature a political and social animal it was necessary that his conceptions be made known to others. This he does through vocal sound. Therefore there had to be significant vocal sounds in order that men might live together. Whence those who speak different languages find it difficult to live together in social unity.[31]

Aquinas would have found this idea in the commentary of Ammonius. John O'Callaghan points out that Aquinas adds the counterfactual with which he begins. The significance of this for Thomas turns on the distinction he makes between two kinds of abstraction. One can understand a red apple as an apple, abstracting from its redness. This is acceptable and indeed necessary abstraction. But to understand the same apple as not-red is a false or vicious abstraction.[32] Aquinas would have considered the solipsistic vantage point of most modern philosophy of language and cognition a vicious abstraction. Human beings are not solitary, and human cognition and language do not function first as solitary, and then as social. This helps to make clearer why Aquinas views language, cognition, and social life, as considered in the *Peri hermeneias*, in the *De anima*, and in the *Politics*, as to some degree interlocking.[33]

If vocal sounds and letters that represent them differ, the passions of the soul, Aristotle says, are the same. This throws up two difficulties that Aquinas notes.[34] The first is equivocation. To take the textbook example, the word "end," with the same vocal sounds and the same letters in English can mean either cessation or goal. Thus, the equivocation: "The end of a thing is its perfection. Death is the end of life. Therefore, death is the perfection of life."

---

[30] *Expositio libri Peryermenias* I, lect. 2, no. 5 (= Leonine ed., vol. 1*/1, pp. 10–11).

[31] *Expositio libri Peryermenias* I, lect. 2, no. 2 (= Leonine ed., vol. 1*/1, p. 9).

[32] *ST* I, q. 85, a. 1, ad 1.

[33] John P. O'Callaghan, *Thomist Realism and the Linguistic Turn: Toward a More Perfect Form of Existence* (Notre Dame, IN: University of Notre Dame Press, 2003), pp. 281–3.

[34] My account of Aquinas's treatment of these two difficulties follows Mark Jordan's elegant unraveling of the arguments: Jordan, *Ordering Wisdom*, pp. 13–14.

Aquinas says that the resolution of the difficulty of equivocation is supplied by Porphyry, who points out that a vocal sound is uttered in order to signify a single conception; when equivocation occurs, the confusion can be overcome by explanation.[35]

The more substantial difficulty is that human opinions differ, yet Aristotle says that passions of the soul "are the same for all." Aquinas distinguishes two kinds of conception, simple and complex. Only at the level of simple conceptions, those signified by the noncomplex vocal sounds, are they the same for all men. Aquinas's example is the use of a simple concept, "man": "If someone truly understands what man is, whatever else than man he apprehends he does not understand as man."[36] The term "passions of the intellect" is important. It implies that the mind's conceptions are acted upon by the world. Aquinas is arguing from the mind as actualized by the world. If there is more than nominal disagreement, this must be due to either a confusion of names or a lack of experience with the world. Understanding is contingent. Thomas does not think that Aristotle is relying on intuition of concepts, but simply defers his discussion of the functioning of the intellect to another place, as does Aristotle.[37]

There is a long and complex history of discussion about the nature of human cognition and speech and their interrelation. I will not enter into its intricacies here.[38] Rather, I will simply point out two aspects of the understanding of human language that Aquinas and Aristotle hold in common. First, human language builds on the capacities of the human being as a rational, social animal to interact with the world around him or her so as to form intellectual conceptions expressed in conventional patterns of speech. In other words, concrete human language is a matter of signifying those conceptions to one another. Secondly, the capacity to do so is evidence of the social and political nature of the human being. Both of those elements are present in the thought of Aquinas and of Aristotle, though Aquinas's exposition of the *Peri hermeneias* brings in aspects of Aristotle's thought expressed in other contexts more explicitly than does Aristotle himself.[39]

---

[35] *Expositio libri Peryermenias* I, lect. 2, no. 11 (= Leonine ed., vol. 1*/1, p. 13).

[36] *Expositio libri Peryermenias* I, lect. 2, no. 10 (= Leonine ed., vol. 1*/1, p. 12).

[37] Jordan, *Ordering Wisdom*, p. 14.

[38] O'Callaghan's *Thomist Realism* offers a lengthy, and to my mind convincing, account of human language and cognition according to Aristotle and Aquinas, in conversation with modern philosophical thinkers.

[39] Aquinas, in his *De regno* I, chs. 6–7, also makes the point that language has an essential communal educative function. It is the burden of MacIntyre's theory of tradition-constituted ethical inquiry to show (quixotically, as he admits) that the seeds of a communal and historical approach to ethical inquiry are present, though not developed, in Aristotle. For this, the concept of Aristotle's dialectic articulated by John D. G. Evans, *Aristotle's Concept of Dialectic* (Cambridge: Cambridge University Press, 1977), pp. 85–9 is important. See Alasdair MacIntyre, *Whose Justice? Which Rationality?* (Notre Dame, IN: University of Notre Dame Press, 1988). The reference to Evans is on p. 114.

When Aquinas takes up Aristotle's definition of a name, "a vocal sound significant by convention, without time, no part of which is significant separately," he stresses the artificial nature of words, which signify "according to human institution deriving from what is pleasing (*beneplacitum*) to man. This differentiates names from vocal sounds signifying naturally, such as the groans of the sick and the vocal sounds of brute animals."[40] Words are made to be sounds by the imposition of a form on vocal sound.[41] The note of human artifice deriving from will comes out in his explanation of why "no part signifies separately," which is Aquinas's explication of the etymological fallacy. He points out the meaning of *lapis*, which he takes to derive from *laesio pedis*, but does not therefore signify an injury to the foot. The meaning is what accords with the intention of the one making the sound into a sign. Aquinas stresses the intentional character of language once again in his commentary on Aristotle's distinction between enunciation and other forms of speech and the unity of enunciations. In all of this, Aquinas takes up elements present in the *Peri hermeneias*, but amplifies and elaborates on them. He clearly does so by appealing to other elements in Aristotle's thought on the social and rational nature of the human being. On Mark Jordan's reading, he also amplifies the intentional aspect of signification through a reading of the text within the tradition of commentary shaped by Christian theologies of Scripture and sacrament. The stress on intention is present in Ammonius, but Aquinas strengthens it further, especially through his appropriation of Augustine's *De doctrina christiana*, and his attentiveness to the issues of spiritual interpretation of Scripture and the signification of words in the sacraments.[42]

Returning to Aquinas's sacramental theology, it is noteworthy that when Aquinas takes up the question "whether determinate words are required in the sacraments" the first objection comes from the *Peri hermeneias*: "As the Philosopher says (*Peri Herm.* i), 'words are not the same for all.' But salvation, which is sought through the sacraments, is the same for all. Therefore determinate words are not required in the sacraments."[43] Aquinas's reply to the objection is a close parallel to the account in the *Peri hermeneias* of the diversity of languages that yet convey the same conceptions of the intellect:

> As Augustine says (*Tract. lxxx super Joan.*), the word operates in the sacraments "not because it is spoken," i.e. not by the outward sound of the voice, "but because it is believed" in accordance with the sense of the words which is held by faith. And this sense is indeed the same for all, though the same words as to their sound be not used by all. Consequently no matter in what language this sense is expressed, the sacrament is complete.[44]

---

[40] *Expositio libri Peryermenias* I, lect. 4, no. 6 (= Leonine ed., vol. 1*/1, p. 21).
[41] *Expositio libri Peryermenias* I, lect. 4, no. 5 (= Leonine ed., vol. 1*/1, pp. 20–1).
[42] Jordan, *Ordering Wisdom*, p. 20.   [43] *ST* III, q. 60, a. 7, arg. 1.
[44] *ST* III, q. 60, a. 7, ad 1.

The sacraments are thus compound signs, composed of sensible things and intelligible words. They are always something sensible, but always compounded with words in order to give them a clear enough meaning that they may be the occasion for faith in the word of God. Natural signs are signs by virtue of their capacity to lead by the apprehension of causal connections, or through association, to something else. This connection or association, however, is not intended by anyone or expressed outwardly in amplification of such apprehension, and so it lacks clarity.[45] Relying on a metaphor going back at least to William of Auxerre, Aquinas compares the relation of the sensible component of sacraments, available to sense perception, and the words used, to the Aristotelian conception of natural things as a compound of matter and form.[46]

It is notable that the response above turns on the centrality of the word as the preeminent type of sign. The sensible element of the sacraments is essential, and the grounds for this will be taken up in the next section (10.3), but the verbal form of the sacrament is what makes it significant with sufficient clarity to become an occasion for the profession of faith. The necessity of words in the sacraments arises from their capacity to signify mental conceptions with clarity. Aquinas cites Augustine as the authority for words as principal signs, and this influence is important. But the concordance with Aristotle's idea that words signify conceptions of the intellect is not far from the surface:

> Augustine says (*De Doctr. Christ.* ii) that "words are the principal signs used by men"; because words can be formed in various ways for the purpose of signifying various mental concepts, so that we are able to express our thoughts with greater distinctness by means of words. And therefore in order to insure the perfection of sacramental signification it was necessary to determine the signification of the sensible things by means of certain words. For water may signify both a cleansing by reason of its humidity, and refreshment by reason of its being cool: but when we say, "I baptize thee," it is clear that we use water in baptism in order to signify a spiritual cleansing.[47]

Further, in understanding sacraments as signs, Aquinas adverts to the idea of institution by artifice that he had used in his commentary on the conventional nature of words. In his *responsio* to the question, "whether determinate things are required for a sacrament?" Aquinas makes use of the principle that God is the one who instituted the sacraments, which he is dealing with in this question under the genus of signs. The first objection turns on the possibility of using different signs to signify the same reality, such as the metaphorical biblical references to God as a rock, a lion, or the sun. In responding to this,

---

[45] Jordan, *Ordering Wisdom*, p. 24.

[46] For background, see Bernard Leeming, S.J., *Principles of Sacramental Theology* (New York: Longmans, Green, and Co., 1956), pp. 403–7.

[47] *ST* III, q. 60, a. 6, corpus.

Aquinas notes the diversity of signs for the same thing, but attributes authority for the determination of sign to be used to the signifier:

> Though the same thing can be signified by divers signs, yet to determine which sign must be used belongs to the signifier. Now it is God Who signifies spiritual things to us by means of the sensible things in the sacraments, and of similitudes in the Scriptures. And consequently, just as the Holy Ghost decides by what similitudes spiritual things are to be signified in certain passages of Scripture, so also must it be determined by Divine institution what things are to be employed for the purpose of signification in this or that sacrament.[48]

In the *responsio* to the same question, Aquinas considers both aspects of sacraments that he takes to be essential to them, worship and sanctification. He points to the divine work of sanctification as the reason for using determinate things, such as water, in the sacraments:

> In the use of the sacraments two things may be considered, namely, the worship of God, and the sanctification of man: the former of which pertains to man as referred to God, and the latter pertains to God in reference to man. Now it is not for anyone to determine that which is in the power of another, but only that which is in his own power. Since, therefore, the sanctification of man is in the power of God Who sanctifies, it is not for man to decide what things should be used for his sanctification, but this should be determined by Divine institution. Therefore in the sacraments of the New Law, by which man is sanctified according to 1 Cor. 6:11, "You are washed, you are sanctified," we must use those things which are determined by Divine institution.[49]

On this principle of God as the one who institutes the sacraments, therefore, divine law determines the things and the words to be used in the sacraments.[50] The significative context is broadened by the fact that God can signify not only things by words, but words by other things,[51] creating a web of meaning within the sacred history, interweaving the ceremonies of the Old Law and New Law.[52]

Aquinas's treatment of the two questions on the necessity of words and the necessity of using determinate things in the sacraments opens up a line of approach to the sacraments as a kind of language. This is potentially fruitful for placing the sacraments in their natural home in the liturgical life of the Christian people. In his monumental *Theological Dimensions of the Liturgy*, Cipriano Vagaggini analyses the liturgy as a whole as "a complexus of signs." The liturgy is a kind of language that is rooted in the revelation of God, which takes place in a sacred history, which is conveyed through the theological

---

[48] *ST* III, q. 60, a. 5, ad 1.   [49] *ST* III, q. 60, a. 5, corpus.
[50] *ST* III, q. 60, a. 5, ad 3.   [51] *ST* I, q. 1, a. 10.
[52] *ST* I-II, q. 101, a. 4; q. 102, a. 5.

interpretation of the Scripture.[53] Vagaggini further defines the liturgy as "a complexus of efficacious signs of the Church's sanctification and worship." The liturgy, and the sacraments that form its core, are like the language of the ecclesial culture of the Christian people. That means that the sacraments are best understood—indeed only understood—both as sanctification and as worship, in the context of the biblical history of revelation.

Languages are acquired in human interaction. The capacity for language is natural but a concrete language is learned. Given its grounding in the Scripture as read in the Christian Church, "full and active participation in the liturgy" is achieved "by means of the necessary instruction"[54] of the Old and New Testaments as read in the tradition of the Church. The very nature of the liturgy is aligned with the principle that grace builds on nature, and more specifically what Vagaggini calls "the law of the Incarnation," that God redeems us in accord with our nature, and indeed by uniting himself to our nature.

The stress on the communal nature of language is not trivial for Aquinas's account of the sacraments. In the *sed contra* of *ST* III, q. 61, a. 1 on the necessity of sacraments, Aquinas quotes Augustine:

> Augustine says (*Contra Faust.* xix): "It is impossible to keep men together in one religious denomination, whether true or false, except they be united by means of visible signs or sacraments." But it is necessary for salvation that men be united together in the name of the one true religion. Therefore sacraments are necessary for man's salvation.

In this larger theological context, Aquinas's interaction with the texts of Aristotle on language, conveyed to him in the commentary tradition, read in the context of the whole corpus of Aristotle's works, in the light of the Church's tradition of biblical interpretation and sacramental life, manifests the transformation of the water of philosophy into the wine of sacred doctrine.[55]

10.3. SACRAMENTS AS SENSIBLE SIGNS

In specifying that the sacraments are sensible signs, Aquinas builds on an Aristotelian anthropology that understands the human being as a composite of body and intellectual soul. In this aspect of his anthropology, Aquinas is as

---

[53] Cipriano Vagaggini, OSB, *Theological Dimensions of the Liturgy: A General Treatise on the Dimensions of the Liturgy*, trans. Leonardo J. Doyle and William A. Jurgens, rev. ed. (Collegeville, MN: The Liturgical Press, 1976).

[54] Vatican II, Constitution *Sacrosanctum Concilium* II,14.

[55] *Super Boetium De Trinitate*, q. 2, a. 3, ad 5 (cf. arg. 5).

solidly "Aristotelian" as he is anywhere in his thought.[56] In the questions on the constitution of the human being as a rational animal in *ST* I, qq. 75–89, Aquinas explicitly appeals to Aristotle, and seems to find in Aristotle the only satisfactory way of thinking about the relationship of intellectual activity and bodily constitution in the human being. This forms important background to his thinking about sacraments as sensible signs.

In *ST* III, q. 60, a. 1 Aquinas established the genus of sacraments as that of signs. In *ST* III, q. 60, a. 2 he narrowed this to a sign pointing to man's sanctification. In *ST* III, q. 60, a. 3 he specifies three ways in which sacraments point to the sanctification of human beings: firstly, to the passion of Christ, as the cause of sanctification; secondly, to the present sanctification of the human being, in the form of graces and virtues; thirdly, to the end of sanctification, which is eternal life. In aa. 4 and 6, he treats two necessary components of the sacraments: that they involve sensible signs, and that they make use of words.

In a. 4, Aquinas asks "whether a sacrament is always something sensible?" The *responsio* relies on a principle drawn from Dionysius:

> Divine wisdom provides for each thing according to its mode; hence it is written (Wis. 8:1) that "she ... ordereth all things sweetly": wherefore also we are told (Mt. 25:15) that she "gave to everyone according to his proper ability." Now it is part of man's nature to acquire knowledge of the intelligible from the sensible. But a sign is that by means of which one attains to the knowledge of something else. Consequently, since the sacred things which are signified by the sacraments, are the spiritual and intelligible goods by means of which man is sanctified, it follows that the sacramental signs consist in sensible things: just as in the Divine Scriptures spiritual things are set before us under the guise of things sensible. And hence it is that sensible things are required for the sacraments; as Dionysius also proves in his book on the heavenly hierarchy (*Cael. Hier.* i).[57]

The sacraments are suited to the nature of human beings, and human nature acquires knowledge of the intelligible from the sensible. The proof from Dionysius comes from the first chapter of his *Celestial Hierarchy*. Wayne Hankey notes that in this article "Aquinas's philosophical authority for understanding the relevant logic is Aristotle and the determining sacred authority is Dionysius the Pseudo-Areopagite."[58] The first objection comes from Aristotle's *Prior Analytics*:

---

[56] James A. Weisheipl, OP, "Thomas' Evaluation of Plato and Aristotle," *The New Scholasticism* 48 (1974): pp. 100–24, at 104 and 110.

[57] *ST* III, q. 60, a. 4, corpus.

[58] Wayne J. Hankey, "Reading Augustine through Dionysius: Aquinas's Correction of One Platonism by Another," in *Aquinas the Augustinian*, edited by Michael Dauphinais, Barry David, and Matthew Levering (Washington, DC: The Catholic University of America Press, 2007), pp. 243–57, at 256.

It seems that a sacrament is not always something sensible. Because, according to the Philosopher (*Prior. Anal.* ii), every effect is a sign of its cause. But just as there are some sensible effects, so are there some intelligible effects; thus science is the effect of a demonstration. Therefore not every sign is sensible. Now all that is required for a sacrament is something that is a sign of some sacred thing.[59]

The response also draws on Aristotle:

The name and definition of a thing is taken principally from that which belongs to a thing primarily and essentially: and not from that which belongs to it through something else. Now a sensible effect being the primary and direct object of man's knowledge (since all our knowledge springs from the senses) by its very nature leads to the knowledge of something else: whereas intelligible effects are not such as to be able to lead us to the knowledge of something else, except in so far as they are manifested by some other thing, i.e. by certain sensibles. It is for this reason that the name sign is given primarily and principally to things which are offered to the senses; hence Augustine says (*De Doctr. Christ.* ii) that a sign "is that which conveys something else to the mind, besides the species which it impresses on the senses." But intelligible effects do not partake of the nature of a sign except in so far as they are pointed out by certain signs.[60]

Aquinas is arguing here on the basis of something he takes to be the position of Aristotle, that all our knowledge springs from the senses. Aristotle is not cited here, but he is associated with the position more explicitly elsewhere in Aquinas's writings, where his anthropology is opposed to what is attributed to the Platonists. For Aristotle, and for Thomas, the nature of man is a composite of body and soul.[61] The intellect is a power of the rational soul, which is at once vegetative, sensitive, and intellectual, since each level of soul contains those that are more basic.[62] Thus, the soul of the human being is the form of the body, in that what characterizes this species, which is man, is that it has the powers that belong to the rational soul united with this body.[63] In both these respects, Aquinas takes himself to be firmly on the side of Aristotle, in opposition to Plato.[64]

---

[59] *ST* III, q. 60, a. 4, arg. 1.   [60] *ST* III, q. 60, a. 4, ad 1.

[61] See *ST* I, q. 76, a. 1, which relies heavily on Aristotle, both in the *sed contra* and in the corpus. After a survey of alternatives, Aquinas bluntly states: "There remains, therefore, no other explanation than that given by Aristotle—namely, that this particular man understands, because the intellectual principle is his form. Thus from the very operation of the intellect it is made clear that the intellectual principle is united to the body as its form." For another lengthy discussion on a similar theme, see *Quaestio disputata de spiritualibus creaturis*, particularly a. 10. See also Chapter 3 in this work.

[62] *ST* I, q. 77, aa. 1–2, citing Aristotle, *De anima* II,2–3.   [63] *ST* I, q. 76, a. 1.

[64] How much direct knowledge Aquinas had of Plato is unclear. See Fran O'Rourke, "Aquinas and Platonism," in *Contemplating Aquinas: On the Varieties of Interpretation*, edited by Fergus Kerr (London: SCM, 2003), pp. 247–79, at 249. But the opposition of Aristotle to Plato is especially clear in the *Quaestio disputata de spiritualibus creaturis*, a. 10.

What characterizes the human being as an intellectual being is the capacity to abstract intelligible forms from the matter in which they inhere.[65] This is opposed to the notion of an intellect substantially separate, which illuminates the human soul, thus giving understanding, to which the human intellect is simply passive.[66] Instead of a passively receptive intellect, Aristotle posited a potential intellect[67] and an active intellect, or possible and agent intellect, which reaches to understanding by a process of movement, from potential understanding to actual understanding.[68] The intellect begins as a tabula rasa.[69] It moves from lesser to greater understanding as it acts.[70]

Aquinas in *ST* I, q. 79, a. 4 raises the question whether the active intellect is something in the soul, a power inhering in the human being. Is understanding something that is proper to the human being? In the *sed contra*, Aquinas cites Aristotle in *De anima* III,5: "The Philosopher says that 'it is necessary for these differences,' namely, the passive and active intellect, 'to be in the soul.'" Aquinas draws in his response on an argument from human experience of moving from lack of understanding to understanding discursively, by arguing. Therefore, he says, there must be some higher intellect, which helps the soul to understand.[71]

On this basis, then, "some have held that this intellect, substantially separate, is the active intellect, which by lighting up the phantasms as it were, makes them to be actually intelligible."[72] In the dense few lines that follow, Aquinas will take hold of the notion of an active intellect in the human soul, as a power, and combine it with the notion that there is, in fact, a higher intellect, separable, enlightening, and indeed personal. He begins, however, by affirming that "even supposing the existence of such a separate active intellect, it would still be necessary to assign to the human soul some power participating in that superior intellect, by which power the human soul makes things actually intelligible."[73] Aquinas is not prepared to let go of the notion that the human intellect is an active, properly human power. Nevertheless, the juxtaposition of the passive and the active intellect has opened a certain door for a notion of participation that is important in Aquinas.

Thus, the notion of an intellectual light in which man participates and a separate intellect is not simply abandoned. Aquinas first takes note that Aristotle compares the active intellect to light received into the air.[74] Then he goes on, citing Ps 4:7, to say that "the separate intellect, according to the teaching of our faith, is God Himself, who is the soul's Creator and only

---

[65] *ST* I, q. 79, a. 4, corpus. Aristotle, *De anima* III,5.
[66] *ST* I, q. 79, a. 4, corpus. Aristotle, *De anima* III,5.
[67] Aristotle, *De anima* III,4. *ST* I, q. 79, a. 2, corpus.
[68] *ST* I, q. 79, a. 3, corpus. Aristotle, *De anima* III,5.
[69] Aristotle, *De anima* III,4.   [70] *ST* I, q. 79, a. 4, corpus.
[71] *ST* I, q. 79, a. 4, corpus.   [72] *ST* I, q. 79, a. 4, corpus.
[73] *ST* I, q. 79, a. 4, corpus.   [74] Aristotle, *De anima* III,5.

beatitude."[75] The kind of participation that Aquinas has in mind here is what marks the human being as the meeting point of spirit and matter.[76]

So, the "philosophical authority" in *ST* III, q. 60, a. 4 does seem to be Aristotle. The human being moves from potential to actual understanding by abstraction of form from matter, and thus, "all our knowledge springs from the senses." Yet, Aquinas's citation of Dionysius as the "sacred authority" in *ST* III, q. 60, a. 4 is perhaps more important, and is perfectly in keeping with the synthesis of intellectual activity and participation in a higher light that he has connected in *ST* I, q. 79, a. 4. Dionysius represents a trend in Neoplatonism in general, present from the time of Iamblichus, to turn toward the sensible in order to rise to the intelligible.[77]

In Christian Neoplatonism, such as that of Dionysius, human interaction with sensible things is the ground for an ascent to the higher, intelligible realities, of which, obviously, God is the supremely intelligible. God is known to human beings only through his effects, and in this life only through his sensible effects, whether in creation, or in the divine sacramental economy of salvation in Israel and the Church.[78] In light of more recent scholarship, many of the old oppositions between Aquinas the Aristotelian and Aquinas the Platonist can no longer be credibly held.[79]

It is important that in his citation of Dionysius, Aquinas does not restrict the principle of movement from the sensible to the intelligible simply to sacramental actions: "Since the sacred things which are signified by the sacraments, are the spiritual and intelligible goods by means of which man is sanctified, it follows that the sacramental signs consist in sensible things: just as in the Divine Scriptures spiritual things are set before us under the guise of things sensible."[80] In light of this double application to Scripture and sacrament, it seems to me that Aquinas suggests, perhaps, the wider linguistic web of interpretation that I have suggested. The point Aquinas makes about learning through the senses should not, it seems to me, be interpreted in a crude manner, as if each sacrament were a lesson, a kind of ritual cognitive exercise. The sacraments have their place within the whole liturgical life of the Church's "complexus of sensible signs."

Aquinas's point, then, that in the sacraments as sensible, significant realities God deals with us according to our mode of being, is closely connected to a set of understandings that, while certainly not simply "Aristotelian," have solid grounding in positions that Aquinas holds in common with Aristotle, and at

---

[75] *ST* I, q. 79, a. 4, corpus.   [76] *ST* I, q. 75, Prologue.

[77] Mark J. Edwards, *Neoplatonic Saints: The Lives of Plotinus and Proclus by their Students* (Liverpool: Liverpool University Press, 2000), pp. xxxiv ff.

[78] See Wayne J. Hankey, "The Place of the Proof for God's Existence in the *Summa Theologiae* of Thomas Aquinas," *Thom.* 46 (1982): pp. 370–93.

[79] See the lengthy list of references in O'Rourke, "Aquinas and Platonism," p. 248, n. 4.

[80] *ST* III, q. 60, a. 4, corpus.

least to some degree has gained from his reading of Aristotle within the tradition in which he has received him. The central correspondences I have considered thus far lie in the realm of anthropology. For both Aquinas and Aristotle, the human being is a rational, social animal, at all points: "The nature that is animal in man, that is rational in man, that is social and political in man, is but one material nature whose principle is the human soul."[81] Human language as conventional signification, interpreted according to intention; language as the expression of concepts derived by rational engagement with the sensible world; language as evidence of man's essentially social and political nature; all of these are grounds on which there is substantial concordance between Aristotle and Aquinas, and where it seems reasonable to say that Aquinas has been strongly influenced by Aristotle. In those respects, an "Aristotelian" anthropology seems to shape Aquinas's sacramental theology, and, indeed, to serve it as an effective handmaid.

10.4. SACRAMENTAL CAUSALITY

Thus far, I have examined the anthropological aspects of Aquinas's thought on the sacraments and have found strong correspondences between his thought and that of Aristotle. Aquinas's anthropology is certainly more elaborate than that of Aristotle, and he at times draws out of Aristotle's anthropology more than it seems Aristotle himself held, particularly regarding the immortality and subsistence of the soul.[82] (This is another case in which the strict opposition of the "Aristotelian" to the "Platonic" in Aquinas's thought must be set aside.) Nevertheless, accepting the premise that "Aristotle" for Aquinas is never a "pure" Aristotle, abstracted from the commentatorial tradition in which Aquinas read him, it seems clear that Aquinas has learned from Aristotle some insights that he puts to work in his theology of the sacraments as sensible signs that form the core of the complexus of signs that is the Christian liturgy.

Thus far, the treatment has stood somewhat aloof from direct engagement with the salient fact that Aquinas's anthropology, especially in *ST* I, qq. 75ff., is obviously a theological anthropology.[83] In the *Summa* above all Aquinas is

---

[81] O'Callaghan, *Thomist Realism*, p. 291.

[82] Frederick Copleston, who credits Aquinas with deep penetration of Aristotle's thought in his commentaries, issues cautions about reading particularly Aquinas's commentary on Aristotle's *De anima* as a straightforward exposition of Aristotle's thought. See Frederick C. Copleston, *Aquinas: An Introduction to the Life and Work of the Great Medieval Thinker* (London: Penguin Books, 1991), pp. 158–9.

[83] *ST* I, q. 75, Prologue.

viewing everything *sub ratione Dei*.[84] The sacraments embody both the divine and the human, not as abstracted from one another, but precisely in their interrelation.[85] The same rule for distinguishing true and false abstraction that we noted above (in section 10.2) applies here.

In his treatment of the causality of the sacraments, and his use of an Aristotelian causal schema, we find Aquinas securing the "realism" or "objectivity" of sacramental acts[86] through a largely analogous use of Aristotelian categories, especially the analogy of craft, to explicate the uniquely divine act of giving grace through the instrumentality of human acts. Aquinas's view of divine causality is not simply the product of a straightforward adoption of Aristotelian categories. It is already marked by the appropriation of Neoplatonic forms of thought that speak of God's self-diffusive goodness as the principle and end of creation. In his use of causal notions in sacramental theology, he further extends the categories of Aristotelian causal theory to accommodate the mode of divine action through the Incarnation and the sacraments which he found especially through reading Scripture in company with the great Greek Fathers, John of Damascus and Cyril of Alexandria.

It is in the discussion of sacramental causality in Aquinas that the influence of Aristotle is most frequently educed, whether in approbation or criticism. Now, paradoxically, Aristotle is almost never cited in the questions dealing with the effects of the sacraments.[87] Why might that be? First of all, in a topic so tightly bound to the details of *sacra doctrina*, Aristotle could not be an authority. By contrast, Thomas frequently cites Aristotle in the questions on anthropology in the *Prima Pars* because much of what is said falls in the realm in which what is revealed and what is known by natural reason overlaps. In the discussion of sacramental causality, however, Thomas deals with something that is instituted by God as part of the New Law; his authorities are primarily and appropriately doctrinal. That is appropriate precisely because Thomas grounds his thinking on the efficaciousness attributed to the sacraments in

---

[84] *ST* I, q. 1, a. 7, corpus.

[85] This is the burden of the excellent answer to Louis-Marie Chauvet offered by Liam G. Walsh, OP, "The Divine and the Human in St. Thomas's Theology of the Sacraments," in *Ordo sapientiae et amoris: Image et message de saint Thomas d'Aquin à travers les récentes études historiques, herméneutiques et doctrinales: Hommage au Professeur Jean-Pierre Torrell OP à l'occasion de son 65ᵉ anniversaire*, edited by Carlos-Josaphat Pinto de Oliveira (Fribourg: Éditions Universitaires, 1993), pp. 321–52. His essay points to a certain oscillation between the symbolic and the metaphysical that characterized the work of theologians who engaged with Thomas after the mid-1960s.

[86] For these modes of speaking about the sacraments, see Colman E. O'Neill, OP, *Sacramental Realism: A General Theory of the Sacraments* (Wilmington, DE: Michael Glazier, 1983); Vagaggini, *Theological Dimensions*, pp. 184ff.

[87] He is cited five times among the sixty explicit citations in *ST* III, qq. 62–63; two of these five citations have nothing to do with causality. This is noted by Jordan, "Theology and Philosophy," p. 243.

Scripture, as read by the Fathers, and refined in his mature sacramental theology especially through close reading of the Greek Fathers.[88]

Secondly, while Thomas certainly uses the causal schema found in Aristotle to good effect, he uses it in a way that goes beyond Aristotle. His sacramental theology explicates a set of relations that Aristotle did not envision; indeed, until the Incarnation, no mind could have conceived of them (1 Cor 2:9–10). Aquinas's use of the Aristotelian schema stretches the notion of what can be counted as a cause.

The account of sacramental causality in the *Tertia Pars* has to be set in the context of the Aristotelian four causes, which Aristotle sets out in two places, *Physics* II,3 and *Metaphysics* V, the latter of which is itself set in the context of the attempt to understand why a thing comes into existence, why it goes out of existence, why it continues in existence. Causation is a problem basic to Aristotle's conception of the world. In contrast to the Platonists, Aristotle saw change not as an illusion to transcend, but as an integral part of the natural world, which must be fully grasped in order to obtain full and reliable knowledge.[89] Therefore, understanding change or persistence is critical to his whole philosophical project. Aristotle's term, traditionally translated as "cause," might better be rendered "explanation" or "explanatory factor" in order to prevent confusion with the more limited modern notion of cause.[90] The Greek term is broader, and bears the sense of "blame" or "responsibility" as well.[91] When Aristotle speaks of causes, he is treating the "why" of a thing.[92]

His four causes encompass explanations for natural things and the processes that generate them, for artistic productions, and for human actions.[93] Aristotle distinguishes four ways in which we answer the question why something is as it is—four ways in which we cite a cause.[94] These are: the material cause, the formal cause, the efficient cause, and the final cause.[95] His four causes are not necessarily four different substances, four distinct

---

[88] See Blankenhorn, "The Place of Romans 6." For a list of patristic texts attesting sacramental efficacy, see Leeming, *Principles of Sacramental Theology*, pp. 38–60.

[89] Aristotle, *Physics* II,3 (194b15–22).

[90] Richard Sorabji, *Necessity, Cause and Blame: Perspectives on Aristotle's Theory* (London: Duckworth, 1980), pp. xi and 10; John D. G. Evans, *Aristotle* (Brighton: The Harvester Press, 1987), p. 83.

[91] Aristotle, *Aristotle's Physics: Books I and II*, trans. William Charlton (Oxford: Clarendon Press, 1992), p. 98.

[92] Aristotle, *Physics* II,3 (194b18–19). Cf. Jonathan Lear, *Aristotle: The Desire to Understand* (Cambridge: Cambridge University Press, 1991).

[93] Aristotle, *Metaphysics* V,2; *Physics* II,3.

[94] Lear, *Aristotle*, p. 28; Wolfgang Wieland, "The Problem of Teleology," in *Articles on Aristotle*, vol. 1, Science, edited by Jonathan Barnes, Malcolm Schofield, and Richard Sorabji (London: Duckworth, 1975), pp. 141–60.

[95] Aristotle, *Physics* II,3 (194b23–33). These are conventional ways of designating the causes, and though they raise issues of translation, will be used here for convenience.

entities; at times the causes may coincide, as when a human being gives birth to a human being, making "human being" the formal, efficient, and final cause.[96]

The material cause is "that out of which as a constituent a thing comes to be."[97] For example, the bronze or silver is the material cause of a loving cup.[98] This is not the whole of the explanation, however, as a lump of bronze or silver is not a loving cup; or, to use Aristotle's own example, a pile of wood is not a bed, except potentially, in that it could be so constructed as to be a bed.[99] Thus, the formal cause is the arrangement of the material, "the underlying thing," into a certain order that makes a thing what it is.[100] Because this order is intelligible, it is possible to give a definition of it.[101] We can say "this is a bed" and "that is a pile of wood" despite the equivalence of the matter. Aristotle does not limit his examples to physical bodies, but is able to apply the scheme to craftsmanship, syllables formed from letters, premises leading to conclusions. The efficient cause is the cause of a thing changing or staying unchanged.[102] Aristotle offers three examples: a man who has deliberated; the father of a child; that which makes something of that which is made, the doer of that which is done.[103] The efficient cause may be either an actual cause or a potential cause; a builder of a house may be called a builder or a builder who is building.[104] Within efficient causes, he distinguishes agents and means employed by them. The final cause is the end or purpose, that which something is for, as health is the cause of a walk. When we ask, "why is he walking?" the response "to keep fit" is a reasonable explanation in the fashion of a final cause, because it tells us what the walking is "for."[105] The final cause is the most important of the four causes, providing the deepest insight into why a thing occurs.[106] It is the key to reconciling Aristotle's whole theory of causation. Only if teleology is true is there a fully adequate theory of causation,[107] apart

---

[96] Aristotle, *Physics* II,7 (198a25–28).   [97] Aristotle, *Physics* II,3 (194b23).

[98] Aristotle, *Physics* II,3 (194b24–25).   [99] Aristotle, *Physics* II,1 (193a34–35).

[100] Aristotle, *Physics* II,3 (195a20).

[101] The phrase "ὁ λόγος ὁ τοῦ τί ἦν εἶναι," argues Lear, should not be understood as "the definition of the essence" as the old Oxford translation gives it. Aristotle is not referring to a linguistic formulation but to a cause, which is a real thing. Nonetheless, the form is related to definability. Because a thing has a form, it is possible to give a definition for it. See Lear, *Aristotle*, pp. 28–9.

[102] Aristotle, *Physics* II,3 (194b29–32).

[103] Aristotle, *Physics* II,3 (194b30–31). This last example is ambiguous, as "τὸ ποιοῦν τοῦ ποιουμένου" can be translated either way. Charlton (*Aristotle's Physics*, p. 48) thinks Aristotle probably means both.

[104] Aristotle, *Physics* II,3 (195b5).   [105] Aristotle, *Physics* II,3 (194b32–33).

[106] Evans, *Aristotle* (1987), p. 91, citing *Parts of Animals* I,1 (639b12–21). Wieland disputes this interpretation, seeing the four causes on a par with one another, but does not deal with the citation in *Parts of Animals*. See Wieland, "The Problem of Teleology," pp. 147–51.

[107] Evans, *Aristotle* (1987), pp. 117–18.

from which the notions of formal and efficient cause alone would not serve to render things intelligible.[108]

In the case of nature most commentators do not hold Aristotle to be committing what modern scientists often label "the teleological fallacy."[109] He does not ascribe purposive decision to nature, nor does he understand nature to be a universal force. What Aristotle is driving at in the realm of nature is that the things we meet in the world are intelligible as things of definite kinds because they contain within themselves principles that make them what they are, and in accord with which they go through certain transformations.[110] He stresses that if we wish to consider natural processes adequately, we must consider them from the point of view of results.[111]

This last point is important for the comparison with Aquinas. Both Aquinas and Aristotle make use of the analogy of craft in their causal schemes.[112] Yet, Aristotle applies it in one of two ways, either to actual human craftsmanship or to natural processes.[113] Sarah Broadie cautions especially against misconstruing the force of Aristotle's analogy between natural processes and craft. The analogy is from nature to craft, and not the other way around, and implies no extrinsic purposive agent.[114] Nonetheless, underlying Aristotle's teleology is a basic conviction that the world of experience is intelligible, that experience may be interpreted in a way that yields a "why."[115] Aquinas uses the Aristotelian model of the artisan as well, and it functions also only as an analogy.

Aquinas uses the Aristotelian causal scheme to demonstrate the Dionysian principle of an ascent from the creaturely to the God who is beyond comprehension. In the question on the existence of God in the *Summa*, he employs the four causes of Aristotle to show a way from the world of sensible creatures to the knowledge that God exists, as the unmoved source of motion, existence, goodness, and perfection.[116] In his understanding of the relation between God

---

[108] Marjorie Grene, *A Portrait of Aristotle* (London: Faber, 1963), p. 135.

[109] Grene, *A Portrait of Aristotle*, p. 135.   [110] Grene, *A Portrait of Aristotle*, p. 134.

[111] Wieland, "The Problem of Teleology," p. 160.

[112] On Aristotle's repeated use of the imagery of craft, see Francis X. Meehan, *Efficient Causality in Aristotle and St. Thomas* (Washington, DC: The Catholic University of America Press, 1940), pp. 31ff.

[113] Grene, *A Portrait of Aristotle*, p. 135. See also Richard Sorabji, "John Philoponus," in *Philoponus and the Rejection of Aristotelian Science*, edited by Richard Sorabji (London: Duckworth, 1987), pp. 1–40, esp. 1; Wieland, "The Problem of Teleology," p. 160.

[114] Sarah Broadie, "Nature and Craft in Aristotelian Teleology," in *Biologie, logique et métaphysique chez Aristote: Actes du séminaire C.N.R.S.–N.S.F., Oléron 28 juin–3 juillet 1987*, edited by Daniel Devereux and Pierre Pellegrin (Paris: Éditions du CNRS, 1990), pp. 389–403.

[115] Aristotle, *Metaphysics* I,1 (981a5–9).

[116] For an exposition, drawing on the more explicitly Aristotelian discussion in the *SCG*, of the relation between the proofs and Aristotle's causes, see Anthony Kenny, *The Five Ways: St Thomas Aquinas' Proofs of God's Existence*, new ed. (Abingdon: Routledge, 2009). For discussion of the variety of assessments of the five ways, see Fergus Kerr, *After Aquinas: Versions of Thomism* (Oxford: Wiley–Blackwell, 2002), pp. 52–72. See also Hankey, "The Place of the Proof."

and the world, Aquinas makes use of Aristotle's four causes, but directed by his notion of God as the utterly self-existent One, whose essence is to be, and who gives being to all else.[117] He asks in the first question on creation "whether God is the efficient cause of all things?"[118] In the *responsio*, Aquinas says:

> It must be said that every being in any way existing is from God. For whatever is found in anything by participation, must be caused in it by that to which it belongs essentially, as iron becomes ignited by fire. Now it has been shown above when treating of the divine simplicity that God is the essentially self-subsisting Being; and also it was shown that subsisting being must be one.[119]

Existence is conceived, then, as a participation in the divine being, whose own proper essence is to exist. Thomas draws here on the Avicennian distinction of essence from existing. Burrell summarizes Aquinas's synthesis:

> Aquinas was seeking for a way of understanding created being using Aristotelian metaphysics, yet the "givens" of that philosophy will have to be transformed to meet the exigency of a free creator . . . the *being* which Aristotle took to characterize substance must become (for Aquinas) an *esse ad creatorem*.[120]

Thus, God creates intentionally, by intellect and will, which are identical in the utterly simple God. The doctrine of the Trinity allows us to perceive the God who created us not by necessity, but out of love:

> There are two reasons why the knowledge of the divine persons was necessary for us. It was necessary for the right idea of creation. The fact of saying that God made all things by His Word excludes the error of those who say that God produced things by necessity. When we say that in Him there is a procession of love, we show that God produced creatures not because He needed them, nor because of any other extrinsic reason, but on account of the love of His own goodness. So Moses, when he had said, "In the beginning God created heaven and earth," subjoined, "God said, Let there be light," to manifest the divine Word; and then said, "God saw the light that it was good," to show proof of the divine Love. The same is also found in the other works of creation.[121]

Creation is a gift, the result of a diffusion of God's goodness, but not a necessary act. Having established all this, Aquinas then puts to work the four causes of Aristotle, and does so even with explicit use of the analogy of the artisan.[122] In the creature, then, God acts in such a way as to impart to it a form, the perfection of which is its goodness:

---

[117] In what follows I rely on David B. Burrell, C.S.C., "Act of Creation with its Theological Consequences," in *Aquinas on Doctrine: A Critical Introduction*, edited by Thomas G. Weinandy, Daniel A. Keating, and John P. Yocum (London: T. & T. Clark, 2004), pp. 27–44.

[118] *ST* I, q. 44, a. 1.   [119] *ST* I, q. 44, a. 1, corpus (with reference to q. 3).

[120] Burrell, "Act of Creation," p. 29.   [121] *ST* I, q. 32, a. 1, ad 3.

[122] *ST* I, q. 14, a. 8, corpus.

Since goodness is that which all things desire, and since this has the aspect of an end, it is clear that goodness implies the aspect of an end. Nevertheless, the idea of goodness presupposes the idea of an efficient cause, and also of a formal cause. For we see that what is first in causing, is last in the thing caused. Fire, e.g. heats first of all before it reproduces the form of fire; though the heat in the fire follows from its substantial form. Now in causing, goodness and the end come first, both of which move the agent to act; secondly, the action of the agent moving to the form; thirdly, comes the form. Hence in that which is caused the converse ought to take place, so that there should be first, the form whereby it is a being; secondly, we consider in it its effective power, whereby it is perfect in being, for a thing is perfect when it can reproduce its like, as the Philosopher says (*Meteor.* iv); thirdly, there follows the formality of goodness which is the basic principle of its perfection.[123]

Failure to take account of the pattern of God's action in creatures to bring them to the perfection of their being, which is their end, leads to a mistaken focus on efficient causality in the sacraments in isolation from formal and final causality.[124] In the sacraments, God acts so as to bring about the perfection of human beings, the fullness of their participation in the divine nature, and to do so by divine action. In this way, sacramental causality is not reduced to efficient causality.

The teleological aspect of the sacraments is implied in the discussion of the necessity of sacraments for salvation. In the first question this occurs implicitly.[125] In *ST* III, q. 61, a. 1 Aquinas states directly that sacraments are necessary for man's salvation. Human salvation for Aquinas is the attainment of the human being's proper end, which is in God, to whom the human being is to direct his or her life.[126] The formal cause in the sacraments is likeness to God through participation in his nature,[127] perfecting the essence of the soul or the powers of the soul that flow from its essence.[128]

The material cause, by implication, is the human being that is the recipient of the grace that brings renewal. In the long course of developing his mature sacramental theology, Aquinas moves from a notion of sacraments as dispositive causes, preparing for the solely divine act of inserting grace, to a perfective causality in which the sacramental action itself becomes a subordinated instrumental cause in the uniquely divine work of imparting grace. There is

---

[123] *ST* I, q. 5, a. 4, corpus.

[124] Liam G. Walsh, OP, "Sacraments," in *The Theology of Thomas Aquinas*, edited by Rik van Nieuwenhove and Joseph P. Wawrykow (Notre Dame, IN: University of Notre Dame Press, 2005), pp. 326–64.

[125] *ST* III, q. 60, a. 1, arg. 3; q. 60, a. 5, arg. 3 and ad 3; q. 60, a. 7, arg. 1. In each case, the objection turns on the necessity of sacraments for salvation. None of the replies denies this premise.

[126] *ST* I, q. 1, a. 1, corpus.

[127] *ST* III, q. 62, a. 1, corpus; q. 62, a. 2, corpus (referring to *ST* I-II, q. 110, aa. 3–4).

[128] *ST* III, q. 62, a. 1, corpus.

a long and somewhat detailed story of this development, and I am going to assume it rather than prove it here, since in both dispositive and perfective causality the underlying causal scheme is Aristotelian.[129] One important piece of this, however, was the discovery that grace is best conceived as an accident of human nature;[130] that is, the renewal that takes place in baptism, though it is described as a death and rebirth in the New Testament, is not a creation of a new substance. If it were, it would allow for no instruments, since God uses no instruments in creating: in creation he acts by the very act by which he himself exists. The recognition that imparting grace in baptism is not literally a new creation opened the way to the mature account of sacraments as instruments, by analogy with one type of efficient cause mentioned by Aristotle.[131] For that reason, it seems to me plausible to see the human being who receives the sacrament as analogous to the material cause.[132]

Thus, Thomas, using the notion of an instrument broadly, explains the effectiveness of the sacraments as that of an instrumental cause, moved by a principal cause. Thomas begins with his understanding of the humanity of Christ as an instrument of his divinity.[133] This idea, found in John Damascene and Athanasius, holds that the flesh of Jesus Christ is the organ of his divinity.[134] Christ as God acts through the organ of his human nature. This view of the relation of Christ's divinity and his humanity is found already in the commentary on the *Sentences*.[135] It remains a constant theme in his Christology. Christ is an efficient cause of salvation, with a twofold agency, principal in his Godhead and instrumental in his humanity.[136]

---

[129] For the best recent accounts of this see Blankenhorn, "The Place of Romans 6" and "The Instrumental Causality of the Sacraments." See also Hyacinthe-François Dondaine, OP, "À propos d'Avicenne et de S. Thomas: De la causalité dispositive à la causalité instrumentale," *RThom* 51 (1951): pp. 441–53; Gallagher, *Significando Causant*; Theophil Tschipke, *Die Menschheit Christi als Heilsorgan der Gottheit: Unter besonderer Berücksichtigung der Lehre des Heiligen Thomas von Aquin* (Freiburg in Breisgau: Herder, 1940). The last cited, which is fairly rare, has appeared in French as *L'humanité du Christ comme instrument de salut de la divinité*, trans. Philibert Secrétan (Fribourg: Academic Press, 2003). For a fairly full argument against such a development, see Leeming, *Principles of Sacramental Theology*, pp. 324–30. The argument, however, seems to presume that elimination of the notion of dispositive cause would render the *res et sacramentum* superfluous. But that seems to suggest that there is no other point to the significative aspect of the sacraments, which does not follow.

[130] See section 2 of Chapter 5 in this work.

[131] Aristotle, *Physics* II,3 (195a1–3); *Metaphysics* V,2 (1013b1–3).

[132] My point here is that in the divine action in the human being who receives the sacrament, God brings the human potency for the virtues, graces, and character to act. For the sacramental action itself, of course, Aquinas makes another use of the concepts of form and matter.

[133] *ST* III, q. 2, a. 6, corpus; cf. ad 4. Note that this is the "humanity" of Christ and not simply the body of Christ. The difference and its import are worked out in *ST* III, qq. 18–19, with respect to Christ's human will and operation. See Chapter 9 in this work.

[134] John Damascene, *De fide orthodoxa* III,19 (*PG* 94, col. 1079); Athanasius, *Contra Arianos* III,31 (*PG* 26, col. 390).

[135] *In III Sent.*, dist. 18, a. 1, ad 4.   [136] *ST* III, q. 48, a. 6.

In his mature sacramental theology, Aquinas adds to this the notion of sacraments as "separated instruments," whereas his humanity in itself is a "conjoined instrument." The necessity of the sacraments, in addition to Christ's efficiency, is justified as the application of a universal cause to a particular individual. A conjoined instrument is like a hand, whereas the separated instrument is like a stick.[137] This scheme allows Thomas to attribute to the sacraments the capacity to impart grace, as an accidental change in the soul, without attributing to the material elements or the human ministers the power to dispense grace, a power which belongs to God alone and to Christ as God incarnate. The humanity of Christ is not an instrument in creation, but is the divine instrument for the restoration of humanity, and that work extends to the sacraments as the acts of human agents subordinated to the incarnate Son of God. In the enactment of sacraments, the instrumental notion is pressed further, to make sense of the role of the minister.[138] The model here is not that of a stick in the hand, but a political minister.[139]

Thus, Aquinas makes use of the Aristotelian schema to account for the properties of sacraments that he wants to affirm, and to avoid the notions that he wants to deny. It allows him to say that the sacraments "contain" grace, which was already a somewhat venerable manner of speaking, yet not as a container, but as a channel, a motion passing from agent to patient.[140]

In all this, Aquinas is making use of the Aristotelian schema in an analogous way, not to account for natural substances or processes, nor to speak of human artisanship, but to explicate the way in which salvation comes to human beings on the basis of the historical work of Christ, within the present-day body of the Church. He is certainly not constrained by the scheme, nor is he dependent on it as an authority for sacred doctrine. In some respects, he can be said to be "exploding Aristotle's understanding of causality, since the Stagirite hardly imagined the possibility of an infusion of a spiritual form through a physical instrument."[141] If what is meant by "exploding" here is that he puts it to an analogous use, stretches it, one might say, to cover instances of causality that the ancient philosopher could not conceive, then that is a reasonable assessment. One might also say that Aquinas upholds the highest form of causality, that by which God brings creatures to share in his life by participation in his likeness, in a manner fully suited to their condition, but far exceeding human capacities.

---

[137] *ST* III, q. 62, a. 5, corpus.   [138] *ST* III, q. 64, a. 1.

[139] *ST* III, q. 63, a. 2, corpus. I do not agree with Jordan that this maxim of Aristotle in *Politics* I,4 (1253b30) is "somewhat disingenuously" applied by Aquinas (Jordan, "Theology and Philosophy," p. 243). To the degree that a minister is in an office that has certain powers derived from another, it seems a reasonable analogy.

[140] *ST* III, q. 62, a. 3, sed contra; q. 62, a. 4.

[141] Blankenhorn, "The Place of Romans 6," p. 140.

The salient question here is: does Aquinas's novel and analogous employment of the Aristotelian causal schema serve its purpose? Does the schema of the efficient causality of Christ, the instrumental causality of his humanity, and the instrumental causality of the sacraments, add anything to the idea of merit or satisfaction?[142] It certainly does not sideline merit or satisfaction as aspects of the work of Christ; these remain vital to Aquinas's account of Christ's work.[143] Yet, I would hold that it affirms, in a direct and striking way, the divine activity of human transformation that cannot be accounted for adequately by the equally analogous employment of human relational terms, such as merit and satisfaction. It allows Aquinas to give expression to the truth that through the sacraments God transforms the human being, without replacing his or her human nature. It also avoids reducing the sacraments to calling attention to a promise of divine action. The action of God through Christ works "from the inside," as it were, through the Incarnation, which establishes a relationship between God and all human beings that cannot be simply mapped onto notions of interpersonal relations such as we know them. The mystery is ineffable, but it is one of which we are compelled to speak as best we can.

---

[142] Philip L. Reynolds, "Philosophy as the Handmaid of Theology: Aquinas on Christ's Causality," in *Contemplating Aquinas: On the Varieties of Interpretation*, edited by Fergus Kerr (London: SCM, 2003), pp. 217–45; Philip L. Reynolds, "Efficient Causality and Instrumentality in Thomas Aquinas's Theology of the Sacraments," in *Essays in Medieval Philosophy and Theology in Memory of Walter H. Principe, CSB: Fortresses and Launching Pads*, edited by James R. Ginther and Carl N. Still (Aldershot: Ashgate, 2005), pp. 67–84.

[143] *ST* III, q. 46, a. 1; a. 2; a. 3, ad 3; a. 6; etc.

Bibliography

Note: the works of ancient authors that are edited in the *Patrologia Graeca* (*PG*) are not included in this list.

Aertsen, Jan A. *Nature and Creature: Thomas Aquinas's Way of Thought* (Leiden: Brill, 1988).

Aertsen, Jan A. "La scoperta dell'ente in quanto ente." In *Tommaso d'Aquino e l'oggetto della metafisica*, edited by Stephen L. Brock (Roma: Armando Editore, 2004), pp. 35–48.

Albert the Great. *Opera omnia*, vol. 27, *Commentarii in II Sententiarum*, ed. Auguste Borgnet (Paris: Louis Vivès, 1894).

Alvira, Tomás. *Naturaleza y libertad: Estudio de los conceptos tomistas de voluntas ut natura y voluntas ut ratio* (Pamplona: Ediciones Universidad de Navarra, 1985).

Amerini, Fabrizio. *Aquinas on the Beginning and End of Human Life*, trans. Mark Henninger (Cambridge, MA: Harvard University Press, 2013).

Anderson, Gary A. *Sin: A History* (New Haven, CT: Yale University Press, 2009).

Aquinas, *see* Thomas Aquinas.

Aristotle. Works edited in the series "Scriptorum Classicorum Bibliotheca Oxoniensis" (Oxford: Clarendon Press).

Analytica priora et posteriora, ed. William D. Ross (1964; rev. repr. 1982).

Ars rhetorica, ed. William D. Ross (1959; repr. 1991).

Categoriae et Liber de interpretatione, ed. Lorenzo Minio-Paluello (1949; repr. 1974).

De anima, ed. William D. Ross (1956; repr. 1986).

De arte poetica liber, ed. Rudolf Kassel (1965; rev. repr. 1991).

De generatione animalium, ed. Hendrik J. Drossaart Lulofs (1965; repr. 1972).

Ethica Eudemia, ed. Richard R. Walzer and Jean M. Mingay (1991).

Ethica Nicomachea, ed. Ingram Bywater (1894; repr. 1979).

Metaphysica, ed. Werner Jaeger (1957; repr. 1978).

Physica, ed. William D. Ross (1950; rev. repr. 1973).

Politica, ed. William D. Ross (1957; repr. 1986).

Topica et Sophistici elenchi, ed. William D. Ross (1958; rev. repr. 1974).

Aristotle. *Aristotle in Twenty-Three Volumes*, "The Loeb Classical Library," 23 vols.: Vol. 7: *Meteorologica*, trans. Henry D. P. Lee (Cambridge, MA: Harvard University Press, 1952; repr. 1987). Vol. 12: *Parts of Animals*, trans. Arthur L. Peck; *Movement of Animals, Progression of Animals*, trans. Edward S. Forster (Cambridge, MA: Harvard University Press, 1937; rev. repr. 1993).

Aristotle. *Politics*, trans. Benjamin Jowett (New York: Random House, 1943).

Aristotle. *The Works of Aristotle*, trans. under the editorship of William D. Ross, 12 vols. (London: Oxford University Press, 1908–1952; rev. repr. 1947–1952).

Aristotle. *The Works of Aristotle*, trans. William D. Ross, 2 vols. (Chicago: Encyclopædia Britannica, 1952).

Aristotle. *Aristotle's Metaphysics*, A revised text with introduction and commentary by William D. Ross, 2 vols. (Oxford: Clarendon Press, 1958).

Aristotle. *Aristoteles Latinus*, vol. I.1–5, *Categoriae vel Praedicamenta*, ed. Lorenzo Minio-Paluello (Bruges: Desclée de Brouwer, 1961).

Aristotle. *Aristotelis opera cum Averrois commentariis*, vol. 8, *Aristotelis Metaphysicorum libri XIII cum Averrois Cordubensis in eosdem commentariis et Epitome* (Frankfurt am Main: Minerva, 1962).

Aristotle. *Nicomachean Ethics*, trans. Martin Ostwald (Englewood Cliffs, NJ: Prentice Hall, 1962).

Aristotle. *Aristoteles Latinus*, vol. XXV.2, *Metaphysica, Lib. I–X, XII–XIV: Translatio Anonyma sive "Media,"* ed. Gudrun Vuillemin-Diem (Leiden: Brill, 1976).

Aristotle. *The Complete Works of Aristotle: The Revised Oxford Translation*, ed. Jonathan Barnes, 2 vols. (Princeton, NJ: Princeton University Press, 1984; repr. 1985).

Aristotle. *Aristotle's Physics: Books I and II*, trans. William Charlton (Oxford: Clarendon Press, 1992).

Aristotle. *Aristoteles Latinus*, vol. XXV.3, *Metaphysica: Recensio et Translatio Guillelmi De Moerbeka*, ed. Gudrun Vuillemin-Diem, 2 vols. (Leiden: Brill, 1995).

Aristotle. *Nicomachean Ethics*, ed. and trans. Terence H. Irwin (Indianapolis, IN: Hackett Publishing, 1999).

Aubert, Jean-Marie. *Le droit romain dans l'œuvre de saint Thomas* (Paris: Vrin, 1955).

Augustine. *Confessions*, trans. Henry Chadwick (Oxford: Oxford University Press, 1991).

Aumann, Jordan, OP. "Thomistic Evaluation of Love and Charity." *Ang.* 55 (1978): pp. 534–56.

Avicenna. *Liber de Philosophia prima sive Divina scientia*, ed. Simone van Riet (Leuven: Peeters, 1989).

Backes, Ignaz. *Die Christologie des hl. Thomas v. Aquin und die griechischen Kirchenväter* (Paderborn: Schöningh, 1931).

Barnes, Corey L. "Albert the Great and Thomas Aquinas on Person, Hypostasis, and Hypostatic Union." *Thom.* 72 (2008): pp. 107–46.

Barnes, Corey L. "Christological Composition in Thirteenth-Century Debates." *Thom.* 75 (2011): pp. 173–206.

Barnes, Corey L. *Christ's Two Wills in Scholastic Thought: The Christology of Aquinas and its Historical Contexts* (Toronto: Pontifical Institute of Mediaeval Studies, 2012).

Barron, Robert. *Thomas Aquinas: Spiritual Master* (New York: Crossroad, 1996).

Barth, Karl. *Church Dogmatics*, vol. 1, The Doctrine of the Word of God, part 1, trans. Geoffrey W. Bromiley, 2nd ed. (Edinburgh: T. & T. Clark, 1975).

Basil of Caesarea. *Contre Eunome, Suivi de Eunome, Apologie*, trans. Bernard Sesboüé (Paris: Cerf, 1983).

Bayerschmidt, Paul. *Die Seins- und Formmetaphysik des Heinrich von Gent in ihrer Anwendung auf die Christologie: Eine philosophie- und dogmengeschichtliche Studie* (Münster: Aschendorff, 1941).

Blankenhorn, Bernhard, OP. "The Instrumental Causality of the Sacraments: Thomas Aquinas and Louis-Marie Chauvet." *Nova et Vetera* 4 (2006): pp. 255–93.

Blankenhorn, Bernhard, OP. "The Place of Romans 6 in Aquinas's Doctrine of Sacramental Causality: A Balance of History and Metaphysics." In *Ressourcement Thomism: Sacred Doctrine, the Sacraments, and the Moral Life: Essays in Honor of*

Romanus Cessario, OP, edited by Reinhard Hütter and Matthew Levering (Washington, DC: The Catholic University of America Press, 2010), pp. 136–49.

Blankenhorn, Bernhard, OP. "How the Early Albertus Magnus Transformed Augustinian Interiority." *Freiburger Zeitschrift für Philosophie und Theologie* 58 (2011): pp. 351–86.

Blankenhorn, Bernhard, OP. "Aquinas as Interpreter of Augustinian Illumination in Light of Albertus Magnus." *Nova et Vetera* 10 (2012): pp. 689–713.

Blázquez, Niceto, OP. "Los tratados sobre la ley antigua y nueva en la 'Summa Theologiae.'" *Scripta theologica* 15 (1983): pp. 421–67.

Blythe, James M. "The Mixed Constitution and the Distinction between Regal and Political Power in the Work of Thomas Aquinas." *Journal of the History of Ideas* 47 (1986): pp. 547–65.

Bobik, Joseph. *Aquinas on Being and Essence: A Translation and Interpretation* (Notre Dame, IN: University of Notre Dame Press, 1965).

Bobik, Joseph. "Aquinas on Friendship with God." *The New Scholasticism* 60 (1986): pp. 257–71.

Boersma, Hans. *Nouvelle Théologie and Sacramental Ontology: A Return to Mystery* (Oxford: Oxford University Press, 2009).

Bonino, Serge-Thomas, OP. "'Toute vérité, quel que soit celui qui la dit, vient de l'Esprit-Saint': Autour d'une citation de l'*Ambrosiaster* dans le corpus thomasien." *RThom* 106 (2006): pp. 101–47.

Bonino, Serge-Thomas, OP. *Les anges et les démons: Quatorze leçons de théologie catholique* (Paris: Parole et Silence, 2007).

Booth, Edward, OP. *Aristotelian Aporetic Ontology in Islamic and Christian Thinkers* (Cambridge: Cambridge University Press, 1983).

Borgo, Marta. "La *Métaphysique* d'Aristote dans le *Commentaire* de Thomas d'Aquin au Ier livre des *Sentences* de Pierre Lombard: Quelques exemples significatifs." *RSPhTh* 91 (2007): pp. 651–92.

Bouillard, Henri. *Conversion et grâce chez S. Thomas d'Aquin: Étude historique* (Paris: Aubier, 1944).

Bourke, Vernon J. "The *Nicomachean Ethics* and Thomas Aquinas." In *St. Thomas Aquinas 1274–1974: Commemorative Studies*, vol. 1, edited by Armand A. Maurer (Toronto: Pontifical Institute of Mediaeval Studies, 1974), pp. 239–59.

Boyle, Leonard E., OP. *The Setting of the* Summa Theologiae *of Saint Thomas* (Toronto: Pontifical Institute of Mediaeval Studies, 1982).

Bradshaw, David. *Aristotle East and West: Metaphysics and the Division of Christendom* (Cambridge: Cambridge University Press, 2004).

Broadie, Sarah. "Nature and Craft in Aristotelian Teleology." In *Biologie, logique et métaphysique chez Aristote: Actes du séminaire C.N.R.S.–N.S.F., Oléron 28 juin–3 juillet 1987*, edited by Daniel Devereux and Pierre Pellegrin (Paris: Éditions du CNRS, 1990), pp. 389–403.

Brown, Stephen F. "Thomas Aquinas and his Contemporaries on the Unique Existence in Christ." In *Christ among the Medieval Dominicans: Representations of Christ in the Texts and Images of the Order of Preachers*, edited by Kent Emery, Jr., and Joseph P. Wawrykow (Notre Dame, IN: University of Notre Dame Press, 1998), pp. 220–37.

Brunner, Fernand. *Platonisme et aristotélisme: La critique d'Ibn Gabirol par saint Thomas d'Aquin* (Louvain: Publications Universitaires, 1965).

Bulgakov, Sergius. *The Lamb of God*, trans. Boris Jakim (Grand Rapids, MI: Eerdmans, 2008).

Burrell, David B., C.S.C. "Act of Creation with its Theological Consequences." In *Aquinas on Doctrine: A Critical Introduction*, edited by Thomas G. Weinandy, Daniel A. Keating, and John P. Yocum (London: T. & T. Clark, 2004), pp. 27–44.

Capizzi, Joseph E. "The Children of God: Natural Slavery in the Thought of Aquinas and Vitoria." *TS* 63 (2002): pp. 31–52.

Carmichael, Calum M. *The Laws of Deuteronomy* (Ithaca, NY: Cornell University Press, 1974).

Chamorro, Juan Fernando, OP. "Ley nueva y ley antigua en Santo Tomás." *Studium* 7 (1967): pp. 317–80.

Chauvet, Louis-Marie. *Symbol and Sacrament: A Sacramental Reinterpretation of Christian Existence*, trans. Patrick Madigan and Madeleine Beaumont (Collegeville, MN: Liturgical Press, 1995).

Chenu, Marie-Dominique, OP. *La théologie comme science au XIIIᵉ siècle*, 3rd ed. (Paris: Vrin, 1957).

Chenu, Marie-Dominique, OP. *Is Theology a Science?*, trans. Adrian H. N. Green-Armytage (London: Hawthorn Books, 1959).

Chenu, Marie-Dominique, OP. *Toward Understanding Saint Thomas*, trans. Albert M. Landry and Dominic Hughes (Chicago: Henry Regnery, 1964).

Christine de Pizan. *The Treasure of the City of Ladies: Or the Book of the Three Virtues*, trans. Sarah Lawson, rev. ed. (London: Penguin, 2003).

Colborn, Francis. "The Theology of Grace: Present Trends and Future Directions." *TS* 31 (1970): pp. 692–711.

Collins, James D. *The Thomistic Philosophy of the Angels* (Washington, DC: The Catholic University of America Press, 1947).

Congar, Yves M.-J., OP. "Avertissement." In *La liberté religieuse: Déclaration "Dignitatis humanae personae,"* edited by Jérôme Hamer and Yves M.-J. Congar (Paris: Cerf, 1967), pp. 11–14.

Constable, Giles. "The Ideal of the Imitation of Christ." In *Three Studies in Medieval Religious and Social Thought: The Interpretation of Mary and Martha, The Ideal of the Imitation of Christ, The Orders of Society* (Cambridge: Cambridge University Press, 1995), pp. 143–248.

Cooper, John M. "Aristotle on Friendship." In *Essays on Aristotle's Ethics*, edited by Amélie Oksenberg Rorty (Berkeley: University of California Press, 1980), pp. 301–40.

Copleston, Frederick C. *Aquinas: An Introduction to the Life and Work of the Great Medieval Thinker* (London: Penguin Books, 1991).

Corvez, Maurice, OP. "L'unicité d'existence dans le Christ." *RThom* 56 (1956): pp. 413–26.

Cross, Richard. "Aquinas on Nature, Hypostasis, and the Metaphysics of the Incarnation." *Thom.* 60 (1996): pp. 171–202.

Cross, Richard. *The Metaphysics of the Incarnation: Thomas Aquinas to Duns Scotus* (Oxford: Oxford University Press, 2002).

Crotty, Nicholas, C.P. "The Redemptive Role of Christ's Resurrection." *Thom.* 25 (1962): pp. 54–106.

Dahan, Gilbert. "*Ex imperfecto ad perfectum.* Le progrès de la pensée humaine chez les théologiens du XIIIe siècle." In *Progrès, réaction, décadence dans l'Occident médiéval,* edited by Emmanuèle Baumgartner and Laurence Harf-Lancner (Genève: Droz, 2003), pp. 171–84.

Dauphinais, Michael, Barry David, and Matthew Levering, eds. *Aquinas the Augustinian* (Washington, DC: The Catholic University of America Press, 2007).

Dewan, Lawrence. *Form and Being: Studies in Thomistic Metaphysics* (Washington, DC: The Catholic University of America Press, 2006).

Diepen, Herman. "L'existence humaine du Christ en métaphysique thomiste." *RThom* 58 (1958): pp. 197–213.

Dionysius, *see* Pseudo-Dionysius.

Dobbs-Weinstein, Idit. "Medieval Biblical Commentary and Philosophical Inquiry as Exemplified in the Thought of Moses Maimonides and St. Thomas Aquinas." In *Moses Maimonides and his Time,* edited by Eric L. Ormsby (Washington, DC: The Catholic University of America Press, 1989), pp. 101–20.

Dobbs-Weinstein, Idit. *Maimonides and St. Thomas on the Limits of Reason* (Albany, NY: State University of New York Press, 1995).

Doig, James. "Aquinas and Aristotle." In *The Oxford Handbook of Aquinas,* edited by Brian Davies and Eleonore Stump (Oxford: Oxford University Press, 2012), pp. 33–44.

Dondaine, Hyacinthe-François, OP. "La définition des sacrements dans la 'Somme théologique.'" *RSPhTh* 31 (1947): pp. 213–28.

Dondaine, Hyacinthe-François, OP. "À propos d'Avicenne et de S. Thomas: De la causalité dispositive à la causalité instrumentale." *RThom* 51 (1951): pp. 441–53.

Doolan, Gregory T. *Aquinas on the Divine Ideas as Exemplar Causes* (Washington, DC: The Catholic University of America Press, 2008).

Dougherty, Jude P. "Wretched Aristotle." In *Indubitanter ad Veritatem: Studies Offered to Leo J. Elders SVD in Honor of the Golden Jubilee of his Ordination to the Priesthood,* edited by Jörgen Vijgen (Budel: Damon, 2003), pp. 126–32.

Duffy, Stephen J. *The Dynamics of Grace: Perspectives in Theological Anthropology* (Collegeville, MN: Liturgical Press, 1993).

Duns Scotus, John. *Opera omnia,* vol. 10, *Ordinatio: Liber tertius, a distinctione vigesima sexta ad quadragesimam,* ed. Commissio Scotistica (Vatican City: Typis Vaticanis, 2007).

Edwards, Mark J. *Neoplatonic Saints: The Lives of Plotinus and Proclus by their Students* (Liverpool: Liverpool University Press, 2000).

Elders, Leo, S.V.D. *La théologie philosophique de saint Thomas d'Aquin: De l'être à la cause première,* trans. Moines de l'abbaye Notre-Dame de Fontgombault (Paris: Téqui, 1995).

Emery, Gilles, OP. *La Trinité créatrice: Trinité et création dans les commentaires aux Sentences de Thomas d'Aquin et de ses précurseurs Albert le Grand et Bonaventure* (Paris: Vrin, 1995).

Emery, Gilles, OP. "La relation dans la théologie de saint Albert le Grand." In *Albertus Magnus: Zum Gedenken nach 800 Jahren: Neue Zugänge, Aspekte und Perspektiven,* edited by Walter Senner (Berlin: Akademie Verlag, 2001), pp. 455–65.

Emery, Gilles, OP. *The Trinitarian Theology of Saint Thomas Aquinas*, trans. Francesca A. Murphy (Oxford: Oxford University Press, 2007).

Emery, Gilles, OP. *Trinity, Church, and the Human Person: Thomistic Essays* (Naples, FL: Sapientia Press, 2007).

Emery, Gilles, OP. "*Ad aliquid*: la relation chez Thomas d'Aquin." In *Saint Thomas d'Aquin*, edited by Thierry-Dominique Humbrecht (Paris: Cerf, 2010), pp. 113–35.

Emery, Gilles, OP. *The Trinity: An Introduction to Catholic Doctrine on the Triune God*, trans. Matthew Levering (Washington, DC: The Catholic University of America Press, 2011).

Emery, Gilles, OP. "*Ad aliquid*: Relation in the Thought of St. Thomas Aquinas." In *Theology Needs Philosophy: Essays in Honor of Ralph McInerny*, edited by Matthew Lamb (Washington, DC: The Catholic University of America Press, 2016).

Erasmus, Desiderius. "Erasmus' Letter to Martin Dorp (1514)." In *The Praise of Folly*, trans. Clarence H. Miller (New Haven, CT: Yale University Press, 1979), pp. 139–74.

Evans, John D. G. *Aristotle's Concept of Dialectic* (Cambridge: Cambridge University Press, 1977).

Evans, John D. G. *Aristotle* (Brighton: The Harvester Press, 1987).

Feingold, Lawrence. *The Natural Desire to See God according to St. Thomas Aquinas and his Interpreters*, 2nd ed. (Naples, FL: Sapientia Press, 2010).

Ferrer Rodríguez, Pilar. "La inmaterialidad de las sustancias espirituales (Santo Tomás versus Avicebrón)" (Diss. Universidad de Navarra, Pamplona, 1988).

Finance, Joseph de. *Être et agir dans la philosophie de saint Thomas* (Paris: Beauchesne, 1945).

Finnis, John. *Aquinas: Moral, Political, and Legal Theory* (Oxford: Oxford University Press, 1998).

Forest, Aimé. *La structure métaphysique du concret selon saint Thomas d'Aquin* (Paris: Vrin, 1931).

Fornerod, Mireille. "La distinction entre *virtus* et *potentia Dei* selon saint Thomas d'Aquin." *Revue théologique de Louvain* 45 (2014): pp. 502–32.

Fransen, Piet F. *The New Life of Grace*, trans. Georges Dupont (London: Chapman, 1969).

Fredriksen, Paula. *Augustine and the Jews: A Christian Defense of Jews and Judaism* (New York: Doubleday, 2008).

Friedman, Russell L. *Medieval Trinitarian Thought from Aquinas to Ockham* (Cambridge: Cambridge University Press, 2010).

Fuchs, Marko. "*Philia* and *Caritas*: Some Aspects of Aquinas's Reception of Aristotle's Theory of Friendship." In *Aquinas and the* Nicomachean Ethics, edited by Tobias Hoffmann, Jörn Müller, and Matthias Perkams (Cambridge: Cambridge University Press, 2013), pp. 203–19.

Funkenstein, Amos. "Gesetz und Geschichte: Zur historisierenden Hermeneutik bei Moses Maimonides und Thomas von Aquin." *Viator* 1 (1970): pp. 147–78.

Gagnebet, Marie-Rosaire, OP. "L'amour naturel de Dieu chez saint Thomas et ses contemporains." *RThom* 48 (1948): pp. 394–446 and 49 (1949): pp. 31–102.

Gallagher, David M. "Desire for Beatitude and Love of Friendship in Thomas Aquinas." *Mediaeval Studies* 58 (1996): pp. 1–47.

Gallagher, John F., C.M. *Significando Causant: A Study of Sacramental Efficiency* (Fribourg: Fribourg University Press, 1965).

Gauthier, René-Antoine, OP. *Saint Thomas d'Aquin, Somme contre les Gentils: Introduction* (Paris: Éditions Universitaires, 1993).

Geiger, Louis-Bertrand, OP. *La participation dans la philosophie de S. Thomas d'Aquin* (Paris: Vrin, 1942).

Gelber, Hester G. *It Could Have Been Otherwise: Contingency and Necessity in Dominican Theology at Oxford, 1300–1350* (Leiden: Brill, 2004).

Gillon, Louis-Bertrand, OP. "La notion de conséquence de l'union hypostatique dans le cadre de III\u1d43, qq. 2–26." *Ang.* 15 (1938): pp. 17–34.

Gillon, Louis-Bertrand, OP. "À propos de la théorie thomiste de l'amitié: 'Fundatur super aliqua communicatione' (II-II, q. 23, a. 1)." *Ang.* 25 (1948): pp. 3–17.

Gilson, Étienne. "Pourquoi saint Thomas a critiqué saint Augustin." *Archives d'histoire doctrinale et littéraire du moyen âge* 1 (1926–1927): pp. 5–127.

Gilson, Étienne. *L'esprit de la philosophie médiévale*, vol. 1 (Paris: Vrin, 1932).

Gilson, Étienne. "La cause de l'être." In *Introduction à la philosophie chrétienne* (Paris: Vrin, 1960), pp. 27–44.

Gilson, Étienne. "L'*esse* du Verbe incarné selon saint Thomas d'Aquin." *Archives d'histoire doctrinale et littéraire du moyen âge* 35 (1968): pp. 23–37.

Gilson, Étienne. "É. Gilson à J. Maritain: 15 avril 1931." In Étienne Gilson and Jacques Maritain. *Correspondance 1923–1971: Deux approches de l'être*, ed. Géry Prouvost (Paris: Vrin, 1991), pp. 46–51.

Gondreau, Paul. *The Passions of Christ's Soul in the Theology of St. Thomas Aquinas* (Scranton, PA: University of Scranton Press, 2009).

Goris, Harm. "Theology and Theory of the Word in Aquinas: Understanding Augustine by Innovating Aristotle." In *Aquinas the Augustinian*, edited by Michael Dauphinais, Barry David, and Matthew Levering (Washington, DC: The Catholic University of America Press, 2007), pp. 62–78.

Gray, Janette, R.S.M. "Marie-Dominique Chenu and Le Saulchoir: A Stream of Catholic Renewal." In *Ressourcement: A Movement for Renewal in Twentieth-Century Catholic Theology*, edited by Gabriel Flynn and Paul D. Murray (Oxford: Oxford University Press, 2012), pp. 205–18.

Gregory of Nazianzus. *On God and Christ: The Five Theological Orations and Two Letters to Cledonius*, trans. Frederick Williams and Lionel Wickham (Crestwood, NY: St. Vladimir's Seminary Press, 2002).

Grene, Marjorie. *A Portrait of Aristotle* (London: Faber, 1963).

Grisez, Germain. "The True Ultimate End of Human Beings: The Kingdom, Not God Alone." *TS* 69 (2008): pp. 38–61.

Grundmann, Herbert. *Religious Movements in the Middle Ages: The Historical Links between Heresy, the Mendicant Orders, and the Women's Religious Movement in the Twelfth and Thirteenth Century, with the Historical Foundations of German Mysticism*, trans. Steven Rowan (Notre Dame, IN: University of Notre Dame Press, 1995).

Guggenheim, Antoine. *Jésus Christ, grand prêtre de l'ancienne et de la nouvelle Alliance: Étude théologique et herméneutique du commentaire de saint Thomas d'Aquin sur l'Épître aux Hébreux* (Paris: Parole et Silence, 2004).

Haight, Roger. *The Experience and Language of Grace* (New York: Paulist Press, 1979).

Hall, Pamela M. *Narrative and the Natural Law: An Interpretation of Thomistic Ethics* (Notre Dame, IN: University of Notre Dame Press, 1994).

Hankey, Wayne J. "The Place of the Proof for God's Existence in the *Summa Theologiae* of Thomas Aquinas." *Thom.* 46 (1982): pp. 370–93.

Hankey, Wayne J. *God in Himself: Aquinas' Doctrine of God as Expounded in the Summa Theologiae* (Oxford: Oxford University Press, 1987).

Hankey, Wayne J. "Denys and Aquinas: Antimodern Cold and Postmodern Hot." In *Christian Origins: Theology, Rhetoric and Community*, edited by Lewis Ayres and Gareth Jones (London: Routledge, 1998), pp. 139–84.

Hankey, Wayne J. "Why Philosophy Abides for Aquinas." *Heythrop Journal* 42 (2001): pp. 329–48.

Hankey, Wayne J. "Reading Augustine through Dionysius: Aquinas's Correction of One Platonism by Another." In *Aquinas the Augustinian*, edited by Michael Dauphinais, Barry David, and Matthew Levering (Washington, DC: The Catholic University of America Press, 2007), pp. 243–57.

Harnack, Adolf. *History of Dogma*, vol. 6, trans. Neil Buchanan (Boston: Little, Brown, and Company, 1899).

Hastings, Adrian. "Christ's Act of Existence." *Downside Review* 73 (1955): pp. 139–59.

Hause, Jeffrey. "Aquinas on Aristotelian Justice: Defender, Destroyer, Subverter, or Surveyor?" In *Aquinas and the* Nicomachean Ethics, edited by Tobias Hoffmann, Jörn Müller, and Matthias Perkams (Cambridge: Cambridge University Press, 2013), pp. 146–64.

Hayen, André. *La communication de l'être d'après saint Thomas*, vol. 2, L'ordre philosophique de saint Thomas (Paris: Desclée de Brouwer, 1959).

Healy, Nicholas M. *Thomas Aquinas: Theologian of the Christian Life* (Aldershot: Ashgate, 2003).

Hibbs, Thomas S. "Divine Irony and the Natural Law: Speculation and Edification in Aquinas." *International Philosophical Quarterly* 30 (1990): pp. 419–29.

Hibbs, Thomas S. "*Imitatio Christi* and the Foundation of Aquinas's Ethics." *Communio* 18 (1991): pp. 556–73.

Hibbs, Thomas S. *Virtue's Splendor: Wisdom, Prudence, and the Human Good* (New York: Fordham University Press, 2001).

Hipp, Stephen A. *"Person" in Christian Tradition and in the Conception of Saint Albert the Great: A Systematic Study of its Concept as Illuminated by the Mysteries of the Trinity and the Incarnation* (Münster: Aschendorff, 2001).

Holtz, Ferdinand. "La valeur sotériologique de la résurrection du Christ selon saint Thomas." *Ephemerides theologicae Lovanienses* 29 (1953): pp. 609–45.

Hood, John Y. B. *Aquinas and the Jews* (Philadelphia: University of Pennsylvania Press, 1995).

Imbach, Ruedi. "Pourquoi Thierry de Freiberg a-t-il critiqué Thomas d'Aquin? Remarques sur le *De accidentibus*." *Freiburger Zeitschrift für Philosophie und Theologie* 45 (1998): pp. 116–29.

Irwin, Terence H. "Generosity and Property in Aristotle's *Politics*." *Social Philosophy and Policy* 4 (1987): pp. 37–54.

Irwin, Terence H. "Historical Accuracy in Aquinas's Commentary on the *Ethics*." In *Aquinas and the* Nicomachean Ethics, edited by Tobias Hoffmann, Jörn Müller, and Matthias Perkams (Cambridge: Cambridge University Press, 2013), pp. 13–32.

Jaffa, Harry V. *Thomism and Aristotelianism: A Study of the Commentary by Thomas Aquinas on the Nicomachean Ethics* (Chicago: University of Chicago Press, 1952).

Janz, Denis R. *Luther on Thomas Aquinas: The Angelic Doctor in the Thought of the Reformer* (Stuttgart: F. Steiner Verlag, 1989).

Jenkins, John I., C.S.C. *Knowledge and Faith in Thomas Aquinas* (Cambridge: Cambridge University Press, 1997).

John Damascene. *De fide orthodoxa: Versions of Burgundio and Cerbanus*, ed. Eligius M. Buytaert (New York: Franciscan Institute St. Bonaventure, 1955).

John Duns Scotus, *see* Duns Scotus, John.

John Paul II. *Memory and Identity: Conversations at the Dawn of the Millennium* (New York: Rizzoli International Publications, 2005).

Johnson, Monte R. *Aristotle on Teleology* (Oxford: Clarendon Press, 2005).

Jolivet, Jean. "Vues médiévales sur les paronymes." *Revue internationale de philosophie* 29 (1975): pp. 222–42.

Jordan, Mark D. *Ordering Wisdom: The Hierarchy of Philosophical Discourses in Aquinas* (Notre Dame, IN: University of Notre Dame Press, 1986).

Jordan, Mark D. *The Alleged Aristotelianism of Thomas Aquinas* (Toronto: Pontifical Institute of Mediaeval Studies, 1992).

Jordan, Mark D. "Theology and Philosophy." In *The Cambridge Companion to Aquinas*, edited by Norman Kretzmann and Eleonore Stump (Cambridge: Cambridge University Press, 1993), pp. 232–51.

Jordan, Mark D. *Rewritten Theology: Aquinas after his Readers* (Malden, MA: Blackwell, 2006).

Jordan, Mark D. "The Alleged Aristotelianism of Thomas Aquinas." In *The Gilson Lectures on Thomas Aquinas*, introduced by James P. Reilly (Toronto: Pontifical Institute of Mediaeval Studies, 2008), pp. 73–106.

Keating, Daniel A. "Justification, Sanctification and Divinization in Thomas Aquinas." In *Aquinas on Doctrine: A Critical Introduction*, edited by Thomas G. Weinandy, Daniel A. Keating, and John P. Yocum (London: T. & T. Clark, 2004), pp. 139–58.

Kenny, Anthony. *The Five Ways: St Thomas Aquinas' Proofs of God's Existence*, new ed. (Abingdon: Routledge, 2009).

Kerr, Fergus. *After Aquinas: Versions of Thomism* (Oxford: Wiley–Blackwell, 2002).

Kerr, Fergus, OP. *Thomas Aquinas: A Very Short Introduction* (Oxford: Oxford University Press, 2009).

Keys, Mary M. *Aquinas, Aristotle, and the Promise of the Common Good* (Cambridge: Cambridge University Press, 2006).

Kleineidam, Erich. "Das Problem der hylomorphen Zusammensetzung der geistigen Substanzen im 13. Jahrhundert, behandelt bis Thomas von Aquin" (Diss. Breslau, 1930).

Klimczak, Paweł, OP. *Christus Magister: Le Christ Maître dans les commentaires évangéliques de saint Thomas d'Aquin* (Fribourg: Academic Press, 2014).

Kobusch, Theo. "Grace (Ia IIae, qq. 109–114)." In *The Ethics of Aquinas*, edited by Stephen J. Pope (Washington, DC: Georgetown University Press, 2002), pp. 207–18.

König-Pralong, Catherine. "Dietrich de Freiberg: Métaphysicien allemand antithomiste." *RThom* 108 (2008): pp. 57–79.

Kraut, Richard. "Are There Natural Rights in Aristotle?" *The Review of Metaphysics* 49 (1996): pp. 755–74.

Kries, Douglas. "Thomas Aquinas and the Politics of Moses." *Review of Politics* 52 (1990): pp. 84–104.

La Soujeole, Benoît-Dominique de, OP. "The Importance of the Definition of Sacraments as Signs." In *Ressourcement Thomism: Sacred Doctrine, the Sacraments, and the Moral Life: Essays in Honor of Romanus Cessario, OP.*, edited by Reinhard Hütter and Matthew Levering (Washington, DC: The Catholic University of America Press, 2010), pp. 127–35.

Lafont, Ghislain, OSB. *Structures et méthode dans la Somme théologique de saint Thomas d'Aquin* (Paris: Desclée de Brouwer, 1961).

Lambert, Malcolm D. *Franciscan Poverty: The Doctrine of the Absolute Poverty of Christ and the Apostles in the Franciscan Order, 1210–1323* (London: SPCK, 1961).

Lamont, John R. T. "Conscience, Freedom, Rights: Idols of the Enlightenment Religion." *Thom.* 73 (2009): pp. 169–239.

Lamy de la Chapelle, Marie. "L'unité ontologique du Christ selon saint Albert le Grand." *RThom* 70 (1970): pp. 181–226 and 533–59.

Lear, Jonathan. *Aristotle: The Desire to Understand* (Cambridge: Cambridge University Press, 1991).

Leclercq, Jean. "La vie contemplative dans S. Thomas et dans la tradition." *Recherches de théologie ancienne et médiévale* 28 (1961): pp. 251–68.

Leeming, Bernard, S.J. *Principles of Sacramental Theology* (New York: Longmans, Green, and Co., 1956).

Leinsle, Ulrich G. *Introduction to Scholastic Theology*, trans. Michael J. Miller (Washington, DC: The Catholic University of America Press, 2010).

Levering, Matthew. *Christ's Fulfillment of Torah and Temple: Salvation according to Thomas Aquinas* (Notre Dame, IN: University of Notre Dame Press, 2002).

Levering, Matthew. "God and Natural Law: Reflections on Genesis 22." *Modern Theology* 24 (2008): pp. 151–77.

Levering, Matthew, and Michael Dauphinais, eds. *Reading Romans with St. Thomas Aquinas* (Washington, DC: The Catholic University of America Press, 2012).

Libera, Alain de. *L'unité de l'intellect: Commentaire du De unitate intellectus contra Averroistas de Thomas d'Aquin* (Paris: Vrin, 2004).

Libera, Alain de. "Les actions appartiennent aux sujets: Petite archéologie d'un principe leibnizien." In *"Ad ingenii acuitionem," Studies in Honour of Alfonso Maierù*, edited by Stefano Caroti, Ruedi Imbach, Zénon Kaluza, Giorgio Stabile, and Loris Sturlese (Louvain-la-Neuve: Fédération internationale des Instituts d'Études Médiévales, 2006), pp. 199–219.

Litt, Thomas. *Les corps célestes dans l'univers de saint Thomas d'Aquin* (Louvain: Publications Universitaires, 1963).

Lombardo, Nicholas E., OP. *The Logic of Desire: Aquinas on Emotion* (Washington, DC: The Catholic University of America Press, 2011).

Lonergan, Bernard J. F., S.J. *Grace and Freedom: Operative Grace in the Thought of St. Thomas Aquinas*, ed. J. Patout Burns (London: Darton, Longman & Todd, 1971).

Lottin, Odon, OSB. "La composition hylémorphique des substances spirituelles: Les débuts de la controverse." *Revue néo-scolastique de philosophie* 34 (1932): pp. 21–41.

Louth, Andrew. *St John Damascene: Tradition and Originality in Byzantine Theology* (Oxford: Oxford University Press, 2002).

Luther, Martin. "The Babylonian Captivity of the Church." In *Martin Luther's Basic Theological Writings*, ed. Timothy F. Lull (Minneapolis, MN: Fortress Press, 1989), pp. 267–313.

MacIntyre, Alasdair. *Whose Justice? Which Rationality?* (Notre Dame, IN: University of Notre Dame Press, 1988).

MacIntyre, Alasdair. *Three Rival Versions of Moral Enquiry: Encyclopaedia, Genealogy, and Tradition* (Notre Dame, IN: University of Notre Dame Press, 1990).

Maimonides, Moses. *The Guide for the Perplexed*, trans. Michael Friedländer, 2nd ed. (New York: Dover, 1904).

Mansini, Guy, OSB. "*Duplex Amor* and the Structure of Love in Aquinas." In *Thomistica*, edited by Eugene Manning (Leuven: Peeters, 1995), pp. 137–96.

Mansini, Guy, OSB. "*Similitudo, Communicatio,* and the Friendship of Charity in Aquinas." In *Thomistica*, edited by Eugene Manning (Leuven: Peeters, 1995), pp. 1–26.

Mansini, Guy, OSB. "Understanding St. Thomas on Christ's Immediate Knowledge of God." *Thom.* 59 (1995): pp. 91–124.

Manzanedo, Marco F. *La imaginación y la memoria según Santo Tomás* (Roma: Herder, 1978).

Maritain, Jacques. *La philosophie bergsonienne*, 2nd ed. (Paris: M. Rivière, 1930).

Marshall, Bruce D. "The Unity of the Triune God: Reviving an Ancient Question." *Thom.* 74 (2010): pp. 1–32.

McCabe, Herbert, OP. "The Immortality of the Soul: The Traditional Argument." In *Aquinas: A Collection of Critical Essays*, edited by Anthony Kenny (Notre Dame, IN: University of Notre Dame Press, 1976), pp. 297–306.

McCord Adams, Marilyn. *Some Later Medieval Theories of the Eucharist: Thomas Aquinas, Giles of Rome, Duns Scotus, and William Ockham* (Oxford: Oxford University Press, 2010).

McInerny, Daniel. *The Difficult Good: A Thomistic Approach to Moral Conflict and Human Happiness* (New York: Fordham University Press, 2006).

McInerny, Ralph M. *The Question of Christian Ethics* (Washington, DC: The Catholic University of America Press, 1993).

McInerny, Ralph M. *Praeambula Fidei: Thomism and the God of the Philosophers* (Washington, DC: The Catholic University of America Press, 2006).

McInerny, Ralph M. "Why I Am a Thomist." *American Catholic Philosophical Quarterly* 83 (2009): pp. 323–30.

Meehan, Francis X. *Efficient Causality in Aristotle and St. Thomas* (Washington, DC: The Catholic University of America Press, 1940).

Meersseman, Gilles G., OP. "Pourquoi le Lombard n'a-t-il pas conçu la charité comme amitié?" In *Miscellanea Lombardiana*, edited by Pontificio Ateneo Salesiano di Torino (Novara: Istituto Geografico de Agostini, 1957), pp. 165–74.

Meyers, Carol. *Exodus* (Cambridge: Cambridge University Press, 2005).

Miller, Jr., Fred D. *Nature, Justice, and Rights in Aristotle's Politics* (Oxford: Clarendon Press, 1995).

Morard, Martin. "Sacerdoce du Christ et sacerdoce des chrétiens dans le *Commentaire des Psaumes* de saint Thomas d'Aquin." *RThom* 99 (1999): pp. 119–42.

Morard, Martin. "Thomas d'Aquin lecteur des conciles." *Archivum Franciscanum Historicum* 98 (2005): pp. 211–365.

Morreall, John. "Perfect Happiness and the Resurrection of the Body." *Religious Studies* 16 (1980): pp. 29–35.

Morris, Thomas V. "St. Thomas on the Identity and Unity of the Person of Christ: A Problem of Reference in Christological Discourse." *Scottish Journal of Theology* 35 (1982): pp. 419–30.

Mulcahey, M. Michèle. *"First the Bow is Bent in Study . . . ": Dominican Education before 1350* (Toronto: Pontifical Institute of Mediaeval Studies, 1998).

Murray, Paul D., OP. *Aquinas at Prayer: The Bible, Mysticism and Poetry* (London: Bloomsbury, 2013).

Narcisse, Gilbert, OP. *Les raisons de Dieu: Argument de convenance et esthétique théologique selon saint Thomas d'Aquin et Hans Urs von Balthasar* (Fribourg: Éditions Universitaires, 1997).

Nicolas, Jean-Hervé, OP. "L'unité d'être dans le Christ d'après saint Thomas." *RThom* 65 (1965): pp. 229–60.

Niederbacher, Bruno, S.J. "The Same Body Again? Thomas Aquinas on the Numerical Identity of the Resurrected Body." In *Personal Identity and Resurrection: How Do We Survive our Death?*, edited by Georg Gasser (Burlington, VT: Ashgate, 2010), pp. 145–59.

Novak, David. "Maimonides and Aquinas on Natural Law." In *St. Thomas Aquinas and the Natural Law Tradition: Contemporary Perspectives*, edited by John Goyette, Mark S. Latkovic, and Richard S. Myers (Washington, DC: The Catholic University of America Press, 2004), pp. 43–65.

Nussbaum, Martha Craven. "Shame, Separateness, and Political Unity: Aristotle's Criticism of Plato." In *Essays on Aristotle's Ethics*, edited by Amélie Oksenberg Rorty (Berkeley: University of California Press, 1980), pp. 395–435.

O'Callaghan, John P. *Thomist Realism and the Linguistic Turn: Toward a More Perfect Form of Existence* (Notre Dame, IN: University of Notre Dame Press, 2003).

O'Donovan, Joan L. "Christian Platonism and Non-Proprietary Community." In Oliver O'Donovan and Joan L. O'Donovan. *Bonds of Imperfection: Christian Politics, Past and Present* (Grand Rapids, MI: Eerdmans, 2004), pp. 73–96.

O'Meara, Thomas F., OP. *Thomas Aquinas Theologian* (Notre Dame, IN: University of Notre Dame Press, 1997).

O'Neill, Colman E., OP. *Sacramental Realism: A General Theory of the Sacraments* (Wilmington, DE: Michael Glazier, 1983).

O'Rourke, Fran. *Pseudo-Dionysius and the Metaphysics of Aquinas* (Leiden: Brill, 1992).

O'Rourke, Fran. "Aquinas and Platonism." In *Contemplating Aquinas: On the Varieties of Interpretation*, edited by Fergus Kerr (London: SCM, 2003), pp. 247–79.

Osborne, Jr., Thomas M. "Perfect and Imperfect Virtues in Aquinas." *Thom.* 71 (2007): pp. 39–64.

Owens, Joseph, C.Ss.R. *Human Destiny: Some Problems for Catholic Philosophy* (Washington, DC: The Catholic University of America Press, 1985).

Parel, Anthony. "Aquinas' Theory of Property." In *Theories of Property: Aristotle to the Present*, edited by Anthony Parel and Thomas Flanagan (Waterloo, ON: Wilfrid Laurier University Press, 1979), pp. 89–111.

Pasnau, Robert. *Thomas Aquinas on Human Nature: A Philosophical Study of* Summa theologiae *Ia 75–89* (New York: Cambridge University Press, 2002).

Pasnau, Robert. "The Latin Aristotle." In *The Oxford Handbook of Aristotle*, edited by Christopher Shields (Oxford: Oxford University Press, 2012), pp. 665–89.

Patfoort, Albert, OP. *L'unité d'être dans le Christ d'après S. Thomas: À la croisée de l'ontologie et de la christologie* (Paris: Desclée, 1964).

Pegis, Anton C. "A Note on St. Thomas, *Summa Theologica*, 1, 44, 1–2." *Mediaeval Studies* 8 (1946): pp. 159–68.

Pegis, Anton C. "Some Reflections on *Summa contra Gentiles II, 56*." In *An Etienne Gilson Tribute: Presented by his North American Students with a* Response *by Etienne Gilson*, edited by Charles J. O'Neil (Milwaukee: Marquette University Press, 1959), pp. 169–88.

Perrier, Emmanuel, OP. *La fécondité en Dieu: La puissance notionnelle dans la Trinité selon saint Thomas d'Aquin* (Paris: Parole et Silence, 2009).

Pesch, Otto H. *Martin Luther, Thomas von Aquin und die reformatorische Kritik an der Scholastik: Zur Geschichte und Wirkungsgeschichte eines Mißverständnisses mit weltgeschichtlichen Folgen* (Hamburg: Joachim Jungius-Gesellschaft der Wissenschaften, 1994).

Philippe, Paul, OP. "Contemplation, VI.7: Saint Thomas, † 1274." In *Dictionnaire de spiritualité*, vol. II/2, edited by Charles Baumgartner (Paris: Beauchesne, 1953), col. 1983–8.

Piché, David, ed. and trans. *La condamnation parisienne de 1277* (Paris: Vrin, 1999).

Pieper, Josef. "Justice." In *The Four Cardinal Virtues: Prudence, Justice, Fortitude, Temperance*, trans. Richard and Clara Winston, Lawrence E. Lynch, and Daniel F. Coogan (Notre Dame, IN: University of Notre Dame Press, 1966), pp. 41–113.

Pieper, Josef. *Guide to Thomas Aquinas*, trans. Richard and Clara Winston (San Francisco: Ignatius Press, 1991).

Pinckaers, Servais, OP. *The Pinckaers Reader: Renewing Thomistic Moral Theology*, ed. John Berkman and Craig S. Titus (Washington, DC: The Catholic University of America Press, 2005).

Plested, Marcus. *Orthodox Readings of Aquinas* (Oxford: Oxford University Press, 2012).

Pollet, Vincent-Marie, OP. "Le Christ d'après S. Albert le Grand." *La vie spirituelle* 34 (1933): pp. 78–108.

Pollet, Vincent-Marie, OP. "L'union hypostatique d'après saint Albert-le-Grand." *RThom* 38 (1933): pp. 505–32 and 689–724.

Porter, Jean. "At the Limits of Liberalism: Thomas Aquinas and the Prospects for a Catholic Feminism." *Theology Digest* 41 (1994): pp. 315–30.

Porter, Jean. "The Virtue of Justice (IIa IIae, qq. 58–122)." In *The Ethics of Aquinas*, edited by Stephen J. Pope (Washington, DC: Georgetown University Press, 2002), pp. 272–86.

Porter, Jean. *Nature as Reason: A Thomistic Theory of the Natural Law* (Grand Rapids, MI: Eerdmans, 2005).

Principe, Walter H., C.S.B. *The Theology of the Hypostatic Union in the Early Thirteenth Century*, vol. 4, Philip the Chancellor's Theology of the Hypostatic Union (Toronto: Pontifical Institute of Mediaeval Studies, 1975).

Pseudo-Dionysius. *The Complete Works*, trans. Colm Luibheid (Mahwah, NJ: Paulist Press, 1987).

Quelquejeu, Bernard, OP. "'Naturalia manent integra': Contribution à l'étude de la portée, méthodologique et doctrinale, de l'axiome théologique 'gratia praesupponit naturam.'" *RSPhTh* 49 (1965): pp. 640–55.

Radde-Gallwitz, Andrew. *Basil of Caesarea, Gregory of Nyssa, and the Transformation of Divine Simplicity* (Oxford: Oxford University Press, 2009).

Reynolds, Philip L. "Philosophy as the Handmaid of Theology: Aquinas on Christ's Causality." In *Contemplating Aquinas: On the Varieties of Interpretation*, edited by Fergus Kerr (London: SCM, 2003), pp. 217–45.

Reynolds, Philip L. "Efficient Causality and Instrumentality in Thomas Aquinas's Theology of the Sacraments." In *Essays in Medieval Philosophy and Theology in Memory of Walter H. Principe, CSB: Fortresses and Launching Pads*, edited by James R. Ginther and Carl N. Still (Aldershot: Ashgate, 2005), pp. 67–84.

Ribeiro do Nascimento, Carlos Arthur. "Thomas d'Aquin et l'histoire de la philosophie grecque." In *Was ist Philosophie im Mittelalter?*, edited by Jan A. Aertsen and Andreas Speer (Berlin: W. de Gruyter, 1998), pp. 293–7.

Rocca, Gregory P., OP. *Speaking the Incomprehensible God: Thomas Aquinas on the Interplay of Positive and Negative Theology* (Washington, DC: The Catholic University of America Press, 2004).

Roland-Gosselin, Marie-Dominique, OP. *Le "De ente et essentia" de S. Thomas d'Aquin* (Paris: Vrin, 1948).

Rondet, Henri. *The Grace of Christ: A Brief History of the Theology of Grace*, trans. Tad W. Guzie (Westminster, MD: Newman, 1966).

Rubenstein, Richard E. *Aristotle's Children: How Christians, Muslims, and Jews Rediscovered Ancient Wisdom and Illuminated the Dark Ages* (New York: Harcourt, 2003).

Ryan, Thomas F. *Thomas Aquinas as Reader of the Psalms* (Notre Dame, IN: University of Notre Dame Press, 2000).

Salas, Jr., Victor. "Thomas Aquinas on Christ's *Esse*: A Metaphysics of the Incarnation." *Thom.* 70 (2006): pp. 577–603.

Schockenhoff, Eberhard. "The Theological Virtue of Charity (IIa IIae, qq. 23–46)." In *The Ethics of Aquinas*, edited by Stephen J. Pope (Washington, DC: Georgetown University Press, 2002), pp. 244–58.

Schoot, Henk J. M. *Christ the "Name" of God: Thomas Aquinas on Naming Christ* (Leuven: Peeters, 1993).

Sherwin, Michael S., OP. "St. Thomas and the Common Good: The Theological Perspective: An Invitation to Dialogue." *Ang.* 70 (1993): pp. 307–28.

Sherwin, Michael S., OP. *By Knowledge and by Love: Charity and Knowledge in the Moral Theology of St. Thomas Aquinas* (Washington, DC: The Catholic University of America Press, 2005).

Smalley, Beryl. "William of Auvergne, John of La Rochelle and St. Thomas Aquinas on the Old Law." In *St. Thomas Aquinas 1274–1974: Commemorative Studies*, vol. 2, edited by Armand A. Maurer (Toronto: Pontifical Institute of Mediaeval Studies, 1974), pp. 11–71.

Sokolowski, Robert. *The God of Faith and Reason: Foundations of Christian Theology* (Notre Dame, IN: University of Notre Dame Press, 1982).

Sokolowski, Robert. "Phenomenology of Friendship." *The Review of Metaphysics* 55 (2002): pp. 451–70.

Sommers, Mary Catherine. "Thomas Aquinas' Polemic of Perfection." In *Atti del IX Congresso tomistico internazionale*, vol. 5, Problemi teologici alla luce dell'Aquinate, edited by Antonio Piolanti (Città del Vaticano: Libreria Editrice Vaticana, 1991), pp. 362–73.

Sorabji, Richard. *Necessity, Cause and Blame: Perspectives on Aristotle's Theory* (London: Duckworth, 1980).

Sorabji, Richard, ed. *Philoponus and the Rejection of Aristotelian Science* (London: Duckworth, 1987).

Southern, Richard W. *The Making of the Middle Ages* (New Haven, CT: Yale University Press, 1959).

Stump, Eleonore. *Aquinas* (New York: Routledge, 2003).

Stump, Eleonore. "Resurrection, Reassembly, and Reconstitution: Aquinas on the Soul." In *Die menschliche Seele: Brauchen wir den Dualismus?*, edited by Bruno Niederbacher and Edmund Runggaldier (Frankfurt: Ontos Verlag, 2006), pp. 153–74.

Suarez-Nani, Tiziana. *Connaissance et langage des anges selon Thomas d'Aquin et Gilles de Rome* (Paris: Vrin, 2002).

Suarez-Nani, Tiziana. *Les anges et la philosophie: Subjectivité et fonction cosmologique des substances séparées à la fin du XIIIe siècle* (Paris: Vrin, 2002).

Synan, Edward A. "Aquinas and the Children of Abraham." In *Philosophy and the God of Abraham: Essays in Memory of James A. Weisheipl, OP*, edited by R. James Long (Toronto: Pontifical Institute of Mediaeval Studies, 1991), pp. 203–16.

Synave, Paul, OP. "La révélation des vérités divines naturelles d'après saint Thomas d'Aquin." In *Mélanges Mandonnet: Études d'histoire littéraire et doctrinale du moyen âge*, vol. 1 (Paris: Vrin, 1930), pp. 327–70.

te Velde, Rudi A. *Participation and Substantiality in Thomas Aquinas* (Leiden: Brill, 1995).

te Velde, Rudi A. *Aquinas on God: The "Divine Science" of the* Summa Theologiae (Aldershot: Ashgate, 2006).

Thomas Aquinas. *Opera omnia iussu Leonis XIII P. M. edita* (= Leonine edition): Vol. 1*/1: *Expositio libri Peryermenias.* Editio altera retractata, ed. René-Antoine Gauthier (Rome: Commissio Leonina, 1989). Vol. 1*/2: *Expositio Libri Posteriorum.* Editio altera retractata, ed. René-Antoine Gauthier (Rome: Commissio Leonina, 1989). Vol. 2: *Commentaria in octo libros Physicorum Aristotelis*, ed. Fratres Ordinis Praedicatorum (Rome: Ex typographia polyglotta S.C. de Propaganda Fide, 1884). Vol. 3: *Commentaria in libros Aristotelis De caelo et mundo, De generatione et corruptione et Meteorologicorum*, ed. Fratres Ordinis Praedicatorum (Rome: Ex typographia polyglotta S.C. de Propaganda Fide, 1886). Vols. 4–12: *Summa theologiae*, ed. Fratres Ordinis Praedicatorum (Rome: Ex typographia polyglotta S.C. de Propaganda Fide, 1888–1906). Vols. 13–15: *Summa contra Gentiles*, ed. Fratres Ordinis Praedicatorum (Rome: Typis Riccardi Garroni, 1918–1930). Vol. 22/1–3: *Quaestiones disputatae de veritate*, ed. Antoine Dondaine (Rome: Editori di San Tommaso, 1970–1976). Vol. 23: *Quaestiones disputatae de malo*, ed. Pierre-Marie Gils (Rome: Commissio Leonina, 1982). Vol. 24/1: *Quaestiones disputatae de anima*, ed. Bernardo Carlos Bazán (Rome: Commissio Leonina, 1996). Vol. 24/2: *Quaestio* *disputata de spiritualibus creaturis*, ed. Joseph Cos (Rome: Commissio Leonina, 2000). Vol. 25/1–2: *Quaestiones de Quolibet*, ed. René-Antoine Gauthier (Rome: Commissio Leonina, 1996). Vol. 26: *Expositio super Iob ad litteram*, ed. Antoine Dondaine (Rome: Ad Sanctae Sabinae, 1965). Vol. 28: *Expositio super Isaiam ad litteram*, ed. Hyacinthe-François Dondaine and Léon Reid (Rome: Editori di San Tommaso, 1974). Vol. 40, pars D: *De substantiis separatis*, ed. Hyacinthe-François Dondaine (Rome: Ad Sanctae Sabinae, 1968), pp. D 39–D 80. Vol. 41: *Contra impugnantes Dei cultum et religionem, De perfectione spiritualis vitae, Contra doctrinam retrahentium a religione*, ed. Hyacinthe-François Dondaine (Rome: Ad Sanctae Sabinae, 1970). Vol. 42: *Compendium theologiae, Responsio ad magistrum Ioannem de Vercellis de 43 articulis, Responsio ad lectorem Venetum de 36 articulis, De regno ad regem Cypri*, ed. Gilles de Grandpré and Hyacinthe-François Dondaine (Rome: Editori di San Tommaso, 1979), pp. 83–205, 325–35, 337–46, and 447–71. Vol. 43: *De principiis naturae ad fratrem Sylvestrum, De unitate intellectus contra Averroistas, De ente et essentia*, ed. Fratres Ordinis Praedicatorum (Rome: Editori di San Tommaso, 1976), pp. 37–47, 289–314, and 367–81. Vol. 44/1: *Sermones*, ed. Louis Jacques Bataillon (Rome: Commissio Leonina, 2014). Vol. 45/1: *Sentencia libri De anima*, ed. René-Antoine Gauthier (Rome: Commissio Leonina, 1984). Vol. 47/ 1–2: *Sentencia libri Ethicorum*, ed. René-Antoine Gauthier (Rome: Ad Sanctae Sabinae, 1969). Vol. 48: *Sentencia libri Politicorum*, ed. Hyacinthe-François Dondaine and Louis Jacques Bataillon (Rome: Ad Sanctae Sabinae, 1971). Vol. 50: *Super Boetium De Trinitate, Expositio libri Boetii De ebdomadibus*, ed. Pierre-Marie Gils and Louis Jacques Bataillon (Rome: Commissio Leonina, 1992).

Thomas Aquinas. *Commentum in librum IV. Sententiarum: Dist. 23–50*, ed. Stanislas E. Fretté (Paris: Louis Vivès, 1882).

Thomas Aquinas. *Scriptum super libros Sententiarum*, vols. 1–2, ed. Pierre Mandonnet (Paris: Lethielleux, 1929).

Thomas Aquinas. *Scriptum super libros Sententiarum*, vols. 3–4, ed. Maria F. Moos (Paris: Lethielleux, 1933–1947).

Thomas Aquinas. *Summa theologiae*, ed. Institutum Studiorum Medievalium Ottaviense (Commissio Piana), 5 vols. (Ottawa: Harpell, 1941–1945).

Thomas Aquinas. *In Aristotelis librum De anima commentarium*, ed. Angelo Pirotta (Turin: Marietti, 1948).

Thomas Aquinas. *In duodecim libros Metaphysicorum Aristotelis Expositio*, ed. Raimondo Spiazzi (Turin: Marietti, 1950).

Thomas Aquinas. *In librum beati Dionysii De divinis nominibus*, ed. Ceslas Pera (Turin: Marietti, 1950).

Thomas Aquinas. *Somme théologique: La Trinité*, trans. Hyacinthe-François Dondaine, 2 vols. (Paris: Desclée, 1950).

Thomas Aquinas. *In Aristotelis libros De caelo et mundo, De generatione et corruptione, Meteorologicorum Expositio*, ed. Raimondo Spiazzi (Turin: Marietti, 1952).

Thomas Aquinas. *Super Evangelium S. Ioannis lectura*, ed. Raffaele Cai (Turin: Marietti, 1952).

Thomas Aquinas. *Catena aurea in quatuor Evangelia*, ed. Angelico Guarienti, 2 vols. (Turin: Marietti, 1953).

Thomas Aquinas. *Quaestiones disputatae*, ed. Raimondo Spiazzi, 2 vols. (Turin: Marietti, 1953).

Thomas Aquinas. *Super Epistolas S. Pauli lectura*, ed. Raffaele Cai, 2 vols. (Turin: Marietti, 1953).

Thomas Aquinas. *On the Truth of the Catholic Faith: Summa contra Gentiles*, trans. Anton C. Pegis, James F. Anderson, Vernon J. Bourke, and Charles J. O'Neil, 4 vols. (Garden City, NY: Image Books, 1955–1957); repr. as *Summa contra Gentiles*, 4 vols. (Notre Dame, IN: University of Notre Dame Press, 1975).

Thomas Aquinas. *Liber de Veritate Catholicae Fidei contra errores Infidelium qui dicitur Summa contra Gentiles*, ed. Pietro Marc, Ceslas Pera, and Pietro Caramello, 3 vols. (Turin: Marietti, 1961–1967).

Thomas Aquinas. *Aristotle On Interpretation: Commentary by Thomas Aquinas Finished by Cardinal Cajetan*, trans. Jean T. Oesterle (Milwaukee: Marquette University Press, 1962).

Thomas Aquinas. *In octo libros Physicorum Aristotelis*, ed. Mariani Maggiòlo (Turin: Marietti, 1965).

Thomas Aquinas. *Super Ieremiam et Threnos*. In *S. Thomae Aquinatis Opera omnia*, vol. 5, *Commentaria in scripturas*, ed. Roberto Busa (Stuttgart-Ban Cannstatt: Frommann-Holzboog, 1980), pp. 96–128.

Thomas Aquinas. *Super Psalmos*. In *S. Thomae Aquinatis Opera omnia*, vol. 6, *Reportationes*, ed. Roberto Busa (Stuttgart-Ban Cannstatt: Frommann-Holzboog, 1980), pp. 48–130.

Thomas Aquinas. *Summa Theologiae*, trans. Fathers of the English Dominican Province, 5 vols. (Westminster, MD: Christian Classics, 1981).

Thomas Aquinas. *Commentary on Aristotle's Nicomachean Ethics*, trans. Charles I. Litzinger (Notre Dame, IN: Dumb Ox Books, 1993).

Thomas Aquinas. *A Commentary on Aristotle's* De anima, trans. Robert Pasnau (New Haven, CT: Yale University Press, 1999).

Thomas Aquinas. *On the Power of God (Quæstiones disputatæ de potentia Dei)*, Three Books in One, trans. English Dominican Fathers (Eugene, OR: Wipf & Stock, 2004).

Thomas Aquinas. *Commentary on Aristotle's* Politics, trans. Richard J. Regan (Indianapolis, IN: Hackett, 2007).

Thomas Aquinas. "St. Thomas Aquinas' Works in English." Dominican House of Studies, Washington, DC, accessed February 20, 2015, <http://dhspriory.org/thomas/>.

Toner, Patrick. "St. Thomas Aquinas on Death and the Separated Soul." *Pacific Philosophical Quarterly* 91 (2010): pp. 587–99.

Tonneau, Jean, OP. "The Teaching of the Thomist Tract on Law." *Thom.* 34 (1970): pp. 13–83.

Torrell, Jean-Pierre, OP. "S. Thomas d'Aquin et la science du Christ: Une relecture des questions 9-12 de la 'Tertia Pars' de la Somme de théologie." In *Saint Thomas au XXe siècle: Colloque du centenaire de la "Revue thomiste" (1893-1992)*, edited by Serge-Thomas Bonino (Paris: Éditions Saint-Paul, 1994), pp. 394–409.

Torrell, Jean-Pierre, OP. "La causalité salvifique de la résurrection du Christ selon saint Thomas." *RThom* 96 (1996): pp. 179–208.

Torrell, Jean-Pierre, OP. *Le Christ en ses mystères: La vie et l'œuvre de Jésus selon saint Thomas d'Aquin*, vol. 1 (Paris: Desclée, 1999).

Torrell, Jean-Pierre, OP. *Saint Thomas Aquinas*, vol. 2, Spiritual Master, trans. Robert Royal (Washington, DC: The Catholic University of America Press, 2003).

Torrell, Jean-Pierre, OP. *Aquinas's Summa: Background, Structure, and Reception*, trans. Benedict M. Guevin (Washington, DC: The Catholic University of America Press, 2005).

Torrell, Jean-Pierre, OP. *Saint Thomas Aquinas*, vol. 1, The Person and his Work, trans. Robert Royal, rev. ed. (Washington, DC: The Catholic University of America Press, 2005).

Torrell, Jean-Pierre, OP. *Christ and Spirituality in St. Thomas Aquinas*, trans. Bernhard Blankenhorn (Washington, DC: The Catholic University of America Press, 2011).

Tschipke, Theophil, OP. *Die Menschheit Christi als Heilsorgan der Gottheit: Unter besonderer Berücksichtigung der Lehre des Heiligen Thomas von Aquin* (Freiburg in Breisgau: Herder, 1940); trans. Philibert Secrétan as *L'humanité du Christ comme instrument de salut de la divinité* (Fribourg: Academic Press, 2003).

Tugwell, Simon, OP, ed. *Albert and Thomas: Selected Writings* (Mahwah, NJ: Paulist Press, 1988).

Vagaggini, Cipriano, OSB. *Theological Dimensions of the Liturgy: A General Treatise on the Dimensions of the Liturgy*, trans. Leonardo J. Doyle and William A. Jurgens, rev. ed. (Collegeville, MN: The Liturgical Press, 1976).

Van Steenberghen, Fernand. *Aristotle in the West: The Origins of Latin Aristotelianism*, trans. Leonard Johnston (New York: Humanities Press, 1970).

Vattimo, Gianni. *After Christianity*, trans. Luca D'Isanto (New York: Columbia University Press, 2002).

Vernier, Jean-Marie. *Les anges chez saint Thomas d'Aquin: Fondements historiques et principes philosophiques* (Paris: Nouvelles Éditions Latines, 1986).

Villey, Michel. "Saint Thomas et l'immobilisme." In *Seize essais de philosophie du droit: Dont un sur la crise universitaire* (Paris: Dalloz, 1969), pp. 94–106.

Villey, Michel. *La formation de la pensée juridique moderne* (Paris: PUF, 2003).

Walsh, Liam G., OP. "Liturgy in the Theology of St. Thomas." *Thom.* 38 (1974): pp. 557–83.

Walsh, Liam G., OP. "The Divine and the Human in St. Thomas's Theology of the Sacraments." In *Ordo sapientiae et amoris: Image et message de saint Thomas d'Aquin à travers les récentes études historiques, herméneutiques et doctrinales: Hommage au Professeur Jean-Pierre Torrell OP. à l'occasion de son 65ᵉ anniversaire*, edited by Carlos-Josaphat Pinto de Oliveira (Fribourg: Éditions Universitaires, 1993), pp. 321–52.

Walsh, Liam G., OP. "Sacraments." In *The Theology of Thomas Aquinas*, edited by Rik van Nieuwenhove and Joseph P. Wawrykow (Notre Dame, IN: University of Notre Dame Press, 2005), pp. 326–64.

Wawrykow, Joseph P. *God's Grace and Human Action: "Merit" in the Theology of Thomas Aquinas* (Notre Dame, IN: University of Notre Dame Press, 1995).

Wawrykow, Joseph P. "Wisdom in the Christology of Thomas Aquinas." In *Christ among the Medieval Dominicans: Representations of Christ in the Texts and Images of the Order of Preachers*, edited by Kent Emery, Jr., and Joseph P. Wawrykow (Notre Dame, IN: University of Notre Dame Press, 1998), pp. 175–96.

Wawrykow, Joseph P. "Charity." In *The Westminster Handbook to Thomas Aquinas* (Louisville, KY: Westminster John Knox Press, 2005), pp. 22–5.

Wawrykow, Joseph P. "Grace." In *The Theology of Thomas Aquinas*, edited by Rik van Nieuwenhove and Joseph P. Wawrykow (Notre Dame, IN: University of Notre Dame Press, 2005), pp. 192–221.

Weinandy, Thomas G., O.F.M. Cap. "Aquinas: God *is* Man, The Marvel of the Incarnation." In *Aquinas on Doctrine: A Critical Introduction*, edited by Thomas G. Weinandy, Daniel A. Keating, and John P. Yocum (London: T. & T. Clark, 2004), pp. 67–89.

Weinandy, Thomas G., O.F.M. Cap., Daniel A. Keating, and John P. Yocum, eds. *Aquinas on Scripture: An Introduction to his Biblical Commentaries* (London: T. & T. Clark, 2005).

Weisheipl, James A., OP. "Thomas' Evaluation of Plato and Aristotle." *The New Scholasticism* 48 (1974): pp. 100–24.

Weisheipl, James A., OP. "Albertus Magnus and Universal Hylomorphism: Avicebron." In *Albert the Great: Commemorative Essays*, edited by Francis J. Kovach and Robert W. Shahan (Norman: University of Oklahoma Press, 1980), pp. 239–60.

Weithman, Paul J. "Augustine and Aquinas on Original Sin and the Function of Political Authority." *Journal of the History of Philosophy* 30 (1992): pp. 353–76.

Weithman, Paul J. "Complementarity and Equality in the Political Thought of Thomas Aquinas." *TS* 59 (1998): pp. 277–96.

West, Jason L. A. "Aquinas on the Metaphysics of *Esse* in Christ." *Thom.* 66 (2002): pp. 231–50.

West, Jason L. A. "Aristotle through the Looking Glass: Aquinas as a Historian of Philosophy." In *Literary Form, Philosophical Content: Historical Studies of Philosophical Genres*, edited by Jonathan A. Lavery, and Louis Groarke (Madison, NJ: Farleigh Dickinson University Press, 2010), pp. 104–14.

White, Thomas Joseph, OP. "The Precarity of Wisdom: Modern Dominican Theology, Perspectivalism, and the Tasks of Reconstruction." In *Ressourcement Thomism: Sacred Doctrine, the Sacraments, and the Moral Life: Essays in Honor of Romanus Cessario, OP.*, edited by Reinhard Hütter and Matthew Levering (Washington, DC: The Catholic University of America Press, 2010), pp. 92–123.

White, Thomas Joseph, OP. "Introduction: Thomas Aquinas and Karl Barth, An Unofficial Catholic–Protestant Dialogue." In *Thomas Aquinas and Karl Barth: An Unofficial Catholic–Protestant Dialogue*, edited by Bruce L. McCormack and Thomas Joseph White (Grand Rapids, MI: Eerdmans, 2013), pp. 1–39.

Wieland, Wolfgang. "The Problem of Teleology." In *Articles on Aristotle*, vol. 1, Science, edited by Jonathan Barnes, Malcolm Schofield, and Richard Sorabji (London: Duckworth, 1975), pp. 141–60.

Williams, Anna N. *The Ground of Union: Deification in Aquinas and Palamas* (Oxford: Oxford University Press, 1999).

Wippel, John F. *The Metaphysical Thought of Godfrey of Fontaines: A Study in Late Thirteenth-Century Philosophy* (Washington, DC: The Catholic University of America Press, 1981).

Wippel, John F. "Thomas Aquinas and the Condemnation of 1277." *The Modern Schoolman* 72 (1995): pp. 233–72.

Wippel, John F. *Metaphysical Themes in Thomas Aquinas II* (Washington, DC: The Catholic University of America Press, 2007).

Wohlman, Avital. *Thomas d'Aquin et Maïmonide: Un dialogue exemplaire* (Paris: Cerf, 1988).

Wolterstorff, Nicholas. *Justice: Rights and Wrongs* (Princeton, NJ: Princeton University Press, 2008).

Wood, Rega. "Angelic Individuation according to Richard Rufus, St. Bonaventure and St. Thomas Aquinas." In *Individuum und Individualität im Mittelalter*, edited by Jan A. Aertsen and Andreas Speer (Berlin: W. de Gruyter, 1996), pp. 209–29.

Yack, Bernard. "Natural Right and Aristotle's Understanding of Justice." *Political Theory* 18 (1990): pp. 216–37.

Zavalloni, Roberto. *Richard de Mediavilla et la controverse sur la pluralité des formes: Textes inédits et étude critique* (Louvain: Éditions de l'Institut Supérieur de Philosophie, 1951).

Name Index

Subject Index

Printed and bound by CPI Group (UK) Ltd, Croydon, CR0 4YY